Your Guide to the Law

Michael Molyneux, BA, Barrister, studied law at Cambridge University. He has been a law lecturer since 1960 and has a wide experience as a journalist and broadcaster.

Charles Blake, LLM, studied law at the universities of Manchester and London. He has been teaching law at Ealing College of Higher Education (ECHE) since 1976. In 1979 he was seconded to Wolfson College, Oxford, to do research on immigration policy.

George Alan Bonner, LLB, BSc (Econ), Barrister, studied at the universities of Hull, London and Vienna. He is the author of *British Transport Law by Road and Rail* and numerous articles on road traffic and transport law. He was for many years a principal lecturer in law at ECHE.

Ann Halpern, LLM, Barrister, studied law at London University. She has been a law lecturer at ECHE since 1972 and has specialized in family law since 1975. She has also been involved in training courses for magistrates on domestic proceedings.

John Hendy, BSc (Econ), LLB, Barrister, studied law at London University and was a law lecturer at ECHE from 1965 until 1979. He was President of the National Association of Teachers in Further and Higher Education in 1976–7. He has had long experience as an active trade unionist and has been a member of the Industrial Tribunal since 1975.

Paul Walker, BA, BCL, is a practising barrister. He studied law at Oxford University and lectured on commercial law at ECHE from 1978 to 1980.

B. Moylett.

36 Meyrick Ave

Luton

Beds

LU1 5JR,

editor: Michael Molyneux

Your Guide to the Law – Revised Edition

contributors: Charles Blake
George Alan Bonner
Ann Halpern
John Hendy
Paul Walker

Secker & Warburg London

First published in England 1981 by
Martin Secker & Warburg Limited
54 Poland Street, London W1V 3DF

2nd printing (revised) 1983
Reprinted 1984

British Library Cataloguing in Publication Data

Molyneux, Michael
Your guide to the law
1. Law – Great Britain
I. Title
344.2 KD664

ISBN 0 436 28453 7

Printed and bound in Great Britain by
Biddles Ltd, Guildford and King's Lynn

How to use this book

The book is laid out in six sections which cover the family, the home, work, goods and services, cars, and the way in which the law works.

To find your way around the book you can either use the table of contents which starts on page vi or you can consult the more detailed general index which is at the end of the book.

To avoid constant repetition, a description of the functions of particular courts, such as the magistrates' court and the county court, is given in a single chapter in the last section of the book on page 413. There is also a chapter in that section on legal aid (see page 428) which sets out the circumstances in which you can qualify for financial help towards the cost of legal advice and assistance in court.

The last chapter (see page 441) is about how to complain, and if you want more advice and help with complaints then turn to the list of organizations and addresses on page 446.

Reading this book will not teach you all you need to know about the law but it may help you to decide whether or not there is a legal solution to your problems.

Law changes very fast these days but we have done our best to state the law as it was in England and Wales on 1 January 1983.

Throughout the book, however, we have drawn attention to proposed changes in the law, and in the section on the family, Chapter 11, 'Money matters', we have included certain changes made by the budget of March 1983.

This book deals only with the law in England and Wales. It must be emphasized that the law, and the legal systems, in Scotland, Northern Ireland, the Channel Islands and the Isle of Man differ in many important ways.

Contents

The Home

At Work

Goods and Services

You and Your Car

The Law and the Courts

The Family

1 What is a family?

The first question which has to be considered here is: exactly what is 'your family'? Most people would say that a family unit is created automatically when a marriage takes place; others would demand that children must first be born. Many people would now approve of a definition which included couples simply living together as though they were husband and wife, especially where there are children, while others would be horrified at such a definition. In some circles the definition would include any situation in which a couple or group of people live together in an emotional bond, whether or not any of them are married, heterosexual, or economically dependent. On the other hand, single parents might in some people's eyes have difficulty in qualifying as a family.

In recent years the traditional view of the proper scope of 'family law' has been steadily extended to meet the needs of families (in the broadest possible sense) living in our present society. These changes have been most apparent in the last ten years. This is because over this period statistics show that the number of marriages has steadily fallen; that the number of children born each year has fallen; that the divorce rate has risen at what some might call an alarming rate; that the number of illegitimate births has steadily increased; and that more homosexual couples are prepared to stand up for their rights and publicize their relationship. Although there are no statistics to prove it, it is generally accepted that a much larger number of people than ever before have chosen to live together without benefit of marriage, and that these relationships are for the most part at least as stable as marriages.

The law has changed so as to be able to provide for all these different types of relationship.

The family and the law

The second question which arises is: what are the functions of law in relation to family life? The major functions would seem to be: to identify the rights and obligations owed by each individual member of the family to each other member of the same family; to protect each member of the family from a failure to exercise any of these rights and obligations; to provide a set of rules and a process for enforcing them; to settle the ownership and possession of money and property, and to provide for the future upbringing of any children when the adult relationship ends; finally to ensure that financial assistance from the state is directed to those in need.

How the law works

The third question which must be posed is: does the law achieve these objectives in relation to the modern family in all its different forms? In most cases it is necessary to compare the law as it affects married people with the law as it affects others in a similar situation. The points of distinction outlined immediately below are only intended to serve as a guide to the system of law; the detailed provisions are dealt with later on.

Choice of partner

It is only possible to contract a valid marriage with people who are outside what is called the 'prohibited degrees'. People within the prohibited degrees, who cannot validly marry each other, are those who are closely related by blood or marriage (see page 77). Provided, however, that no question of incest arises from a sexual relationship, it is possible to cohabit with anyone at all.

Right of abode

A British citizen (see page 21 for definition) may bring into the UK his or her spouse, fiancé or fiancée. The immigration authorities will demand evidence that the marriage is in fact genuine and not undertaken merely to get round the immigration rules. They will therefore check whether the parties are living together one year after the spouse has been admitted. Similarly, the authorities will check up to see that engaged couples have in fact married, they will do this three months after admission to the UK. A man who is ordinarily resident in the UK and has been given indefinite leave to remain, with no conditions on his passport (which means that he is settled here), may also bring in his wife or fiancée. Women, under the present rules, are not given the same opportunity. This matter is at present pending before the European Commission, and the rule may therefore be changed in the future.

A couple who are not married, but are living in permanent association, are given some rights under the new rules. The male partner, if a British citizen or settled in the UK, may bring in with him a woman who has been living with him as though she were his wife, provided that he can support her without recourse to public funds.

A spouse who is brought in by a British citizen is entitled to apply for an accelerated form of naturalization: he or she may apply after three years, no language test will be applied, and no evidence of an intention permanently to reside will be required.

A wife who is brought in by her settled husband will have to wait the normal five years before being able to apply for naturalization and pass a language test and show all intention to remain here permanently, unless her husband naturalizes.

Children

Only married couples have automatic joint rights and duties in respect of their legitimate and adopted children. For illegitimate children (those born or conceived out of wedlock) only the mother has automatic rights and duties; the father has to have the authority of a court to exercise them. It should be noted that some of these distinctions may be removed in the near future because the Law Commission has recommended the abolition of the status of illegitimacy (see page 26).

Financial support

Each party to a marriage must support the other and both spouses are obliged to support their legitimate children. These obligations can be enforced by the husband or wife taking action in the courts (see page 91) or by the state taking action to recover money spent on support where one party has failed in his or her obligations (see page 115). Cohabiting couples have no duties of financial support to one another, and consequently no action can be taken by either partner or by the state. However, a woman who lives with a man is unable to claim supplementary benefit in her own right because the law assumes that the man is supporting the woman whatever the reality of the situation (see page 117). The reasoning behind this rule is that it would be unfair if unmarried people were treated more favourably by the social security system than married people, who can only claim through the man, after their resources have been aggregated. In 1983 the rules are to be changed so that families will be able to nominate a 'breadwinner' who alone will be entitled to make a claim. This need not be the male partner.

The mother of an illegitimate child has the sole duty to maintain the child unless the mother or the state takes affiliation proceedings against the reputed father (see page 37). It is also possible for the mother of an illegitimate child to get an allowance for herself as well as support for the child from the father provided that he is wealthy enough and the woman cannot work because she is caring for the child (see page 38).

Taxation

Married couples are treated as a single unit for taxation purposes unless they make different arrangements with the tax authorities. Unmarried couples are always treated as separate individuals for purposes of taxation. The state encourages marriage by giving a special married man's tax allowance whether or not there are children of the marriage. The married man's allowance is lost if the parties decide to be taxed separately – an arrangement which is only immediately of value to those with very high incomes. Unmarried couples with children can claim an additional allowance to bring one of their allowances up to that of a married man however high their income is; as a result, they may be better off than an equivalent married couple (see page 96). There is an exemption from capital gains tax for gifts between married couples; this exemption does not apply to gifts between people who are living together (see page 110).

Housing

Local authority housing is usually only available to families with children who are unintentionally homeless. This is because these homeless families have a priority need (see page 213).

The idea of the family is also important in connection with the right to succeed to a tenancy protected under the Rent Acts and to secure local authority tenancies. Where a protected tenant dies the tenancy will pass automatically to any member of the tenant's family who was living in the rented property on the tenant's death (see page 171). The definition of the family for these purposes can include unmarried people of the opposite sex living together in a stable relationship, as though they were husband and wife.

Therefore couples who live together maintaining their independence by keeping separate names and bank accounts may not be members of the same family for these purposes; adults who live together in an emotional relationship which is non-sexual, are excluded, and so may be those who live in a homosexual relationship.

Ownership of property
Married couples are treated by the law of property as strangers, and consequently, whatever the relationship, strict property ownership rules are applied to them. The only advantage in being married is that a wife may be able to establish that property bought by her husband and registered in her name was meant to be a gift to her (see page 123).

Rights of occupation
Each party to a marriage has an equal right to occupy the matrimonial home (see page 128); people who live together without being married have to prove that there is a legal agreement granting them a right to occupy (see page 124).

Where an unmarried couple have been living together as if they were married, and the relationship breaks down, then in some circumstances one of them may be granted a temporary right to occupy that home to the exclusion of the other (see page 67).

Death
The rules governing the distribution of property on death are more generous to the surviving partner of a marriage than to the survivor of a relationship between two unmarried people. For example, if a husband or wife dies without having made a will the surviving spouse has certain automatic rights of succession. This does not apply to unmarried couples; and even where there is a will, a court can still in effect alter the terms of it if it fails to make reasonable provision for a surviving spouse. The survivor of an unmarried couple can only upset a will in this way if he or she was actually at least partly dependent on the dead person (see page 136).

Cohabitation contracts
Unmarried people can enter into a 'cohabitation contract' which could contain an agreed set of rules providing for lesser or greater rights and obligations than those given by general law. If you want to make a cohabitation contract you should consult a solicitor.

Single parents
Single parents are treated more generously by the state than are two-parent families. There is an additional child benefit payment (see page 122), and the rules about entitlement to other social security benefits are less severe (see page 121).

2 Names

This chapter looks at the registration of names and how they can be changed.

The registered name

Although all children must be registered within six months of birth at the Registry of Births Deaths and Marriages, the names by which a child is registered do not have to be the names by which the child is actually called. This is because a name is something which a person acquirès by repute rather than by operation of the law.

The rules which cover the registration of children merely require the registered name to be that by which it is 'intended' that the child shall be known.

Registration can be done by the mother and father acting together, or by either of them acting alone. It is therefore possible to register as the surname of a child one which is the same as that of both parents, one that is the same as that of one parent, or a name which is completely unconnected with either parent.

In the same way it is perfectly possible for the mother of an illegitimate child to choose the surname of the father as the child's surname, even though she cannot register the man as the 'father' without his permission, unless either he has made a statutory declaration that he is the father or there is an affiliation order against him.

Re-registration of names

This can be done in three cases.

1 It is possible to add or register a forename (where none was entered on the original registration) within twelve months of the original registration. The Registrar is able to add information to the original record, but cannot erase any of the original information.
2 In the case of an illegitimate child, where the original registration left the father's name blank, it is possible to add the father's name where:

- both parents ask for it; or
- an affiliation order has been made; or

- where the father has made a statutory declaration admitting paternity.

In any situation where a child has reached the age of sixteen, his consent to any re-registration must also be obtained.

3 Where the parents of an illegitimate child marry after its birth, the child is legitimized, and the parents *must* then re-register the birth so that the record can be amended.

Adopted children

An application for an adoption order will ask the court to order that the child be known by the adopters' surname. (It is also possible to change the forenames of an adopted child as part of an adoption order.) The new name will then be entered in the Adopted Children Register, and a copy of this entry operates as if it were the birth certificate of the adopted child. The original registration details are confidential and will only be disclosed after a court order, or when the adopted child reaches the age of eighteen and, after being counselled, wants to discover his true origins. (For adoption proceedings see page 9.)

Marriage

It is the custom for a married woman to change her surname to that of her husband on marriage. There is, however, no legal rule which requires this change, so it is perfectly acceptable for a married woman to retain her maiden name and, if she wishes, to denote her change in marital status simply by the use of the word 'Mrs' before her surname. If a woman changes her surname on marriage the wedding certificate serves as proof of the change.

Divorce, etc.

A divorced woman may make a conscious decision to revert to her maiden name after a decree of divorce, nullity or judicial separation. Women in these circumstances are also entitled, if they wish, to retain their married surname.

Cohabitation

A couple who live together as man and wife, although not married, will often be known by one of their surnames among their friends and neighbours. So if the man takes the woman's name, his surname will have been changed to hers by repute.

Changing your surname

The registered name of a person merely serves as evidence of that person's name; it is perfectly possible therefore to acquire a new surname without any legal formalities provided it is not done for dishonest purposes. This is because all surnames are said to be names 'by repute'. All that is necessary to achieve the change is a conscious decision to change that surname, so that the person becomes generally known by the new name. Since a 'conscious' decision is required, a child of tender years (probably under sixteen) is not considered capable of making such a decision and so cannot change his name 'by repute'; his parents, however, could do it on his behalf.

There are times when formal evidence of a change of name is needed – when applying for a passport, for example, or proving entitlement under a will – and there are three main ways of providing this evidence: by advertisement, by statutory declaration, and by deed poll.

Advertisement

This is the simplest and cheapest way of providing evidence of a change of name and giving publicity to the change. All that is needed is an advertisement in a local paper giving the name by which the advertiser wishes to be known in future.

Statutory declaration

This is a formal statement in writing giving the name that the writer was called by at birth and the name by which he or she is now known. The writer must swear to the truth of the statement and sign it in the presence of a solicitor. The solicitor will charge about £2 for this service.

Deed poll

This, like the statutory declaration, is a formal legal document. The main difference between the two is that a statutory declaration usually declares that the writer's name *was* changed at some time in the past, whereas a deed poll is used to announce a change that is to take effect for the future. Anyone over the age of eighteen can change his or her name by deed poll, and the same deed can be used to change the names of all the members of a family who are over eighteen provided that each of them signs the deed.

The deed can be registered at the Central Office of the Royal

Courts of Justice, The Strand, London. This is not essential but if the deed is registered then anyone who needs proof of your new name – such as the Inland Revenue or the Passport Office – can be supplied with an official copy.

A deed poll is a fairly complicated and technical document and it is sensible to get it drawn up by a solicitor.

3 Becoming a parent

This chapter looks at the immediate consequences of becoming a parent, either naturally or by adoption, and looks at the practical problems of avoiding children or coping initially with pregnancy and parenthood.

By giving birth

A child *conceived* as a result of normal intercourse during a marriage, or one *born* during a marriage, is deemed to be the legitimate child of the married couple. If, however, it can be shown – by blood tests, for example – that the husband could not be the father of the child, then the child becomes illegitimate.

A child conceived by a woman who is not married to the father is illegitimate unless she marries the father of the child. So a child conceived as a result of a course of treatment of artificial insemination by a donor who is not the woman's husband is an illegitimate child. This means that the husband has no automatic rights over the child and is, in reality, a kind of step-parent. A child born as a result of treatment by artificial insemination by the husband will, however, be the legitimate child of the parties to the marriage and so will a child created in a test tube (from the mother's egg and the father's sperm) and then implanted into the mother's womb.

By adoption

At present, people who want to adopt a child can approach either an approved adoption society or a local authority, known collectively as adoption agencies. It is now illegal for anyone other than an adoption agency to place a child for adoption, unless the adopter-to-be is a relative of the child, for example, grandparents, the natural father of an illegitimate child, or an uncle. Not all local authorities provide an adoption service, but in the future (no date has yet been fixed) they will all have to provide an adoption service themselves or ensure that one is provided in their area by an adoption society approved by the Secretary of State. (The address of local adoption societies can be obtained from the Association of British Adoption Agencies, 4 Southampton Row, London WC1 01 836 1373.)

In English law, 'adoption', which transfers all parental rights from the natural to the adoptive parents, can only be effected by court order. Private agreements intended to create an adoption are therefore ineffective and payments for adoption arrangements are forbidden, although approved adoption societies may make a charge to cover their expenses, and the government has introduced for an experimental period of seven years the opportunity to pay an allowance to adopters. This will allow payments to be made to foster parents who agree to adopt children they have been fostering but who would otherwise suffer a loss of income because the fostering allowance would be withdrawn on adoption. It is also hoped that more 'hard to place' children will find adoptive parents in this way.

In making an adoption order the court must consider all the circumstances of the case, and the first consideration is the need to promote the welfare of the child. Courts will also take account of the wishes and feelings of the child, according to its age and understanding, through the guardian *ad litem*, who must be appointed to represent the interests of the child.

If the child does understand he will have to attend the court to answer any questions the court may want to ask.

Who can adopt a child?

Adopters must be at least twenty-one years of age. Married couples and single people, but not cohabiting couples, can adopt a child. A lone married person can adopt a child, provided that the other spouse cannot be found, or is incapable of applying, or the couple are separated in circumstances where the separation is likely to be permanent. There are further restrictions which are likely to be applied by the court when the adopter is a step-parent of the child, a natural parent of the child, or a relative of the child.

Step-parent
Courts are required to dismiss applications by step-parents if they consider that the application could be better dealt with as an application for custody made in divorce proceedings between the natural parents. In these cases the courts would see adoption as a last resort. The views of the natural parent who does not have custody would be highly relevant, especially since courts attach great importance to maintaining links between parents and their children, unless it can be shown that the absent parent has nothing to offer the child. This was held to be so in a case concerning a father who was a practising homosexual and in others where the father had dropped out of the children's lives.

A natural parent
Courts are required to dismiss applications by one natural parent, unless it can be shown that the absent natural parent is dead, cannot be found, or there is some good reason justifying the exclusion of that person.

Relative
This includes step-parents. In these cases the court will in the future have to consider instead making a custodianship order where the continuation of the links between a child and its natural parents would be beneficial. These orders are not yet available, but when they are they will have the effect of transferring to the custodian all the parental rights and duties that concern the physical possession of the child (see page 29).

Who can be adopted?
Any child over the age of nineteen weeks and under the age of eighteen years who has not been married can be adopted.

Steps in making an adoption order
There are three things that must happen before a court will consider making an adoption order: the child must have lived with the people who want to adopt it for a certain length of time; a guardian *ad litem* must be appointed (see page 12), and the consent of the child's natural parents must be obtained or dispensed with by the court.

Child residing with potential adopters
When a child has been placed with the people who want to adopt it by an adoption agency, or the potential adopters are close relatives,

then the child must have lived with them for thirteen weeks immediately before the order. In all other cases, the child must have lived with the potential adopters for twelve months. Temporary absences, say, for hospital treatment, will be ignored. Where the potential adopters are a married couple, this requirement will be satisfied even if one of the spouses is temporarily absent from the home, provided that there has been a sufficient opportunity of assessing the relationship of the child with both spouses.

The guardian ad litem

As the law now stands a *guardian ad litem* (that is, a person who represents the interests of the child) must be appointed in all adoption proceedings. However new rules are to be made which will require a guardian to be appointed only in certain cases – for example, where the adoption application is contested.

Agreement of natural parents or guardians

The basic rule is that natural parents (or guardians) must agree to the adoption order; that is, they must agree to the severing of the ties between themselves and the child. Agreement must be given voluntarily, unconditionally and in full knowledge of the consequences of an adoption order.

In the following circumstances, however, the court can dispense with the agreement of a parent or guardian:

- where the parent cannot be found;
- where the parent is incapable of giving consent because he or she lacks the mental capacity;
- where the parent is withholding his or her agreement unreasonably. Once a child has been placed with a view to adoption the longer a parent delays in giving consent, the more likely it is that the court will hold the parent to be unreasonable;
- where the parent has persistently failed without reasonable cause to discharge his or her parental duties (the parental duties of protection, education and maintenance are described in Chapter 5, pages 31 to 42);
- where the parent has abandoned or neglected the child. This seems to mean that the parent must have neglected his or her parental duties to the extent of being criminally liable;
- where the parent has persistently ill-treated the child;
- where the parent has seriously ill-treated the child and the rehabilitation of the child within the parent's household is unlikely.

The problem with the present system of obtaining and dispensing with parental consent that is described above is that people who want to adopt a child do not really know where they stand until the adoption order is finally made by the court. Under a new system, to be introduced shortly (probably early in 1983), a procedure called 'freeing a child for adoption' will be used. Under this system adoption agencies will be able to ask a court to make an order freeing a child for adoption, and parental consent will be given or dispensed with at this stage. The order will transfer the parents' rights over the child to the adoption agency. When the child is then placed with the potential adopters they will at least know that they don't have to worry about the consent of the child's parents when they apply for the final adoption order.

Which courts can make adoption orders?

Three courts have jurisdiction in adoption matters: the Family Division of the High Court, the county court, and the magistrates' court. Hearings are in private. In practice most adoption proceedings take place in the county court (see page 413).

Conditions attached to adoption orders

The court can attach to an adoption order a condition that the child shall be brought up in a particular religion. In some cases the courts have been prepared to attach an access condition to an adoption order. This has occurred in the past where the adopters are one natural parent and a step-parent and where the court considers that the excluded natural parent should maintain contact with the child.

Effect of adoption order

Adopted children are entitled to succeed to the property of their adoptive parents as though they were natural children. An adopted child is deemed to have been born on the date of the adoption order.

Adopted children are still bound by the prohibited degrees so far as marriage is concerned: they cannot marry their natural or adoptive parents (see page 77).

Children who are brought into the UK for adoption

The immigration rules do not provide for the entry of children for this purpose. The Home Secretary does however have a discretion to admit children in these circumstances, provided that he believes that the intention to adopt is genuine.

Adoption orders made overseas
Provided that the adoption is genuine and the child's parents are unable to care for the child, a child will be admitted with its new adoptive parents.

Right to discover natural parents
An adopted child who has reached the age of eighteen is entitled, after counselling, to find out who his natural parents are (see page 7).

Avoiding children

Family planning advice, supplies, 'substances and appliances', vasectomy and sterilization operations are available free of charge under the National Health Service. These services are available from Family Planning Clinics (ring 01 636 7866 for the address of your local clinic), from some general practitioners, and from some hospitals. Leaflets describing the different methods are available from the Health Education Council. The method of contraception chosen by the patient or advised by the doctor will fall within the doctors' code of ethics and is absolutely confidential. A wife can choose to use the contraceptive pill without telling her husband in the absolute knowledge that her doctor will not tell her husband without her consent. Unmarried girls over sixteen are entitled to consent to medical treatment themselves, so a doctor who prescribes the pill will have to ask for the girl's permission if he wants to tell her parents. Doctors have discretion to decide whether to prescribe the pill to girls under sixteen without first consulting their parents.

It is worth pointing out that many doctors will not perform sterilization operations without the consent of the other spouse.

Abortion

Abortion is available under the National Health Service but in some areas it is difficult to get the operation performed. There are, however, charitable organizations from which help can be obtained: the British Pregnancy Advisory Service (Guildhall Buildings, Navigation Street, Birmingham 2) and the Pregnancy Advisory Service (58 Petty France, London SW1 01 582 8871). These organizations usually charge a small fee for their advice. Entitlement to an abortion is based on medical grounds, which must be certified by two medical practitioners, acting in good faith. The medical grounds for an abortion are: a risk to the life of a pregnant woman or to her physical or mental health; a risk of physical or mental injury to any existing children of *her* family greater than the risk involved in having an abortion; a substantial risk that if the child is born it will suffer from serious physical or mental abnormalities.

In deciding whether there is a risk to the pregnant woman's physical or mental health, the doctors can take her home conditions into account. So, for example, if the birth of another child would mean that the existing family had to live in seriously overcrowded conditions, grounds for abortion would exist. The Medical Defence Union, which provides legal advice and assistance to doctors, has said that in cases where it is alleged that the health of existing children is threatened by the birth of another child the doctors should discuss the situation with the husband.

In any event, doctors prefer to discuss the pros and cons of abortion with a woman's husband, but they cannot do so without the woman's consent. In theory a husband's knowledge of, or consent to, an abortion is irrelevant but it may be very difficult to find two doctors who are willing to act without first consulting the husband.

The rule that a doctor must keep his dealings with his patients confidential is not a rule of law but merely a part of the doctor's own code of professional ethics. This means that he can be forced to give evidence in court about his patients and their treatment. For example, he could be called to give evidence in a divorce case if a wife had had an abortion without her husband's consent and the husband wanted to use this as proof of his wife's unreasonable behaviour.

Pregnancy

The right to maternity leave

Working women are now entitled to have time off in order to attend antenatal clinics and to be paid during absences from work for this purpose.

A woman who has been employed for the 104 weeks up to the 11th week before the expected week of confinement is entitled to maternity leave, provided that she has worked at least sixteen hours in each week. Maternity leave entitles a woman to take 11 weeks off before confinement and 27 weeks off after the birth, before she returns to work. A woman who is employed for less than sixteen hours each week may also be entitled to maternity leave if she has worked for the same employer for the previous five years.

A woman who wants to return to work after having a child must inform her employer in writing of her intention to do so, giving the date or week of confinement. This written notification must be made 21 days before leaving, or as soon as is reasonably practicable (to take account of premature birth or miscalculation). The woman will also have to inform her employer in writing 21 days before her return to work of the proposed date of her return. Employers will be able to write to the woman at any time after 49 days from the birth asking her to confirm in writing her intention to return to work. She must then confirm her intention within 14 days unless this is not reasonably practicable.

An employer can refuse to take back a woman if he and any associated employer has five employees or less at the time of her leaving and it is not reasonably practicable to take her back either in her old job or in a suitable alternative job. In these circumstances the refusal to take her back does not amount to an unfair dismissal and no compensation can be claimed.

An employer can also refuse to take back a woman if he or an associated employer offers her suitable alternative employment and she does not accept the offer.

Maternity grant

This is a single lump sum payment of £25 to a woman who has given birth or is expected to give birth within eleven weeks. Entitlement is based on the woman's own national insurance contributions, or on those of her husband. The contribution record of the mother or her husband ceased to be relevant in July 1982. From this date onwards every mother will qualify for the grant provided that she has resided in the United Kingdom for at least 26 weeks out of the last 52 weeks before confinement.

Maternity allowance

This is a weekly sum payable to a woman from fourteen weeks before confinement. Entitlement to the allowance depends on the woman's own insurance contribution record; if this is insufficient then the allowance will be paid at a reduced rate. The rate at the moment is £25.00 (part of this sum may however be 'clawed back', as the government expected the rate of inflation to be higher than in fact it is).

The allowance is payable for eleven weeks before confinement and for seven weeks after, that is for a total period of eighteen weeks.

It is also possible to claim an allowance of £0.30 for each dependent child and an allowance of £15.45 for a husband who cannot support himself. Sickness benefit can be claimed instead of maternity allowance. A woman who works during the time when she could be claiming maternity allowance is disqualified from claiming.

Maternity pay from an employer

A woman who is entitled to maternity leave is also entitled to be paid maternity pay by her employer. Certain conditions must however be fulfilled before a claim can be made:

- She must have been in full-time (defined as sixteen hours' work each week) work for a minimum of two years with the same employer, or in part-time work (defined as eight hours' work or more each week) for over five years with the same employer.
- She must remain in work until the eleventh week before confinement.

The employer is then bound to pay her maternity pay, which is now (since the abolition of the earnings-related supplement to the maternity allowance) her normal pay less the maternity allowance, national insurance contribution, and tax, for a maximum period of six weeks.

It is important to note that this is what the state requires the employer to do at the very least. Consequently, many employers have given far greater maternity rights to their employees under their contract of employment.

4 Rights over children

This chapter is about the rights that parents and others may exercise over children under the age of eighteen. The rights are described at the beginning of the chapter; the rest of the chapter deals with the extent to which each of these rights can be exercised by different categories of people. The rights are numbered from **1** to **17** and this numbering is used throughout the remainder of the chapter for easy reference.

The rights described

1 *The right to physical possession*

(Sometimes known as either 'custody' or 'care and control'.) This right can best be defined as the right to determine the place and manner in which the child's time is spent. In particular it covers the child's place of residence.

In most cases the parents will have the best claim as against any other person to the physical possession of their children.

2 *The right to choose the child's name*

There is a duty to register the birth of a child within forty-two days of the birth, and the parents have the right to choose the name to be entered on the birth certificate. This applies not only to the child's first names but also to the surname. Although it is usual to choose the family married name for the child this is not compulsory; if they wish the parents can give the child a surname which has no connection with either of them. The only limitation to this is that although the mother of an illegitimate child can choose the father's surname she cannot register him as the father of the child unless he gives his consent or has already admitted paternity. (See Chapter 2 for a fuller explanation of names and the naming of children.)

3 *The right to determine the child's religious education*

This is a right to choose whether or not the child should have any form of religious education, and if such education is thought desirable to determine what form it should take.

4 *The right to consent to medical treatment*

This covers the right to consent to normal medical treatment. This right ends when the child reaches the age of sixteen.

5 *The right to have a child educated and to choose the form of that education*

This is in effect a right which can be enforced by action against the local education authority, who are under a duty to provide sufficient schools in the district. Parents also have the right to choose between private and state education. If the parents choose state education they have a limited right to express a preference for a particular school. (See Chapter 8 for a fuller explanation of rights and duties connected with a child's education.)

6 *The right to discipline a child*
A parent has the right to punish a disobedient child, but the punishment inflicted must be a reasonable one. What is reasonable will depend on the age, sex, physical condition and build of the child. (See Chapter 9 for more details.)

7 *The right to services from a child*
The services in question can be such things as making cups of tea and doing the washing-up, which the child could be expected to perform without payment. In reality this right is no more than a legal fiction; its only real importance is that it gives parents a right to claim damages from a third party who has caused injury to their child and so deprived them of his or her services.

8 *The right to administer the child's assets and income*
The effect of this is probably no more than to oversee the way in which a child disposes of his or her income. Once again, the extent of this right will depend to a large extent on the age of the child.

9 *The right to represent the child in legal proceedings*
This is the right to act as the child's 'next friend' in order to bring proceedings in a civil case on behalf of the child. The right is of limited application where the child is the subject of a care hearing (see page 43).

10 *The right to consent to the issue of a passport*
The effect of this right is that the passport office will not issue a passport to a child over 16 but under 18 on his own application; nor will it issue a separate passport to a child under 16, without the consent of a parent.

11 *The right to object to the passing of a Section 3 resolution by a local authority*
This right will only arise when a child has been received into the care of a local authority when the family has been in temporary difficulties, perhaps because of the ill health of one or both parents. The passing of the resolution is an attempt by the local authority to

keep the children in care on a more permanent basis. It is to this that a parent can object. (See Chapter 6.)

12 *The right to refuse to agree to the making of an adoption order*
An adoption order can only be made when the parents of a child have agreed that the child should be adopted. The right to refuse to agree to an adoption order may be taken away from a parent if the parent is thought to be exercising the right in an unreasonable way. (See Chapter 3, page 12.)

13 *The right to consent to the marriage of a child aged between 16 and 18 years*
If a child wishes to marry before his or her eighteenth birthday the child must first obtain consent from *both parents*. The consent of only one will do where the parents are divorced, separated, or one has deserted the other. If one or both parents refuse consent, the child can apply to the court, and if the court approves, the child can marry without parental consent.

14 *The right to appoint a guardian*
Either parent can, by will or by deed, appoint any person to become the guardian of the child after that parent's death. In these circumstances the guardian can exercise his rights jointly with the surviving parent.

15 *The right to succeed to the property of a child on that child's death*
This right will arise in cases where the child dies without having made a will. The only people under eighteen who can make valid wills are service personnel on active service and merchant seamen.

16 *The right to access: 'visitation rights'*
This right, which is to maintain contact with the child, is only likely to be of importance in circumstances where one parent has left the family home, or where the child is no longer living with his or her parents.

17 *The right to choose domicile and nationality*
All children have by birth a domicile of origin, which, if they are legitimate, is the domicile of their father at the date of the birth, and if illegitimate, is the domicile of their mother at the date of birth. Until the age of 16 a child's domicile is said to depend upon that of the father (if legitimate) and that of the mother (if illegit-

imate), so that any change in that parent's domicile will automatically change the domicile of the child. If married parents are living apart, then the domicile of the child may follow that of the mother if his or her home is normally with the mother. (In law, domicile means more than just a home or place of residence. It is the country with which a person has his closest connection, and the law of the country of domicile governs most aspects of marriage and divorce among other things.)

From 1 January 1983 a new Nationality Act came into force. This provides for three new types of nationality: British Citizenship, British Dependent Territories Citizenship, and British Overseas Citizenship. Only British citizens will automatically have the right of abode in the UK.

For children born before January 1983: Any patrial citizen of the UK and Colonies will automatically obtain British citizenship. Any child who was born, adopted, registered or naturalized in the UK or Islands, or whose parent or grandparent was, is a patrial citizen and will therefore obtain British citizenship.

For children born after January 1983: Any child who is born in the UK and is the legitimate child of a British citizen or settled mother or father will automatically obtain British citizenship. Similarly, an illegitimate child of a British citizen or settled mother will also obtain British citizenship if born in the UK.

Any child who is not born in the UK but whose parents were, will automatically obtain British citizenship. However, if the child is of the second generation born abroad, then transmission of British citizenship is no longer automatic. If the child has resided in the UK with his parents for three years, then during his minority (whilst under 18 years) he is entitled to register as a British citizen. If the parent of the child has resided in the UK for some period of three years ending before the child is born, and one grandparent of the child was born in the UK, then the child may be registered as a British citizen within one year of its birth. If neither of these residence requirements are fulfilled, then the child will have to qualify in his own right for admission to the UK, and if he desires British citizenship will have to qualify for naturalization. The Home Secretary does however have an absolute discretion to register any minor as a British citizen provided that the child has a close link with the UK, for example, if the child has been schooled there.

Any child who is born in the UK but does not have British

citizenship may, if he has lived here for ten years, register as a British citizen. Similarly, a child who is stateless may register as a British citizen, provided that he is aged between 10 and 22 years, and can prove five years' residence at any time.

If the parents of a child become settled in the UK or British citizens of the UK, then the child may register as a British citizen.

Natural parents of legitimate children and parents of adopted children

All the parental rights described above, with the exception of the choice of domicile and nationality (**17**), can, in the absence of a court order, be exercised separately by each natural parent and by each parent of an adopted child without consultation with each other. This can obviously lead to disputes between the parents. The next section of this chapter is therefore intended to identify the circumstances which are likely to lead to disputes and to suggest some of the remedies that are available in law.

Permanent breakdown of parents' marriage

If the parents of a child have obtained a decree of divorce, nullity or judicial separation (see Chapter 10) the court is obliged to consider the arrangements which the parents are proposing to make for the future of their children.

The final order by the court will, however, be made in accordance with what the court believes to be in the best interests of the child. The order may take one of the following forms:

Custody to both parents, care and control to one

The term custody does not, strangely enough, include physical possession. This means that, where both parents have custody, all the rights described above except for the right to the physical possession of the child will continue to be exercisable by both of them. The right to physical possession will be exercisable exclusively by the parent who is granted care and control. In most cases the parent who has not got physical possession of the child will have a right of access. The court will only make an order of this kind where both parents still get on well with each other and are likely to be able to agree on the upbringing of the child.

Where an *interim* custody order is made, the courts sometimes divide the physical care of the child equally between the parents so as to maintain each parent's links with the child until a final decision can be made.

Custody to one parent, care and control to the other

The parent granted custody will be entitled to make all the major decisions affecting the child's future upbringing, and so will be entitled to exercise all the parental rights except the right to physical possession. This right is given to the parent who is granted care and control.

Particular problems may arise on the making of this kind of order. For example, there would appear to be no right to change the surname of a child without the prior consent of either the other parent or the court.

The parent with care and control must make all the decisions about the day-to-day upbringing of the child, but of course these decisions may conflict with the rights retained by the parent with custody.

The parent granted custody will normally be granted a right of reasonable access by the court.

Custody and care and control to one parent only

This means that all the parental rights will be granted to one parent, although the other will usually be granted the right of access. Once again there is no right to change the surname of the child without the prior consent of either the other parent or the court.

This type of order is likely to be made in cases where there remains, after the divorce, continuing disagreement between the parents.

Temporary marital difficulties where the parents are still cohabiting

Since all the parental rights described above are exercisable equally, but separately, by each parent, disputes may well arise in the exercise of any particular right. If the parents cannot resolve such a dispute by discussion, they can apply to the court for directions.

Some examples of possible disputes

Education One parent wants the child privately educated, while the other parent wants the child educated within the state system. The court will decide which form of education is preferable, keeping as the paramount consideration the interests of the child.

Medical treatment Parents in dispute about non-therapeutic treatment, such as circumcision, can ask the court to decide what is in the child's best interests.

Temporary marital difficulties where the parents have ceased to cohabit

This section applies not only where the parents' marriage has been experiencing temporary difficulties, but also where the marriage has broken down completely, although the parents have not yet obtained a divorce. If the parents are unable to agree about the upbringing of their child they can make application to the court so that the court can determine which of them should be given the 'legal custody' of the child. 'Legal custody' in this context includes all the parental rights that concern the physical possession of the child. 'Legal custody', therefore, does not include the following rights:

- the right to change the child's surname (**2**);
- the right to administer the child's assets and income (**8**);
- the right to arrange for the child's emigration from the UK (**10**);
- the right to object to a Section 3 resolution (**11**);
- the right to succeed to the child's property on his death (**15**);
- the right to refuse to agree to an adoption order (**12**).

These excluded rights continue to be exercisable by both of the child's natural or adoptive parents.

Disputes with the child

The law has very little to offer a parent who is in dispute with a child over the exercise of any of the parental rights. A parent could, if the child were beyond his control, ask the local authority to initiate proceedings to have the child taken into care, but this course of action would be likely to destroy any existing emotional relationship between the parents and the child.

All kinds of disputes can arise between parents and children; a few examples are discussed below:

Your child wants to leave home (**1**)

This will interfere with the parental right to physical possession. A court, however, would be unlikely to order a child who has reached the age of discretion (normally sixteen) to return home. In other circumstances, although the court might be willing to make an order directing the child to return home, the enforcement of such an order without locking the child up is almost impossible.

Your daughter aged under sixteen is taking the contraceptive pill (4)
This would seem to be a breach of the parental right to consent to medical treatment for a child under sixteen. This right, however, conflicts with the code of practice which applies to medical practitioners. They will not, unless the child first gives her consent, consult parents before prescribing oral contraceptives, although most doctors prefer not to prescribe at all without consulting the parents.

Your child wants to leave school at sixteen (15)
Although parents have the right to choose the form of their child's education, this does not include a right to force the child to remain at school beyond compulsory school-leaving age (currently sixteen).

Disputes with third parties
This kind of dispute is most likely to arise between parents and either foster parents or relatives. In the last resort these disputes will have to be dealt with under the wardship procedure available in the Family Division of the High Court (see page 73). The effect of making a child a ward of court is that the court takes over the parental role so that no important step in the upbringing of the child can be taken without the court's authority. In effect the court grants custody to itself, but it then has to decide which of the disputing parties is the most suitable to have the care and control (i.e. physical possession) of the child. The welfare of the child is the most important consideration and dictates the court's decision.

Action against foster parents to obtain the return of the physical possession of the child
It is often said that the parents have the best claim to the physical possession of the child. Whether the court will be prepared to uphold this view will depend on the child's best interests. In circumstances where a private fostering arrangement has lasted for some time, the court will usually take the view that the child's interests are best served by causing as little disruption to his upbringing as possible. Therefore if the child has become very attached to his foster parents, the court may decide that it would be best to leave the child with them. In that case the parents will usually be granted access because of the possibility that, at some time in the future, the child might again be transferred to their care.

Action by a third party to prevent a parent exercising a particular right
This could happen where a parent has consented to a child's undergoing a form of non-therapeutic medical treatment, such as a sterilization operation or circumcision. Any interested third party can apply to the court to have the child made a ward, so that the court can decide whether the proposed medical treatment is beneficial or not.

Natural parents of illegitimate children

The mother of an illegitimate child has the sole right to exercise all the parental rights described at the beginning of this chapter except two: choice of registration of father (**2**) and succession to property (**15**).

The father of an illegitimate child therefore has no original rights over his child.

Limitations to mother's rights
Choice of registration
The mother can use the father's surname for the child, but she cannot register the man as the father unless she has already obtained his consent, or he has made a statutory declaration acknowledging his parenthood of the child, or an affiliation order has been made by a court against the father.

The right to succeed to property
In this case both parents are equally entitled to inherit the estate of a child who dies without having made a will.

The father's rights
Although the father of an illegitimate child has no original rights, he may acquire rights in the following ways.

Legitimization
If the parents of an illegitimate child subsequently marry, the child will become legitimate and all rights over him or her will then be exercisable equally by both parents as though the child had been born legitimately.

Adoption
The father of an illegitimate child can adopt it and so obtain all the parental rights. But the father can only do this if the mother is dead

or the court has ordered that the mother be excluded from the upbringing of the child.

In deciding whether to make such an order the court must first consider the welfare of the child and, depending upon its age, its views.

Guardianship

The mother may appoint the father to be the guardian of the child on her death. The father can also apply to be made guardian on the mother's death. In each case the father will acquire all the rights which the father of a legitimate child would have (and see below).

Legal custody

The father of an illegitimate child can apply to the court for an order granting legal custody to him.

An order for legal custody gives the successful applicant all the normal parental rights except for (**2**), (**8**), (**10**), and (**15**). It is unlikely, however, that a father who is a stranger to his child would succeed in such an application. If the father were successful, the mother of the child would probably be allowed to retain some of her original parental rights and would anyway continue to exercise those rights which relate to the property rather than the possession of the child – that is, (**2**), (**8**), (**10**), and (**15**). Here again the court's decision would be taken with the child's best interests in mind.

Access

The father of an illegitimate child may apply to the court for access to that child, and this will be granted in cases where it coincides with the child's welfare.

Guardians

The natural parents of a legitimate child, the parents of an adopted child and the mother of an illegitimate child are known as their child's 'natural guardians'. A natural guardian automatically has by law all the parental rights described at the beginning of this chapter.

It is, however, possible to appoint a guardian to act in place of a parent after that parent's death. The guardian can be appointed either by the parent or by the court on the application of the person who wants to be appointed. Once a guardian has taken over he or she is entitled to exercise all the parental rights described above.

If the guardian is to exercise his or her rights jointly either with the surviving parent or with another guardian it is possible that a dispute may arise in the exercise of the parental rights. In these circumstances an application can be made to the court for directions as to how the dispute should be settled. The court will act only in the interests of the child. Where the dispute is particularly deep-rooted the court can remove the guardian.

It is sometimes possible for the father of an illegitimate child, or any other person who has been granted the legal custody of that child, to appoint a guardian.

A guardian appointed in this way would only be entitled to exercise the parental rights which relate to the person of the child. This excludes (**2**), (**8**), (**10**), and (**15**).

Grandparents

Grandparents have no automatic rights over a child but they may apply to court if they want to obtain some rights.

Right to apply for access

There are several ways in which a grandparent can apply for access to a grandchild:

1 On a decree of divorce, nullity or judicial separation the court has power to make whatever order for custody it thinks fit; this could include an order for access by grandparents.

2 If an application for the legal custody of a child is before a court, grandparents can intervene and ask for an access order.

These rights of application apply whether the child concerned is legitimate or illegitimate. Once again the grant of access will depend on whether the court believes that it will be in the best interests of the child.

Grandparents as guardians

It is open to a parent of a child to appoint the child's grandparents to act as guardians after that parent's death. Alternatively a grandparent can apply to the court to be made the guardian of a child on the premature death of the parent. The grandparents will then exercise all the parental rights either alone or jointly with the surviving parent, if there is one.

Disputes between grandparents and others over the exercise of parental rights

The wardship procedure

A grandparent can apply to the court to have the child made a ward of court (see page 73). If the court accepts that the child should be made a ward the effect will be that custody is taken over by the court. This means that the court will in future make any major decisions concerning the upbringing of the child. At the same time it will be decided who should in future have the care and control of the child (that is, the physical possession). This will again be decided in accordance with the best interests of the child. If the grandparent is not granted care and control he or she can ask the court to consider instead making an order for access.

Grandparents might use this procedure where their grandchildren have been taken into care by a local authority. The hope would be that the court considering wardship would grant physical possession of the children to the grandparents rather than allow the children to be placed in a home or with foster parents.

Custodians

(*Warning:* These new rules about custodians have already been approved by Parliament but, at the time of writing, they are not yet in force.)

An application for a custodianship order can be made, with parental consent, by a relative of the child or by a step-parent if he or she has had possession of the child for three months; a person who is not related to the child can apply after twelve months' possession.

Where the parents of a child do not consent, an application can be made by a person who has had the physical possession of that child for three years, and in particular, possession for the three months preceding the application.

Whether or not the order is made will depend on the best interests of the child.

The effect of a custodianship order is to give legal custody to the applicant. This means that the applicant will be entitled in the future to retain the physical possession of the child and exercise all the parental rights which relate to the physical possession of the child. This excludes (**2**), (**8**), (**10**), (**15**), and (**17**).

People who might wish to make use of this procedure could include: any blood relative, any person related by marriage, including a step-parent, and any foster parent with whom the child has been placed, either privately by the parents, or by the social services department of a local authority after a care order or resolution (see page 42).

Local authorities

A local authority may acquire parental rights or powers in one of two ways: by obtaining a care order, or by passing a resolution about a child who is already in their care (discussed in detail in Chapter 6).

The most important of these parental rights which a local authority may acquire is the right to the physical possession of the child (which is then lost to the natural parents until such time as the order or resolution is discharged). The local authority has no power either to change the religion of the child or to agree to the child's adoption. It is not clear, however, whether the local authority's parental rights and powers include the right to consent to the marriage of a child (**13**) or any of those rights which relate to the property of the child – i.e. (**2**), (**8**), (**10**), and (**15**). In cases of doubt, local authorities will usually ask parents to give their written consent to any exercise of these powers by the authority.

Once a local authority has a child in its care it must exercise its parental rights in such a way that the welfare of the child is always the first consideration. If a parent considers that the local authority is not exercising its powers properly he or she can apply to the High Court to have the child made a ward. The High Court will, however, refuse to intervene in cases where parents are in reality using the procedure as a method of appealing against the order which places the child in the care of the local authority. This is discussed in more detail on page 46.

If the local authority has, in the exercise of its parental rights, placed the child with foster parents, it would seem that the authority can consent to a custodianship order (see page 29) being made in favour of the foster parents. A foster parent who has had the physical possession of a child for three years will be entitled to apply to become the custodian of the child, so as to prevent the local authority from exercising its right to take back the physical possession of the child.

5 Duties of parents

There are three duties that parents owe to their children. They are the duty to ensure that a child receives education, the duty to maintain a child, and the duty to protect a child. Although called 'parental' duties they will sometimes have to be carried out by people who are not parents. There are also variations in the meaning of 'child': some duties apply only to children under the age of sixteen, others to children even after they have reached the age of eighteen.

The legal results of not performing parental duties vary. In some cases the state (through a local authority social services department) may try to have the child removed from parental control; or the local authority may itself have a duty to receive the child into care. In other cases a failure to perform a parental duty may lead to criminal charges being brought against the person who should have performed the duty.

Duty to educate

This duty begins when the child is five and lasts until the child reaches the age when compulsory schooling ends. A child who becomes sixteen between 1 September and 31 January must remain in school until the end of the next Easter holiday; any other child who reaches the age of sixteen during that school year (Jan.–Sept.) must remain in school until the end of May.

The duty must be carried out by any person who has the physical possession of a child and so may have to be carried out by people other than parents or guardians.

The duty is to ensure that the child receives efficient full-time education suitable to his age, ability and aptitude. Thus it is possible to comply with the duty either by sending the child to school or by providing a proper education at home. If the local education authority takes the view that the education which is provided for the child is unsuitable, it can order the child to attend a specified school by making what is called an attendance order. If the attendance order is not complied with, then the actual custodians will have committed a criminal offence. The local education authority may then have them brought before the magistrates' court. (For choice of school and stating a preference see page 52.)

Parents must also ensure that the child attends school regularly. So a parent will be guilty of a criminal offence if the child's attendance at school is irregular and the absences are not caused by sickness or other proper reason.

A local education authority that is considering taking criminal proceedings against the parents of a child must also consider whether to start care proceedings against the child in the juvenile court. The effect of successful care proceedings is to transfer the child into the physical possession of the local authority, which must then carry out the parental duties itself. The authority may, for example, place the child in a children's home and have him taken to and from school.

To obtain a care order the local authority will have to establish two things:

- that the parents have broken their duty to have the child educated; and
- that the child will not receive proper care and control unless the care order is made.

Lack of 'care' in this context means that the child is being deprived of education which is necessary for normal social and intellectual development. It has happened that parents who were politically opposed to a system of comprehensive school education have lost the physical possession of their children to local authorities because they refused to send their children to school.

Duty to maintain

This is a duty to provide the child with adequate food, clothing and lodgings and, if necessary, to seek the help of the state to achieve these ends by, for example, claiming supplementary benefit or the family income supplement (see Chapter 11, page 115).

It is a criminal offence to neglect a child by failing to maintain it, and charges may be brought against a parent, guardian or anyone else who has possession of the child.

As well as facing criminal charges, a parent who fails to maintain a child properly may find that the child is compulsorily taken into the care of a local authority under a *care order*.

A care order is usually made by a juvenile court on the application of a local authority, but it can be made by any court which is considering the custody of a child – for example, in divorce proceedings.

A parent who is having difficulty in maintaining a child can also ask a local authority to *receive* the child into its care.

Receiving a child into care

A parent who is unable to provide properly for a child because of permanent or temporary difficulties may ask the local authority to receive a child who is under the age of seventeen into its care. The local authority will then take over the obligation to provide accommodation and maintenance for the child, although the parent may be asked to contribute to the cost of such provision (see below). A local authority is obliged to give any guidance and assistance that may eliminate the need to receive the child into its care, provided that this is in the interests of the child. Assistance can take the form of provision in kind or in cash. For example, the authority might provide day care facilities so that a parent could work to support the family; or the authority could provide a cash grant to cover the cost of outstanding gas or electricity bills or arrears of rent. A child who has been received into care may be returned to its parents at their request. If the child has been in care for six months the parents must give twenty-eight days' notice of their intention to apply for the return of the child.

It is also possible for a person who has the physical possession of the child to get a *court order* requiring the parent whose duty it is to maintain the child to make a *financial contribution* to the child's support (see page 34 onwards). In some circumstances the child himself can apply to the court for such an order (see page 39).

What parents must do when a child is in care

When a child is in the care of a local authority because a care order has been made by a court, or because the parents have asked the authority to receive the child into its care, the parents must notify the authority of any change in their address and they may also be asked to contribute to the upkeep of the child.

Change of address

There are two reasons for notifying a change of address to the local authority. First, because the local authority will wish to keep in touch with the parents, and cooperate with them, in the hope that the child can one day be returned to their care; and second, because the parents may be required to make a financial contribution to the upkeep of the child while it is in the care of the local authority.

Contribution to upkeep: parents of legitimate children and mothers of illegitimate children
The amount of any contribution will be assessed by the local authority and it will not be greater than the boarding-out allowance paid to foster parents even though the actual cost of maintaining the child is much greater. If the parents do not agree with the assessment the local authority can apply to the magistrates' court for a 'contribution order'. In making the order the court will take into account the means of the parent and will not in any case order the parent to pay an amount greater than the original assessment. An order can last only so long as the child is in care and can be varied if the means of the parents change.

Contribution to upkeep: reputed father of an illegitimate child
If there is an affiliation order in existence (see page 37) then the local authority can apply to a magistrates' court to have the order varied so that payment is made to the local authority rather than to the mother of the child. In cases where there is no affiliation order the local authority can apply for one to the magistrates' court within three years of the child's coming into its care. The mother of the child does not have to give evidence although an order cannot be made unless the evidence proving the paternity of the father is corroborated, possibly by a blood test.

Instead of going to court, the local authority may try to get the putative father to agree voluntarily to contribute to the maintenance of the child.

Once again these arrangements last only for as long as the child is in the care of the local authority.

Enforcing the duty to maintain by application to a court for a financial provision order

(a) *Application to the magistrates' court for financial provision*
Either party to a marriage can apply to a magistrates' court for an order to enforce the duty to maintain a child. There are three possible grounds for the application:

- first, that the respondent is failing to make a proper contribution towards the maintenance of the child (in deciding a case on this ground the court will take into account all the circumstances of the case and in particular the guidelines set out on page 36);
- second, either party can apply to the court for a consent order. This will only be approved by the court if the arrangement appears proper or reasonable (see page 36 for details);

- third, if the parties have separated voluntarily and maintenance payments have been made over the three months preceding the application, the court can convert these payments into an order (see page 92 for details).

Whenever an application has been made to the court on any of these three grounds the court cannot make a final order or dismiss the application without first considering the future actual custody (that is, physical possession of the child). If an order for actual custody is made, then an order for financial support can be made against either party to the marriage, payable to the actual custodian for the benefit of the child or to the child directly.

Orders which a magistrates' court can make The court can order a periodical and/or a lump sum payment of up to £500, to the applicant for the benefit of the child or to the child directly.

Duration of orders Orders which are made payable to the applicant for the benefit of a child come to an end if the parties to the marriage continue or resume cohabitation for a continuous period of six months. Orders payable to a child directly are not subject to this limitation unless the court says so. All orders for continuing support are subject to the rules on age (see page 39) and will terminate in any event on the death of either the person to whom they are payable or the person by whom they are paid.

(b) *Applications to the Divorce County Court and High Court (Family Division) for financial support*

These cases are based on a failure to provide or make proper contribution to the maintenance of a child of the family (see page 36). The procedure is the same as that in the magistrates' court, which is described above, except for the following:

Orders which the court can make In addition to periodical payment orders the county court and the High Court can make secured periodical payment orders (see page 97) and there is no limit to the size of lump sum orders.

Duration of orders Orders made by these courts only cease when the child ceases to be eligible in terms of age (see page 39) or when the person to or by whom payment is made dies.

A secured periodical payment order, however, is unaffected by death.

Interim orders Interim orders can be made by all the courts described above and are temporary orders for financial support available in cases where the court considers there is need. Such orders can last for three months with the possibility of a further three months being available if the full hearing cannot take place within that period.

(c) *Orders for financial support available in proceedings for divorce, nullity or judicial separation*

Financial support in this context may include both orders for money payments and property adjustments (see page 97). The opportunity to order a property adjustment only arises when a decree of divorce, etc. is actually granted, whereas an order to pay money can be made even if the application for the divorce is refused. Money payments in this context include periodical payments, secured periodical payments and lump sums (see page 97 for a definition), and can be ordered to be paid to the party to the marriage who is given actual custody, to an unconnected third party given actual custody, or to the child himself. Property adjustment orders include transfers, settlements and variations of settlements made on or in contemplation of marriage (see pages 98–9 for definitions).

Property adjustment orders and a lump sum order are mainly used by the court to ensure that a child is adequately housed whilst a dependant. Otherwise orders will be made which ensure that a child is given shelter, food and education which accords with the financial standing of the parties to the marriage.

The guidelines

These guidelines, with some small points of distinction, apply equally to sections (a), (b), and (c) above. The guidelines require the court to consider the following:

- the current and future financial position of the parties to the marriage, including their ownership of property;
- their current and future financial needs and obligations;
- the financial needs and position of the child;
- any disabilities suffered by the child;
- the standard of living enjoyed before the application;
- the manner and expected manner of education of the child.

In divorce proceedings the court is also required to place the children in the position that they would have been in if the marriage had not broken down and if each party to it had properly performed his obligations to the child.

In any case which involves the support of a child of the family, who is not the child of the person against whom an order is made, special guidelines are applied by the court. The court must take into account:

- whether the person assumed responsibility for the child;
- the extent, basis and length of time of that assumption;
- whether there was knowledge of the real situation;
- and the liability of any other person to maintain the child.

Financial orders made in custody dispute cases under the Guardianship of Minors Act

Custody in this context means the actual custody or physical possession of a child. In any situation where the court decides to make an order for actual custody, the court can order financial support to be paid either to the actual custodian for the benefit of the child, or to the child directly.

Three courts have power to make orders in this area, the magistrates' court, the county court, or the High Court (Family Division). Each court can order periodical or lump sum payments. In the magistrates' court lump sum payments will be limited to £500.

An order cannot be made in this area of the law for the support of an illegitimate child. (The Law Commission has recommended that this rule should be abolished.)

Where the court makes a preliminary decision about custody it may also make a periodical payments order, which will last for three months. If the final decision about custody has not been made by then, the order for payment can be extended for another three months.

In any case in which the parents of the child either continue to live together or resume living together for a continuous period of six months, the order for maintenance will terminate. If it is made payable directly to the child, however, the maintenance order will not terminate, even if the parents are living together, unless the court says so.

Financial support orders against the reputed father of an illegitimate child

These proceedings are known as affiliation proceedings and can only be brought in the magistrates' court, either by the mother of the child, the custodian of the child (see page 29) or a local authority in whose care the child is (see page 30).

The mother can claim if she was a single woman at the time of either the birth of the child or the application to the court. A 'single woman' for these purposes includes an unmarried, divorced, widowed and in some cases separated woman.

An application must be made within three years of the child's birth, unless it can be shown that the father actually supported the child at some time during that three-year period, or that the father left England during that three-year period, in which case an application can be made within the year of his return.

If the man denies that he is the father of the child the mother will have to give evidence of paternity, and this evidence must be 'corroborated in a material particular'. Evidence that will suffice includes:

- an admission of paternity to a third party;
- registration of the man's name as father;
- evidence of sexual intercourse at the relevant time;
- a blood test which shows a strong probability that the man tested is the father.

Blood tests are expensive (approximately £80), although this cost can, if the person seeking the tests is legally aided, be paid by the state out of the Legal Aid Fund. If the court directs that blood tests are to be taken, any refusal will allow the court to draw inferences against the person refusing. The court will not direct a blood test unless this is in the best interests of the child and this would normally be the case if it was likely to establish paternity.

If the case is found proved, the court can order periodical payments and the payment of a lump sum (maximum £500) against the reputed father. These payments can be ordered to be made to the mother for the benefit of the child, or to the child directly. The father may also enter into an enforceable agreement with the mother to maintain his illegitimate child. Any default in this contractual obligation could be remedied by an order from a county court.

The court may be prepared to make a periodical payment order for the child which includes an element of support for the mother whose earnings or capacity to earn are reduced or lost as a result of caring for the child.

(The Law Commission has proposed that the law relating to legitimate and illegitimate children should be brought more closely into line.)

Orders for financial support attached to a custodianship order
(See *Warning* on page 29.) Whenever a custodianship order is made, an order for periodical payments or a lump sum order (limited to £500 in the magistrates' court) can be made against the parents of a legitimate child, or against any adult within whose marriage the child was treated as a member of the family. Orders can be paid to the custodian for the benefit of the child or to the child directly.

A custodian is given the power to apply for an affiliation order against the reputed father of an illegitimate child within three years of the custodianship order.

Orders for maintenance made under the wardship jurisdiction
When a child is made a ward of court, the court will decide who should have the care and control (i.e. physical possession) of the child in the future. The court is empowered to order the parent without physical possession to make periodical payments for the support of the child. The court will decide what is a reasonable sum bearing in mind the means of the parent, and orders will not be made if the parents are residing together and will terminate if they resume cohabitation for a continuous period of three months.

A child who has reached the age of 18 (the date when wardship ends) will be entitled to apply for an order of financial support until he or she is 21, provided that the child's parents are not then residing together.

No orders can be made under these provisions if the child is illegitimate.

Age limitations
Orders for periodical payments will continue until a child is 17, although there is discretion to extend support until the child is 18. If there are special circumstances (for example, if the child suffers from some disability making independence at 18 impossible), then extension is possible until the death of the payer (and beyond in the case of secured periodical payment orders). Similarly, if a person of 18 is receiving education or training, such as an apprenticeship, the court is empowered to extend support beyond the age of 18.

These age limitations do not apply to property adjustment orders made in divorce proceedings (see page 98).

Applications for support by the child himself
Children are not entitled to enforce the duty of maintenance through court action, unless there is an existing dispute between their parents

or step-parents. It is, therefore, impossible for an eighteen year old to force his parents to pay their assessed contribution to any educational grant obtained from a local authority.

There are three exceptions to this rule:

- first, where there is an existing order which has ended between the ages of 16 and 18. In this case the child can apply to have the order revived (and increased if there has been a change in the circumstances) at any time before his 21st birthday. An order revived in this way could continue in force beyond the 21st birthday of the child;
- second, a child of 16 is entitled to ask for a variation of an existing order if there has been a change in the circumstances which could include an application to extend the order beyond his 17th or 18th birthday;
- third, if the parents of a child have divorced, or are in the process of divorcing, a child of the family aged 18 can apply in his own name for an order for his support if he is following a course of education or there are other special circumstances.

Variations

If there has been a change in the circumstances an application can be made to the court for a variation of a periodical payment order.

Obligations of support imposed by the state

In any situation in which a parent (including the mother of an illegitimate child, but excluding the reputed father) who could afford to comply with the duty to maintain a child but fails to do so (so that the state, through the supplementary benefits scheme, has to step in and support the child), the state may recover its payments from the defaulting parent. This is known as the 'liable relative rule'. A supplementary benefits officer will make an assessment against the liable relative, calculated in such a way that the person is not reduced to below subsistence level.

Subsistence level means the basic householder scale rate (which depends on whether the person is single or remarried or cohabiting); all reasonable housing costs; the stated allowance for any dependent child and one quarter of net earnings or £5 whichever is the larger. If agreement cannot be reached then application can be made to the magistrates' court for an order, which will be made on the basis of whatever the court thinks appropriate, bearing in mind the resources of the person brought before the court.

A persistent refusal to maintain, or neglect to maintain, also amounts to a criminal offence in supplementary benefits cases.

So far as illegitimate children are concerned, the reputed father can be forced to make payments to the state to reimburse payments of supplementary benefit made to the mother for her dependent illegitimate child. This can be done by varying an existing affiliation order so that payment is made to the supplementary benefits authority instead of to the mother or, if there is no existing order, by applying to the magistrates' court for an order payable to the authority. The authority has three years from the start of the payment of benefit to make the application.

Duty to protect

The criminal law

The duty to protect a child may be enforced by criminal action against the parent or other person with physical possession of the child. The extent of this duty depends to a large extent on the age of the child; the older the child becomes, the less far reaching the duty to protect.

Examples of criminal offences that can be committed include:

- a failure in the duty to protect resulting in death (if the failure is intentional, this will amount to murder; if the failure is not intentional, it will amount to manslaughter);
- leaving a child aged under 12 in a room with an unguarded fire, resulting in death or serious injury;
- allowing a child aged under 16 to take part in or train for dangerous performances;
- giving intoxicating liquor to a child aged under 5;
- being drunk in a public place whilst in charge of a child under 7;
- failing to notify the local authority of an intention to foster a child privately (not yet in force);
- encouraging or causing the seduction or prostitution of a daughter under 16;
- allowing a child aged over 4 and under 16 to be in a brothel;
- allowing a child to be photographed for or take part in pornographic films;
- leaving a child in the care of a baby-sitter who is too young for the job, or a child-minder who is not registered.

The civil law

A parent who fails to exercise reasonable care to protect his child from foreseeable dangers may be liable to compensate the child for any injury caused as a result of the breach. For example, a parent who allows a young child to cross a busy road without supervision will be liable if the child is injured by an oncoming car.

Care proceedings

A parent who fails to protect his child properly may run the risk of losing the care of that child to a local authority. This can occur where the failure in duty amounts to neglect or ill treatment, or exposure to moral danger, and a juvenile court is satisfied that the child would be unlikely to receive proper protection unless placed in the care of a local authority. If the duty of protection could be fulfilled by the parent with help from a social worker, then a supervision order could be made instead.

6 Children in care

There are three ways in which a child can come into the care of a local authority:

- where the authority *receives* a child into its care;
- where a *juvenile* court makes a *care order* as a result of an application to it by the authority; and
- where any *other* court makes a *care order* during a hearing about custody.

Child received into care

Local authorities have a duty to care for children whose parents are prevented from doing so either permanently or temporarily and who ask the local authority for help. A child received into care in this way must be returned to its parents at their request unless the local authority has already assumed full parental rights over the child, or the child has already been in the care of the local authority for six months. If the child has been in care for six months the parents must give 28 days' notice of their intention to take back the child. This effectively gives the authority 28 days in which to pass a resolution (see below) taking over the care of the child.

In caring for a child who is received into care, authorities are expected to work towards a solution that ensures that the possession of the child is taken over by a parent, guardian, relative or friend provided that this appears to be in the best interests of the child. In other words it is accepted that institutional care of children, even for short periods of time, should be avoided wherever possible. If the child is finally placed in the care of relatives or friends they must ensure that the child is brought up in accordance with the religious persuasion chosen by the child's parents.

Passing a resolution

The effect of a resolution passed by a local authority is to transfer all parental rights and duties, except the duty to contribute to the support of the child, to the authority.

A resolution can only be passed where one of the following conditions exists:

- if the parent or guardian is dead and the child has no other guardian or custodian;
- if the parents have abandoned the child;
- if one parent suffers from a permanent disability making him or her incapable of caring for the child, or from a mental disorder rendering him or her unfit to have the care of the child;
- if the habits or way of life of one or both parents make them unfit to have the care of the child (this might apply if one of them is an alcoholic or a drug addict);
- if the parents have consistently failed to discharge their obligations and are unfit to have the care of a child;
- if a person who is unfit or incapable of caring for a child is, or is likely to become, a member of the same household as the child;
- if, throughout the three years preceding the passing of the resolution, the child has been in the care of the local authority.

The authority must notify parents in writing, by registered or recorded delivery post, of the resolution. This notice must inform the parents that they have the right to object to the passing of the resolution. An objection, in order to be effective, must be made in writing, and served on the authority within one month of receipt of the notification of the passing of the resolution. An objection made in this way means that the resolution lapses after fourteen days unless the authority applies to a juvenile court for an order that the resolution shall not lapse. In deciding whether or not to support the authority's resolution, the court will investigate whether the grounds for passing the resolution still exist and whether the transfer of rights and duties is in the interests of the child. (Resolutions continue to have effect until the child is eighteen, is adopted, a guardian is appointed, or the authority repeals the resolution. Parents, guardians or anyone who would have parental rights and duties but for the resolution can apply to the juvenile court for discharge of the resolution.)

The resolution will be discharged if there were no grounds for passing it in the first place, or if the resolution is no longer in the interests of the child. The power of the authority to pass a resolution lasts only for so long as the child is physically in its care. It is likely that the resolution process will be reformed in the near future, and that all children will be referred to the juvenile court, which will decide after a full hearing whether the child should remain in care. Parents will then be able to put their own point of view to the court.

Care orders by a juvenile court

These can be applied for by a local authority, a police constable or an NSPCC officer. Applications are made to the juvenile court and an order can be made placing the child in the care of the authority if certain conditions exist *and* the child is in need of care and control. Most of the conditions that must exist relate to a failure in the parental duties and they are explained on page 31, but in this context there is one additional condition known as the 'offence precondition'. This means that the child has been found guilty of an offence (excluding homicide) and is beyond the control of the parents or guardian. So children who commit criminal offences, which include criminal damage to property after a football match, may be removed from parental control. And children who terrorize their parents so that the parents ask the authority to take the children away may be removed by order from parental care.

The powers of juvenile courts are limited to children under the age of 17, (or 16 if they are or have been married). Orders last until the child is 18, unless first made when the child is 16, in which case they last until 19.

The local authority, the parents or guardians, or the child can apply to the juvenile court at any time for an order of discharge from care.

It is important to note that parents are *not* parties to care proceedings, although they (and any foster parents) must be notified of such proceedings and at the hearing they are entitled to meet any allegations made against them by calling or giving evidence. They are not, as of right, entitled to cross-examine the local authority's witnesses, although they may be allowed to do so. Parents are entitled to act as their child's representative and, if they can afford to, they can pay for a lawyer to do so on their behalf. Parents are not at the moment entitled to legal aid in order to be represented. Only the child is entitled to legal aid for representation.

The government has announced that certain provisions of the Children Act 1975, which do allow for both children and parents to be legally aided, are to be brought into force in 1983.

In some cases there may well be a conflict of interests between the views held by the parents about the future of their child and the interests of the child. At present, if, in an application to discharge a care order, the court is of the opinion that there is a conflict of interest, and the local authority is not opposing the application, the court must order that the child be separately represented unless the court thinks that this is unnecessary to safeguard the interests of the child. In these circumstances both the parents and the child will be able to claim legal aid for legal representation. It is worth pointing out that the legal aid which is available is under the criminal legal aid scheme, and will therefore be determined by the magistrates' court. If all the provisions mentioned above are brought into effect, then the court *may* order that the parents are not to represent the child if the court believes that there may be a conflict of interest. Once again this will entitle both the child and the parents to legal representation, and where the court considers it appropriate, the parents may obtain legal aid. The right of parents to be heard in these circumstances is to meet any allegations made against them, to make representations to the court, and with the permission of the court to cross-examine any witnesses.

In cases where parents are allowed to represent their child and instruct a solicitor, or where the court orders that the child be separately represented, the solicitor may well refuse to follow the parents' instructions if it appears to him that those instructions do not coincide with the interests of the child. It is also open to the court to grant legal aid for the child and instruct a solicitor on the child's behalf or, if the child is old enough, to allow the child to instruct a solicitor himself.

The powers of the court are not limited to making care orders; it can instead make an order for the supervision of the child, who will then remain with his parents. These orders can be challenged in the same way as care orders.

Care orders in custody hearings

In custody or wardship proceedings courts will only commit children to the care of a local authority where there are exceptional circumstances making this desirable. The welfare of the child is the first and paramount consideration.

The duty of the local authority
Once a child has been placed in its care, the authority's first duty is to safeguard and promote the welfare of the child, taking into account the child's own wishes.

Challenging care orders

1 The wardship procedure
This procedure allows the High Court to protect those who, because of their youth, are not able to protect themselves, but it is of limited application in challenging a local authority's exercise of its rights over children in care.

Courts will refuse to use their powers so as to interfere with the exercise of an authority's discretion to deal with the child as it thinks best. The only exceptions are where the authority is acting in breach or disregard of its statutory duties or where its statutory powers are inadequate. The wardship procedure is not available as a means of appealing against a decision of a juvenile court in making or refusing to discharge a care order.

The wardship procedure has, however, been used in a case where the High Court felt that the local authority's statutory powers were inadequate to meet a particular situation. The parents were foreign nationals who were suspected of having battered their baby and they wanted the baby back in order to return to their own country. No order for discharge of the care order was made by the juvenile court because of fears that the child might again be injured before the parents actually left the country. Under the wardship procedure in the High Court, however, the parents were able to get the physical possession of the child, but only as they left the country and not whilst they were making their arrangements to leave.

Allegations of improper action on the part of a local authority are difficult to establish. For example, in one case allegations by a mother that social workers were reacting to her with hostility and that their decisions about the future upbringing of the child were clouded by this hostility were not clearly proved and the court refused to act under the wardship procedure.

Similarly the wardship procedure cannot be used to challenge the decision of a local authority to place a child with a view to adoption because such a decision is wholly within the proper exercise of the authority's discretion.

2 Powers to make custody orders over children who are in care

There is apparently nothing to prevent a court making an order for the custody of a child who is in the care of a local authority. Custody orders made by a divorce court will have the effect of superseding a care order.

3 The local ombudsman

Whenever it can be shown that a person has suffered injustice as a result of maladministration by a local authority a complaint can be made through a local councillor (or directly, if the councillor refuses to act) to the local ombudsman. He has the power to investigate and report on cases of maladministration. Maladministration means delay, incompetence, ineptitude and arbitrariness. Any decision therefore which causes obvious hardship may amount to maladministration. For example, an authority which had the care of two brothers might be deemed to be acting improperly if it separated them.

An investigation by the ombudsman followed by a finding of maladministration and a report, although not strictly speaking binding on the authority, will in most cases encourage the authority to act properly in the future. (For address see page 499.)

Responsibilities of the authority once a child of 16 or 17 leaves their care

Until the child reaches the age of eighteen the authority is obliged to advise and befriend the child for as long as the child's welfare requires it. And until the child reaches twenty the authority has power to make financial contributions for the accommodation and maintenance of anyone who is working, seeking work, or receiving education and training.

7 'In the best interests of the child'

Disputes can arise between parents and guardians about the exercise of parental rights, and between parents and others about the future physical possession of a child, and over the parental rights which automatically go with physical possession. In all these cases the courts will exercise their powers in accordance with the welfare principle: that the welfare of the child is the first and paramount consideration, whatever the rights of the parents. The courts have adopted a series of principles, or guidelines, which help them to determine what is best for the child. The courts' discretion is absolute, so that a description of these principles can only provide a rough guide to what is likely to happen in any future case. Where there is a dispute about physical possession the court will normally ask a welfare officer to make a report which will contain the welfare officer's conclusions about the future upbringing of the child. It is the normal practice of the courts to disclose these reports (and in fact this is a requirement in the magistrates' court) so that parents can know to some extent how to meet the case against them. It is also possible for parents to use private social workers as expert evidence to challenge the welfare officer's report. Legal aid can cover these costs. The court is not bound to follow the welfare officer's recommendations, although if it does not do so it will normally give reasons. The rest of this chapter is a description of the guidelines which help the court to reach its decision.

The guidelines

1 Young children, especially female children should be with their mothers

This is a basic rule, but not an invariable one. Courts believe that women are in the main best suited to bring up young children, especially when if a man were to do the job he would have to give up work and rely on state financial support. Provided that a court considers this basic guideline, it can on other evidence decide that a child should instead be with its father.

2 Siblings should not be separated

Courts will try to achieve this objective even if it means disrupting the life of one of the children. Courts may be prepared to depart from this principle in cases where one of the children might be able to exercise a disruptive influence over the others. With teenage children it is assumed that girls should be with their mothers and boys with their fathers; this may outweigh the disadvantages of separating them from their brothers and sisters. This would seem to ignore the particular difficulties which often arise between teenage girls and their mothers.

3 Custody orders should not be used as a means of punishing a 'guilty' spouse

At one time courts took the view that an adulterous mother was automatically a bad mother and they would therefore award custody to the father. It is clear that this is no longer the case and the fact that the mother's adultery was the cause of the breakdown of the marriage is irrelevant if the mother is in all other respects a 'good' mother. Promiscuity of itself, provided that the children are shielded from its effects, will not stop a court from granting custody to the promiscuous parent.

4 The wishes of the child should be taken into account

The relevance of this guideline will depend to a considerable extent on the age of the child. The younger the child is the less likely it will be for the court to take its wishes into account. Judges may see the children privately to find out their wishes, and a child of twelve who expresses very strong views would be likely to be heeded. A parent who argues to the court that the children wish to live with them will be ignored if the court considers that this view has been influenced by that parent. This is a subject which the welfare officer will explore and report on to the court.

5 Educational and material advantages

These will be assessed and taken into account by the court, but will normally only be decisive where the differences are very considerable.

6 Religious upbringing

Courts are reluctant to become involved in making choices between different types of religion and will decide the future custody of the child with little regard to religious upbringing. If, however, this is clearly a matter about which one parent feels very strongly the court may require an undertaking to bring the child up, say, as a Roman Catholic before giving custody to the other party. This is the usual approach except in cases which involve religions which according to English standards would force the children into isolation (no television, music, football, etc.). In these circumstances the courts may prefer the parent with 'normal' religious convictions. This has occurred in two cases; one involving a Jehovah's Witness (although if practice is moderate, normal rules will apply), and the other a member of the Exclusive Brethren.

7 Preserving the *status quo*

This is probably the most important factor which is taken into account by the courts. Over the years evidence from psychologists and others has shown that any interference with the upbringing of a child, even holidays, causes disruption and can be very damaging. In many cases, therefore, rather than disrupt the child's life, the court prefers to leave it where it is unless there is clear reason not to. This has certainly been the case where a mother's physical possession of the children is being challenged; it is less certain in the case of fathers. There have been some cases where, regardless of the potential disruption, courts have been prepared to transfer young children from their father to their mother. In one recent case a child who had from its birth been in the sole care of the father was transferred, when it was eighteen months old, to the mother. In the same way homosexual parents may be deprived of the physical possession of their children however long the original arrangement may have lasted.

Access

Courts take the view that a child has as great a right to know its parents as parents have to know their children, and it is extremely rare for a parent to be denied access to his or her child. A child may, however, indicate that he or she wants nothing to do with one parent, and if the child is old enough for the court to have confidence in his or her judgment, the court will agree with the child and refuse access.

If the custodian parent consistently frustrates the other parent's rights to access in accordance with the court's order, this can eventually lead the court to a conclusion that the original decision relating to custody was misguided, and whatever the *status quo*, transfer the child to the other parent.

8 Education

Education is compulsory for any child between the ages of five and sixteen, although this does not mean that a child must attend school. All that is required is that a child receives full-time education which is suitable to his age, aptitude and ability.

Educating a child at home

If a child is already in school, then parents should notify both the head-teacher of the school and the Education Welfare Officer. It will be necessary to explain to the welfare officer what alternative arrangements are to be made for the future education of the child. Acting on the views of the welfare officer, the local education authority will probably arrange a discussion meeting to consider whether the education proposed by the parents is adequate or not. It is usually necessary to provide the authority with clear plans for the education of the child and, if possible, a timetable showing the daily educational programme. Local education authorities are likely to cooperate with arrangements made by parents who are themselves teachers, or at least educated to a high level. If the arrangements are approved, advisers may visit from time to time, both to give advice and to check that the approved arrangements are being carried out. An organization known as Education Otherwise, Manor House, Thelnetham, near Diss, Norfolk, will be able to help with advice.

If the authority thinks that the arrangements are unsatisfactory, it will probably make a school attendance order. Before serving the order the authority must send written notice of its intention to serve the order, and indicate which school or schools it considers the child should attend. If the parents decide to send the child to one of the schools selected by the authority in the notification they can, within fourteen days, select the school, and the authority must then name that school in the order. The authority can also name any other school at which the child has been offered a place. A failure to comply with a school attendance order could lead to an appearance before a magistrates' court, with a potential £200 fine, or imprisonment, and possibly a care order placing the child with the local authority.

Education at school: the state system

Local education authorities are bound to allow parents to express a preference for a particular school and to give reasons for their preference. The duty of the LEA is to comply with that preference unless such compliance would either prejudice efficient education or efficient use of resources; or unless the preferred school is an aided school, and the preference falls outside the arrangements made between the school and the authority; or unless selection of pupils for the school depends on ability or aptitude, and preference is incompatible with the selection requirements. LEAs are required to publish information about the schools in their area. Information which is published includes, for example, the number of children in the sixth form of the school, the number of GCE passes and the number of CSE passes. Parents are therefore expected to make informed choices before stating their preferences. Reports by school inspectors are also published and these may help parents in making their selection.

It is possible for a parent to state a preference for a school which is not in his local education authority's area. In order that parents can make informed choices, authorities have to publish information about the arrangements for the admission of children to schools both within and outside their own areas. The published particulars will also include the number of pupils in each age group to be admitted to each school each year; the admission functions of each relevant body; the policy followed in deciding admissions; and the arrangements for pupils from outside the authority's area.

Parents are asked to give reasons for selecting a particular school, and in the past good reasons have included religion, medical considerations, transport, and in Wales the availability of Welsh language classes at a particular school.

If the local authority refuses to give effect to the parental preference, the parents will be able to appeal against that refusal. The appeal will be heard by an appeals committee whose decision is binding on the authority. The committee will consist of members of the LEA, other people who have experience of education and some knowledge of local conditions, and parents. The LEA members of the committee must outnumber the others by more than one, although none of them can be chairperson, nor can they be involved if they took part in the original refusal.

Parents who wish to appeal must do so in writing, setting out the grounds for the appeal (for example, that a Roman Catholic child should be educated at a Roman Catholic school). The parents can appear themselves, or through a friend, or through a legal representative. The committee is required to consider the expressed preference and the published arrangements for the admission of pupils in reaching their decision. The decision, and the reasons for it, will be sent in writing to the parents and to the authority.

In some education areas it is possible for children to be admitted to primary school before the age of 5, provided that they reach that age within six months of entering the school. Similarly, in areas where the division between primary and secondary schooling comes at 11, some authorities allow pupils of 10½ and over to be counted as secondary school pupils. In either situation the arrangements for choice of schools can then be exercised by the parents at the earlier age.

Rights once the child is in school

(a) *Free transport*

Children aged under eight who live more than two miles from their schools by the shortest walking route are entitled to free transport. Children aged over eight are only entitled to free transport if they live more than three miles from the school by the shortest walking route. If the authority has failed to provide free transport to those entitled, then parents will have a defence to any criminal action instituted against them by the authority if their children fail to attend school.

(b) *School meals*

Authorities have the power to provide pupils with milk, meals and other refreshments and must provide facilities which they consider appropriate for the consumption of meals brought in by pupils. Authorities now have the power to charge what they like for meals, but they can, in appropriate cases, charge less than the full fee or nothing at all. For parents who are claiming supplementary benefit or the family income supplement, the authority is obliged to provide milk and meals which are appropriate for the children.

(c) *Equipment*
Local education authorities are under a duty to ensure that schools have sufficient equipment and are forbidden to charge fees for basic educational services. In the current economic climate schools have been requesting parents to try to raise money to buy certain equipment or books for schools; this may amount to a failure by the LEA to carry out its duty to provide efficient education. The difficulty is that each local authority is entitled to set its own levels for necessary equipment and it is difficult to challenge their assessment of needs. But where parents are being asked to contribute for what appear to be essentials, they should at least write to the Education Committee to challenge the request. The Advisory Centre for Education, an educational pressure group, has published an information sheet, *School Books: Is your LEA breaking the law?*, advising parents what to do in these cases. This sheet is available free from the Centre at 18 Victoria Park Square, London E2 9PB.

(d) *Membership of the governing body*
The governing body of a school is responsible for the conduct and curriculum of its school, the appointment and dismissal of teachers and the suspension of pupils. All schools are run in accordance with their articles of government, which set out how the school is to be run and describe the functions of the head-teacher, managers, governors, and local education authority. These can be inspected at the relevant local education authority office. There must be at least two parents (elected by parents of pupils registered at the school), and two teachers (elected by teachers) on the governing body. This means that there is, at least, some opportunity for parents to put their views as to how the school should be run. The rest of the governing body is nominated by the authority, which can appoint as many people as it chooses. This means that parents are invariably outnumbered and are therefore unlikely to have much muscle-power.

Governing bodies are required to act reasonably and the Secretary of State is responsible for seeing that they do. If the Secretary of State is of the opinion that the authority or governors are failing to carry out their duties properly, he can make an order indicating the default and giving directions as to how the duty should in future be carried out. If the authority were to refuse to comply, these directions could then be enforced through the courts.

(e) *Establishing, closing and altering schools*
Any proposals of this kind must be published by the local education authority and, within two months of this publication, any ten or more local government electors can submit objections to the proposals. Any objections made must then be passed to the Secretary of State with the authority's observations. Proposals for the maintenance of county schools or voluntary schools, or the ending of maintenance of a voluntary school must be approved by the Secretary of State. Any other proposals only require the approval of the Secretary of State if he gives notice within two months of receipt of the proposals, or there have been objections made which have not been withdrawn. If the Secretary's approval is required, then he can approve, reject or modify the proposals made to him. So, in this area, there is at least an opportunity for parents to make their views known, and for them to be taken into account by the Secretary of State.

Complaints about schools and local education authorities

Complaints about head-teachers
Complaints should initially be addressed to the local education authority. If the authority upholds the actions of the head, then application can be made to the Secretary of State. He can direct that the LEA is acting unreasonably in supporting the head.

Local authority acting unlawfully
It is unlawful for the local authority to deprive children of education to which they are entitled. There are three avenues of action open to parents:

- they can apply to the Secretary of State and ask him to give directions on how the authority should act in the future;
- parents can take independent action in the courts on the grounds that the authority is acting *ultra vires* (outside its powers). If the claim is upheld, the court can issue an injunction requiring the LEA to cease the unlawful act and it can award damages to compensate the parents for any losses they have suffered;
- parents can make a complaint, normally through a local councillor, to the local ombudsman on the basis that injustice has been caused by the authority's maladministration. If the ombudsman

upholds the complaint he can make a report which could be followed by a further report if the authority fails to comply with the first. This would probably force the Secretary to embody the recommendations in an order.

Religious education

Parents can request that their children be excused attendance at the school's daily act of worship and classes for religious instruction. If the particular form of religious instruction chosen by a parent is not available at the school, and could not be made available by transfer to another school, arrangements can be made which ensure that the child receives the instruction elsewhere during school hours. The authority must approve these arrangements which may interfere with school attendance only at the beginning and end of the school day.

Sexual discrimination

It is unlawful for maintained schools and universities, unless they are single-sex establishments, to discriminate against women in terms of admission, or in the provision of any benefits, facilities, or services. (The same rules also apply to some independent schools and special schools.)

The specific duty not to discriminate may be enforced by civil action in the county court. The court can order that, in future, the discrimination shall cease and can also award damages for any loss suffered.

Only one case has in fact been heard under these provisions. In that case a female pupil claimed damages because she was originally excluded from metalwork classes and then exceptionally allowed to attend on the understanding that she would be the only girl. She was not entitled to damages, as the court found that the entire action had been instituted as a matter of principle and not because the girl had genuinely wanted to join the class.

Education authorities also have a general duty to ensure that facilities and benefits are provided without sexual discrimination. The only way to enforce this general duty is by a complaint to the Secretary of State that the authority is acting unreasonably.

Special educational needs

Under the Education Act of 1981, LEAs are to be obliged to ensure that provision is made for all children who have special educational needs. These are defined as including both children with learning difficulties (identified by reference to the child's age group) and those with disabilities which prevent them from using ordinary education facilities. The provision which the LEA makes will, however, remain totally within its own discretion. If the LEA decides that the child has special needs it will make a formal statement. Parents must be informed that the LEA intends to make a statement about the needs of their child and the provision which it intends to make for the child. Parents are entitled to be present and to take part in any decision which is taken by the LEA. If the parents disagree with the statement made they may appeal to the local appeals committee (see page 53). The committee may recommend some other provision to the LEA.

The LEA may decide that a child does not need special provision and refuse to make such a statement. In these cases it is possible for the parents to appeal against the refusal to make a statement. This appeal goes to the Secretary of State, who can direct the LEA to reconsider its decision. If the authority confirms that it does not consider that the child needs special provision then the rights of the parents are merely to state their preference as to the school they wish their child to attend (see page 52).

Special schools

It is now accepted that children with special educational needs should as far as possible be integrated into ordinary schools. However, LEA's are not entitled to close special schools without the advance approval of the Secretary of State. Approval will only be given if the Secretary approves the alternative suggested by the LEA. (This provision is in force.)

Nursery schools

Local education authorities are *empowered* to establish nursery schools but are no longer under any duty to do so. This means that an authority which decides to avoid expenditure on education by refusing to establish a nursery school can now properly do so. However, an authority which decides to cease to maintain a nursery school will have to submit its proposals to the Secretary of State for his approval if at least ten local government electors object to the closure. Authorities can, however, reduce the number of children in a nursery school without having to get the approval of the Secretary of State.

The provision of education otherwise than in school
Authorities are under a duty to provide education for children who need it, not only by the provision of schools, but also, for example, by providing a child with teaching at home in appropriate cases. This has been used in the past to provide for pregnant schoolgirls aged under sixteen, and for children with physical or psychological disorders, such as school-phobia. If parents want their children to be taught at home they should get a report from an educational psychologist to prove the advantages of such education to the authority. (These powers can also be used to provide education for children suspended from school.)

Local authorities, on the same principle, may also provide daycare facilities for the under-fives, so that parents are able to work.

A blanket refusal to provide any of these provisions could be challenged as a breach of duty by application to the Secretary of State or to the courts.

Education at school: the private sector

Any parent who can afford to do so can pay to have his child educated outside the state system. The government has introduced a new system for the parents of bright children who cannot afford to educate their children at private schools. This scheme is known as the 'assisted places scheme'. Schools taking part in the scheme have to apply to the Department of Education and Science for approval. Parents wishing to take part will have to fall within the means limitations laid down under the scheme. (At the time of writing parents with incomes up to £11,000 p.a. will be entitled to some assistance with the costs of fees and other incidental expenses. A parent whose income is £5,266 p.a. or less will have all the costs paid for him.) Children must be aged eleven or above. Those entering the sixth form directly have to obtain the permission of the education authority before being able to take up an assisted place. (This rule is soon to be abolished.) All funds for the scheme are provided by central government.

Since the government lifted the ban on local authorities buying places in independent schools, many authorities now have their own locally funded schemes. The schemes available vary from area to area, but mostly apply to children who are very able or have specialized gifts – such as outstanding numerical ability.

In some cases, boarding school provision may be felt desirable and, if this cannot be obtained in the state sector, authorities may be prepared to pay the costs of an independent boarding school.

(The government is considering the introduction of education vouchers which parents could use in either the public or the private sector.)

Higher education

Any student who is admitted to a 'designated' course of higher education will qualify for a maintenance grant the amount of which will vary according to his parents' income. The fees for the course will also be paid.

The following full-time courses are 'designated': degree courses; diplomas in higher education; teacher-training courses; TEC and BEC courses. Any other course does not qualify for an automatic grant so that, although authorities are empowered to provide assistance, they are under no duty to do so and at the present time some authorities are giving no discretionary awards at all.

Discretionary awards, if any, are available from local authorities for any further education course; that is, one which begins after the pupil has passed the end of compulsory schooling.

Financial help is also available in the form of industrial scholarships which are given to people taking full-time courses at universities and colleges, where that course is relevant to a career in industry. Similarly, special grants are available to help with the cost of providing education in Welsh in Wales.

9 Protection from domestic violence

This chapter deals with applications that can be made to the civil and criminal courts by a person who is the victim of domestic violence. It also deals with the circumstances in which a local authority will provide housing for someone who leaves home because of violence, and the ways in which children can be protected from violence in the home.

The civil law

Civil actions in the magistrates' court

This section deals first with applications to a magistrates' court for *personal protection orders* and *exclusion orders*, and then with methods of enforcing these orders.

The applications described below are heard by the magistrates' domestic court, staffed by magistrates who have a special interest in this area of the law. Applications can be made to any magistrates' court within the county in which the parties to the marriage live.

It is possible, in cases where the court considers that an application for a personal protection order or exclusion order should be heard without delay, for a court which is not a domestic court to hear the applications. This power is most likely to be exercised by a magistrates' court sitting as a criminal court, when criminal charges are being brought by the applicant or the police against the violent spouse.

Who can apply?

Either partner in a marriage. A child cannot make an application in his own right, although the court can make orders for the protection of any child of the family.

Who is a child of the family?

Any child who is the natural or adopted child of the parties to the marriage and any child who is treated as though he were a natural child, even if mistakenly, is included.

The orders which the court can make include personal protection orders and exclusion orders.

A personal protection order

This is an order not to use or threaten to use violence against the applicant or child of the family, or an order not to encourage some other person to use or threaten to use violence.

An exclusion order

This can take any, or all, of the following forms: an order that the respondent leave the matrimonial home; an order that he or she be prohibited from entering it in the future; an order that he or she must allow the applicant to enter and reoccupy it.

How to get a personal protection order

The applicant must prove to a magistrates' court that the respondent has used, or threatened to use, violence and that such an order will help to ensure the future protection of the applicant or a child.

How long will the order last?

The order may be made without limit of time or may be made for a limited period. In either case it is possible to return to court and ask for the order to be removed or extended: recent comment suggests initial limits of three months.

What to do in an emergency

A procedure known as the 'expedited personal protection order' is available in cases where there is imminent danger of physical injury. A hearing can take place immediately, probably in the absence of the respondent, even if the emergency occurs at night or at the weekend. All that is required is that the applicant certifies in writing that there is imminent danger. If the problem arises outside court hours, the police should be contacted as they will know how to set the procedure in motion (by telephoning the clerk at home).

How long will an expedited order last?

The order will last until the date of a full hearing to which the respondent is invited, or for twenty-eight days, whichever comes first. The court can grant a further expedited order if more time is needed.

How to get an exclusion order

Here the jurisdiction of the magistrates' court is very restricted. There must be strong evidence of violence, which means that the applicant must prove that the respondent has used violence against her or him, or against a child of the family; or that he or she has threatened such violence and is known to have committed violent acts against others (for example, where the respondent has previous criminal convictions for violence); or that he or she has acted in breach of an existing personal protection order (by continuing to make threats or by actually using violence). Furthermore, the applicant must also satisfy the court that he, she or the child is in danger of physical injury, or would be in such danger if the respondent were to remain in the matrimonial home. 'Physical injury' would seem to require evidence of the existence of, at least, cuts or bruises. It is, therefore, sensible to visit a doctor immediately after the injury is caused so that this evidence can be certified. 'Danger' suggests that the violent act is likely to be repeated or, where the application is based on threats, that they are likely to be carried out.

As already indicated, exclusion orders relate only to the matrimonial home. Although not defined by statute, 'matrimonial home' probably indicates the last residence in which the parties to the marriage lived and might therefore include the respondent's parents' home, if that is the place where they last lived together. If the matrimonial home incorporates both business and private accommodation, then an exclusion order will only be made where it is possible to divide the private parts from the business parts (e.g. where there are separate entrances and no internal connection).

How long will an exclusion order last?

Generally speaking, exclusion orders are viewed by the courts as temporary solutions to the problems of domestic violence, giving the applicant a 'breathing space' to make alternative arrangements for accommodation either by finding somewhere new to live or by instituting proceedings for a divorce and property redistribution (see page 80). Consequently an exclusion order is unlikely to be made for more than three months on any one application. It is possible to return to the court after the three-month period has elapsed and ask for a new order which would almost certainly be granted where, for example, the divorce settlement although pending has not been finally resolved.

What to do in an emergency

There is no equivalent to the 'expedited personal protection order' (see page 61) so that, in an emergency, it is much better to use the similar procedure available in the county court and the High Court. Where there is no emergency the hearing will normally take place within two weeks of the application being filed. In an emergency the only other alternative is to contact the Women's Aid Federation who will then help you to find accommodation in one of their hostels. This arrangement will probably only be temporary because hostels tend to be overcrowded.

It can, however, be very helpful to discuss these kinds of problems with others who have themselves had similar experiences, and legal advice and assistance will often be available. If an order is made excluding the violent spouse from the matrimonial home, then the absent spouse will be able to obtain an order of reentry and reoccupation of the matrimonial home.

How to enforce a personal protection or exclusion order
There are two methods of enforcement available to the applicant:

1 Having a power of arrest attached to the order A power of arrest is a direction to a police constable to arrest without warrant any person whom he has reasonable cause to suspect of having broken one of the above orders. This provides a speedy method of defusing a potentially dangerous domestic situation, by removing the spouse in breach of the order from the scene, and placing him out of harm's way in a cell at the police station. This method could clearly be used oppressively to interfere unjustifiably with the liberty of the individual and it is therefore only available in very serious cases. In order to have the power of arrest attached the applicant must prove that physical injury has been caused (that is, some bruising or cuts as a minimum) and that, despite the existence of the order, the respondent is likely to cause her physical injury again. This requires the applicant to establish that the respondent has broken an order before.

Theoretically it is also possible to attach a power of arrest to an 'expedited personal protection order', but this is unlikely in cases where the respondent is not present in court, as it is generally accepted that the respondent must be given an opportunity to argue against the power being attached.

The power of arrest will not come into operation until the respondent has been notified of the order, immediately after which it will be filed with the relevant police station. In most cases the power of arrest will now be limited in duration to three months. Extensions will only be granted where there is evidence that the danger of a breach of the protection order, etc., continues.

2 Obtaining a warrant for the arrest of the respondent Once the respondent has notice of the order and the applicant can prove by sworn evidence that the order has been broken then the court can issue a warrant.

A warrant is a direction to a policeman to arrest the respondent and bring him before the court.

When the accused has been arrested in either of the above ways he must be brought before the court. If the hearing cannot take place immediately, the respondent must still be brought before the court, in the case of arrest under a power of arrest, within 24 hours (excluding Christmas Day, Good Friday and Sundays), and in the case of an arrest under a warrant, within a reasonable time, normally 48 hours.

At these appearances before the court, the court can decide whether the respondent should be retained in custody or released on bail pending the hearing. Once brought before the court the respondent can be punished for the breach of the order by a fine or imprisonment. Magistrates do not have the power to sentence to consecutive periods of imprisonment for each breach of the order.

Financial support from the state for an application to the magistrates' court

Any person who would be entitled to receive free legal advice (or such advice subject to a contribution) is entitled to obtain free legal assistance (perhaps subject to a contribution) for legal representation before the magistrates' court on any domestic matter. This can be a more generous method of entitlement because all the calculations as to the means of the parties are undertaken by the solicitor conducting the case.

Going to the magistrates' court without representation

The court staff will help an applicant to prepare an application for protection orders and will give advice during the hearing.

Civil actions in the county court and the High Court

This section deals with the powers of county courts and the High Court to grant *anti-molestation injunctions*, *exclusion orders* and orders allowing the applicant to *reoccupy the matrimonial home*.

The Domestic Violence and Matrimonial Proceedings Act 1976

This Act was passed expressly to simplify the procedure for getting an injunction in the county court, and these simplified procedures are now also available in the High Court, without the need to present a divorce petition.

The injunctions

It is possible to obtain any one or all of the following injunctions or orders:

- an anti-molestation injunction to protect the applicant or any child living with the applicant;

- an order excluding one party from the matrimonial home, its surrounding area, or some part of the matrimonial home;
- an order entitling the applicant to enter and reoccupy the matrimonial home, or a part of it.

Any exclusion order must have as its focal point the matrimonial home, which probably means the place in which the parties to the marriage last lived together.

An anti-molestation injunction
Although obviously covering cases of domestic violence, this type of injunction can also be used in cases of general interference; for example, abusive telephone calls or cases where someone is generally making a nuisance of himself by pestering the applicant.

Who can apply? Either party to a marriage can make an application and so can either party to a relationship where the parties are living together as though they were husband and wife. It has been held that a relationship of three months' cohabitation was sufficient for these purposes, and that the powers of the court were not lost after the parties had separated, even where the separation had lasted a few months. In either case an application can be made on behalf of any child living with the applicant (whether or not that child is a child of the family).

Emergencies
In cases where there is a real and immediate danger of serious injury or irreparable damage being caused, an application can be made to the court *ex parte*. An *ex parte* hearing means that the application will be decided by the court even though the respondent is not in the court and has not been notified that a hearing is about to take place. The applicant will have to attend the court and either present evidence by way of a sworn statement setting out the facts (an affidavit), or by giving evidence orally and answering any questions put by the court. Recently it has been established that an injunction excluding one party from the matrimonial home should not, because of its drastic effects, be made *ex parte*. Solicitors have been warned that if they make unnecessary *ex parte* applications they will be held personally responsible for the costs of the action. It may well be impossible to find a solicitor willing to institute an *ex parte* application for exclusion.

Time limits An *ex parte* injunction, because it is made without hearing any argument from the respondent, will only last for a matter of days. A full hearing will normally take place four days after application is made so *ex parte* injunctions will usually last for four days.

Which court? In cases for which legal aid has been granted, because the jurisdiction of the High Court and county court is identical, costs under the scheme will only be approved on the lower county court scales. Any county court situated in the district in which the applicant or respondent lives, or in which the matrimonial home is situated, has jurisdiction. Both courts operate arrangements that ensure that a judge can be found at any time of the day or night, including Christmas Day.

Legal aid Legal aid is available for *ex parte* proceedings, so that solicitors are able to make what is called an emergency application. There is, therefore, no delay to the legally aided litigant.

Circumstances which the court will take into account when granting a full injunction

Anti-molestation injunctions

These can only be granted in cases where there is clear evidence of molestation or violence: they may last initially for three months.

Exclusion injunctions

The general principle, which is applied in those cases where the marriage has clearly broken down, is that the court should think essentially in terms of homes especially for the children, bearing in mind the difficulties which exist in finding alternative housing. Consequently the court must consider the facts of the case and decide on that basis what is a fair, just and reasonable order. The court must consider:

- the behaviour of the applicant and respondent;
- the effect on the children of the respondent's remaining in, or being removed from, the home;
- the respondent's own personal circumstances; and
- the likelihood of injury to either party's health, both mental and physical.

Most recent cases have suggested that it is the interests of the children which are paramount so that, if the applicant will not remain in the matrimonial home whilst the respondent is there, and the applicant is the party who would be expected to care for the children (normally the mother), the court will exclude the respondent because the interests of the children require that they should continue to live or return to live in the matrimonial home. This may be the result even where there is little or no evidence of domestic violence. However, in some recent cases, the courts have refused to make an exclusion order where they felt that the decision to end cohabitation was not reasonable.

Even in cases where there are no dependent children the courts have been prepared to exclude a husband from the matrimonial home. This would happen where it would clearly be unreasonable to expect the parties to continue living together (that is, where the marriage has broken down) and the applicant refuses to remain with the respondent in the matrimonial home. This could be proved, for example, by the applicant's seeking accommodation from a battered women's home even if she has not, in fact, been battered. This is because the applicant is entitled to a peaceful existence in congenial surroundings.

An injunction has been refused in a case in which the husband respondent successfully established that there was some doubt as to whether the mother should have the custody of the children, and consequently the court adjourned the injunction hearing until a decision on custody could be made.

The position of unmarried people living together

After some initial confusion the case of *Davis* v. *Johnson* 1978, heralded in the press as the 'Mistresses' Charter', made clear that unmarried people were to be treated under the Act in exactly the same way as married people. Consequently, even where the applicant has no legal rights to remain in the 'matrimonial home', the court will be willing to exclude the respondent where a failure to do so would in effect force her to leave, especially where there are children, and their interests require that the applicant remains with them in the 'matrimonial home'.

How long will an exclusion order last?

It has been said that the Act was intended to provide no more than first-aid help. Exclusion injunctions will usually not last for more than three months, although it is possible to get a further order in cases where a long-term solution to the ownership or possession of the property has not yet been achieved. For example, court processes for divorce and redistribution of property mostly take longer than three months.

Ensuring compliance with an injunction
There are two methods of enforcement:

1 Attaching a power of arrest This can be attached to injunctions against the use of violence and injunctions excluding one party from the matrimonial home. The applicant must prove that actual bodily harm has already been caused to him or her (that is, any hurt or injury calculated to interfere with health) and that it is likely to happen again. The courts have made clear that the power of arrest is not to be regarded as a routine remedy. It must be made clear that the respondent has previously broken an exclusion injunction or some similar order. It has also been made clear that the respondent must be notified that a power of arrest is to be applied for, so that he can raise arguments against its attachment. A power of arrest is a direction to a police officer to arrest a person whom he reasonably believes has broken an injunction. It will be limited initially to three months in duration.

2 Committal for contempt of court If no power of arrest is attached, then the applicant must apply to the court for a warrant of committal, by which the court orders the respondent's imprisonment as punishment for breaking the court's order.

Punishment for breach of an injunction
Any failure to comply with an order of a court is a contempt of court and, as such, may be punished by a fine, or a term of imprisonment. It has been said that imprisonment should, in family matters, be imposed only in the last resort, and courts will often give the respondent another chance, by suspending the imprisonment order, unless or until the respondent commits further breaches.

Undertakings
In some cases the court will accept an undertaking from the respondent not to molest the applicant, or to leave the matrimonial home, instead of issuing an injunction. The effect is the same and breaches are punished in the same way.

Injunctions obtainable without using the 1976 Act
It is possible to approach the High Court or a divorce county court for an injunction where other domestic proceedings are already taking place. The most likely situation would be where a petition for divorce has been presented and then the petitioner asks for an injunction. The only requirement is that the divorce proceedings are closely related to the injunction application (for example, the granting of custody of the children is related to exclusive possession of the matrimonial home). In cases where no proceedings have yet been started, the court will still grant the injunction provided that the applicant agrees to present the divorce petition without delay. The injunction will automatically expire when the related divorce proceedings have been resolved.

When to use this procedure This procedure is particularly useful in emergency exclusion applications, since a hearing will take place within two days, as compared to four days under the 1976 Act.

Entitlement to local authority housing

The Housing (Homeless Persons) Act 1977 places a duty on local authority housing departments to provide accommodation for any person who is unintentionally homeless and has a priority need (see page 212 for details).

In the context of domestic violence, a party to a marriage (or a cohabitee) who leaves the matrimonial home because of violence, or threats of violence, is treated as homeless. Local authorities are specifically required to treat battered women sympathetically and to recognize that just because there has been no violence at the date of the application (only threats) this does not mean that violence will not take place if the woman is forced to remain in the home.

In this area priority needs arise whenever the applicant has dependent children living with her, or dependent children who might reasonably be expected to live with her, where the applicant is pregnant or where she is a battered woman at risk if she returns home. Similarly, if the children are at risk from violence in the matrimonial home, the non-violent adult has a priority need for rehousing.

In these cases the housing department of the local authority must do one of three things:

- make accommodation available to the applicant, for example by offering other permanent accommodation;

- secure accommodation for the applicant from some other person; or
- offer advice and assistance to ensure that she will obtain accommodation from some other person.

To this extent therefore the local authority can obtain, through a third party, accommodation outside its area provided it is sure that the applicant and children will not run any risk of violence in that area. For example, if a woman has suffered violence in the Liverpool area, and has fled to London, the London housing authority could perform its duty to house her by ensuring that the Liverpool housing authority offers her accommodation – provided that it has considered, and dismissed as unlikely, the possibility that violence may occur again. If a housing authority refuses the applicant's claim then it must give reasons.

Violence and children

The civil law

As can be seen above (page 60), it is possible for a party to a marriage to apply to the magistrates' court for a personal protection order or an exclusion order to safeguard any child of the family. Similarly it is possible (page 64) for an applicant (married or not) to use the 1976 Act to obtain court orders to protect any child living with the applicant.

There are two other ways in which an application can be made for an injunction to protect a child:

- first, an application in the county court or High Court as a part of other proceedings. This means that in a dispute as to the custody of a child, the party given actual custody of the child may be able to have the non-custodian excluded;
- second, the High Court can, as part of its inherent jurisdiction, act as the protector of children under the wardship jurisdiction and make injunctions against any person whom the court feels might cause the child injury, including an injuction excluding an adult from the place in which the child is living. In one case, a mother, in making her child a ward, was held to be entitled to an anti-molestation order for her own protection, since the court held that this would be in the child's best interests.

Battered children and the state

Place of safety orders – emergencies

Any person can apply to a magistrate at any time or place if he has reasonable grounds to suspect that a child is being ill treated, or neglected so that his health or development is being affected, or if this situation has already arisen in the case of another child in the same family. The applicant will then be authorized to take the child to a place of safety (police station, hospital, child care clinic) for a maximum period of twenty-eight days. The parents of a child who is the subject of a place of safety order do have to be told what has happened 'as soon as practicable'.

This 28-day period is usually used by the social services department of the relevant local authority to call a case conference of all professionals involved with the family, so as to decide what action to take; they could, for example, decide to apply for a full care order (which has the effect of transferring parental rights to the local authority). If the 28-day period is insufficient to allow for a full investigation, the local authority can apply for an interim care order, which is a temporary order lasting until the full hearing.

This form of interim care order application can be made by the parents of a child who are attempting to have the place of safety order removed because the effect of a refusal of such an application is that the child will be sent home. The only other form of appeal open to parents is an application to the High Court showing that the magistrates have wrongly interpreted the law. Since there is very little opportunity to interpret law in these cases, such an application is unlikely to succeed. A police constable who has reason to believe that a child is being ill treated can, through a senior police officer, keep such a child in a place of safety for eight days without a court order. Information should be given to the parents, who can then apply to a magistrate to have the child released.

In some cases social workers or the police may believe that a child is being ill treated, or that criminal offences of a sexual or violent nature are being committed against a child, but be unable to enter premises to follow through inquiries. In these cases applications can be made to a magistrate for an order allowing a police officer to enter and search the premises and remove the child to a place of safety. Once again, this form of place of safety order can last for only twenty-eight days but may be followed by an interim or full care order.

The public giving information to social services, police or the NSPCC
It is clear that these bodies will avoid where possible having to give the name of any informant in later care proceedings and they are entitled to keep as confidential any informant's name when there are other legal proceedings envisaged. So, for example, if the parents are attempting to initiate proceedings to obtain damages for libel or slander they cannot force the NSPCC to disclose the name of the informant whom the parents now wish to sue.

Care proceedings – permanent
After a place of safety order has been obtained, or at any other time, a social worker, police constable or representative of the NSPCC can apply to a juvenile court (that is, a magistrates' court specially constituted to deal with young persons and children) for a care order.

There are three ways in which this might happen in cases of violence to children:

- a child is being neglected or ill treated, which would include cases of both physical injury and mental injury;
- a care order is being or has been made on grounds of neglect or ill treatment of any other child in the family. This means that when one child in a family has already suffered, the others can be protected;
- a person who has been convicted of sexual or violent crimes against a child is about to become a member of the same household as the child. Thus a person who is known to have been convicted of cruelty to children in the past would not be given the opportunity to repeat his crimes.

The court must also consider whether the child is in need of care and control which he would not receive without the care order. In this context care means protection.

Even if these conditions are satisfied, the court, on the basis of the child's welfare, can decide not to make a care order. The court might instead leave the child where it is and arrange for a social worker to supervise it in its home environment. This course of action will generally be taken in cases where it is felt that, with proper support, the problems of neglect or ill-treatment can be avoided. Difficulties arise because there are no clear guidelines to indicate how the supervision should be carried out and, since so many social services departments are understaffed, such orders will rarely provide sufficient support and consequently are less likely to be made.

If the court does make a care order, the effect is that all parental rights (see Chapter 6) – except the right to change the child's religion, and the right to agree to an adoption – are transferred to the local authority. The authority, through its social service department, can then decide how the child is to be cared for; they may, for example, decide to board the child out with foster parents or with relatives.

Once a care order is made it will continue in force until the child is eighteen, unless an application for its discharge is successful. Such an application can be made by the parents of the child, but the court will only discharge an order when they are sure that the child will receive adequate protection. The considerable amount of publicity which has surrounded cases in which magistrates have made mistakes in discharging care orders (for example, Maria Colwell and Wayne Brewer) has meant that they will beware of discharging a care order when there is some fear that the child might be unprotected despite the substitution of a supervision order for the care order.

In cases where the local authority does not oppose the discharge of the care order (as happened in the Maria Colwell case) then, to be sure that the court can safeguard the interests of the child, the court will order that the parents should not act as the representative of the child. So both the child and the parents may be entitled to legal aid to pay for representation before the juvenile court (for details see page 45).

Using the wardship procedure as a form of appeal

In general the High Court will not allow the wardship procedure to be used as a means of interfering with the local authority's discretion in dealing with a child who is in their care, unless it can be shown that the authority is acting improperly, *ultra vires* (outside its powers) or without considering relevant matters. Similarly the wardship procedure is not available as a method of challenging a decision reached by a juvenile court, either in making a care order or on refusing to discharge it.

General advice on domestic violence

The National Women's Aid Federation provides hostels in many parts of the country to which battered women and their children can go both for accommodation and for help and advice. The addresses and telephone number are *not* in the telephone book, but can be obtained from local social services departments, Citizens' Advice Bureaux, or from a police station.

If things are becoming difficult and you feel that there is a chance that you might batter your own child there are now various self-help groups which run emergency telephone advice and assistance schemes. Most of these groups are local and will have posters displayed in Citizens' Advice Bureaux, post offices and Department of Health and Social Security offices. They are run by many different organizations such as Parents Anonymous and Family Lifeline.

If there is no group near you then, in an emergency, if talking to someone might help, ring the Samaritans; their number is in the telephone book.

The criminal law

This section deals with the powers of the criminal courts to deal with domestic violence against children and adults.

Children

If a child dies as a result of action by a parent which is deemed to be unlawful and intentional, that parent will be guilty of murder. If there is no intention to cause death or serious injury then that parent will be guilty of manslaughter. Any physical injury short of death will fall within the criminal offences defined in the Offences Against the Person Act 1861 (for example, common assault or inflicting grievous bodily harm).

A further offence is defined in the Children and Young Persons Act 1933, which makes any person over the age of sixteen who has the custody or care of a child guilty of an offence if that person wilfully assaults, ill-treats, neglects or abandons the child so that the child is caused unnecessary suffering or injury to health. In this context a failure to provide adequate food, clothing or medical aid will amount to wilful neglect.

It is also a criminal offence to allow a child under the age of twelve to be in a room containing an unguarded fire if, as a result, the child is killed or seriously injured. Similarly where the parent allows the child to train for or take part in dangerous performances resulting in injury, that parent is guilty of an offence.

Adults

Binding-over orders

Any person who has just cause or fear that some other person might do him physical harm can ask the magistrates' court to bind over that person to be of good behaviour or to keep the peace. A person who is bound over for a year to keep the peace 'in the sum of £100' will only have to pay that money into court if he fails to be of good behaviour within the year. There is no right of appeal against a binding-over order, although it does not count as a conviction.

In a case decided in 1744, Lord Vane, who had previously molested his wife and had her kidnapped, was said at the time of the application to the court to be plotting to have his wife returned to him 'dead or alive'. He was bound over to keep the peace.

Offences Against the Person Act 1861

This Act lays down the various offences with which an adult can be charged when violent acts are committed against anyone, including a cohabitee or spouse. In any case in which there has been a serious assault (according to the Metropolitan Police) the police will take positive action (probably by arrest) and conduct a prosecution whenever there is sufficient evidence. Sufficient evidence in these circumstances requires the injured person to make a statement and agree to act as a police witness at the trial. Married women can, if they wish, give evidence against their husbands in this sort of case, although they cannot be forced to do so. Unmarried women can be compelled to act as police witnesses.

In cases of non-serious injuries or assaults where there is no direct evidence of injury, the police may refuse to prosecute. In these cases the injured person is entitled to bring a private prosecution but, since legal aid for representation is not available for private prosecutions, this may not be a suitable course of action.

In any case in which the police are prepared to act, the violent person will usually be held in police custody overnight and then brought before the magistrates on a bail application. It is open to magistrates to grant bail but they could, for example, impose a condition that the accused should not return to the matrimonial home.

Criminal injuries compensation scheme

The scheme has been extended to cover people who are the victims of violence within the family. Compensation will be paid when the offender has been prosecuted and where the injuries are such that compensation in excess of £500 would be payable, provided that the offender will not benefit from the award.

10 Ending a marriage

A marriage may be formally brought to an end by a decree of nullity, a decree of divorce, or a decree of presumption of death. A decree of judicial separation, which is also dealt with in this chapter, does not formally end the marriage; it merely releases the parties from their duty to live together.

Nullity

A decree of nullity will be granted where the marriage is either void or voidable. A void marriage is one that strictly speaking never existed at all; a voidable marriage will cease to exist from the date of the decree absolute of nullity, but is treated as valid until that time.

In the case of a void marriage it is not strictly necessary to obtain a decree setting the marriage aside, but since the court can only make orders for the division of propery and financial support (see page 97) where the marriage has been dissolved by decree, it is often sensible to obtain a decree.

Applications for a decree of nullity are made by petition, and if undefended, are heard in the divorce county courts; if defended they are heard in the Family Division of the High Court. There will always be a full hearing before a judge to establish whether the grounds for a decree exist and, consequently, those with small means will be entitled to legal advice and representation paid for either wholly or partly from state funds.

1 Void marriages

These are marriages which are not valid within the Marriage Acts 1945–1970:

- A marriage between people who fall within the 'prohibited degrees'. The prohibited degrees include close relationships by blood or marriage, so that a marriage between a blood brother and sister or a step-brother and a step-sister is prohibited. (It is possible, especially in step relationships, to obtain a private Act of Parliament so as to be able to marry validly. Although there are no specific requirements it is unlikely that permission would be given to a couple who, through their relationship, have caused some other relationship to break down in divorce.)
- A marriage between people who are under the age of sixteen at the time of the marriage.
- A marriage in disregard of certain of the requirements as to formation of a marriage. This would include, for example, the solemnization of a marriage by a person who is not in holy orders, where both parties to the marriage were aware of this irregularity at the time of the marriage.
- A marriage between people either of whom is already lawfully married to someone else.
- A marriage between two persons of the same sex. In this context the sex of an individual is determined at birth, so that a sex change operation will not legally change a man to a woman or vice versa, so as to enable a valid marriage to be contracted. This also means that as far as the law is concerned homosexual couples cannot enter into a valid marriage.
- A marriage between people domiciled in England or Wales (that is, intending to make England or Wales their permanent home) which is actually or potentially polygamous. Polygamy means that a husband is entitled to more than one wife. Consequently a Muslim who is domiciled in this country cannot, whatever his beliefs, legally marry in such a way as to be entitled at some time to take a second wife during the lifetime of the first.

Who can apply for a decree?

Any interested person can apply to the court to have a marriage declared void. This is because the validity of a marriage can have considerable effect on property inheritance rights (see page 129). Consequently, an interested person includes anyone who stands to gain financially from having a marriage declared to be void.

Effect on any children born

Since a void marriage has never existed logically all children born to the parties to it are illegitimate. However, if both or either of the parties to the marriage believe it to be valid, either at the time of its celebration or at the time of the sexual intercourse leading to conception, any child born will be legitimate.

Declarations

It is possible instead of applying for a decree to ask the court to declare that a marriage is void. In this case, however, the court will have no power to redistribute income and property.

2 Voidable marriages

There are six grounds available for having a voidable marriage brought to an end:

- The marriage has not been consummated owing to the incapacity of either party to consummate it. 'Consummation' means sexual intercourse between the parties after the celebration of the marriage; 'intercourse' must be 'ordinary and complete and not partial and imperfect', and the act must last for a reasonable length of time. The incapacity can be either physical or mental; if it is a physical incapacity it must be incurable. 'Incurable' means that the incapacity can be cured only by a dangerous operation, or by a simple operation which the incapable party refuses to undergo. In order to establish the truth of the allegations, the court may order both parties to undergo medical examinations. Any refusal to comply with such an order would allow the court to draw adverse conclusions against the party refusing. Either party can petition.
- The marriage has not been consummated owing to the wilful refusal of the respondent to consummate it. In order for this ground to apply the respondent must have decided not to consummate the marriage and have no good reason for having reached that decision. A good reason might be that the parties have agreed to marry by a civil ceremony, but have decided not to behave as married people until after a religious ceremony or blessing. There can be no wilful refusal until after the religious ceremony, but a failure to go through such a ceremony could itself amount to a wilful refusal.
- The parties to the marriage did not validly consent to it, because of duress, mistake, unsoundness of mind or otherwise.

  The definition of marriage according to English law is that it is a 'voluntary union'; so if it can be proved to a court that the union is not voluntary, the marriage can be voided. Duress exists where, because of a threat to life, limb or liberty, the consent of one party amounts to no more than a 'yielding of the lips' and not of the mind. Consequently, shotgun marriages, where the gun is real, can be set aside on this ground. And in the past, threats of political detention have been sufficient to avoid the consequences of a marriage entered into so as to escape political regimes. But a 'sham' marriage, contracted merely to obtain a different nationality or immigration status, without fear of injury, death or imprisonment, will not be voidable for duress.

'Mistake' will make a marriage voidable when the mistake affects consent. If, for example, a heavily veiled bride turns out not to be the girl he intended to marry, the mistaken bridegroom can have the marriage voided. A mistake as to the nature of a ceremony will have the same effect; so if the party believes himself to be going through a ceremony of formal betrothal which turns out in fact to be a ceremony of marriage, that marriage can be set aside. 'Unsoundness of mind' requires that one party at the time of the marriage was incapable of understanding the nature of marriage and the duties and responsibilities it creates, and so could not be said to have consented to undertake these duties and responsibilities.

To have a marriage set aside on these grounds the petition must be presented within three years of the celebration of the marriage.

- At the time of the marriage either party, though capable of giving a valid consent, was suffering (whether continuously or intermittently) from mental disorder within the meaning of the Mental Health Act 1959 of such a kind or to such an extent as to be unfitted for marriage. The kinds of illness covered here include mental illness, arrested development, psychopathic disorder, and any other disorder of the mind, which lead to an inability to cope with the duties and responsibilities of marriage. Once again, application must be made within three years of the celebration of the marriage.
- At the time of the marriage the respondent was suffering from venereal disease in a communicable form. This is available as a ground because the petitioner, if aware of this disease, might not have consented to the marriage. Once again action must be taken within three years and the petitioner must not have known of the disease at the time of the marriage.
- At the time of the marriage the respondent was pregnant by some person other than the petitioner. The assumption here is that the

petitioner was led into marriage because he believed himself to be the father of the unborn child. Action must be taken within three years of the marriage and the petitioner must have been ignorant of the fact that he was not the father at the time of the marriage.

Defence to a petition for nullity
The only defence available to any of these grounds is that the petitioner knowing his rights acted in such a way as to lead the respondent to believe that he would not petition, and that it would therefore be unjust to the respondent to grant the petition. For example, a couple who set about adopting a child are confirming the future existence of their marriage, and consequently the respondent to an action to have the marriage set aside at some future date could ask the court to refuse the application. However, if both parties want to be free of the marriage, the court will refuse to see the adoption as confirmation of the marriage.

Effects of decree of nullity
A decree of nullity brings a voidable marriage to an end on the date of the decree absolute, and therefore any children conceived before that date are legitimate. The effect of such a decree is very much the same as a decree of divorce and the rights of the parties to property and money are the same (see page 97).

Divorce

There are two ways in which a valid marriage relationship can be terminated:

- by decree of divorce;
- by decree of presumption of death and dissolution of the marriage.

In each case, the applicant for a decree is known as the petitioner, and the person against whom the action is taken is known as the respondent. The action is begun by a petition.

What is a decree?
A decree is an order by the court that in future the marriage and any obligations arising from it will cease to exist. There are two stages to the decree, the *decree nisi* and the *decree absolute*.

The decree nisi does not formally bring the marriage to an end, but gives a short breathing space to the parties to settle such matters as:

- the division of any matrimonial property (see page 97);
- the provision of maintenance for either party to the marriage or for any child of the family; and
- decisions about the future custody, care and control, or access to, any children of the family (see page 22).

This period of delay also gives any other person an opportunity to prove to the court that the marriage ought not to be terminated because, for instance, the parties have manufactured the evidence.

The decree absolute can be granted on the petitioner's own application, usually six weeks after the granting of the decree nisi. If the petitioner does not apply, the respondent may do so three months from the date of the decree nisi unless the court decides to delay the grant (see page 87). But if there is a delay of more than twelve months, then it may be necessary to give reasons for the delay, and if these are insufficient, the application for the decree to be made absolute will be refused. In these circumstances a fresh petition for divorce would have to be filed. The effect of the decree absolute is formally to bring the marriage to an end.

Which court?

In an undefended petition, the divorce county court has jurisdiction to grant the relevant decree. In defended actions, cases will be heard in the Family Division of the High Court.

When do the courts in England and Wales have jurisdiction?

The court must be satisfied that either the petitioner or the respondent is *domiciled* in England and Wales, or has been *habitually resident* in England and Wales for the twelve months immediately preceding the presentation of the petition. (When application is made for a decree of presumption of death – then it is only the position of the petitioner which can be considered.)

What is domicile?

This normally means the country which a person considers to be his or her permanent place of abode. Domicile is acquired:

- by origin (the country of domicile of a person's father at birth or, if the person is illegitimate, the mother); or
- by choice (which means that, after reaching the age of sixteen, a person may choose any country to become the country of

domicile by taking up residence there with the intention of making a permanent home in that country).

What is habitual residence?
The stronger a person's ties with, say, England, the easier it will be to prove habitual residence. For example, a person who takes a job, buys a home, and sends his children to school in this country will undoubtedly be held to be habitually resident in England.

What is a marriage in this context?
An English court will accept jurisdiction to terminate a marriage, provided that the marriage is broadly similar in type to an English one, and provided also that it was valid according to the law of the country in which it was celebrated. Polygamous marriages are now accepted as valid marriages over which an English court has jurisdiction to grant relief.

Obtaining a decree of divorce
The three-year rule
This rule prevents a petition for divorce from being heard unless the parties have been married for at least three years. If one of the parties does not want to wait that long, then the court has a discretion to grant permission to apply for a decree within the three-year period. The court will normally give permission if the petitioner proves that to be forced to remain married would cause exceptional hardship or that the respondent has behaved with exceptional depravity making it essential to grant the decree without delay. The courts have recently been expressing the view that applications based on exceptional depravity are unsatisfactory, and consequently when faced with such applications they have preferred to conclude that the facts amount to 'exceptional hardship'. The extent of the proof required for 'exceptional hardship' has in any event been diminishing, so that now it seems that all the petitioner has to do is prove that he or she has suffered more than ordinary upset as a result of the breakdown. The information which is included must however show the extent of the suffering complained of, for example, evidence of ill health, nervous sensitivity and tension.

In any event this is a complex issue for which legal aid is available provided that the applicant falls within the means limits (see page 429). It seems likely that the three-year rule will be abolished in the near future. Instead there will be an absolute bar on divorce within one year of marriage.

The grounds for divorce

Since 1971 there has been only one ground available to establish entitlement to a decree of divorce, and this is that the marriage has 'irretrievably broken down'. It is only possible to prove that a marriage has irretrievably broken down by proof of one of the five factors specified in the Matrimonial Causes Act 1973. Even if the petitioner is able to prove the existence of one of these five factors, it is still open to the court to take the view that the marriage has not in fact irretrievably broken down, although very clear evidence will be necessary before the court takes such a view.

The five factors proving irretrievable breakdown

(a) *The respondent has committed adultery and the petitioner finds it intolerable to live with the respondent* The petitioner must prove at least one act of adultery on the part of the respondent. Adultery is defined as voluntary sexual intercourse between a married person and someone of the opposite sex who is not that person's spouse. The easiest way to prove such an act will be by getting the respondent to confess to the adultery; otherwise evidence from a private inquiry agent may be used to establish the opportunity for adultery. This will be enough unless the respondent can provide a satisfactory explanation.

Similarly, a finding against a husband that he is the father of a child born illegitimately will be sufficient; so will a finding that a husband could not (because of a clear result achieved by blood tests) be the father of a child born to his wife.

Having proved the act of adultery the petitioner must next show that he or she finds it intolerable to continue living with the respondent. It is not, however, necessary that the marriage should have become intolerable because of the adultery if this can be established from other circumstances. A petitioner who believes in an 'open' marriage would be able to succeed under this provision if there were other evidence, such as the respondent drinking to excess or consistently ignoring the petitioner, which made the marriage intolerable.

Time limits A petitioner who is seeking to rely on the respondent's adultery will lose this right if the parties continue to live together, for a period or periods of over six months, after the petitioner has knowledge of the adultery. If the petitioner is alleging that the marriage has become intolerable because of the respondent's adultery, then any period of continued living together which amounts to no more than a total of six months will be ignored by the court in deciding whether the marriage has become intolerable. This is a recognition by the law that the parties should be encouraged at least to attempt to keep the marriage alive, by having one more go. This is more likely to happen if the intended petitioner will not thereby lose the opportunity to apply to the court for a divorce if things do not work out.

(b) *The respondent has behaved in such a way that the petitioner cannot reasonably be expected to live with the respondent* This would seem to require the petitioner to prove three distinct elements:

- that the behaviour is more than trivial;
- that the impact of the behaviour is quite severe; and
- that, taken objectively, all husbands or wives with the same character as the petitioner would be likely to be affected equally severely.

It is therefore possible for a decree to be given to a wife who is extremely sensitive, because of her husband's obscene language, whereas a decree would not be granted to a wife who was not in the least sensitive about such language.

Misbehaviour may take the form of one single act or a course of conduct. For example, in one case (in 1975) a husband wrote a letter to his wife's solicitor suggesting that he was not the father of the children born to his wife during the marriage. This was held to be sufficiently unreasonable behaviour to entitle the wife to a decree of divorce. In the same case, the husband had also decided to attempt to eliminate all traces of damp from the matrimonial home. To this end he removed all the floorboards, mixed cement on the living-room floor and removed the door from the lavatory for eight months. Even when the lavatory door had been replaced he would continually pop up between the floorboards to talk to people using the lavatory. The court held that this conduct itself amounted to sufficiently unreasonable behaviour to entitle the wife to a decree of divorce.

Unreasonable behaviour caused by the respondent's mental illness may also entitle the petitioner to a divorce. But in this case the petitioner will have to prove that the effects of the behaviour were more serious than could be tolerated from a person not suffering from mental illness. This means that a petitioner will normally have to wait longer in these cases, or will have to show a much more severe impact from the behaviour.

Time limits It is provided that, if the parties continue to live together for a period or periods of six months or less, then no account of this shall be taken by the court in assessing how reasonable or unreasonable it is to expect the parties to live together. If the parties continue to live together for more than six months, then the court has a discretion to ignore any such longer period of cohabitation. This will most often be the case in circumstances where it would be impossible for the petitioner to move out of the matrimonial home or, because of overcrowding or fear of the respondent, even out of the matrimonial bed.

(c) *The respondent has deserted the petitioner for a continuous period of at least two years immediately preceding the presentation of the petition* The meaning of this provision is that the respondent has left the petitioner, intending never to return, without any good reason for having done so and without the permission of the petitioner. It has been said that desertion amounts to a complete repudiation of the obligations of marriage.

Respondent has left the petitioner This means that the parties to the marriage cease to live together as man and wife. If they still remain under the same roof the respondent must refuse to have anything to do with the petitioner.

Intending never to return This requirement must be present throughout the two-year period, so that if the respondent makes a genuine offer to return to the petitioner the desertion comes to an end. (This must be read subject to points made under *Time limits*, below.)

Without the permission of the petitioner If the petitioner consents to the desertion, then it is immediately converted from desertion into separation.

Without any good reason If the petitioner has acted in such a way that the respondent cannot be expected to continue cohabitation, by committing adultery for example, then the respondent's departure will not amount to desertion.

Constructive desertion This occurs when the respondent has behaved in such a way as to force the petitioner to leave the matrimonial home. The respondent will then be considered to have deserted the other spouse even though it was not the respondent who left. The respondent's behaviour must make continued cohabitation impossible, and amount to a form of expulsion of the petitioner from the matrimonial home.

Two years Time begins to run only from the day following the actual desertion. The desertion must have lasted for two years before the petition is presented and be continuous.

Time limits It is provided that a period of six months' resumed living together can be ignored by the court when seeking to establish whether the two-year period of desertion has been continuous or not. But the court will still require the period of desertion to amount in all to two years. For example, if the respondent deserts the petitioner on 1 January 1981, normally the petitioner would not be able to institute proceedings until 2 January 1983. If the respondent returns to the matrimonial home for one month in the middle of this period of desertion, the continuity of desertion will not be broken but the earliest possible date on which the petitioner will be able to petition would be 2 February 1983.

(d) *The parties to the marriage have lived apart for a continuous period of at least two years immediately preceding the petition, and the respondent consents to the petition being granted* This means that if the parties to a marriage live separately for two years, and then both agree, a divorce can be granted.

What does living apart mean? Living apart means that the parties cease to live with each other as part of a marital unit. So they can remain living under the same roof, provided that each avoids doing things for the other which might be referrable to the marital relationship. For example, a wife must stop cooking, cleaning, eating with, or sharing the marital bed with, her husband and a husband must stop changing plugs, helping with cooking or cleaning, eating with his wife or sharing the marital bed. It is possible for the parties to be seen by the court as still living together despite the fact that they may be separated by several thousand miles. If, for example, the husband is working under contract in the Middle East and his wife has remained throughout this period in the UK, but both parties consider the marriage to be subsisting, then this will not amount to living apart for the purpose of the act.

Time limits The same principles apply here as under point (c) above. Namely, a period or periods of resumed cohabitation, amounting to no more than six months, will not break the continuity of the period of separation although the parties must actually have lived apart for the required two years.

Respondent's consent The respondent must give a positive consent to the decree being granted: this means more than just not objecting. It normally means that the respondent gives his consent in writing. To this end, the forms sent to the respondent by the court will warn him of the consequence of giving his consent. (For example, he will lose the automatic right to inherit if his wife dies without having made a will.)

(e) *The parties to the marriage have lived apart for a continuous period of at least five years immediately preceding the presentation of the petition.*
What does living apart mean? (See page 86.)

Time limits The same principles apply here as under parts (c) and (d) above. Namely, a period or periods of resumed cohabitation, amounting to no more than six months in all, will not break the continuity of the five years' separation, although the spouses must actually have lived apart in total for the required five-year period before starting action.

Defence The Act provides the respondent with a defence to a claim for divorce under the five-year separation rule. This arises where the respondent can prove that the decree of divorce will cause 'grave financial hardship' or 'other grave hardship'. No known claim based on 'other grave hardship' has been successful. 'Grave financial hardship' would seem to be limited to circumstances where the parties are at least in middle age, and usually nearing the age of retirement, so that the hardship envisaged on the grant of the decree is the loss of a chance of receiving benefits under an occupational pension scheme. It is possible for the petitioner to propose methods of offsetting this potential loss which, if acceptable, would cause the defence to fail. For instance, if the occupational pension scheme allows for the nomination of a beneficiary, then the petitioner will be able to nominate the respondent and so obtain the decree. If there is no possibility of nomination, then the petitioner could propose the purchase of a life assurance policy, with the respondent nominated as beneficiary.

In any event, the court will grant the decree (even if grave financial hardship has been established and no proposals to offset it have been made) if it decides that the circumstances are such that a decree ought still be to be granted. The shorter the marriage and the longer the separation, the more likely it will be for the court to reach such a conclusion.

Delaying decree absolute

(See page 80 for the normal rules.) Where a petition has been based on either of factors (d) or (e) above, then the respondent can ask the court to delay the grant of decree absolute until proper financial provision has been made for the respondent (see page 97 for financial provision orders). The court can then make one of three declarations, after which decree absolute will be granted without further delay. These declarations are:

- that no financial provision should be made for the respondent; or
- that the financial provision made is reasonable; or
- that, in any event, there are circumstances making it desirable to grant a decree absolute without delaying at all, provided that the petitioner undertakes to make adequate financial provisions for the respondent.

Where there are children of the family

Where there is a child aged under sixteen, or an older child (including one of eighteen or more) receiving education, a decree cannot be made absolute unless the court makes one of the following declarations:

- that arrangements have been made for the welfare of the named children, and these are reasonable; or
- that no arrangements should be made; or
- that in any event there are special circumstances making it desirable for a decree absolute to be granted without delay.

This amounts to statutory recognition of the fact that, in marital breakdown, the people most likely to suffer are the children and that the court must therefore consider their needs and requirements before giving the spouses their freedom.

Who is a 'child of the family'? This term is broadly defined to include any child treated as a child of the family, whether a child by blood or not (this does not include a foster child).

What does welfare mean? This include such matters as financial support, future custody, and care and control, and the education of each child.

So far, the legal rules which govern entitlement to a decree absolute of divorce have been described. The amount of government financial assistance available to a spouse seeking a divorce, and the court procedure necessary in order to obtain a divorce will depend on whether the application for a divorce is defended or undefended. The respondent may believe that the marriage has not irretrievably broken down, and consequently may want to argue this issue out before the court; or, for example, the respondent may deny allegations of adultery or unreasonable behaviour, thereby denying that the marriage has broken down in the required way. In these types of case, the petition will become a defended one.

Undefended cases

If the case is undefended then what is known as the 'special procedure' (a divorce by post) comes into play. This means that provided the court is satisfied that all the documents are in order and the legal requirements for providing entitlement to a divorce are established in the documentation, a divorce will be granted without the petitioner having to appear in court. If the petitioner comes within the income limits, legal advice may be available either totally free or subject to a contribution. This initial advice will cover the divorce stage of the petition so that if there are subsequent difficulties over other things, like the future custody of any children or the ownership of the matrimonial home, further sums will be available for advice and legal representation in court, should this become necessary. (For legal aid see page 429.) Where there are children involved, it will be necessary for the spouses (either or both of them) to attend the court to discuss privately with a judge in his room the proposed future arrangements for the children.

Defended divorces

These are automatically transferred to the Family Division of the High Court. For an applicant who falls within the means limits laid down, free advice from a solicitor and free representation by a barrister will be available. For applicants who are not entitled to completely free representation, but nevertheless fall within the basic limits, such advice and representation will be available subject to a contribution (see page 430).

Warning Because so many other rights and obligations depend on the continued existence of a marriage, it is inadvisable to divorce without having first sought advice from a solicitor, a Citizens' Advice Bureau, or a legal advice centre.

Presumption of death

This decree is available in cases where there is no positive evidence that one spouse is dead, although there are reasonable grounds for supposing this to be the case.

Evidence on which the court will act
If one spouse has been absent from the other for at least seven years, and the petitioner has had no reason to believe that the other spouse has been living during that time, then the court will assume the absent party to be dead unless there is evidence to the contrary.

The court may act even if the seven-year period has not elapsed, provided that the petitioner can show reasonable evidence to support the contention that the spouse is dead. For example, a spouse who went missing after an earthquake when he was known to be in the area of greatest danger could be presumed dead by the court.

The decree puts the petitioner in the position of a widow or widower, even if it subsequently transpires that the other spouse is still alive.

Judicial separation

A decree of judicial separation does not formally bring the marriage to an end; it merely brings an end to the requirement that the spouses cohabit. It is particularly useful where spouses do not want a divorce (for example, because their religion forbids it) but nevertheless want the court to make orders about the future custody, care and control of any children of the family, and make orders about financial provision (see page 97) and property redistribution (see page 98).

How to get a decree
The court will grant such a decree provided the petitioner can prove the existence of any one of the five factors proving entitlement to a divorce described above (see pages 83 to 87). This means that

- proof of adultery making the marriage intolerable;
- unreasonable behaviour;
- desertion for two years;
- separation for two years with consent; or
- five years' separation with or without consent will entitle the petitioner to a decree.

Undefended cases
These are determined in the divorce county court under the special procedure without the need for a hearing.

Defended cases
Where there is doubt about the existence of the ground relied upon by the petitioner, then the case will be heard by the Family Division of the High Court.

Decree absolute
No such decree can be granted where there are children of the family, unless the court makes one of the three declarations described on page 88.

There is a booklet called *Undefended Divorces*, available free from any divorce county court, which describes how to bring a petition for an undefended divorce without a solicitor.

11 Money matters

This chapter is about financial support in the form of periodical payments, lump sum payments and property settlements that can be awarded by the courts to people during marriage and on divorce. It also deals with the tax position of married and separated couples and summarizes the state benefits that are available for the support of families.

Financial support during marriage

Parties living apart
Actions in the magistrates' court
The powers of magistrates to make orders for financial support were overhauled in 1978, and there are now three types of case in which the court can act.

First, an applicant can establish any one of the following three grounds:

- that there has been a failure to provide reasonable maintenance;
- that the respondent has behaved in such a way that the applicant cannot reasonably be expected to live with him or her; or

• that the respondent has deserted the applicant.

What is a failure to provide reasonable maintenance? The court will decide whether the applicant is entitled to an order by following the statutory guidelines to see what would amount to reasonable provision and then compare that with the payments made by the respondent. If no payments are being made, or the payments are less than might have been expected, then there is a failure to provide reasonable maintenance (see page 101).

What is unreasonable behaviour? This concept is defined on page 84. The only point of distinction is that an application to magistrates must take place within six months of the last provable act of unreasonable behaviour.

What is desertion? This concept is explained on page 85. The only point of distinction is that in magistrates' courts there is no need to wait for two years.

The second way in which a magistrates' court can make financial provision is by making a *consent order*. This will arise in cases where the parties have reached full agreement on all aspects of financial support and, because of the tax advantages to be gained, want the agreement to be turned into a court order. The court must be satisfied that the respondent has truly given his consent and that the agreement is not contrary to the interests of justice. An agreement which requires excessive payments or insufficient payments would be contrary to the interests of justice. In these cases the court can, with the parties' consent, make an order which will accord with the interests of justice.

The third way in which magistrates can make financial provision is where the parties have *separated by agreement*. If voluntary payments for financial support have been made over the three months immediately preceding the application to the court, the court can convert these payments into obligatory ones by making them the subject of a court order. (The court cannot order a lump sum payment.) The only limitation on the power of the court is that the ordered payments cannot exceed, over a three-month period, those which had been paid voluntarily over the relevant three-month period. If these voluntary payments are either excessive, or insufficient, the court can make any order which it thinks fit.

Orders that the court can make The orders that the court can make are:

- a periodical payment order (that is, a maintenance payment order, or alimony); and
- a lump sum order which cannot exceed £500. (For an explanation of these concepts see page 97.)

Legal advice and representation Hearings in magistrates' courts are relatively informal, and both court staff and magistrates will be helpful to any unrepresented person. Any person may make use of the new form of legal assistance, which allows a solicitor to calculate the means of an applicant (to decide whether he or she falls within the financial limits of the scheme) and then represent the applicant in court. Calculations made in this way ensure that delay is kept to a minimum.

Variation Once the court has made an order, it may be that the circumstances change so that the original order ceases to be fair. Consequently either party can reapply to the court to have the original order varied in some way. The court is also empowered to make a further order for the payment of a lump sum, and in the case of a variation of a consent order, to approve payment of a lump sum in excess of £500.

In the divorce county court or High Court (Family Division)
This area of law was also amended in 1978, so that an application can now be made in cases where there has been a *failure to provide reasonable maintenance*. This means that the respondent has failed either wholly or in part to give the applicant sufficient financial support, given each party's financial situation.

This jurisdiction duplicates that which is available in the magistrates' court (see page 91).

The distinction in the two parallel jurisdictions relates to the orders which can be made; the power of the magistrates is more restricted.

Orders which the county courts and the High Court can make are:

- a periodical payment order;
- a secured periodical payment order; and
- a lump sum order without financial restriction.

(For an explanation of these types of order see page 97.)

Cases transferred from magistrates' court In cases of a complicated nature, where the parties are particularly wealthy, or where allegations of misconduct are particularly nasty, the magistrates can transfer the case to the High Court.

Cases transferred from the divorce county court Once again, cases which involve substantial allegations of misconduct will be taken in the High Court.

Legal advice and representation Legal advice is available under the 'green form scheme' to those who fall within the means limitations. The costs of legal representation can be paid if the applicant's means fall within the limits laid down, and the cause is considered worthy of state support (see page 428).

Parties living together

The court can exercise its powers to make an order despite the fact that the parties are living together at the time of the application. In other words, it is possible to obtain an order that the respondent pay reasonable housekeeping expenses to the applicant.

This power is of limited application in the magistrates' court, since an order for periodical payments must terminate if the parties continue to live together for a continuous period of six months. Living together means as part of the same household, which requires both eating and sleeping together as part of one family unit. The six-month period must be continuous, so an order will not terminate in cases where the parties have resumed living together for one month each year for six years!

Orders made in other courts do not have to terminate in this way.

Interim periodical payment orders

The court has power to make an order for periodical payments before hearing full argument on the issues. This will usually happen in circumstances where there will be some delay between application to the court and final decision, either because the court's diary is heavily booked or because the applicant needs time to prepare the case.

In the magistrates' court such an order will be limited to three months' duration initially, although it may be extended for a further period not exceeding three months.

The tax position

Income tax

This tax is payable by all of us on income earned from any source. It is known as a 'progressive' tax: the more you earn, the higher the rate at which you pay. The basic rate of tax is currently 30%; rising, for high-income earners, to a rate of 60%. If our income arises from investments rather than earnings, then an additional 15% tax is payable on investment income in excess of £6,250. Investment income is added to the top slice of earned income for taxation purposes. We all have certain tax allowances which we can set against our income before we reach the part which is taxed. These allowances include, for example, the personal allowance (which everyone gets), married man's allowance, child allowance, mortgage interest relief, and so on. From April 1983 mortgage interest relief will be deducted from monthly instalments.

Married couples

Married couples, with or without children, are entitled to claim the married man's tax allowance (if they live together) and the wife's earned income allowance against their joint income. The responsibility for payment of tax is the husband's, so that even if the wife is paying tax, the husband may be liable to pay an additional sum at the end of the tax year.

It is only very recently that married women have been recognized as separate individuals by the tax authorities; tax offices will now write to married women about their own tax affairs, and pay rebates to a wife, rather than, as in the past, to her husband. The wife's earned income relief can only be offset against earned income and not against investment income.

So, on this basis, a married couple's tax bill (much simplified) might look something like this:

MARRIED COUPLE (husband and wife working)

Earnings	£	£
Husband's earnings	15,000	
Wife's earnings	5,000	
		20,000
Allowances		
Married man's allowance	2,795	
Wife's earned income allowance	1,785	
		4,580
Total taxable income		15,420

On this total, tax would be payable as follows: 30% on the first £14,600,

40% on the next £2,600. This would result in a total tax bill, for the year in question, of £4,708.

There are two other ways in which a married couple can arrange their tax affairs: they can opt for separate assessment or separate taxation.

Separate assessment If husband and wife ask for this then each will make a separate tax return, and the obligation to pay tax will then be apportioned according to each party's income. The total bill is the same, it is just that each party is now obliged to pay his or her own share.

Separate taxation In this case, each party to the marriage is treated as a single tax-paying individual, and for high earners there are considerable tax benefits to be gained. It is important to calculate the potential benefits each year, since tax allowances tend to change with every budget. The effect of deciding to be taxed separately is that:

- the married man loses his married man's allowance, and becomes entitled only to the single person's allowance, while
- the wife loses her married woman's tax relief and becomes entitled to the single person's allowance.

Each party is then treated as a separate individual (except in so far as investment income is concerned) and each pays the basic rate of income tax until his or her income reaches the level of higher rate tax (which, as you will see from the above example, starts at £14,601). There is no real advantage in separate taxation until the parties' joint earned income gets to £20,000 or more.

(Proposals made by the government would allow married couples to choose to be treated equally and divide all allowances equally between them.)

Single parents

Any unmarried person who has a child living with him or her, and is financially maintaining the child, is entitled to the 'additional child tax relief' of £1,010 p.a. This relief brings the single person's tax relief up to the married man's tax allowance and means that, in effect, cohabiting couples with children can draw the equivalent of the married man's tax allowance.

Married couples living apart

If the parties to a marriage are living apart, as a result of a separation order or an agreement, or in such circumstances that the separation is likely to be permanent, then the man loses his right to claim the married man's tax allowance. The party who has the children and is maintaining them may, however, claim the additional child tax relief of £1,010 p.a.

Mortgage interest relief
Interest paid on a loan to finance the purchase or improvement of land or buildings within UK attracts full tax relief, provided that the property is used as the only or main residence of:

- the borrower, or
- a former or separated spouse of the borrower, or
- a dependent relative of the borrower.

This relief is available only on the interest on loans of less than £30,000, and is now deducted from payments made to the lender, not from income at source.

(The figures in this section take account of the budget changes in 1983.)

Financial support on divorce, etc.

Both the divorce county court (the Divorce Registry in London) and the High Court (Family Division) have power to hear applications. The former hears all undefended cases, and the latter defended cases and those which are transferred from the county court because they involve serious allegations of matrimonial misconduct or large sums of money. Cases which are dealt with in the divorce county court are usually heard by the registrar. The registrar is an administrative assistant to the judge, who can also act judicially in cases that are not contested. If the registrar's decision is thought to be wrong, then it is possible to appeal to the judge. Cases are normally heard in the registrar's or judge's room and not in open court.

Orders which the court can make

A periodical payment order
This is an order which can be paid weekly, monthly, bimonthly, etc. and is usually intended to provide sufficient income to cover, either wholly or in part, the normal expenses of life.

A secured periodical payment order
This kind of order is to provide maintenance and to ensure that any default in payment can be made good against a capital sum which is set aside and held by trustees. The fund remains the property of

the payer to the extent that the maintenance obligation is met. This form of order is only available in cases where the payer has a capital asset which can be set aside, and will only usually be selected in cases where the respondent is likely to default and where the normal methods of enforcement would not be appropriate (for example, where the respondent is living abroad).

A lump sum order

This is an order for the payment of a large sum of money, and can be ordered to be paid by instalment. Lump sums will often be used to cover expenses incurred before the application is made, and in the magistrates' court (where an order is limited to £500 per member of the family) will often be used to cover an outstanding debt (for example, an outstanding rates or heating bill).

The lump sum could also be used to fund a specific project of the petitioner's (for example, to buy a new house or begin a business). Generally, these orders are only appropriate where the payer has enough capital to raise the lump sum, either by sale or by using capital as security for a loan. Consequently the court will bear in mind that, although many assets will have a high paper value, the reality of the situation may be that they cannot be converted into money without unnecessary loss.

In cases where there is only one capital asset (for example, the former matrimonial home), and the applicant has a share or is granted a share in it by the court, the court may order the respondent to buy out the applicant's share by making a lump sum order. If the respondent still needs the former matrimonial home this will only be ordered where the lump sum can be raised by mortgage; otherwise the property will be sold and the proceeds divided.

A property transfer order

This is an order which gives all or part of a specific piece of property to the applicant. In most cases the only property which the parties to a marriage have is the matrimonial home, and in cases where the applicant's name does not appear on the title documents, the court may grant the applicant a share in it. A home which is being rented privately may fall outside the powers of the court. This will be the case where the lease or tenancy agreement expressly prevents the tenant from transferring the property to another person. Since 1980 the court has had power to transfer a secure (local authority) tenancy on a decree of divorce or nullity. In such cases the transferee becomes the secure tenant.

Where an applicant is receiving legal aid, any property which is received as a result of the legally aided action is caught by the Law Society's charge. This means that apart from an exempt £2,500, the whole of the value of the property received in the action may be used to pay back the costs of the action. This does not mean that the house must immediately be sold; but if it ever is the Law Society is entitled to recover its costs. The Law Society has a discretion to postpone the operation of the charge so that if the home has to be sold in order to buy something cheaper, the Society may agree to delay taking out its share until such time as this second house is sold.

A property settlement order

This is an order whereby the court ensures that family property (which may be either jointly owned or owned by one party) is retained for the use of the family. The most obvious example is the matrimonial home. In cases where the value of the matrimonial home is too small to allow each party to be provided with a new home out of the proceeds of sale, the party who has the physical possession of any dependent children will have to live in the house until such time as the children become independent. Each party's entitlement to a share in the value of the house will then be delayed until the property ceases to be needed as a home.

When to apply for an order

An application for property transfers and settlements must be made before remarriage. This does not mean that the court must make its decision before remarriage, just that an application will not be entertained once the applicant has remarried.

Duration of orders

Periodical payment orders automatically cease on the remarriage of the person to whom payments are made. Similarly, periodical payments will cease on the death of the payee or payer. A secured periodical payment order will continue after the death of the payer until the remarriage or death of the person to whom it is payable. A property settlement will state in the settlement how long it is intended to last.

Maintenance pending suit

This application can be made once a petition for divorce, etc. has been presented to the court, and can be compared to an interim periodical payment order. The purpose of this form of order is to provide the applicant with some financial support until a final order is made. Normally the court will refuse to order payment of more than one quarter of the parties' joint gross income.

Legal advice and representation

This area of the law is very complex and the powers of the court so extensive that legal advice should be sought. For people who satisfy the means limitations laid down for free legal advice or representation, it should be noted that free help, or help subject to a contribution, is available even though the divorce element of the action is undefended. In undefended divorce cases only legal advice is covered by the legal aid scheme for the actual divorce – but where financial relief and property settlements are involved, money is available for representation by a lawyer in court.

Maintenance agreements intended to take effect on divorce, judicial separation or nullity

Parties who can reach an agreement on all financial and property matters (an agreement which is to take effect when the marriage is dissolved) would be well advised to do so. Such an agreement does not depend on court approval for its validity, although it is possible to refer the agreement to the court for approval. The court does not act as a rubber-stamping agency, but will look at the terms of the agreement and see whether the proposed arrangements appear reasonable. The court will take special care in cases where one party has acted without legal advice, or has agreed not to be maintained (leaving the state to support that party instead), or where there are children in the family.

In all other cases it is possible for the parties to agree that there should be no future obligations of support owed, and once such an agreement has been implemented it will be enforced by the court. This is known as the 'clean break' principle and is encouraged because each party will then be able to organize his or her life without the continuing worry of a new or further applications for support being made in the future. It has been recognized, however, that this is very difficult to achieve in cases where there are dependent children.

Guidelines for assessing support

These guidelines are relevant when application is made to a court for any of the kinds of financial relief dealt with in this chapter. Men and women are treated equally to the extent that applications can be made by either, but in most cases the level of relief granted or approved will depend very much on the sex of the applicant, so that men will usually get less than women.

The general rules

In cases where the parties are not poor, the court will normally start with the so-called 'one third rule'. This means that the party claiming financial support will normally be entitled to *one third of the parties' joint gross income*, and to *one third of any family property*. This basic rule is only used as a starting point (although in many cases it will also be the finishing point!), but the following specific factors will be taken into account in deciding whether the basic rule should be varied up or down:

- The rule is generally ignored when the parties are particularly wealthy, as a sum of less than one third will usually produce justice and equality in living standards between the parties.
- When the claimant is a man, as already suggested, it is rare for him to be awarded as much as one third of the other party's income and property. But this very much depends, of course, on the relative financial strengths and weaknesses of both parties.
- For families who have very little income and property the basic rule is meaningless, so instead the courts have adopted a different starting point; namely, that the respondent's income must not be reduced to below subsistence level. Subsistence level is defined by reference to the supplementary benefits scheme (see page 115). The basic single or two-person householder's rate, all reasonable housing costs (that is, rent or mortgage interest, rates, and an allowance for repairs and insurance), and the scale rate allowance for any dependent children, will be added together to establish the subsistence level of the respondent. Any income which falls above this level is then considered to be available for redistribution. Normally the court will then split the difference between the parties.
- When one party is called upon to pay a lump sum to the other the court will look to the source from which the lump sum is to be raised.

- The courts have recently stated that the rule is of little use when the parties are dividing capital assets.

The statutory guidelines

(a) *Income and earning capacity*

The court requires full information about the parties' financial positions and details of any property which might be available for redistribution.

In the magistrates' court each party will have to fill in a means questionnaire. This is a form which requires each party to provide information about income from all sources (including overtime payments, whether regular or not) and expenditure. In the county courts and High Court, each party is required to complete an 'affidavit of means' (a sworn, signed and witnessed statement) covering all aspects of income, expenditure, property ownership and entitlements.

The courts are entitled to draw adverse inferences against any party who fails to complete the form honestly. For example, if one party fails to disclose income from overtime, the court can estimate the income from such earnings and this may well exceed the real earnings. The court is concerned to ensure that the real financial situation of each party is adequately reflected, and to this extent will also want to know the financial position of any person living with each party.

The court may be prepared to impute an earning capacity to a party who is not working at all but could do so, or who could work in a more highly paid job but chooses not to. So, if the respondent is unemployed but could find employment, the court will pretend that the respondent has the same income as what could be earned if the available job were taken. Similarly, the courts have been prepared to attribute an income to a non-working mother who could take employment, if she has children who are at school. It has been said that 'marriage is not a meal ticket for life', and consequently most women will be expected to become at least partly financially independent.

If one party has refused to make a full declaration of his financial position to the court, then the other may obtain an order from the court to go and search for papers or documents which have been withheld and make copies of them. If it is feared that one party may attempt to transfer assets out of the jurisdiction of the court, then the court may be willing to grant an injunction to prevent this from happening.

(b) *Financial needs and obligations*

When considering each party's financial needs, the court will try to ensure that financial resources are distributed in such a way that each party will be able to meet his or her financial obligations. When there is insufficient money available to achieve this object, the court will discount those needs which are not essential.

In cases where a second marriage has broken down while the respondent is still supporting the first wife and/or children, the second wife's claim will take second place to that of the first wife.

The court can also take account of moral obligations of support (for example, where the husband is supporting an aged parent), as part of the respondent's financial obligations.

In cases where the court must decide on the future occupation or ownership of the matrimonial home, the needs of each party will be fully explored. In many cases a sale of the matrimonial home will not provide sufficient cash for both parties to be able to acquire a new home. Consequently, where there are dependent children (that is, children under the age of 17 or 18) the court will have to ensure that the party who has the physical possession of the children can remain in the house at least until those children become independent. This can be achieved in several ways. For example:

- The whole of the interest in the matrimonial home might be transferred to the custodian parent, at the same time reducing all obligations to maintain.
- The house could be transferred to the custodian parent and a charge to the non-custodian then created over the property. A charge is an acknowledgement of indebtedness secured against the house or flat which ensures that the agreed debt is paid off under certain clearly stated conditions. The events which would make the debt payable might be any of the following: the death or remarriage of the other party, the sale of the house, or the youngest child's reaching the age of 17 or 18.
- The party whose name does not appear in the title documents might be given a share, so that the house then becomes partly owned by each spouse. Each of them could then be prevented from selling out until, say, death or the remarriage of the spouse still residing in the house, or the youngest child's reaching the age of 17 or 18.

(c) *The standard of living enjoyed by the parties during the marriage*

So far as it is possible the courts try to ensure that standards of living do not suffer as a result of marital breakdown. It is, however, recognized that two families cannot live as cheaply as one, so the aim is to achieve equality between spouses; each should be able to live at roughly the same standard as the other.

(d) *The age of the parties and duration of the marriage*
In cases which involve young couples who have been married for only a short time and have no children, it is rare for the court to make an order for financial support. In these cases, entitlement to property will depend on the contributions made towards the acquisition of that property (see page 123), or on any economic loss sustained as a result of the marriage (for example, if one party has to give up employment, or a council tenancy, on marriage).

In long-lasting marriages, where the wife is approaching or in middle age and has completed the job of bringing up the family, she can expect to be financially supported and receive a substantial share of any family assets.

In general, periods of cohabitation before marriage are excluded from calculating what is a short marriage, but this will depend on the quality of the cohabitation. If a woman gives the best years of her life to a man during cohabitation, and is faithful, loving, hard working and mother to that man's children, then the court will have to take this into account when assessing the woman's entitlement on the breakdown of a short marriage, otherwise it would be impossible to achieve justice between the parties.

(e) *Physical or mental incapacity of either party*
This allows the court to enforce an obligation of support where, other things being equal, there might have been none. So that a disabled man may have to be maintained by his wife; or a person who, because of a disablement, cannot work will not have an earning capacity imputed to him or her.

(f) *Contributions made to the welfare of the family, including looking after the house or caring for the family*
This provision is an attempt to equate housekeeping and caring for children and the benefits arising from these activities with going out to earn money and then applying that income to the needs of the family.

The former is deemed to be a contribution in kind, which will automatically entitle the wife (or, if relevant, husband) to share in the assets acquired for the family's use, as though the money for the acquisition had been provided at least partly by the wife. The same principle is applied when considering entitlement to any savings in, say, a building society account.

It has been suggested that in cases where the wife actually leaves her husband, children and the matrimonial home without having completed the job of bringing up the family, her entitlement to share in the family assets will be reduced to take account of this fact.

(g) *Value of any benefit which will be lost on the grant of decree of divorce or nullity*

This is not relevant unless the marriage has been dissolved by decree (see page 80). The purpose of this provision is to ensure that the court keeps in mind the fact that a wife will, on dissolution, cease to be a 'wife' and therefore lose all benefits from the state widow's pension scheme and from any occupational pension scheme to which the husband has contributed. The older the parties are when the marriage is dissolved, the clearer is the need to offset this loss. This may be done by giving the wife a higher property settlement than might have been expected, or by purchasing an annuity for the wife which will then automatically offset any loss, or, if it is possible, by ordering the husband to nominate his ex-wife as beneficiary under the pension scheme.

Conduct of the parties

Although a court is directed to have regard to the conduct of the parties in the breakdown of the marriage it is rare for misconduct by itself to affect the amount of any order. This is because only conduct of a 'gross and obvious' nature will be taken into account. This means something more than mere blameworthiness; it is something which would make the normal entitlement to financial relief or property redistribution unacceptable to society.

Therefore adulterous conduct by itself will be ignored by a court. However, adultery with a close relative by blood or marriage may be taken into account; similarly an adulterous association which takes place at a time when a matrimonial home is bought in the names of both parties to the marriage will indicate that the conveyance into joint names would not have taken place had the innocent party been aware of the adultery.

Similarly, violent conduct which leads to serious injury will often be taken into account by the court, and so will action which is intended to affect one party's employment or employment prospects, such as disparaging remarks to an employer.

In those cases where conduct has been held to be relevant, the so-called guilty party will not always lose all entitlement, but it may well affect the size of his or her share in the family income and property.

It is exceptional for conduct to be deemed a relevant consideration, and it has been said that everything should be done to avoid 'costly, indecent and time wasting investigations'. In any case involving serious contested issues as to conduct, the divorce county court, or magistrates' court will normally transfer the case to the High Court.

The taxation position

(See note on page 122 for April 1983 change in tax relief and allowances.) As already mentioned, when the parties are separated and the separation is likely to be permanent, the husband loses his entitlement to claim the married man's tax allowance. This will clearly be the case where a decree of divorce, etc. is envisaged, or where application for one has been commenced. In these circumstances each spouse will only be entitled to claim the single person's tax relief, and the spouse with the care of any children may claim additional child tax relief.

As has been seen, the usual situation will be that the ex-husband will be expected to maintain his former wife and any children of the family. If from the date of separation he is merely making voluntary payments of maintenance (that is, payments not made under a separation agreement or court order) then such an arrangement has no effect whatsoever on either party's liability to pay tax.

If, however, payments are being made under an agreement or court order, then the payments cease in reality to be part of the husband's income. This is because the income comprised in the payments is deemed to belong to the wife and children. There are two possibilities in these circumstances.

Small maintenance payments

If the payments are made by court order and amount to no more than *small maintenance payments*, they can be deducted before the payer's income is subjected to tax.

Payments of up to £33 per week or £143 per month to a former spouse are small maintenance payments. There are two ways of making such payments to children. First, when by an unambiguous order maintenance is paid directly to the child, the payments are considered small maintenance payments if they amount to no more than £33 per week, or £143 per month. This means that they are paid in full (without deduction of tax by the payer) and that the child will only pay tax on the maintenance if his income from all sources exceeds his personal allowance (currently £1,565 p.a.). For the order to qualify the words of the order must take the following form:

The Respondent pay to (name of the child) £00.00 per week/per month from (date) to (date).

Payments which qualify are those made after 6 April 1983, those made under an order made on or after 30 July 1982, and those varied or revived on or after 30 July 1982.

If payments are made to some other person (usually the custodian parent) for the benefit of the child, then these will amount to small payments if they are made for a maximum of £15 per week or £78 per month. Once again, such payments are made without deduction of tax by the payer, but will be subject to tax in the hands of the recipient, if that person is liable to pay tax.

It is now extremely advantageous to have maintenance payments ordered to be paid directly to the child. It is possible to seek a variation of an existing order on this basis.

For example: Husband's income = £5,500 p.a. Maintenance order to wife £12 per week = £624 p.a. Maintenance order to each of two children under the age of twenty-one £7 per week = £728 p.a.

Tax relief	= single person's tax relief	£1,565
	= maintenance to wife	£624
	= maintenance to children	£728
		£2,917

Total taxable income = £5,500–£2,917 = £2,583
Total tax payable at 30% = £774.90

The wife's position is then that she pays tax on her own income, which includes income from earnings and income from maintenance payments, but excludes maintenance payments ordered directly payable to a child. For example:

Wife's earned income	£2,000
Income from maintenance	£624
Total income	£2,624

Tax allowances:
Single person's tax relief = £1,565
Additional child tax relief = £880
Total tax relief = £2,445
Total tax payable = 30% of (£2,624–£2,445) = £53.70

The taxation position of each child is that each has income of £364 p.a. and since each child's personal tax relief is £1,565, no tax will be payable.

It is worth noting here that one of the most important matters considered by the courts, in deciding how much maintenance to order, is to reduce as far as legally possible the tax liability of each person. Consequently in the example detailed above if part of the maintenance payment ordered to be paid to the wife (that is, that part on which she pays tax, £29) were instead ordered to be paid directly to the two children, that sum would escape tax altogether, both in the husband's hands and in the wife's.

Other payments

If the payments ordered are greater than small maintenance payments, or the payments are made under an agreement, then the husband payer is entitled to deduct tax at the basic rate before making the payment. If his income has already been subjected to tax (because he is a PAYE employee) then he can retain the tax so deducted, and if his income has not been taxed (because he is a Schedule D taxpayer) then he must account for the taxation deducted to the revenue. So far as the wife or children are concerned, maintenance payments which have already been subjected to tax are 'grossed up' (this means that the tax deducted is added to the payments made) so that a figure representing the maintenance before tax can be added to the wife's and childrens' incomes. The Inland Revenue can then assess the liability of the wife and the children to pay tax. If there would be no obligation to pay tax, then the wife and children are entitled to claim back from the revenue the tax deducted by the husband, for example:

Husband's income = £12,000 p.a.
Less personal tax relief £1,565
Taxable income = £10,435
Tax paid (PAYE) = £3,130.50
Payment to wife of maintenance = £4,000
Deduct tax at standard rate = £4,000–£1,200 = £2,800
Husband pays to wife £2,800

Husband's tax liability reduced to £1,930.50 (being tax paid less tax deducted from maintenance payment to wife)

Wife's income from maintenance = £4,000
Less personal tax relief £1,565
Taxable income = £2,435
Tax payable = £730.50
Tax paid = £1,200 (deducted by ex-husband)
Tax rebate = £470.50

Once again, if there are children also being maintained by the husband directly, there are considerable tax advantages to be gained by ensuring that each child can use up the whole of his or her personal tax allowance. It can be financially advantageous to direct certain of the maintenance payments legally due the wife to the child instead. For example:

Wife maintenance/income = £4,000 p.a.
Less reliefs £1,565
£880 = £2,445
Taxable income = £4,000–£2,445 = £1,555
Tax payable at 30%, £466.50
Tax deducted by husband £1,200
Tax reclaim £1,200–£466.50 = £733.50
Child's maintenance/income = £1,040 p.a.
Less relief £1,565 = – £525
Tax paid by deduction by father £312
Tax reclaim £312

The tax reclaimed by the wife and children together amounts to £1,045.50. If £525 were paid directly to the children instead of the wife the calculation would be as follows:

Wife's income = £3,475
Less reliefs £2,445 = £1,030
Tax at 30% = £309
Tax paid by husband = £1,042.50
Tax reclaim £1,042.50–£309 = £733.50
Child's income £1,565
Less relief £1,565
Taxable income *nil*
Tax paid by husband = £469.50
Tax reclaim = £469.50

The tax reclaimed by the wife and children will now amount to £1,243. The increase in income to the wife and children will be £200.50.

Capital gains tax

This tax is payable on gains made from the disposal of assets. During the currency of a marriage disposals between spouses are exempt from tax, but after a decree absolute any disposal between ex-spouses is treated as a disposal between 'connected persons' and is considered to have been made at market price. Tax is payable on the difference between the cost price and the market price on the day of transfer. In each financial year the first £5,300 of gain is exempt tax; for gains over this sum, tax is charged at the rate of 30%. (This is the April 1983 figure which is index-linked to retail prices.)

In the divorce context, the majority of chargeable transfers will relate to the matrimonial home. Houses are exempt from tax if the house disposed of was the transferor's only or main residence. If the house is being sold as the result of the breakdown of a marriage relationship, then the exemption will still apply if the house was the disposer's only residence twelve months before the sale. If this rule does not apply, it may be possible for the transfer or sale still to be exempt if the house was the transferee's only residence, and the transferor has elected no other house to be treated as his 'only residence' before the transfer.

Capital transfer tax

This tax is charged on the value of property disposed of in such a way as to reduce the transferor's estate, either by gift (more than three years before death) or on death (see *Death and the family*, page 132).

For purposes of this tax, transfers between husbands and wives are exempt. However, since most transfers in the divorce context are likely to take place after a decree absolute, the husband and wife exemption will cease to apply. Whether or not property transfers are subject to tax in these circumstances will depend on whether or not they are gifts. It is likely that an arrangement to transfer assets as part of a divorce settlement will *not* be seen as a gift and consequently will not attract the tax. In any case the tax only becomes payable once there have been transfers over the years which amount in value to over £60,000. If this is the case, then the rate of tax chargeable on gifts is 15% rising to 50%. Each year it is possible to give away £3,000 of assets without this amount being accumulated for the purposes of the £60,000 total, and it is possible to carry forward the £3,000 exemption to the next tax year. Gifts are now only accumulated for a period of ten years ending with the date of death (April 1983 figures).

A further exemption is available for transfers of capital made in order to provide maintenance for a party to a marriage, or child (up to the age of eighteen), made as part of a divorce, etc. settlement.

Examples of financial provision

Example 1

The parties married in 1954. Immediately after their marriage, the parties, pooling their earnings, moved into a flat. In 1956 the matrimonial home was bought for £5,000 with a 100% mortgage. This was conveyed into the husband's name alone. The wife worked until 1958, when their first child was born; thereafter she stayed at home, and also helped as receptionist and clerk in the husband's dental practice. The husband paid all the mortgage instalments. The wife left in 1972. The son stayed with the father, and the daughter went with the mother.

The value of the matrimonial house at this time was £22,000, with £2,000 outstanding on the mortgage. The husband's income was over £6,000 p.a. The wife's earning capacity as a dental nurse was £750 p.a.

The wife had made full contributions over the eighteen years of the parties' marriage:

Income

Parties' joint gross income	£6,750
One third	£2,250
Wife's earning capacity	–£750
	£1,500

So using the 'one third' calculation, the wife was entitled to £1,500 p.a. in periodical payments.

Property

Value of house	£22,000
less outstanding mortgage	£ 2,000
	£20,000

One third £6,666

The court ordered a lump sum payment of £6,000, which was approximately one third of the value of the matrimonial home. An order for a payment of £300 per annum to the daughter was also made.

Example 2

The parties married in July 1965 and separated in October 1967 at a time when the husband was 21 and the wife was 34. There was one child of the marriage living with the wife. A decree of divorce was obtained in February 1971.

The husband had earnings of £74.50 per week. After deductions for national insurance and the expenses of getting to work this left him with about £69.50 per week. The husband's financial obligations considered reasonable by the court, including outstanding debts, amounted to £50.00 per week. This left the husband with £19 in his pocket. He maintained his daughter at the rate of £5 per week, this then left him with a balance of £14, out of which he was ordered to pay his ex-wife £12 per week in periodical payment:

Gross income £69.50
One third £23.16

But this was a short marriage, so ignoring the one third rule, £12 was a fair payment.

Example 3

Here the parties married when they were both over fifty in May 1970. The wife left in 1972, and the parties divorced in 1975. On her marriage the wife had sold her house and given the proceeds to her son, and had also given up her full-time teaching job, which resulted in a certain loss of pension rights. The wife's position on divorce was that she had earnings from part-time teaching of £450 p.a. and income from her pension of £350 p.a. and no capital. The husband on the other hand had income of £14,000 p.a. and a house worth £28,000.

The wife clearly needed a house and some income to help her run it. She was awarded a £2,000 lump sum payment and periodical payments of £2,000 p.a. less tax; a good deal less than one third of the parties' joint gross income, because of the shortness of the marriage. The court also made a settlement on her of £11,000 until her death or remarriage, which would allow her to obtain a new home and remain in it for as long as she needed.

Example 4

This case involved poorer parties; the two children remained with the mother after the breakdown. The court applied both the one third rule and the subsistence level rule to the facts and compared the outcome.

The one third rule

Gross income of husband,	£75
less National insurance, travelling expenses, leaves	£68
Gross income of wife (child benefit)	£ 3
Joint gross	£68 + £3 = £71
One third =	£34

Less the wife's own income this would have given a payment of £31 per week to the wife.

The subsistence level rule

Husband's entitlement scale rate for single person	£12.70
Rent addition	£ 9.50
	£22.20
Wife's entitlement scale rate for single person	£12.70
Rent addition	£ 8.50
Rate for two dependent children	£ 8.70
	£29.90

To reach this subsistence level the wife would need £26.90 to add to her own income of £3.

The husband was ordered to make periodical payments to the wife of £12 per week, and £5 for each child, and further ordered to pay mortgage and rates of £8.50. This meant his total payments amounted to £30.50 each week, giving the wife a total income of £33.50 compared with the one third calculation which would have given her £34.00 each week. The husband meanwhile retained £15.30 of his income above his basic needs.

Variations

The court is empowered to vary any order made under these powers whenever there has been a change in the circumstances which the court could have taken into account when making the original award.

The powers of variation are limited to orders for maintenance pending suit, periodical payments, and secured periodical payment; orders for lump sum and property orders will not be varied.

Variation in this context includes a power to raise or lower the amount of payment, to suspend the operation of a payment order or discharge a payment order, or revive a suspended order.

The 'clean break' principle

It is possible for the parties to agree between themselves on a settlement of all financial and property claims. This agreement will be enforced by the courts. The form of such a settlement would be that the party who might ordinarily be expected to claim a continuing financial provision will forgo all such claims (both current and future) in return for a larger than normal property or capital settlement. When an agreement of this kind has been made (whether embodied in a consent order or not) and acted upon by the parties, the court will, in the absence of any evidence of oppression, refuse to depart from the terms of the agreement. Consequently no future claims to maintenance would be entertained by the court. The purpose behind this principle is to allow each party to begin a new life without that new life being overshadowed by the relationship which has broken down. This objective, however, is impossible to achieve in any situation where there are dependent children. The parties to the marriage will have to maintain contact with each other, and therefore it has been said that clean breaks are not possible where there are children.

It has also become clear that the consent of the parties is necessary in order to achieve a clean break, and therefore such arrangements cannot be imposed by courts on unwilling parties. Seemingly courts may not be prepared to embody such arrangements in consent orders where the effect will be to place the burden of supporting a family on to the state when this could be avoided by making a periodical payment order against the party with income. (These principles are likely to be changed in the near future to give priority to support for children and to encourage the wife to become financially independent.)

Collection and enforcement of periodical payment orders

Orders for periodical payments made by the magistrates' court can be ordered to be paid to the clerk of the court. This ensures that there are proper accounts to prove payment of the order. Also, if requested in writing, the clerk can, in his own name, take proceedings for enforcement of the order. Money collected in this way can then be forwarded by post to the payee.

Periodical payment orders obtained in other courts can be registered with the magistrates' court so that this special collection and enforcement procedure can be used. Once registered such an order can only be varied by the magistrates' court.

Enforcement may be: by *distress warrant* – where the defaultee's goods are seized and sold to help cover the arrears; *attachment of earnings* – which allows a sum of money to be deducted by the payer's employer and then paid direct to the court, the payer being left with sufficient to cover his needs; *committal* – this may commit the payer to prison and will be used only in cases where the payer deliberately avoids paying the order. Such an order can be suspended on condition that the payer keeps up with the payments.

State support for families

1 The supplementary benefits scheme

This provides income for families whose breadwinner is not in full-time work, and whose resources fall below requirements as defined by the state. The scheme has recently been overhauled, with amendments becoming operative from November 1980. The overhauled scheme is intended to reduce discretion and make clear from published information exactly what each claimant's entitlement is (information can be obtained from DHSS offices, Post Offices and CABs).

Who can claim?

Benefit can only be claimed by people who are:

- not in full-time employment;
- available to be employed.

Full-time work is defined as averaging 30 hours or more each week (35 hours for the disabled).

Registering for employment. All claimants for a supplementary allowance (that is those not claiming supplementary pension) must be available for work. The regulations provide certain exceptions to this rule; these include single parents, blind people and people who have been out of employment for so long that they have no relevant experience, or are nearing the age of retirement.

Available for employment. Certain people will not be entitled to benefit because they are considered not to be available for work; for example, students and persons who have unreasonably refused an offer of employment.

Other people excluded from benefit include people under the age of 19 years and receiving full time education and those involved in an industrial dispute, who are not entitled to claim benefit for themselves, but may claim for their dependants.

When benefit is payable
Benefit will be paid when the claimant's resources are insufficient to meet his requirements.

Resources may be divided into income and capital.

Income resources. All income from whatever source, including child benefit, is added together. However, when earned income is considered, only such sums are counted as remain after deduction of the costs of earning it. Deductions include: income tax, national insurance, fares to and from work, and child-minding costs. Certain income is totally disregarded; for example, attendance allowances and mobility allowance. Some income is partially disregarded; for example, the first £4 of weekly earned income. Single parents are entitled to an additional disregard of one half of their earned income between £4 and £20. Lump sum payments of less than £2,500 are treated as income, spread over a period of weeks calculated in accordance with the following formula:

$$\frac{\text{Lump sum}}{\text{supplementary benefit} + £2}$$

For example a payment of a lump sum of £1,000 when the claimant is entitled to £18 per week supplementary payment, would deny the claimant benefit for a period of 50 weeks:

$$\frac{1,000}{18 + 2} = 50.$$

Capital resources. Under the new rules claimants whose capital amounts to more than £2,500 are not entitled to benefit. 'Capital' excludes such items as the claimant's home and the furniture within that home. Claimants whose capital amounts to more than £300, although entitled to benefit, may not be entitled to claim a single payment or an additional requirement.

Resources and the aggregation rule. All members of a family (the assessment unit) will have their income and capital aggregated (added) together, so that the assessment of resources takes into account the reality of the whole family's financial position.

Whose resources are aggregated? Resources of married and unmarried couples are aggregated, and at the moment only the male partner may claim benefit (this rule will be changed at the latest in 1984, to bring the law into line with that of the EEC). In relation to unmarried couples, this rule, sometimes known as the cohabitation rule, means that the female partner is deemed to be financially supported by the man whether this is the case or not. To avoid too hasty a decision, the benefits officer may continue to pay benefit for any children belonging to the female, at least for a period of four weeks (with extension to six weeks in some circumstances). Similarly the resources of any dependent person will be aggregated with those of the claimant. A 'dependent person' is a child under the age of 19, receiving full-time education, when the claimant is responsible for that child. Responsibility apparently ceases to exist if the child has income from earnings which exceeds the basic scale rate for a child of his age, but not if some other person is paying maintenance for that child above the scale rate. In the latter situation, the application of the aggregation rule reduces the whole assessment unit's claim by the amount of the maintenance payment, whereas in the former situation the claim is reduced only by the scale rate applicable to the particular dependant.

The effect of the aggregation rule on capital. A dependant's capital may be disregarded if, when aggregated with that of the claimant, it exceeds in total £2,500. The claimant will then not be entitled to claim benefit for that dependant. Special rules apply to capital, when the dependant receives this by way of a lump sum payment. If the lump sum is itself less than £2,500, then it is deemed to provide for all the requirements of the dependant for a period calculated in accordance with the following formula:

$$\frac{\text{lump sum}}{\text{dependant rate}} \quad \text{e.g.} \quad \frac{\pounds 730}{\pounds 7.30} = 100 \text{ weeks.}$$

If maintenance is also being paid at an amount above scale rate then the lump sum can be ignored.

Requirements are calculated by reference to the scale rates laid down in November each year.

Supplementary benefit (rates at November 1982)

	Short-term	Long-term
Single householder	£25.70	£32.70
Married or cohabiting couple	£41.70	£52.30
Non householder 18+	£20.55	£26.15
Non householder 16–17	£15.80	£20.05
Children 0–10	£ 8.75	
11–15	£13.15	
Housing addition for a non householder	£ 3.10	

As can be seen the rates vary depending upon how the assessment unit is created. Householders are treated more favourably than non-householders. because of the additional financial cost of taking on responsibility for housing. Couples are treated as one thereby following the principle of aggregation. Non-householders are given a specific allowance for their housing costs. In order to obtain more they will have to prove, for example, that they actually pay more, and that without the extra they would suffer hardship. People who are responsible for a child under the age of 19 (in full-time education) can claim additional scale rates depending upon the age of the child.

Housing payments. There are two schemes now available for the payment of housing costs. For those who live in rented accommodation, their housing costs will now be paid by their local authority under their rent allowance (private accommodation) and rent rebate (public housing) schemes. Rates, water rates and sewerage costs will also be met by the authority. The only limitation on these payments is that the authority must consider the housing costs reasonable. For those who live in owner-occupied property, their housing costs will continue to be met by the supplementary benefits officer. Payments will cover the whole of any mortgage interest, ground rent and service charge, provided once again that these are deemed to be reasonable. Rates and water rate payments will be made by the local authority. In either case, if the claimant is responsible for repairs and insurance, £1.70 will be added to weekly benefit to cover these expenses (from 6 April 1983).

What housing costs are reasonable? The benefits officer is entitled to refuse to meet any housing costs which he deems to be excessive. Costs might be deemed to be excessive if the premises are thought to be too large, too expensive by comparison with other rents in the area, or the property is situated in an area which is deemed to be too expensive. However, if the claimant was able to meet the obligations at the time when he entered the accommodation, then he will be given six months of full payment of his housing costs. Even then he may not have to find alternative accommodation if it can be shown that there is no suitable alternative accommodation, bearing in mind such matters as age, health, length of residence and prospects of obtaining or retaining employment; or if a move would interfere with the education of a member of the claimant's family.

Long-term rates are payable to supplementary pension claimants, and claimants who are not considered available for work: for example, single parents. In the latter case the long-term rate becomes payable after the claimant has been on benefit for 52 weeks.

Additional requirements may be met by adding the relevant sum to the basic requirement rate. The rates for most additional requirement payments are laid down each November. These were, in November 1982:

Heating addition £3.80 or £1.90
Age addition 80+ 25p
Blind person's addition £1.25
Special diets, e.g. diabetes £3.35, convalescent diet £1.45, dialysis £9.60

Additional payments can also be made to cover the cost of HP payments for such things as essential furniture, except where the claimant's capital exceeds £300 by an amount that would cover the cost of the goods. Payments can also be made to cover such expenses as home helps, fares, laundry costs and clothing replacement or repair. In all cases the circumstances surrounding the claims must be pretty exceptional. For example, in order to be able to claim a heating addition, the higher rate will be payable if a member of the 'assessment unit' is confined to the home through ill health: it can be claimed at the lower rate when, because of ill health, additional heating is required, or a member of the 'assessment unit' is aged under 5 or over 70, or the house is difficult to heat.

Single payments (SPs)
These payments are available in very limited circumstances to those who are in receipt of supplementary benefit or would be so entitled if they made a claim. SPs are only paid to meet costs which are not intended to be covered by the basic scale rate; for example, the replacement of worn-out clothing or shoes is, unless the need is caused by extra wear and tear due to mental or physical disability, intended to be covered by the basic scale rate. SPs can be made to cover such items as maternity needs (e.g. cots, bedding) and the installation of prepayment gas or electricity meters. The claimant must be able to prove that his need falls within the provisions specified, or prove that the payment is necessary to prevent serious damage or serious risk to the health and safety of any member of the 'assessment unit'. If a payment is agreed, its amount is also now fixed as the cost of new goods for personal items and second-hand prices for other goods.

The effect of capital on entitlement is that if the claimant has more than £300, this excess sum should be used to meet the need.

NB Such things as free prescriptions, school meals, and dentistry may be obtained by those claiming supplementary benefit or family incomes supplement.

Appeals can be made against the decision of a benefits officer to an appeal tribunal, and from there to a commissioner, but only on a point of law.

Strikes
Strikers are not entitled to benefit, and although claims can be made by them on behalf of members of their family, any entitlement will be reduced by £14.50 which it is assumed they have received as strike pay. Occasional gifts of £100 or less will be disregarded.

Liability to maintain
During the currency of a marriage, whether the parties are living together or apart, each party is required to maintain the other, and any of their children. A failure to maintain in these circumstances will entitle the benefits officer to claim a refund of all or part of the costs paid by the state in support of the family. The refund depends on the means of that person, and payment can be enforced by bringing that person before the magistrates' court. Fathers who have been ordered to maintain children through affiliation proceed-

ings and mothers of illegitimate children are also required to support them in the same way. A persistent failure to maintain amounts to a criminal offence which could lead to imprisonment for a maximum period of three months, and to a fine of up to £400.

2 The family income supplement (FIS)

This benefit is a supplement payable to the low-paid family breadwinner who is in full-time work. A family is defined as consisting of one or two adults (married or unmarried but living together as husband and wife) and at least one child. Entitlement depends on whether the claimant is in full-time work, which is 30 hours per week, but in the case of single parents, 24 hours a week. This distinction is so that single parents can choose which of the two basic state schemes is likely to be most beneficial financially, i.e. supplementary benefits scheme or the FIS scheme.

The supplement is calculated by adding the incomes of all the members of the family together. It is the gross income before deduction of tax and other expenses which is used. Regulations now provide that maintenance payments received from any person legally obliged to maintain a child should be aggregated with the income of the family. Child benefit is excluded from the calculation, as are some other benefits. The supplement is half the difference between the income of the family and the prescribed amount, which is normally updated each November. The prescribed amount varies according to how many children there are in the family.

Family income supplement as at November 1982
One-child family: prescribed amount £82.50
Increase for each additional child £9
Maximum payment for one-child family £21
Increase for each additional child £2

3 Rent and rate rebates

These benefits are paid by local authorities, who are required to operate schemes which reduce the amount of money payable in rates or rent by people with low incomes.

Each authority runs its own scheme, so entitlement may vary. Entitlement under the national scheme is based on a needs allowance of £41.40 for a single person, £61.00 for a couple or single parent with child, and additions to the basic rates of 75p for pensioners, and £11.40 for each further dependent child. When income is greater than the needs allowance, then the rent rebate/allowance will be 60% of reasonable rent less 21% of the excess of income over needs; the rate rebate will be 60% of eligible rates less 7% of the excess of income over needs. When income is less than the needs allowance, the rebate is 60% of the rent or rates, plus for the former 25% of the shortfall and for the latter, 8% of the shortfall.

4 Other benefits which are available

These are based on the national insurance contributions of the contributor or his spouse. They include the retirement pension, and widow's allowances, and maternity allowance.

Retirement pension £32.85
Additional payment for adult dependant £19.70

It is intended in future that widows' allowances should be increased annually at 5% below the increase in prices. In 1982 the government intends to tax these benefits.

Child benefit

This benefit was first introduced in 1975 to replace both child tax relief and family allowances, and to put the money directly into the hands of the person caring for the child. The benefit is not taxed and is not counted as income for purposes of FIS, and is not means-tested. The rate payable from November 1982 is £5.85 per child. If the claimant is a single parent, then an additional weekly supplement of £3.65 is payable. (From November 1983 the rates will be £6.50 and £4.50.)

Child benefit is payable to a person who has a child actually living with him or her, or who contributes at a rate not less than the child benefit rate to the maintenance of the child. The former type of claimant takes precedence over the latter. Where a husband and wife are living together with the children, then the wife is entitled to claim. In cases of cohabitation without marriage, the mother is entitled. In cases of equal entitlement, the Secretary of State will decide who should claim.

'Child' in this context means a child under the age of 16, or a child under the age of 19 who is receiving full-time education.

Note: except where otherwise stated, the calculations in this chapter do not take account of the 1983 budget. The principal changes in that budget were as follows:

married man's tax allowance	from £2,445 to £2,795
single person's allowance wife's earned income relief	from £1,565 to £1,785
additional personal allowance	from £880 to £1,010

12 Ownership of family property

This chapter is about the sharing of all kinds of property between husband and wife, whether they are married, separated or divorced, and between unmarried couples. It also deals with the rights of wives and others to occupy the 'matrimonial home'. Lastly, it looks briefly at the problem of gifts between engaged couples and at the impact of tax on family property.

The matrimonial home

Owner occupiers

The law about the ownership of land and houses is extremely complicated. It is not enough simply to look at the title deeds or the entry in the Land Register to see whose name appears as the legal owner. There are many ways in which other people can acquire rights to a share in the property.

One way by which a wife, or even a mistress, may acquire a legal right to a share in the matrimonial home, even though it is registered in the man's name alone, is through the mechanism of the trust. A trust is an arrangement under which one person holds property – whether land or money – wholly or partly for the benefit of someone else. A trust can be created expressly in writing, or it can come into existence as a result of the conduct of the parties.

Resulting trusts

These trusts come into existence when the person who provides all or part of the purchase money is not the person named in the deed. The person named in the deed is considered to hold the property on behalf of the person who provided the money. This is not always the case, however, and where the purchase money is provided by the husband and the deed is in the wife's name, the husband is presumed to intend the purchase money as a gift to his wife so that she will not hold the house on trust, but in her own right.

Implied trusts

Here the courts will look to the intentions of the parties. If the property was bought for cash then joint contributions towards the price will indicate that the parties intend joint ownership to result.

Buying on mortgage

If the property is acquired by mortgage the position is more complicated. Contributions to the legal charges and the deposit indicate an intention that the property is to be jointly owned. Regular and substantial contributions to the mortgage instalments also indicate an intention that the property is to be jointly owned. This will be the case even if the contributions cease during a period when the wife is unable to work because she is having a baby. Therefore it can be seen that where there are direct contributions, the courts can with little difficulty decide that both parties are entitled to a share.

When it comes to indirect contributions, however, the position is less clear. Indirect contributions occur where one party pays all or some of the household expenses and the other pays the mortgage instalments. In these circumstances, if it is clear that the person named in the deed and paying the mortgage instalment could not pay the other household expenses out of his income, this indicates that the parties intended joint ownership of the property. Similarly, if all the parties' income is paid into a joint bank account, from which all costs including the mortgage are met, this also shows the intention of joint ownership. But other forms of indirect contribution may not entitle the wife to a share.

Constructive trust

The existence of such a trust will depend on whether the wife acts to her detriment in the reasonable belief that she would receive a share in the property as a consequence of the contribution. Consequently a wife who spends time or money improving the home will be entitled to a share which accords with the increase in the value of the property brought about by the improvement. So in one case a mistress, who used a 14-lb sledgehammer to break up concrete laid in the front garden, replaced it with turf and did extensive decorations within the home, was held to be entitled to a share in the property, because she would not have done the work had she not expected to obtain a share.

It can be seen from the above that there are many ways of proving entitlement to a share in the home.

How big a share?

Where the whole of the purchase price is paid jointly the general rule is that each party will be entitled to a share which equals his or her contribution. So if the total purchase price is £20,000 and the husband pays £15,000 and the wife £5,000, the property will be owned in the proportion 75% to the husband and 25% to the wife. Where the property is being bought by mortgage then the value of contributions to the deposit, legal charges and the mortgage instalments will be taken into account. If there has only been a contribution to the deposit, this will determine the amount of the share. Where contributions include regular and substantial payments towards the mortgage instalments it may be very difficult to quantify the exact contribution made, in which case courts often give each party a half share.

When the names of both the husband and the wife appear on the title deeds they may be either what the law calls 'joint tenants' or 'tenants in common'. The difference between these two forms of ownership is important – particularly when one of the parties dies.

If the deeds say that the house is 'held on trust for themselves as joint tenants beneficially' then the husband and wife will be joint tenants. The most important consequence of this is that when one of them dies the other will *automatically* inherit the dead person's share.

If the deeds use another form of words such as 'held by the parties in equal shares' then they will be tenants in common and there will be no automatic right of inheritance. Each party can leave his or her share by will, like any other property. (For more details see page 132.)

When are interests in property important?

On the breakdown of marriage

Courts have been empowered since 1882 to resolve disputes about the ownership of property, between husbands and wives whose marriages are still going concerns. The procedure is relatively quick and simple but the courts have to apply the complicated rules described above. Where a marriage has already broken down, the courts prefer to use the much wider powers of redistributing property which exist in divorce proceedings to achieve justice between the parties (see page 97). Of course, since only married couples can get divorced, questions as to the ownership of property between cohabiting couples can only be settled in accordance with the ordinary rules described above.

Intervention by creditors or the trustee in bankruptcy

Questions as to the ownership of property are likely to arise when a husband or wife runs into debt. Usually the house is their only major asset of any real value and creditors will be anxious to obtain vacant possession of it so that it can be sold and the proceeds applied to reduce the debt. It is important in these cases for anyone with a right to a share in the ownership of the house to be able to prove it. The creditors will then be entitled to claim only the debtor's share. This area of law has, however, become somewhat confused since the decision of the House of Lords in the case of *Boland* in 1980. This decision suggests that people with a share in a house who are in actual occupation of it are automatically entitled to retain possession of it.

Since the full value of property is only realized if it is sold with vacant possession, a person in actual occupation who insists on retaining possession can, for some time at least, frustrate attempts by creditors to recover the value of the debts by selling the house.

Creation of mortgages to secure loans

It now seems that a person in actual occupation of the land under the *Boland* rule has an interest which has priority over any later attempts to deal with the property, say, by using it as security for a mortgage. Consequently, the mortgage company will not be able to obtain possession of the property and sell it to realize the loan. In practice this means that in future mortgage companies will approach any people in actual occupation to obtain their agreement before they will be prepared to make a loan to the legal owner.

On divorce

If a marriage ends in divorce the court can reopen or stop any transaction entered into by the legal owner affecting the matrimonial home (or other property) when it appears that such a transaction was entered into with the intention of defeating a claim to the property. Any transaction occurring within three years of the application is assumed to have been made with the intention of defeating a claim. The court is however precluded from acting in this way if the sale is made to a person acting in good faith, without knowledge of the intention of defeating the claim.

Transactions which defraud creditors

Courts are empowered to set aside any transaction affecting land which is made with the intention of defrauding creditors. Any person who has made contributions towards the acquisition of the property is treated as a creditor. So that if the legal owner sells the land at a price which is very much below market value so as to ensure that the creditor's claim in the proceeds is reduced, such a transaction can be set aside.

Joint ownership and sale

Property which is jointly owned is said to be subject to a trust for sale. A trust for sale means that the property is held on the basis that it must be sold and the proceeds divided according to the size of each party's share. The sale can, however, be postponed indefinitely so long as all the interested parties agree. If one party wishes to sell and the other party does not, then application can be made to court to ask the court to postpone the sale.

The court will exercise its discretion according to whether it believes that the purpose of the trust has been fulfilled. More recently the courts have adopted a new test: Whose voice in equity ought to prevail? On this basis the court must decide whether it would be fair to order a sale, taking into account such matters as the ease of finding alternative accommodation and any disruption to children by a forced change of school.

If the house has been purchased to provide a home for two adults who are within an emotional relationship and that relationship breaks down (there being no children to complicate the issue) the court will order a sale.

Rented accommodation

Rent Act accommodation

(For details of the rules which apply, see Chapter 16, page 164.)

The most important protection under the Rent Act is security of tenure, which exists for as long as the tenant remains in personal occupation and pays the rent. The effect is that the tenant cannot be removed from the premises. If the tenancy is granted in joint names, then this protection applies to both tenants, whatever their relationship. However, if the tenancy is in one name alone and the tenant leaves, then the protection granted may be lost unless the remaining adult was married to the tenant, or the landlord accepts rent from the remaining tenant in such a way as to make it clear that a new tenancy has been created. Where the tenancy of the matrimonial home is in the name of the husband and he leaves, his wife will be entitled to remain in occupation. She will continue to have security of tenure so long as she pays the rent.

On the breakdown of a marriage the court is empowered to transfer a Rent Act tenancy to the non-tenant spouse. The only limitation is that such a transfer can only be made on the grant of a decree of divorce, nullity or judicial separation.

Local authority housing

It is possible for local authorities to grant tenancies in joint names; this should always be requested, whether the potential tenants are married or not. Protection is now given to a local authority tenant, who will now be a secure tenant. Proposals have also been made which would give a non-tenant spouse a right of occupation by the automatic application of a joint tenancy in the home. A court can now transfer such a tenancy on the grant of a divorce.

There is no equivalent power to transfer a secure tenancy from one cohabitee to the other on the breakdown of the relationship. In fact the tenant has an absolute right to remain in the premises provided that he continues to pay the rent. If the female cohabitee is therefore forced to leave and has the children with her, she will have to approach the local authority for new housing as a homeless person with priority need. It may well be safer for such a woman to try to encourage the local authority to grant the tenancy in her own sole name, or at best into their joint names, rather than in the man's name.

The right to occupy the matrimonial home

A married person whose name does not appear in the title deed as owner is, by statute, given a right of occupation in the matrimonial house. This right of occupation must, however, be registered to be effective. Registration of the right can take one of two forms: for registered land, a caution can be entered on the land register, and for unregistered land a class F land charge can be registered. Although the protection given here is limited (it only entitles the person with registered rights to continue residing in the property with the purchaser), in practice it is highly unlikely that anyone would wish to buy land against which such a right is registered unless agreement on removal of the right is reached. A registered right of occupation is not, however, effective against the trustee in bankruptcy, who may take over the land and sell it as though there were no right of occupation, registered or not.

A married person with a registerable right of occupation, who is not in occupation, may apply to the court for an order to be entitled to enter and occupy the matrimonial home. Furthermore, in cases where the right to occupy would be meaningless (because of an intolerable marital situation) if the other party to the marriage were also to continue in occupation, that person may ask the court to exclude the other party.

Contractual licences

A contractual licence is not a tenancy but it may nevertheless create valuable rights to occupy property. Licences are not important where two married people live together, because spouses automatically have rights of occupation in the matrimonial home. But where people are living together, without being married, licences are important. There are two different kinds of licence: a bare licence, which merely entitles the non-property-owning person to remain in the accommodation for as long as the property-owning party consents; and an irrevocable contractual licence, which is granted in return for money or services, is intended to have legal force, and can last for as long as the parties intend. This kind of contractual licence has been held to exist where one party gives up a secure home to move in with the other and agrees to care for children. Such a licence to occupy premises only ends when the children cease to need the house, usually when they are seventeen or eighteen. A licence, because it can last for such a long time, may have a high capital value. This does not mean that it could be sold on the open market, but the legal owner may well be prepared to buy out the licence holder's interest so as to recover full possession of the property.

A woman who was the mistress of a wealthy man, but did not live with him as though she were his wife, failed in an attempt to establish an irrevocable contractual licence. She argued that in return for such a licence she had subordinated her choice of residence and mode of life to his, but the court was not prepared to accept this argument. The relationship would seem to have to be more akin to marriage than was apparent in this case. Even if there is no clear agreement to grant a licence, the court may still decide that there is a limited obligation to provide housing, so that the right to remain on the premises may only be terminated after giving reasonable notice. Where there are children, reasonable notice would be about twelve months.

So it can be seen that someone who gives up clearly defined economic advantages in order to move into someone else's home may be able to prove an obligation on that person to continue to provide accommodation even after the relationship has broken down.

Joint bank accounts

If both parties pay money into the joint account it is generally assumed that each owns fifty per cent of the money in the account and that any property bought by both of them with money from the account is also jointly owned. Property which is purchased by one party only using the account money will be owned by that party alone, unless there is evidence to show that the property was acquired by them both.

If only one party pays money into a joint account, the general rule is that all of the money belongs to that person. This rule may not operate between a husband and wife, where it is the husband who pays into the account, because it is assumed, unless there is evidence to the contrary, that he intends the money as a gift to her, so the money will then be equally owned.

Housekeeping money

If a husband makes a housekeeping allowance to his wife, then any savings from the housekeeping and any property bought from these savings is deemed to be owned jointly and equally by the husband and wife for all purposes.

Other property

Any property acquired by any person is owned by that person. It is possible within a marriage for a spouse to contribute money for the substantial improvement of property owned by the other. If this is the case, then the contributing spouse obtains a share (or an extra share if the property is already jointly owned) in the property. Therefore a spouse who pays for respraying the other's car, or physically resprays it, will be entitled to a share in it. This will occur unless the spouses have reached agreement to the contrary.

Special rules which apply to engaged couples

Disputes are likely to arise here if an engagement is broken. There are two rules which apply:

Engagement rings

The gift of an engagement ring is treated as an absolute gift and the ring cannot be recovered by the donor if the engagement is broken.

This rule will not apply if it is clear that the gift was not made absolutely, as may be the case where the ring has been in the donor's family for generations.

Other property
Whether other property can be retained or must be returned on the breaking of an engagement will depend on whether the gift was made conditional on the marriage. If it was then the property can be recovered, provided, seemingly, that the donor has not acted wrongfully in causing the engagement to be broken.

Gifts

In order to pass ownership by gift the donor must intend to pass ownership and there must either be a deed made by the donor or delivery of the goods by the donor.

Since it is rare for cohabiting couples to execute deeds, the usual means by which a gift passes the ownership of property will be by delivery. When the articles concerned are personal, for example a diamond necklace or a man's watch, it will be clear that delivery has taken place; but where the articles concerned are for general use, for example the dining-room table, there is more difficulty. The required result of passing ownership can be achieved by actually passing the goods over, or by executing a deed, the latter being preferable, where evidence of the gift is necessary to prevent the goods being seized by the creditors of the donor.

The tax position

Capital gains tax
This tax is payable at a rate of 30% on gains which arise as a result of the disposal of an asset. Even gifts may be seen as disposals. A disposable gain is calculated as the difference between the purchase price and the market value of the gift on the day of the gift. No tax will be payable on gains of less than £5,300 in any one year. Gifts between spouses who are living together are exempt from tax. Tax will, however, be payable if the donee spouse sells the property given, and the gain will then be calculated on the original acquisition costs to the donor. In all cases where the parties have been separated for more than one year, they are treated as 'connected persons' and not spouses, and any transfer is deemed to have been made at market value. There are some specific exemptions, for example the

taxpayer's dwelling house (his or her main residence), in which case no tax will be payable. Applications to court which merely quantify already existing interests in property will not be subject to the tax as they do not amount to the disposal of an asset.

Capital transfer tax

This tax is levied on every chargeable transfer occuring ten years before death. Chargeable transfers are those which diminish the transferor's estate. Transfers between spouses are exempt, but not transfers between people who are cohabiting. A person who can establish an already existing equitable interest in the property transferred can argue that the transferor's estate is not reduced by the transfer. In any situation in which the transfer is not a gift but made as a result of an arm's-length transfer (probably for a price) there will be no charge to capital transfer tax. Similarly dispositions for the maintenance of the family, which include the education or training of a child up to the age of eighteen, are exempt. This can include capital payments, but must relate to a former marriage and be referrable to a divorce settlement.

There are further exemptions which allow gifts in any one financial year which amount to no more than £3,000 and gifts of £250 or less to any person, also gifts forming part of normal expenditure. The charge to tax is levied once the total amount of gifts or transfers on death amount to over £60,000. In the case of gifts the rate starts at 15% and on death starts at 30%. The scale rate increases with the size of the transfer.

13 Death and the family

This chapter deals with the distribution of property on the death of a member of the family. It describes what happens to the family home and other property when someone dies, whether or not they have made a will; and it explains the state benefits that may be payable on death.

The home – rented house or flat

A home which is a statutory tenancy under the Rent Act (see page 164) or a secure council tenancy (see page 180) will automatically pass on the death of the tenant to a member of his family. The tenancy will automatically be transferred to the widow of the tenant, if she was living with the tenant at the time of his death. If the deceased tenant left no widow, then any other member of the tenant's family who was living with him at his death and for the six months immediately preceding the death is entitled to succeed to the tenancy. Succession to the same tenancy under these principles can occur on a maximum of two occasions.

It is now clear that a couple who have been living together as though they were husband and wife can create a 'family' unit for these purposes, so that a mistress would, if outwardly appearing to be a wife, be able to succeed to a tenancy on the tenant's death. The position is the same where a mistress has had children by her lover; she and the children fall clearly within the phrase 'members of the tenant's family'.

The home – jointly owned

Where the matrimonial home is jointly owned by the husband and wife the effect of the death of one of them will vary according to the form of joint ownership. If the house is in both their names and declared to be 'held on trust for themselves as joint tenants beneficially' then, when one dies, the survivor will automatically become the owner of the whole interest in the house. If these words are not used but some other form, for example 'held by the parties in equal shares', then the survivor will not automatically inherit the dead spouse's share. In that case the dead spouse could have left his share in the house to someone else – and if he did not make a will it would be disposed of according to special rules (see page 134).

Leaving a will

Only adults can make a will. (There are, however, special rules for those under eighteen serving in the armed forces.) An adult of full capacity (that is, one who is not so insane as to be incapable of knowing what he is doing) can decide in his will to leave his money and property to anyone he chooses. Although originally sacrosanct, the wishes of a testator (the person who makes a will) may now be overridden by a court (see page 135).

In any event, in order to be valid and enforceable, a will must comply with the provisions of the Wills Act 1837. The requirements of this Act are very complex and in cases where it is intended to make a number of gifts, or where there is a fair amount of property involved, it is sensible to seek the advice of a solicitor.

The effect of marriage

When a person who is domiciled in England (see page 81) marries, this has the effect of revoking any will which was made before the marriage, unless the will was clearly drawn up in contemplation of that marriage.

The effect of divorce

Where a decree of nullity or divorce is granted, this has the effect of revoking any gift by will by either party to the marriage to his or her former spouse. This rule will apply to testators who die on or after 1 January 1983.

Bequests to children

A gift stated in a will to be to 'my children' or 'Fred's children' will automatically include legitimate and illegitimate children. This will be the case unless a contrary intention appears.

Not leaving a will

The rules applied in these cases are known as the 'intestacy rules' and entitlement under them depends on the survivors left by the deceased:

Spouse (widow or widower) only

In these circumstances everything which the deceased had will pass to his surviving spouse.

Spouse and children, whether legitimate, illegitimate or adopted

The surviving spouse is entitled to all the deceased's personal possessions; these include jewellery, clothes, car, domestic animals, china, glassware, etc. but will exclude such things as money and business property. The surviving spouse also gets a legacy of £40,000 and a life interest in one half of any balance. (For people who died before 1 March 1981 the figure is £25,000.) If there is anything left after the surviving spouse has had his or her share then it is held on trust for the children during their minority (that is, until eighteen). This means that the income from the property can be applied for the maintenance and education of the children and up to one half of the capital can be used for their benefit, for example to buy one of them a flat in which to live. When the children reach eighteen they take their appropriate shares absolutely.

Spouse and parents or brothers and/or sisters

Spouse

In these cases the surviving spouse is entitled to the personal possessions absolutely (see page 134); a legacy of £85,000 and one half the balance of anything which remains, absolutely. (For people who died before 1 March 1981 the figure is £55,000.)

Parents

The balance left after the deceased's spouse's entitlement is then the deceased's parents' absolutely, in equal shares.

Brothers and/or sisters or, if deceased, their children

The balance will be held on trust during minority and divided equally between them at eighteen.

No surviving spouse but children

Then the whole of the estate will be held on trust for the children.

No surviving spouse and no children but parents

Then to the parents equally and absolutely.

No surviving spouse, no children, no surviving parents but brothers and/or sisters (or, if deceased, their children)

They take equally and absolutely. If there are no brothers or sisters then grandparents take equally and absolutely; if no grandparents, then uncles and aunts take equally and absolutely.

Illegitimate children

On the death of an illegitimate child, only his parents are entitled to succeed to his property in cases where the illegitimate child leaves no surviving spouse or children.

Objecting to a will or the effect of intestacy rules

Applications can be made to the High Court or the county court, depending upon the value of the estate. These rules apply to anyone who dies domiciled (see page 81) in England and Wales after 31 March 1976.

Who can apply?

- *Spouses* can apply, including former spouses, who have held the decree dissolving the marriage for no more than one year, and for whom no financial provision has yet been made. It is also possible to put into a divorce settlement, etc., a clause which prevents any claims being made under this provision. So where such a clause exists, no claim for financial provision will be entertained by a former spouse.
- *Former spouses* who have not remarried.
- *Any offspring of the deceased* including those born legitimately, illegitimately, and any children adopted by the deceased.
- *Any child of the family*, that is, a child falling outside the provisions of 'offspring of the deceased', but treated as such a child would be.
- *Any other person* whom the deceased was maintaining either wholly or partially immediately before his death. This can include relatives, mistresses, and lovers, but will exclude anyone who is being paid rather than 'maintained', so that a housekeeper working for a salary or just for her keep would fall outside the definition. A woman who initially acts as a housekeeper but then becomes the deceased's mistress and has a child by him will be entitled to apply.

The few cases which have so far been decided on this part of the law would seem to indicate that men will find it much more difficult to substantiate claims. This is because the man will have to prove that the deceased was responsible for his maintenance before his death. In a relationship where each party contributes towards living costs, it has been said that this shows that neither party is undertaking any responsibility for the other's future maintenance, and consequently no claim will be entertained.

Entitlement

A successful claimant will be entitled to 'reasonable financial provision' out of the estate of the deceased. Statutory guidelines are provided to help the court decide what is reasonable. The court is required to balance the claims of competing applicants against each other, and, where relevant, against a beneficiary under the will. In balancing these claims the court must consider the future and current financial resources and needs of each claimant; any obligations and responsibilities owed by the deceased to each; any physical or mental disabilities suffered; the nature and size of the estate, and any other relevant matter, including the conduct of the applicant. This means that conduct which would indicate to an ordinary member of society that no provision ought to be made will be relevant. Similarly if a couple live together as though they were husband and wife for fifty years, this 'conduct' would be relevant to ensure that proper provision could be made out of the estate for the survivor. There are also specific guidelines which apply to each different class of applicant. They are as follows:

For spouses and former spouses The court is required to consider:

- the age of the survivor and the duration of the marriage;
- the contributions made to the family, including looking after the home and caring for the family;
- and what provision the court would have made had the marriage ended in divorce rather than death.

In essence this allows the court to start from the minimum standard of the one third rule (see page 101). This will be the minimum since the whole basis of the one third rule is that provision is made both from existing capital assets and from future income, usually earned, whereas, in the context of death, earnings will obviously have ceased.

For children and 'children of the family' The court is required to consider the manner, or expected manner, of the child's education.

For children of the family (any child treated as a member of the family) The court is required to consider:

- whether the deceased assumed responsibility for the child;
- the extent and length of time of that assumption;
- whether the deceased knew the truth;
- and the liability of any other person to maintain the child.

For others wholly or partly maintained by the deceased The court is required to consider the extent, length of time and basis of the assumption of responsibility for maintenance.

The standard
There are two standards applicable in these cases, one which is applied to surviving spouses, and the 'basic standard', which is applied to others.

The surviving spouse's standard This is for reasonable financial provision, whether or not that provision is required for that spouse's maintenance. This means that a spouse who is wealthy in his or her own right, and has a high income from a job, could nevertheless be given as much as one third of the deceased spouse's estate under these provisions.

The basic standard This is such financial provision as it would be reasonable in all the circumstances for the applicant to receive for maintenance. This is a lower standard than that applicable to spouses, and only provides for some kind of income to cover some (or all) of the day-to-day costs of living.

Orders which the court can make
The court can order:

- periodical payments;
- lump sums;
- transfers and settlements of property;
- variations of settlements made on or in contemplation of marriage (see page 97 for definitions); and
- orders that property be bought and transferred to the applicant. For example, if the mistress of the deceased needs a roof over her head, a house could be bought for her to own or to use until her death, as part of the provision.

State benefits on death

Payments are available to provide support to families when death is deemed to have affected the family's income.

To widows

The widow's allowance
This is payable for the first twenty-six weeks of widowhood (provided that the husband was contributing to the national insurance scheme) regardless of the age of the widow and whether or not there are any dependent children. It is intended to alleviate the immediate

hardship caused by the death of a husband, who is usually the main breadwinner.

The payment is a flat rate of £49.95 per week with an addition of £7.95 for each dependent child. The rates are increased each November. The rates quoted are those applicable in November 1982.

The widowed mother's allowance

This payment serves to support a widow who has children living with her who are aged under nineteen and are still dependent on her; she is entitled to claim child benefit (see page 122). The rates payable as at November 1982 are £32.85 for the widow and £7.95 for each additional dependent child. Entitlement will be based once again on the dead husband's contributions to the national insurance scheme. Once the children are independent, entitlement to this benefit ceases

The widow's pension

This benefit is payable to any widow who was over 40 at the time of the husband's death, or over 40 at the time she ceased to be entitled to the widowed mother's allowance. Payments are calculated according to a sliding scale for a widow aged between 40 and 50, with the full rate payable once a widow reaches the age of 50. The rationale is that a woman of 40 who no longer has the care of dependent children can be expected to work at least part time and thereby supplement her state income.

The full rate as at November 1982 is £32.85 per week, reduced by 7% for each year the claimant is below the age of 50. For example, a 45-year-old woman's entitlement would be 65% of the full rate. Once again, entitlement to this benefit depends on the dead husband's contributions to the national insurance scheme.

Duration of payments All payments from the state cease if a widow remarries. Similarly a widow who cohabits with a man as though she were married to him loses, for the duration of the cohabitation, the right to claim state widowhood support, both for herself and, if relevant, for her dependent children.

Who is a widow? Only people who were validly married according to English law at the time of the husband's death are widows. Consequently if a decree absolute of divorce had been obtained before the husband's death the ex-wife cannot be a widow. A decree nisi does not bring a marriage to an end, and hence a husband who dies between decree nisi and absolute leaves a widow who can claim (see page 80).

Persons who are married polygamously (that is, a man who has more than one wife – and is entitled to do so according to the law of his domicile) leave no widow for these purposes. However, if a couple have married according to a polygamous form of marriage ceremony, but the husband at the time of his death has no second wife, the surviving wife will be a widow.

The effect of earned income The above benefits are not means-tested, so that entitlement will be unaffected by income from any other source but they will soon be taxed.

Entitlement to supplementary benefit These benefits are counted as income, so claims to supplementary benefit will be reduced by the amount of the widow's entitlement to other state benefits.

Widowers

At the present time widowers are excluded from state death benefits. However, membership of the EEC requires that there be no sexual discrimination in the availability of national insurance benefits, and widowers will be able to claim these benefits in the not too distant future.

Divorced women

A special child's allowance is payable to a divorced woman if, at the time of her ex-husband's death, he was contributing in excess of £0.25p per week to the maintenance of a child, or was legally obliged to do so. Entitlement once again depends on the dead husband's contribution record. The claimant must be entitled to claim child benefit for the child, and child benefit must have been payable either to her or her husband at the time of his death. The claimant is entitled to £7.95 for each child (November 1982). There is no payment for the divorcee herself. Entitlement ceases on remarriage or cohabitation. These provisions also apply to decrees of nullity obtained by parties to a voidable marriage. The entitlement is lost if the claimant claims the single-parent addition to the child benefit. It is clearly financially advantageous to give up the single-parent addition to child benefit, and instead claim the child's special allowance.

Guardian's allowance
Any person who cares for a child and is entitled to child benefit may claim the guardian's allowance, provided also that:

- both the child's parents are dead;
- one of the child's parents is dead and the claimant is unable to trace the whereabouts of the other parent;
- one of the child's parents is dead and the other is in prison for at least five years starting with the other's death.

In cases concerning illegitimate children, the above rules apply only as regards the child's mother, unless the father has been found by a court to be the father, or he admits he is the father, or parenthood has been established. In cases concerning children whose parents are divorced, entitlement arises on the death of the parent who had a custody order in his or her favour, provided the other parent has had no order granting him custody or obliging him to pay maintenance for the child.

The payment in November 1982 was £7.95 per child per week.

Death grant
The national insurance scheme provides that where a deceased was, before death, contributing to the national insurance scheme, or was married to or the child of a contributor then a grant will be paid to the estate of the deceased or to any person who agrees to be responsible for the whole or part of the funeral expenses. The grant is £30 where the deceased was aged over 19 at death, £22.50 where the deceased was aged between 6 and 19 at death (£15.00 aged 3–6 and £9.00 aged under 3).

The tax position

The widow's bereavement allowance
Any woman whose husband was entitled to the married man's allowance at the time of his death is entitled to claim this allowance for the rest of the financial year in which the husband died and the following year. The allowance amounts to the difference between the single person's tax allowance and the married man's tax allowance. So that if the husband dies in January, the widow will be entitled to claim two-twelfths of £1,010 for that tax year and the full £1,010 for the following year.

Additional child tax relief
This is payable to a single person, which means either a widow or widower, who has a child living with him or her who is financially maintained. This allowance brings the single person's allowance up to the married man's tax allowance.

Housekeeper allowance
This is an allowance of £100 available to a widower or widow in respect of a relative who resides with him or her to act as housekeeper.

Dependent relative allowance
This is an allowance of £100 given to a person who maintains a poor incapacitated relative, or widowed mother or mother-in-law. A single woman claiming the allowance is entitled to £145.

The age allowance
This is a claim to tax relief by persons over the age of sixty-five. The age allowance for a single person is £2,360. Where a married couple are claiming the allowance, the amount is £3,755. This allowance is given instead of the personal tax allowance of £1,785. However, the benefits of the allowance are lost if the person earns in excess of £7,600, because for every £3 of earnings the age allowance is reduced by £2, until it reaches the lower limit of £1,785, or £2,275 in the case of a married couple. These reliefs will be increased yearly in line with the retail price index.

Capital transfer tax
Liability to pay this tax can arise on the transfer of a deceased's estate, when the death occurs after 13 March 1975. The tax is only payable on an estate worth over £60,000. In deciding whether there is likely to be a charge to tax, the value of the estate must be added to gifts made within ten years of death, less those which are exempt. Exempt gifts include transfers between husbands and wives, gifts totalling a maximum of £3,000 in any one year, and gifts of £250 or less to any individual. Lifetime gifts attract tax at a lower rate.

Retirement pension

This depends on contributions made to the national insurance scheme. A married woman's claim can be based on her husband's contribution record if she has never worked (a category A pension) and if she has worked on her own contribution (category B pension). If she has not worked throughout the marriage, entitlement will depend on a combination of hers and her husband's contribution record (category B). Divorced and widowed women are also entitled to draw on their husband's contribution record if they were 60 at time of death or divorce. If there has not been a full contribution record, then the pension is payable on a *pro rata* basis. The pension is payable to a man aged 65 and a woman aged 60. The married couples' pension is payable when the man reaches the age of 65 even if his wife is under 60. Pensions are payable in full, unless the pensioner has earnings of over £57 per week, in which case a reduction of 5p will be made for every 10p above £57 to £60 earned in any week. If earnings exceed £60, each 5p earned reduces the pension payable by an equivalent of 5p. A married woman claiming a pension on her husband's contribution record will start to lose her entitlement when her earnings reach £45 per week.

The Home

14 Buying your home

In 1900, 15 per cent of the people in England and Wales owned the houses they lived in; by 1980 the figure was 55 per cent. This is really not surprising because there is today every reason to become a home owner. Investment in property has proved an excellent hedge against inflation. The combination of tax relief for mortgage interest and freedom from any other form of taxation for the rise in value of homes has proved a major incentive to ownership. Of course, it is true that while you are living in a house or flat the year-by-year increase in value (recently as high as twenty per cent) is not available for your immediate use. It is a paper increase but it does enable you to keep up with market values so that if you decide to move the increase can be used to acquire a larger property. And although interest on mortgages has recently risen to fifteen per cent (an all-time record), repayment is made in money which loses its value by an even greater amount each year because of inflation. As a result the real interest rate, taking tax relief into account as well, is probably a negative one.

Of course, you may prefer to be a tenant if your need for accommodation is short term or if you simply cannot raise the deposit to buy a property. And you may prefer to let someone else worry about major repairs.

House or flat?

This is not always a matter of simple choice. Price is obviously important because flats are usually cheaper than houses. In some areas few flats are available for purchase and older maisonettes or conversions in houses are not to everyone's liking. Also some building societies will not lend on conversions. One problem is often overlooked: a modern flat in a block may be conveniently situated for transport, shops and main routes, but someone will have to pay for the upkeep of the exterior of the whole block, staircases, lifts, corridors and gardens. Usually this will be carried out by a residents' association in accordance with the various leases, but it may be done by the landlord who is then reimbursed. Either way the owner of each flat will have to meet, out of taxed income, an amount for maintenance and repair of the block as a whole which can only increase year by year. (The question of the owner's precise rights will be dealt with later.) Flats are usually leasehold properties; this means that you buy the right to live there for, usually, ninety-nine years or whatever is left of a lease granted to someone else.

If you do decide to buy your home, whether it is to be a house or a flat, there are three points to consider:

- how will the purchase be financed?
- how can the physical state of the property be checked?
- how will the legal formalities be handled and what will the cost be?

Financing the purchase

Very few buyers have the cash available to pay for a property outright. Many look to a building society to lend them money. The building society movement came into being when people moved from the country to the towns at the time of the Industrial Revolution. The original aim of the movement was to assist those who had insufficient resources to acquire the land on which to build. At first the societies were composed of small groups of people who came together to form a mutual aid organization. But the function of acquiring land and erecting properties is no longer one carried out by the societies. Instead they now provide a means of depositing savings on which a competitive rate of interest is paid and from which fund a source of finance is available to lend money to those who wish to acquire properties as homes. Although building societies are not the only institutions prepared to lend money for house purchase they are the most important source of funds. So we need to ask how they operate and in what circumstances they will lend.

How building societies work

The amount of money available for lending at any one time by the societies as a whole, or by a particular society, depends upon how much money is being invested balanced against the demand for funds. In recent years demand for money has always exceeded supply and a rationing system of one sort or another has operated.

Usually societies will give preference to existing investors. After that, societies base the amount they will lend on the borrower's income multiplied by 2.5 or 2.75. (These figures vary from time to time.) If a couple wish to borrow, this multiplier is either applied to their joint incomes or the society will at least be prepared to take into account a part of the income of the partner as well as that of the main wage earner.

The societies are reluctant to make general statements about their lending policies, and each borrower will have to conduct his own negotiations with the manager of the local branch. Even then the societies do not like to commit themselves to lending a specific amount before it is certain that the sale will go through. There will always be a valuation of the house or flat and as a further limitation on lending societies will usually only advance between 75 and 90 per cent of the amount of the valuation (which may be less than the purchase price). It is sometimes possible to borrow more by taking out a single-premium guarantee policy with an insurance company to cover the extra amount that would not normally be lent. You should try to resist this but you may have to pay the extra premium as a condition of getting a loan. The exact figure will depend upon the age of the property, its location and the current policy of the society. These statements may seem vague but the reason for this is the absence of published details of lending policies.

If you invest in a building society with a view to borrowing money in the future it is a good idea to get a clear statement from the local branch manager about the conditions on which a loan will in fact be made.

Types of mortgage

There are two principal types of mortgage that a society will make. First, it may lend on a *repayment* (sometimes called an annuity) basis, and second, it may do so on an *interest only* basis, the loan being linked to a life assurance policy which will eventually repay the capital advanced. The differences between the two are quite important.

Repayment loan	*Interest only loan*
(a) Payments are made each month of an amount of capital and interest. Tax relief is available on the	(a) Payments are made each month to the society of an amount of interest and to an insurance company (a

amount of interest paid each month	premium) for a life policy equivalent to the amount of the loan. Tax relief is available on both interest payments at whatever the highest rate of tax is that you pay and on the premium for the whole period – the latter at 15% per year.
(b) In the early years of the loan more interest than capital is repaid so higher tax relief is available initially but this tapers off in later years.	(b) The same interest payment is made throughout the term of the advance on the whole amount of the loan.
(c) The interest rate can vary so that monthly repayments may go up or down.	(c) The interest rate can vary so that monthly payments may go up or down, but the premium payment will not change.
(d) If the property is sold during the period of the loan the society will be repaid from the proceeds leaving the profit from any increase in value to the owner.	(d) If the property is sold during the period of the loan the capital will be repaid to the society out of the proceeds of sale (interest having been paid monthly). The life policy will remain in existence for the benefit of the borrower provided that the premiums continue to be paid.

	Repayment loan	*Interest only loan*
(e)	The capital is repaid gradually or on an earlier sale.	The capital is only repaid at the end of the loan (or on an earlier sale of property). If the life policy is 'with profits', although the premium each month is higher, the bonus at the end of the policy is likely to be large. (The basis of a 'with profits' policy is that you participate in the general prosperity of the insurance company by getting a share in its annual profits.)
(f)	The main disadvantage is that tax relief eventually reduces. If the property is sold during the early part of the loan the amount repaid may be almost as high as the amount borrowed. This is because interest is added yearly. For example: January 1982 £25,000 borrowed – interest added 10% = £2,500. Debt immediately becomes £26,500. January 1986 – property sold. Repayments of capital made by then may be no more than £1,000. As interest will have been added each January the amount needed to repay the loan will be about £26,300. (Of course the value of the property will have increased – at least in a time of inflation.)	The main disadvantage is that the scheme only works well on a long-term basis. If the property is sold at an early date during the term of the loan the insurance policy will not have a very great value if surrendered. If another property is bought the policy cannot always be used together with a new loan. A fresh policy may be needed. Sometimes a new policy can be taken out to top up the old policy in connection with a new loan. You should inquire carefully about this before taking out the first policy.

You should think carefully about these alternatives. It is best to select an interest-only loan linked to a life assurance policy only if you can afford a 'with profits' policy and do not intend to sell the property at a very early stage during the loan. And this scheme will be preferable to a repayment mortgage if you can afford rather more than you would otherwise pay each month but are interested in receiving a substantial capital sum when the loan is finally paid off.

There are some schemes where you start off with a low-cost policy and convert to a 'with profits' policy later. These are well worth considering. From April 1983 the way in which tax relief on mortgages is given has changed. Previously the relief was built into each person's tax code. This meant that frequent adjustments had to be made to codes when interest rates altered. This was administratively expensive. Now each borrower no longer receives relief via the tax code. Instead the amount of monthly payments is reduced by the amount of tax relief. The sums will be calculated by the lender and the government will pay the tax relief due direct to the lender. For technical reasons this may tend to increase the net amount of monthly repayments in early years of mortgages.

If you select a repayment scheme it is sensible to take out a *mortgage protection policy*. This is a form of life cover which will pay off the mortgage if you die during the period of the loan. This will leave the capital value of the property intact. Premiums depend on age but are relatively low.

Other sources of funds

Local authorities do lend money for home purchase but in recent years they have lacked substantial funds. They do, however, look at older and less well-maintained properties than those acceptable to building societies. Recently, banks have begun to make funds available for long-term lending but the interest rate is usually higher than that charged by building societies. Insurance companies have always been involved in lending for house purchase but they are mainly concerned with large loans in excess of £30,000 (building societies generally being unwilling to lend sums much above this). Interest rates again tend to be higher and the loan will always be linked to an insurance policy. Sometimes you can combine a loan from a building society for the bulk of the purchase price with a 'top up' loan from an insurance company for the balance not covered by your own resources.

Mortgage brokers

You will often see advertisements by people offering their services as agents to enable you to obtain a loan. Frequently such people are also insurance brokers. They will either charge a fee for obtaining a loan or, if it is linked with a life policy, receive a commission from the insurance company. You should only deal with a firm which is a member of a recognized professional body. A proper fee to pay if no life policy is taken out is no more than one per cent of the loan. If no loan is forthcoming you cannot be charged more than £1.

Mortgage brokers do seem to have access to a variety of funds and can provide a useful service. But you should make sure that the loan offered is what you want. Often estate agents acting for sellers can help you find a mortgage and may not make a charge. But make sure it is the type of loan you want.

Tax relief and 'option' mortgages

We have already seen that the interest element of a mortgage is allowable against income tax. There are two conditions: that the maximum amount of capital on which interest is paid is fixed at £30,000 (including any 'top up' mortgage), and that the property is the only or principal home of the borrower.

To help the low-income borrower the option mortgage scheme was set up in 1967 under which the government subsidized the mortgage but no tax relief was available. This scheme came to an end in April 1983. Now all mortgage payments are reduced by tax relief deducted at source. This benefits non-taxpayers as the option mortgage used to.

Closing the gap

A great problem for first-time buyers is to find the difference between the amount they can borrow and the purchase price of the property. This may run to several thousands of pounds. The government introduced a Homeloan scheme for first-time buyers in 1978. It is rather limited in effect. If you save under the scheme with a building society or bank for two years and for the last twelve months have had between £300 and £1,000 in your account you will at the end of the two years be given a tax-free cash bonus of between £40 and £110 depending on the exact amount saved. In addition you can qualify for an extra loan of £600 provided you have saved at least £600 yourself with that institution. This is above the amount the financial institution would normally lend you and you do not have to repay any part of the £600 or any interest on it for five years. To qualify for the bonus and the extra loan the savings of joint purchasers can be added together.

However, there are limits to this scheme. You must be a first-time buyer and the help is only available for lower priced homes. The scheme does not, by itself, guarantee that you will be given a loan, but if you are, these terms will apply. Building societies are the best people to help you get a loan under such a scheme.

Finding a property at the right price

Most buyers go to local estate agents or look at advertisements in newspapers. Do not be afraid to bargain with the seller or his agents if you think the price is too high. Many advertised prices are deliberately set too high and are no more than a starting point. It may also be possible to negotiate for carpets or other fittings to be included in the price.

Although in law you need not pay a deposit before you enter into a contract it is often sensible to pay a preliminary sum as a token of good faith. It shows you are seriously interested. Do not, however, hand over more than £250 and only pay the seller's reputable agent or his solicitor – not the seller himself. This deposit is returnable if the purchase falls through. Do not enter into an agreement to buy before having legal advice. You can, however, make an agreement 'subject to contract' and you should not put anything in writing without using this phrase. If you make an agreement 'subject to contract' neither party is committed until a formal agreement is drawn up and exchanged.

The state of the property

Once you have found a property you will need to see that it is in a good physical condition. A survey will cost between £75 and £100 plus VAT for a medium price-range property, and often will not cover matters like drains or electrical wiring because these may require highly specialized tests. The reason for having a survey is to ensure that the large investment you will make will not be wasted on a property in a bad state. Also you can sue the surveyor if he did not notice a defect that he should have seen. If he does report that there are some minor faults in the property you may be able to negotiate a reduction in the price. Obviously you may be looking at more than one property, so having a number of surveys carried out will be expensive and time-consuming. If prices are rising rapidly you will be competing with many others for any one property, so there will be a need to move quickly.

There is no simple answer to the problem of whether you should instruct a surveyor as soon as you find a suitable house. First make sure that the seller is serious in his or her intentions. Is the seller moving into another property? If you obtain a survey, what is the likelihood of the purchase falling through with the result that you have wasted money? Remember that investing in property shows high returns but if you have neglected to have a survey carried out the costs of repair may also be very high. The building society's 'survey' is not sufficient because it is only a valuation. And the seller does not have to disclose to you any defects in the property even if he knows about them. He must not actively conceal them but that is the limit of his duty.

Reducing the cost of a survey

There are three possible ways of reducing the cost of a survey. First, the seller may himself have had a survey carried out when he bought the house and you may be able to see that. Obviously if the survey is more than five years old it is unlikely to be of much help, and even if it is more recent it still needs to be treated with some caution. If the report turns out to be inaccurate then because it was prepared for someone else you will not be able to sue the surveyor. So this method saves money but involves risks.

Second, and more helpful, is the practice of finding out, from whoever is lending you the purchase money, who will be carrying out the valuation on their behalf. Although you pay for this valuation it is not a full survey and you will not usually be shown the report. (Some building societies have recently begun to show borrowers these reports.) It is possible that the lender will bring defects to your attention because he wants them attended to as a condition of the loan. But you will then be able to instruct the same valuer as is employed by your lender to carry out a full survey and you will normally be charged only a modest sum on top of the valuation fee. This arrangement cannot always be made but it is worth trying to effect it.

Finally, you can instruct a surveyor but ask for an oral report or perhaps accompany him on his visit. Some surveyors do not like this approach because if there is no written report disputes may arise later.

Whatever you decide to do you should only employ someone who is fully qualified and a member of a recognized professional body such as the Royal Institution of Chartered Surveyors or the Incorporated Society of Valuers and Auctioneers (see list of useful addresses on page 446).

The legal formalities

In recent years there has been a great deal of criticism of solicitors in relation to their work dealing with the formality of buying or selling properties known as conveyancing. There are a number of books available which indicate how you can do this work for yourself and space does not allow for any such guide to be included here. But there are some points to consider before deciding whether to tackle your own conveyancing or to leave it to a solicitor.

Saving the solicitor's fee

You will, if successful in doing the work yourself, save money. Not all legal fees are avoidable, however. What you will not pay will be the solicitor's own fees. You will still have to meet the cost of stamp duty, search fees, and (sometimes) land registry fees. Scale fees for solicitors' conveyancing work were abolished some years ago in favour of a charge based on the time taken and the importance of the work to the client. As a rough guide, solicitors charge about 1½ per cent of the purchase or sale price. So on a purchase for £15,000 of a house or flat you will save £225. But following the various books on do-it-yourself conveyancing is often not easy, although once you have handled one transaction successfully it will be much easier to repeat the task on a later occasion.

The main argument in favour of doing your own conveyancing is that most purchases and sales are a routine operation once you have grasped the use of the forms involved and the initially complex procedures. Also the whole matter is in your hands and time will not be taken up with letters and telephone calls to and from your solicitor.

Against this is the fact that you will have to spend time referring to reference books or guides if something out of the ordinary occurs. And you will be learning as you go along (which takes time), as abstract instructions on technical matters may be very hard to follow.

On the whole it is better to instruct a solicitor unless you have the time and resources to follow quite complex guide books and deal with letters and telephone calls without delay.

Registered and unregistered land

It is usually much easier to handle the purchase of a house in a large built-up area than the same property in a rural location. This is because the title to the former will almost certainly be registered at the Land Registry. This means that the government has entered details of the property on a permanent register which it maintains. Future sales of such registered titles are much simpler than if the title is unregistered. In the latter case the title deeds may consist of numerous technical documents which will have to be examined with care each time there is a sale; equally, if you are buying a new flat, then the wording of the lease is crucial. Leases can be very complex documents and a non-lawyer will find them difficult to follow.

Paying the building society's solicitor

Whether you act for yourself or not, if you are borrowing money to help you to acquire a property the lender will still instruct solicitors to handle the formalities of the mortgage. You will have to pay their costs which are, strangely enough, still subject to a scale as follows:

Building society solicitor separate from your solicitor		Building society solicitor same as your solicitor	
Loan	Costs	Loan	Costs
£10,000	£72.00	£10,000	£45.00
£15,000	£80.00	£15,000	£50.00
£20,000	£86.40	£20,000	£54.00

(Intermediate amounts are charged at a proportionate rate.)

Instructing a solicitor

If you do not know of a solicitor who could act for you, then friends, relatives or even the building society manager may be able to suggest one. There is every reason to 'shop around', even if you have a recommendation, until you find a solicitor who will quote you an inclusive price and guarantee that figure barring wholly unforeseen events like the seller's withdrawing before entering into a contract or having done so refusing to move out when the time comes. Do not accept what you may be told: 'I cannot give you a price until the work is finished because I cannot foretell how much work may be involved.' In the vast majority of cases the amount of work can be predicted from the outset. Also, ask that you be kept closely informed about everything that happens. Discuss any special problems or requirements at the beginning so that no difficulties arise later.

What your solicitor does

In outline this is what happens if you are buying a property with registered title. We shall assume that your solicitor is also acting for the building society; you should try to achieve this because it will save you money.

1 A search is made (by post) at the local authority to see if there are any plans to redevelop the area, any breaches of planning law, smoke control orders, plans to build roads near by or other local matters which affect the property. This takes between 7 and 21 days but in urgent cases may be done personally.

2 The contract is received from the seller's solicitors. This gives details of the property and includes information about the title, the way in which the seller's solicitor or agent will receive the deposit (usually ten per cent of the purchase price) and details of any fixtures and fittings which were agreed as included in the sale price. If the property is a flat a copy of the lease would also be sent.

3 Your solicitor will send off preliminary inquiries to the seller's solicitor. Because the seller's duty to disclose defects is so low the purpose of this document is to draw him out by asking specific questions about the state of the property, his use of it and (in the case of a flat) the amount of any service charge. If the answers turn out to be incorrect you may be able to avoid the purchase altogether or recover compensation if you suffer loss and the seller was careless.

4 With all this information gathered together your solicitor will be able to report to you on the purchase telling you everything you need to know about the property. This should take about 3 to 4 weeks from the time you first approached him, but if matters are urgent it can be done in much less time – even within one day. Obviously this will be more expensive.

5 If all is well you will sign one part of the contract and the seller will, separately, sign the other part. You will now need the ten per cent deposit. The contracts are then *exchanged* – that is, each part is sent by post to the other solicitor (your part goes off first). You are now committed to buy and the seller is equally bound to sell.

6 At this stage your solicitor will inform the building society that contracts have been exchanged. (Exchange should not take place until a firm offer of a loan has been sent to you.) The reason for telling the society now is, first, so that it will insure the property

on your behalf (the risk of destruction passes with the contract) and, second, that it will send instructions to your solicitor to enable him to prepare the mortgage documents.

7 Your solicitor now prepares the document actually transferring the property to you and then makes a search (by post) at the Land Registry in order to check that the seller's title is in order. The transfer document is then sent to the seller's solicitor for signature.

8 You will now be asked to sign the mortgage documents (which will be explained to you) and to pay the balance of the purchase money, if any, and the costs.

9 Your solicitor will then complete the purchase by obtaining the amount of the loan from the building society, paying the seller's solicitor and collecting the title documents. All the papers are then sent to the Land Registry so that your name may be registered as owner and the building society's interest may be noted. Any stamp duty will now have to be paid.

Falling behind with the mortgage

If payments due are not kept up the building society or other lender can ultimately evict the borrower and sell the property. However, most lenders are reluctant to do this and will often come to an arrangement with the borrower. In any case the court has power to keep the lender out of possession of the property if any arrears can be paid off reasonably quickly.

If the owner becomes unemployed the DHSS may pay the interest, but not the capital, due on a mortgage by way of supplementary benefit.

If problems arise it is best to contact the lender as soon as possible to discuss matters.

Insurance

Building insurance

Once you have 'exchanged contracts' to purchase, the risk of the property's being destroyed or damaged passes to you. So you must insure. If you are buying with the aid of a mortgage, or the property is leasehold, you will probably find that the lender or landlord will have arranged this for you. But you must take great care (with your solicitor's help) to check the following points:

- Is the amount of cover adequate? Remember that you are insuring the building only. The land on which it stands cannot be destroyed (unless an earthquake occurs which is not very likely) so your interest is that the building should be rebuilt if it is, for example, burnt down or severely damaged by flooding. Building costs are now very high, particularly if the property is fairly old and built to a standard not seen today. So it is no good insuring for the market value. The cost of rebuilding may be very much more than this. Architects' fees must also be covered.
- Does the amount insured increase automatically in line with inflation? Anything less is false economy and most unwise. The risk of under-insurance is that you may not even recover the total amount you have insured for. The reason for this is that your claim is scaled down by the percentage amount of under-insurance. This seems unfair but protects the insurance company. If you had insured for the full amount you would have paid a higher premium. Incidentally the cost of insuring is now about 15p for each £100 of value. So cover of £20,000 would cost £30 a year.
- Does the cover include liability for injury to visitors, subsidence, flood damage and the cost of temporary accommodation? Unless it does it does not represent a worthwhile expenditure of the premium. To repeat the point, cutting corners and saving relatively small sums with insurance is not worth the great risk involved.

Contents insurance
This can be more expensive – about 25p a year for each £100 insured. Again, it is not worth having a policy that does not provide for the replacement cost of items damaged, destroyed or stolen. If you do not have such a policy you will only recover the second-hand value of the goods. In days of high inflation it only makes sense to have a 'new for old' policy. Again the policy should be index-linked to cover inflation in future years.

Buying a leasehold home

The practical differences between buying a house and a flat have already been explained. Without going into technicality the legal distinction is that in the case of a house it will almost always be a 'freehold' property and belong to the owner. Nobody else will have an interest in it. A flat will almost always be 'leasehold'; that is, a landlord will grant the right to a tenant or 'lessee' to have the use of the flat as his or her own for a limited period of time. The longer that period the more valuable the lease. Most flats today are sold on leases for ninety-nine years. A premium or lump sum will be charged and the owner will also have to pay a relatively small rent known as a 'ground rent'. If a full or market rent is paid then the home is rented and not bought. This is dealt with fully in Chapter 16, page 164.

A long-leasehold property as a home

The terms of the lease will often be complicated and will vary from property to property. Legal advice should be obtained as to the advantages and disadvantages of any particular document. If a new property is being bought there may be room for negotiation on the wording, but if an existing lease is being bought from an owner this will not be possible.

Most leases require the owner to keep the property fully repaired, not to use it for business purposes and not to alter it without the landlord's agreement. But one problem occurs in all flats – whether in a block or conversions within a house – and that is the question of service charges.

Who pays for services?

This will be dealt with in the lease. In modern leases of flats in blocks the developer will not wish to retain any responsibility for repairs to the gardens, halls, lifts and other common parts. The usual scheme is to set up a limited company in which each resident has a share. The residents themselves then carry out such work and often will be responsible for insurance of the block, painting and decorating the outside, and porterage. This arrangement needs careful thought. Is the company properly run? Are there enough residents who take an interest in it? Will the accounts it has to file each year with the Registrar of Companies be properly prepared? Is there a resident who looks after the accounts? Are all the contributions paid on time? Have there been disputes in the past about these accounts? All these questions must be asked and answered before the purchase goes ahead. If a new lease is being bought, a lot of these matters have to be taken on trust.

The other arrangement – which is less common today but is still found in older blocks or conversions – is where the landlord does the work and charges the owners of individual flats. Their rights have been increased in recent years.

For the years before 1980

- The owners have the right to see properly audited accounts.
- A clause in the lease that accounts shall be 'final' or 'not questionable' is not enforceable. The amounts charged may still be challenged.
- If the charge paid is more than £80 a year then the landlord must obtain two estimates before work costing more than £250 is carried out. At least one estimate must be from an independent person and not a builder connected with the landlord.
- If work is likely to cost over £2,000 then each owner or the residents' association, if there is one, must first be consulted before estimates are obtained.
- A landlord can only charge for work or service provided it is done to a reasonable standard, and he cannot charge more than a reasonable amount. This means that poor work does not have to be paid for at all. Over-lavish work or excessive charges can also be resisted. But court action is often needed to establish this.

For the years after 1980

The above rules apply in their entirety except that the figure of £250 (for work above which the landlord has to get two estimates) is altered to £25 multiplied by the number of flats or £500 (whichever is the greater). As well as obtaining two estimates in the manner described above, the tenants or any tenants' association must be given the chance to make comments on the proposed work and the costs. But the county court can waive any of these requirements if it thinks it reasonable to do so.

Criminal penalties are now imposed for failure by the landlord to meet any duty imposed on him or her by the law.

Breaking the lease

If a leasehold owner does not follow the terms of his or her lease the landlord may ultimately be able to get the property back. However, there are many provisions to protect owners. The landlord must first serve a notice saying in what way the owner has broken the lease. Only if this is ignored can court proceedings be taken. If the breach of the lease concerns repairs the landlord is very restricted in what he can do and needs the permission of the court even to begin proceedings. He will not get this unless there is some very good reason for having the work done now. In most cases matters can be resolved by negotiation without the need for court action.

When the lease runs out

The general rule is that when a long lease of a flat comes to an end the owner does not have to leave. He or she can stay but will not get another long lease. Instead the owner can claim the protection of the Rent Act 1977 and will have to pay a full rent for the property. The landlord will only be able to evict the tenant if he or she does not pay the rent or there is some other ground for possession. These matters are dealt with in full in Chapter 16, page 168.

If an owner has a long lease of a house and it runs out then it may be possible to buy out the landlord or get a new fifty-year lease. This does not apply to the owners of flats.

The owner must have lived there for at least three years and the price is fixed by a complicated formula. It is almost always better to borrow some money and buy the freehold because this is a very valuable investment. The landlord can insist on certain restrictions being included in the sale document if he owns other property in the area. There may be a detailed management scheme laid down for the locality if many houses have been bought in this way.

A ten-year guarantee

Most new homes – houses or flats – will have the benefit of a ten-year guarantee of good workmanship. This is issued by the National House-Building Council and it may not be possible to obtain a mortgage without it. The Council inspects properties in the course of construction and lays down standards to be followed in building.

For two years after purchase the builder is bound to make good any defects. For the next eight years the Council takes on the liability but only gives cover for major damage caused by structural defects. If the builder goes bankrupt then the Council will step in even during the two-year period. The guarantee lasts for the benefit of future owners but there are some limitations to the scheme. First, it may be necessary to go to an arbitrator to establish how much work is faulty. Second, there is a limit to the overall amount that is paid out for any one builder so that a mistake repeated in many properties by a builder could cause problems.

15 Selling your home

This chapter is about how to set about selling a house and how to deal with estate agents; what your solicitor should do for you; and how much it will all cost.

How to achieve a sale

The first problem is whether or not to instruct an estate agent. If you do he will charge a fee of about three per cent of the sale price – there is no longer any scale fee. The main reason for having an agent is that purchasers make use of their services and he will advise you as to the price to ask and will prepare printed particulars to advertise the property. You may have to pay at least part if not the entire cost of a newspaper advertisement under the agent's name but some agents will meet the cost of one advertisement. This is a matter for negotiation.

The agent may offer you a reduction of the fee to two per cent if he is given 'sole selling rights' for a certain period. Sometimes the agent may omit mentioning any specific period at all. It is usually unwise to do this. The amount saved will be relatively small and you will have to pay the commission even if you sell the property by your own efforts. If you are tempted by the lower commission rate try to limit the period to a short one.

'Sole agency' is quite different. This means simply that you agree not to instruct any other agents but if you sell the property yourself you will not have to pay any commission. However, even this agreement may not be sensible as you may wish to instruct two or three agents.

If you do not want a board placed outside your home then say so at the beginning. Otherwise you are likely to find that one has been erected very quickly.

What a solicitor does

In short it is usually rather less than on a purchase. It can be summarized like this:

- The solicitor obtains the title deeds if you do not have them – for example, if the property is mortgaged the lender will have them.

- The draft contract is prepared and sent to the buyer's solicitor. (See page 156 for details of what the draft contract contains.)
- Answers are sent to preliminary inquiries made by the buyer's solicitor. These should be sent to you for checking.
- Your signature is obtained to the contract, and exchange takes place.
- The document transferring legal title is approved – it is prepared by the buyer's solicitor – and signed by you.
- A statement is prepared showing how much is due from the buyer including any rebate of rates if you have paid them in advance.
- Details are obtained from any lender as to how much is needed to pay off loans.
- Completion is arranged and takes place. Payments are made to lenders and to any estate agents owed commission.

If a sale and purchase are taking place as a linked transaction the solicitor will have to ensure that both proceed simultaneously. If, as is usual, a chain of sellers and buyers is involved this can become very complicated.

The cost

It may be useful to set out in summary form the approximate costs connected with a sale and purchase of houses at £20,000 assuming the title to the land is registered and that your solicitor on the purchase also acts for the building society.

Sale	£	*Purchase*	£
Estate agents' commission:	400	Solicitors' costs and land registry fees:	360
VAT:	60	VAT:	54
Solicitors' costs:	340	Stamp duty	nil
VAT:	51	Removal expenses:	400
Removal expenses:	400	VAT:	60
VAT:	60		
Total deductions:	£1,211	Total extra cost:	£874
Net to seller:	£18,789		

Stamp duty is chargeable on purchases at £25,000 upwards. It is on a sliding scale from ½% rising to 2% for purchases at above £40,000.

16 Renting a house or flat

About fifteen per cent of the housing market is controlled by private landlords with a further thirty per cent within the public sector, principally housing provided by local authorities. These are national figures and the pattern may be very different in some areas. For example, in some inner city areas public housing may account for sixty to seventy per cent of local provision. In other areas there may be no private rented accommodation available at reasonable rents. This is rapidly becoming the case in Central London although there is no shortage of flats or houses at very high rents – over £100 per week.

Within the percentage given for the public sector there is concealed the small but growing role of housing associations. These will be dealt with separately.

The first thing to be said about renting a property is that the law governing the relationship of landlord and tenant is extremely complicated. The main source of that law is the Rent Act 1977, but by itself that Act is not a complete code. The Act is a consolidation of previous measures and has to be read subject to a vast body of case law. Moreover the Housing Act 1980 makes important changes to the scheme of the Act. But certain points can be made quite simply.

The nature of Rent Act protection

The aim of the Act is twofold. First, it is designed to protect the tenant who occupies a property as his or her home. The landlord can only recover possession of the property on certain stated grounds; some of these grounds are only discretionary, but some are mandatory – the court must make an order for possession whether it thinks it fair or not (see page 170). Second, while the tenant is in occupation the rent that the landlord can charge is limited to that which is fixed as a 'fair rent' by a rent officer, an official independent of both parties (see page 172).

In some cases the protection given by the 1977 Act is of a restricted nature. This depends on the form of the tenant's occupation. First, let us look at full Rent Act protection and then compare this with the lesser protection given to some tenants.

Full protection

For full protection the following conditions must apply:

A letting

There must be a letting of a house, a flat or even a room. A *letting* is contrasted with a *licence*, which is purely personal to the occupier and gives no rights of tenancy. The distinction between the two is often very difficult and has come before the courts on many occasions. It is necessary to look at all the facts to see what relationship was intended. Unfortunately for the person trying to claim Rent Act protection the usual position is that the owner of the property produces a written or printed document which has been prepared by lawyers and is expressed to be a licence. While this is not conclusive it is very hard to show that the owner is trying to avoid the Rent Acts by using such a document. Most recent attempts to treat a piece of paper which is headed 'licence' as a lease have failed and, if the question arises, expert legal advice should be obtained.

Separate dwelling

The letting must be of a *separate dwelling*. This is a technical phrase and means that the tenant must have exclusive occupation of some separate living accommodation. It can be large or small, one room or twenty rooms. If there is a degree of sharing of living accommodation with the landlord then only the lesser degree of protection described on page 166 will apply. If there is a sharing with other tenants then each tenant is fully protected under the Rent Acts. The sharing with the landlord so as to remove full protection must be of living-rooms, i.e. a kitchen or a sitting-room, but not a bathroom or toilet.

Rateable value

The *rateable value* of the property let must be under £1,500 in Greater London and under £750 elsewhere. Sometimes it is possible to go back to the values in 1965 or 1973, but this is unusual. The reason for this limit is not entirely clear but it seems to be that more expensive properties attract very high rents and those who can afford to pay such amounts do not need any protection.

Amount of rent
The *rent* must be greater than two-thirds of the rateable value of the property let. If it is not, then another scheme of protection may apply (Landlord and Tenant Act 1954).

Lesser protection

Where full protection under the Act does not apply it may be possible to claim the lesser degree of protection given by another part of the Rent Act 1977. There are a number of cases in this category, and it is simpler to set them out without lengthy comment. The rateable value limits mentioned above apply here as well.

Payment for services
Where property is let at a rent which *includes* payment for services.

Services
This is defined to include the provision of heating, lighting, the supply of hot water and any other privilege or facility connected with the occupation of a dwelling. Some of these terms are rather obscure but the idea is that if the landlord provides a degree of service that goes beyond the mere supply of somewhere to live, then the lesser protection will apply.

Licence – exclusive possession
Even if there is no tenancy the lesser degree of protection will apply where there is a mere *licence* to occupy residential property, provided that it gives the occupier *exclusive possession.*

Resident landlord
Where the landlord lives on the same premises as the tenant: this is perhaps the most important category of lesser protection available today. The idea behind this provision is that a person may live in a house rather too large for his or her immediate needs yet not want to have someone else living there who would be able to stay indefinitely. To come within this category the landlord must have been resident in the same building as the tenant at the beginning of the

tenancy and at all times during its continuation. Difficulties may arise as to exactly what is meant by a 'building', but it seems to be a question of fact in each case whether the two parties are living close enough to each other to justify the application of the limited protection the tenant obtains. There cannot be a resident landlord where the tenant lives in one flat in a purpose built block and the landlord in another.

No protection

In some cases neither full Rent Act protection nor the lesser degree of protection is available. Some of these exceptions have been removed by the Housing Act 1980 which extends full protection to local authority and government tenants as well as to some others. The main categories where there will be no protection of either kind are as follows:

Licence – no right to exclusive possession
Most licences granted these days are of this kind; they expressly deny the occupier's right to exclusive possession of 'the whole or any part of the premises'.

Holiday lettings
Where the letting is for the purpose of a holiday: this can lead to abuse. Advertisements may often be seen for 'holiday lets' in unlikely inner-city areas or in suburbs. The courts will be ready to detect sham lettings which are not for holiday purposes at all.

Board and lodging
Where the provision of *board* forms a substantial part of the rent: this word is not defined but is taken to mean the daily provision of at least one meal. But the board provided must account for a major part of the whole rent which can only be determined on the facts of each case.

Student lettings
These are lettings to students by genuine educational bodies, but not by private landlords, although in practice the resident landlord exception will often apply.

Public houses
These are lettings of a public house even where the tenant lives on the premises.

In all these cases the tenant or licensee does not have any security of tenure. But the landlord or owner must usually obtain a court order before evicting the occupier. The court may suspend the operation of the order for a week or two to give the occupier a chance of being rehoused (see Chapter 23 on homelessness).

Full protection – security

Provided that the tenant pays the rent regularly and keeps to the other terms of the tenancy the landlord cannot evict him or her without a ground for possession. The way in which security of tenure operates is quite simple. When the tenancy is initially granted it may be on a weekly or monthly basis or for a fixed term. A weekly or monthly tenancy will run on indefinitely until brought to an end by notice to quit. This notice must be at least twenty-eight days in length; it must be in writing; and it must expire on a day on which the rent is due to be paid. It must also tell the tenant about his legal rights.

A tenancy for a fixed period will simply come to an end by expiry of time.

Whether the tenancy comes to an end by notice or by expiry of time the tenant will not have to leave at once. The Rent Act says that once a tenancy has come to an end in either of these ways what is called a *statutory tenancy* comes into existence. A statutory tenancy has several special features the most important of which is that the landlord can only sue for possession of the property if he can prove that one or more of the grounds for possession set out in the Rent Act apply.

The grounds for possession fall into two groups. The first group consists of *discretionary* grounds. To get possession on one of these grounds the landlord must also prove that it is *reasonable* to grant possession. This gives the judge a discretion to refuse possession to the landlord even though one of the grounds exists. The second group consists of *mandatory* grounds. If one of these grounds exists the judge has no discretion and must grant possession to the landlord.

Discretionary grounds

Alternative accommodation

1 The landlord can provide suitable alternative accommodation for the tenant. This must be broadly comparable to the existing property in terms of size, rent, proximity to the tenant's place of work and that of members of his family and be generally suitable for the needs of the tenant and his family. If the landlord can persuade the local authority to rehouse the tenant or to certify that the landlord can provide accommodation similar to that which the authority itself would provide, then the landlord will succeed.

Arrears of rent and breach of tenancy

2 The tenant has failed to pay rent or broken some other term of the tenancy.

Causing a nuisance

3 The tenant has caused a nuisance or annoyance to neighbouring occupiers or has been convicted of using the property for illegal or immoral purposes.

Neglect of property

4 The tenant has neglected the property or damaged it or any furniture provided with the property.

Notice to quit by the tenant

5 The tenant has given notice to quit and the landlord, in reliance on this, has agreed to sell or let the property or taken some other step and his position would be prejudiced if he could not evict the tenant.

Tenant sublets

6 The tenant has sublet or transferred the whole property to somebody else.

Tenant was employee

7 The landlord requires the property for an employee and the tenant was once his employee and occupied the property as a result of his employment.

Occupation by landlord

8 The landlord requires the property to live in himself or for his adult children or his mother or father (or parents-in-law). But in this case two special points arise. First, the landlord must have granted the tenancy himself and not bought out some earlier landlord. Second, if the tenant can show that he or she would suffer greater hardship if he or she were evicted than if the

landlord were refused an order for possession, then the court will not make an order. In practice this is hard to prove.

Tenant sublets at high rent

9 The tenant has sublet part of the property at an excessive rent. (Rents are dealt with on page 172.)

In each of the above cases the landlord must show that it is *reasonable* to make an order for possession. The court can make an order but suspend it. For example, if the tenant is behind with the rent the court may make an order for possession suspended for several months. If the tenant pays the current rent during that time and an amount towards the arrears then the order will be automatically cancelled. If the tenant has failed to carry out repairs then an order for possession might be suspended for six months to see if the repairs are in fact done as they should be.

Mandatory grounds

In some cases the policy of the Rent Act is to encourage certain groups of people to let their property because they do not require it for immediate occupation, but to let it in such a way that when the need arises they can be sure of getting the property back. Of course, the ordinary rules set out above, about terminating the tenancy by notice or expiry of time still apply, but if they are complied with then the court *must* make an order for possession. The landlord need not prove that it is reasonable for the court to do so nor can the order be suspended. At most the tenant will be given twenty-eight days in which to make arrangements to move. The mandatory grounds for possession are:

Owner occupier

1 Where property has been let by an owner occupier (interpreted in a common-sense way) and the tenant was informed in writing on or before the grant of the tenancy that this provision would be used to obtain possession: the landlord must require the property to live in himself or for a member of his family who previously lived there. It is also enough if the owner occupier wants to sell the property in order to buy another more conveniently located for his or her work. If the owner occupier had died and the tenancy later comes to an end it is enough that the estate of the landlord wants the property back to sell it.

Retirement home

2 Where a property has been bought for or is now intended for retirement purposes and until then has been let to a tenant: the landlord must again inform the tenant, before the tenancy begins, that this ground will be used to recover possession at the end of the tenancy.

(In either case the court can waive the rule that the landlord must give notice at the start of the tenancy if it thinks it right to do so.)

There are other such cases – the most important being where an out-of-season holiday let has been arranged and where a property was previously let to students in such a way that the Rent Act would not apply.

In the Housing Act 1980 a new 'shorthold' tenancy is created. This is a letting for a fixed term for up to five years which, on its expiry, is not renewable and the court must order possession. This is a very important change in the law. The tenant must be told that the letting will be a 'shorthold' before it begins.

The nature of a statutory tenancy

If the landlord does not have grounds for possession then the statutory tenancy continues for as long as the tenant lives at the property. 'Tenancy' is a misleading term although it is found in the Act. The true position is that the tenant has no rights recognized by the general law relating to land and interests in land, but rather has a 'status of irremovability'. The tenant need not live in the property for 365 days a year so long as it is his or her home. The tenant may have another home elsewhere and may only occupy the property in connection with a job or for some other special reason, but that is enough. The tenant cannot, however, sell the tenancy or move out entirely for to do so would be an abandonment of his or her rights. It is purely a personal right of occupation.

Inheritance

On the tenant's death the tenancy does not pass by will or under the laws applicable if no will has been made (known technically as intestacy). Instead the Rent Act provides its own machinery for succession. A widow or widower living with the tenant on his death succeeds automatically to the tenancy so long as she lives there. Any other person living in the property with the tenant at the time of, and for six months before, his death as a member of the tenants' family is also entitled to succeed to the tenancy. 'Member of the family' is not defined but the courts have decided that it includes a son, daughter, brother, sister, parent or perhaps a remoter relative. It has also been decided that it includes a person of the opposite sex to the tenant who was living with him or her in a stable 'common law' relationship of husband or wife.

Full protection – fixing the rent

The general rule is quite simple. The landlord and tenant can agree on any rent they choose but either party is free at any time to approach the rent officer to ask him to fix a 'fair rent'. Once fixed, this is in general the maximum that can be charged. The rent officer acts informally although he will inspect the property and call the landlord and tenant to a meeting to discuss the matter. Once fixed, the rent is entered on a public register kept by the local authority. It is always worth looking at the register before any hearing in order to see if there are any comparable properties near by for which rents have been previously registered.

The registration lasts for two years unless there has been a change of circumstances in the mean time; if, for example, the landlord has effected major works to the property.

When fixing a fair rent the rent officer ignores the personal circumstances of the landlord and the tenant as well as the scarcity value of the property. This produces a discount on what the rent would be under a system entirely free of control. Also local amenities and facilities are disregarded. There are complex rules about increases permitted in rent on account of an increase in rates or improvements to the property where the landlord has to bear the costs of these. Also any increase in the rent after an application to the officer has to be phased. The rules here are extremely complicated but broadly the phasing has to be spread over two years.

If either party is dissatisfied with the finding of the rent officer an appeal may be made to a rent assessment committee. This has a legally qualified chairman, a surveyor or property valuer and one other member. It exercises its powers relying partly on its own knowledge and expertise and it is often worthwhile for tenants in a block of flats faced with demands for an increased rent to seek professional advice from a solicitor or surveyor because the landlord is usually well prepared with ample documentary evidence to support his case. If the landlord has charged a rent in excess of the registered rent it can be recovered by the tenant within two years, either by suing the landlord in the county court or by deducting it from the current rent.

Premiums or 'key money'

A tenancy which is fully protected by the Rent Acts is a valuable asset. As long as a statutory tenancy has not yet come into being the tenant has something he or she may sell unless the tenancy prohibits this. In order to prevent the tenant from turning this statutory protection into an unfair advantage the Rent Act prohibits the tenant from receiving a premium – a lump sum often known as key money – for the sale of a tenancy protected by the Act. Equally the landlord cannot demand a premium for granting such a tenancy. This includes a sum as a deposit against, for example, breakages which is unreasonably high. The tenant can, of course, sell the fixtures and fittings in the flat but any amount he or she receives in excess of a reasonable price is treated as a premium. There are two dangers in breaking this law. First, there are criminal penalties for doing so. Second, the incoming tenant can sue within six years to recover the premium. In practice, prosecutions are rare and incoming tenants do not sue because they are glad to have found somewhere to live and hope to repeat the process in due course. But the danger of losing the premium and being prosecuted is still there.

Lesser protection: security of tenure and fixing the rent

Everything depends on whether the tenancy was granted before the Housing Act 1980 came into force in November of that year.

Tenancies made before the Housing Act 1980

If a tenancy, granted before November 1980, has only the lesser form of protection given by the Rent Act 1977 (see page 164) it is technically known as a restricted contract and the landlord will usually be able to obtain possession much more easily than he could with a fully protected tenancy. The landlord will not have to prove the existence of one of the grounds for possession described on pages 168–70, nor will the court have to be satisfied that it is reasonable to make an order (see page 170).

If the tenancy is for a fixed term then it will automatically come to an end and there is no possibility of the tenant acquiring any security of tenure at all. However, if the tenancy is a periodic one (usually weekly or monthly) then some security can be obtained. If the landlord serves a notice to quit (as with fully protected tenancies, it must be at least four weeks in duration, inform the tenant of rights he or she may have, and it must expire on a day when the rent is due to be paid) then the tenant has certain rights.

- The tenant can apply to a rent tribunal for an extension of the tenancy. (In 1980 the old rent tribunals were abolished and their functions transferred to rent assessment committees. Somewhat confusingly, however, when the rent assessment committees are exercising the functions described here they are known as rent tribunals!)

  The application must be made before the notice expires. The tribunal has wide discretionary powers to delay the operation of the notice for up to six months. The tenant can make repeated applications but in practice he is unlikely to obtain more than one period of security.
- The rent tribunal also has power at any time, on the application of the landlord or tenant, to fix a reasonable rent which will override any amount the parties have agreed between themselves. Once fixed, this rent will last for two years.
- If the landlord serves a notice to quit on the tenant after the tenant applies to the tribunal for a rent to be fixed the length of the notice is automatically extended until six months after the tribunal reaches its decision unless a shorter period of security is granted.
- Where the tribunal grants security of tenure the landlord can come back and apply for the period to be shortened if the tenant, during the period of security, fails to pay the rent or breaks the terms of the lease.
- There is no power to give security where an owner occupier has granted the right to occupy to another person and given notice that he or she is an owner occupier. To take advantage of this provision the landlord must need the property for himself or herself or for some other member of the family who lived with him or her when the house was last occupied by the landlord.
- As with fully protected tenancies no premium can be charged on the grant or sale of a restricted contract letting.

Tenancies granted after the Housing Act 1980

Drastic changes have been made to the previous rules relating to security which are set out above. There is no power to apply to the rent tribunal for even the limited form of security it could previously give. Instead the county court is given the power to postpone an order for possession for up to three months only. Only one period of postponement is allowed. So that although the rent tribunal (see page 173 for its new form) can still *fix rents* there is no automatic *security* where the landlord serves a notice to quit after the tenant asks for the rent to be fixed.

Eviction by the landlord

Whether the tenant has a fully protected tenancy or a restricted contract the landlord must always go to court to obtain an order for possession before evicting the tenant. If the tenant does not leave after the order takes effect then court officials, known as bailiffs, will come along and evict him or her. (The rights of homeless people to be housed by the local authority are dealt with on page 212.)

Harassment

The landlord must not harass the tenant. This is a serious criminal offence and consists of things like cutting off gas, electricity or water supplies, disturbing the tenant for no good reason, creating a noisy environment or, more simply, locking the tenant out. Recently the courts have given heavy sentences for this sort of behaviour.

A landlord is not prohibited from paying a tenant money to give up a protected tenancy, but anyone considering an offer ought to take legal advice and not accept the first figure put forward. Any sum which is not substantial is unlikely to compensate the tenant for the abandonment of his or her home.

Some special cases

A number of tenants face special problems or have special rights. These result mainly from historical circumstances but need careful attention because of the complexities involved.

Tenants in properties that are mortgaged

As between the landlord (who will have borrowed money on mortgage to finance the purchase) and the tenant, the tenant can claim either full Rent Act protection or the lesser protection of a restricted contract, but most lenders expressly state that the borrower must not let the property. This is because a tenancy created with the lender's agreement will prevent the lender from evicting the tenant if the borrower fails to keep up the payments due under the mortgage. If the landlord does let the property in breach of a condition in the mortgage and later fails to keep up the payments then the tenant will have no protection against the lender and can be evicted at will. Anyone in such a position should take legal advice immediately because it may sometimes be possible to persuade the lender not to evict the tenant immediately or even to raise technical legal arguments showing that the lender had previously done some act which recognized the rights of the tenant.

Homes that go with jobs

There are three problems here. First, what happens where a small business man takes a lease of, say, a shop and uses the living accommodation above as a home? Can the tenant claim Rent Act protection? The general answer is no. If the main purpose of the letting is to give the tenant somewhere in which a business can be carried on then the Rent Act will not apply. This does not mean that the tenant receives no protection at all. Part 2 of the Landlord and Tenant Act 1954 will apply in such a case. This is a complex measure but the main difference between it and the Rent Act is that the landlord can obtain possession if he intends to demolish or reconstruct the property (which is not a ground under the Rent Act). Also the tenancy does not become a statutory tenancy when the term granted runs out or a notice to quit is served, but has to be brought to an end by a further special notice and the question of whether the tenant is entitled to a new lease is resolved by the court (usually the county court). A tenant in this position ought to take legal advice if any notice to quit or similar document is received from the landlord.

The second problem arises when the tenancy goes with a job. These are sometimes known as *tied cottages* or *houses* and may be let for a low rent or for no rent at all. As stated previously such a 'tenancy' is outside the Rent Act because it is not truly a tenancy at all. Rather it is a requirement of the job to live in premises provided by the employer.

If, however, the employee is truly a tenant – where, for example, the employer happens to provide accommodation, but it is not part of the job requirement that the tenant lives in it, then the Rent Act will apply unless the rent is below two-thirds of the rateable value. The problem here is the calculation of the rent. If the accommodation is offered with the job but no rent is payable the wage paid will usually be fairly low. This may seem attractive but unless the rent can be worked out in money terms the Rent Act will not apply. It is better to accept a job at a salary of, say, £70 per week with a deduction of, say, £10 per week for rent. Then the tenant can see if the Rent Act applies or not. But even if the Act does apply it has already been seen (page 169) that the landlord can recover possession if the employment comes to an end and the property is needed for another full-time employee provided, of course, that the county court judge thinks it is reasonable. (Special rules apply to farm workers and these are dealt with on page 178.)

The third general problem concerns the use of a property, let as a home, for some business or professional purpose. Apart from the possible need for planning permission the general rule is that the Rent Act will not apply where the business use is more than minimal or occasional.

Caravans as a home

The housing shortage experienced in this country since the Second World War has led to many problems. Some have been solved by imposing duties on local authorities to house certain categories of homeless people. But some other people have chosen – usually as a temporary measure – to live in a caravan on a permanent site. These are sometimes called 'mobile homes' but once on such a site they usually remain.

The law needs special rules in this context because a caravan is quite separate from the land on which it rests.

The Mobile Homes Act

This Act gives caravan dwellers a degree of security of tenure, but the Rent Act does not apply and the nature of the protection is rather limited. First, the law is designed to cover the person who buys a caravan and then rents land for a fixed term or on a monthly or quarterly basis. The site owner cannot evict the caravan dweller without a court order. As with residential lettings it is an offence to harass the tenant. Protection extends to widows, widowers or (if none) members of the family living with an original occupier if he or she has died.

The court can suspend any order for possession for up to twelve months at a time and the tenant can apply for a renewal. In general the tenant is much more likely to obtain a suspension if he or she has met the terms of the lease and complied with any site rules. Also the court must ask if the site owner has offered to renew the tenancy and if so on what terms. This is because a notice to quit may have been served to obtain a rent increase. (The rent officer system does not apply.)

If the caravan dweller wishes to move he or she may want to sell the caravan to an incoming tenant as well as the lease of the site. The site owner often states in the letting agreement that he will have a monopoly of supply of caravans to be placed on the site. The relevant legislation does not protect the tenant from this sort of agreement and it is unwise to accept an agreement with such a clause in it. (A bill at present before Parliament (January 1983) will improve the rights of caravan dwellers.)

It is worthwhile investigating the planning permission granted to the site owner to make sure that any conditions laid down as to the number of caravans allowed on the site, or the length of time it can be used as a caravan site, have not been broken. Also the necessary right to use the site facilities – electricity, water, gas and sewerage – should be included in the agreement.

Mortgages are not available on caravans and the rate of interest charged by a bank or finance company on a loan to buy a caravan will be much higher than a building society would charge on a mortgage.

Farm workers

In 1976 the Rent Act was extended to protect farm workers with tied cottages whose jobs came to an end. Unlike other 'tied cottagers or householders' the farm worker does not have to leave at that time. He or she becomes a statutory tenant with the usual rights of succession. There is a qualifying period of employment of two years to take advantage of these provisions.

The farmer may of course be in difficulties if he cannot recover possession of a cottage which he needs for an incoming worker. He has a right to ask the local authority to rehouse the tenant. Although the authority has no duty to do so if an offer of rehousing is turned down by the tenant the court may later find that the tenant acted unreasonably and order him or her to be evicted. Therefore, any such offer needs to be considered very carefully.

The rent payable under a statutory tenancy will be fixed by a rent officer even if previously the tenant paid no rent. As an interim measure the tenant must pay 1½ times the annual rateable value as an annual rent.

Discovering who your landlord is

Many tenants experience difficulties in identifying exactly who the landlord is. Unless you know this you may have problems in getting him to carry out repairs. A tenant now has the right to discover who the landlord is. This right can be exercised against the agents who collect the rent or the person to whom the tenant last paid his rent. There are criminal penalties for failing to comply with such a request. Also the tenant can require the names and addresses of all the directors of any company which is the landlord.

If the landlord sells the property to a new landlord then the tenant must be given details of the new landlord within two months of the sale or, if later, when the next instalment of the rent becomes due. Failure to meet this requirement is also a criminal offence.

17 Renting from public bodies

For many years this sector of the housing market (which includes local authorities and housing associations) has catered for about thirty per cent of the population. This level is likely to remain static or even to diminish because little new building is possible under present financial restraints. Also, as we shall see, many properties may be bought by the tenants within the next few years following recent (and very important) changes in the law. Even if a tenant decides not to buy (or is not qualified to do so for one of a number of reasons) the rights given to such a person have increased substantially as a result of the Housing Act 1980 whenever the tenancy began.

Local authority tenancies

This phrase includes tenancies granted by new towns, development corporations or the Housing Corporation. Tenancies granted by housing associations are subject to complicated legal rules and will be dealt with separately.

Before October 1980 tenants of the above bodies had few legal rights. Their tenancies were not protected by the Rent Act 1977, and so in theory the tenants could be evicted at the choice of the landlord. However, in practice tenants were not evicted arbitrarily and could feel secure in their homes unless they failed to pay the rent, broke some other condition of the tenancy or, perhaps, were living in a property that had become rather too large for their needs. The law has now changed to give most of such tenants formal security of tenure and certain other new rights.

Security of tenure

Broadly, the scheme we have already looked at in relation to private sector tenancies protected by the Rent Act 1977 has been adopted for public sector tenants. They are now called 'secure tenants'. But there are some differences.

- When a fixed-term tenancy (e.g. for two years) comes to an end, a statutory tenancy does not come into existence immediately. Instead a periodic tenancy arises. This makes no difference to the tenant's protection. Indeed, it is somewhat greater than that of a private sector statutory tenant. A notice to quit of at least four weeks in length must be served by the landlord before court proceedings can be begun for possession. The notice must be in a fixed form and give the tenant notice of his or her rights to stay on until the court orders possession. It must also state the grounds upon which possession will be claimed (see page 183).
- The rules about succession on the death of a tenant are the same as those in the private sector prevailing after 1980 (see page 171) except that a person living with the tenant as husband or wife is specifically defined as 'a member of the family' and, as such, entitled to succeed to the tenancy.

'Member of the family' is, for secure tenants, further defined as being the husband or wife, parent, grandparent, child, grandchild, brother, sister, uncle, aunt, nephew or niece. (This is broadly the position in the private sector reached by interpretation of the phrase by the courts.) However, only one succession is allowed rather than two as in the private sector. This means that on the death of the successor the tenancy comes to an end. But anyone living in the property at that time might have a claim to be rehoused under the Housing (Homeless Persons) Act 1977 (This is dealt with in Chapter 23, page 212.)

A secure tenant, like a statutory tenant in the private sector, cannot leave the secure tenancy to somebody by will except that he or she *can* do this if the tenancy is left to someone who would (or might) have succeeded to it under the rules about automatic succession. If the tenant does try to leave the property to somebody who would not be so qualified then the gift is valid but the tenancy is no longer a secure tenancy and the landlord could repossess the property simply by going to court and not having to prove any grounds for possession.

Similarly the tenant cannot sell (or even give away) the tenancy during his or her life without its ceasing to be a secure tenancy. The only exception to this is where a divorce court orders a husband or wife to make the tenancy over to the other as part of a divorce settlement.

Terms of the tenancy

Subletting

The tenant has certain rights implied by law in the tenancy whatever it may say. These are that the tenant may take in lodgers and may, with the permission of the landlord, sublet part of the property. A lodger is an occupant of part of the property on an informal basis whereas a sub-tenant is someone with a formal right to occupy. The landlord can only withhold permission to sublet on reasonable grounds. For example, if the landlord had a blanket policy of refusing all such applications then refusal would be unreasonable. On the other hand, if the sub-tenant was to be charged a very high rent and the tenant lived elsewhere then refusal might be reasonable.

If the tenant is allowed to sublet the whole property or, having sublet part then sublets the remainder, then the tenancy is no longer a secure tenancy. It is not entirely clear as to whether the sub-tenant in such a case loses his rights as against the landlord. What is clear is that the landlord must respond to a request for consent to subletting within a reasonable time (probably no more than two to three weeks) and if consent is refused the reasons must be given.

Improvements

The landlord has the power (but does not have a duty) to compensate the tenant for improvements carried out by the tenant during the tenancy. Any work done must have been begun after October 1980 and it must have added to the value of the property. The amount of any payment is also in the discretion of the landlord and the landlord must have given consent before any work was begun. As with sublettings, consent cannot be unreasonably withheld. The landlord can withhold consent if, for example, it can be shown that the works would make the property dangerous or reduce its value. Similar rules as with subletting apply to the period of time within which any request for consent must be answered and reasons for any decision must be given. The landlord can impose reasonable conditions when giving consent and, if these are not met, then that gives the landlord a ground for possession.

Although the power to compensate the tenant for improvements is discretionary, grants for some or all of the cost of the work may be available. This topic is dealt with fully under the heading *Improving your home* on page 196.

The rent charged cannot be increased because the tenant carries out any such improvements.

Consultation

One frequent complaint about local authorities and other public sector landlords was that they often failed to consult their tenants about the management or maintenance of estates. This has now changed. Such a landlord must set up arrangements for consulting its tenants about questions of management, repair or demolition, and must consider any views the tenants may have. It seems that the landlord does not have to act on such views so the possibility of influencing decisions may not be very great. Questions of increases in rent are not included within the process of consultation.

Notice and variation of terms

The tenant must be given full information about the terms of the tenancy and the landlord must publish details of the terms of the lettings and make these generally available.

The terms of a public sector tenancy can only be varied by notice given to the tenant. He or she must first be given an opportunity to comment on any proposed variation. This rule does not apply to any increase in rent as to which see below.

Fixing the rent

One major difference between the public sector and the private sector is that rent officers have no power to decide what rents public sector landlords shall charge. Instead the landlord may charge a 'reasonable' rent. This is bound to vary with inflation and as different governments increase or reduce payments by way of subsidy to such landlords – notably to local authorities. It is very hard to show that a rent charged is not reasonable and the few attempts to do so in court proceedings have not been successful.

Grounds for possession

A secure tenant can only be evicted after service of a notice to quit (as mentioned above) and the landlord must prove a ground for possession. In addition, as with private sector tenancies, the landlord must show that it is *reasonable* for the court to make an order for possession. The comments made on this in relation to private sector tenancies apply here equally (see page 170).

The grounds for possession are broadly the same as for the private landlord (see page 169). But there are some differences. The following are *additional* grounds for possession:

Making false statements
That the tenant deliberately or recklessly made a false statement to the landlord which brought about the grant of the tenancy: this could occur where the tenant deceives the landlord about his or her personal circumstances and is provided with housing as a result.

Temporary occupation
Where the tenant was housed temporarily pending repairs or other works at another property owned by the landlord.

In the following two cases the landlord does not have to show that it is reasonable to make an order for possession, but must provide suitable alternative accommodation for the tenant and his or her family. In this connection the court must look at all the facts, e.g. nearness to the tenant's work, the sort of accommodation available and the terms of any proposed tenancy.

Overcrowding
That the property is overcrowded so that a criminal offence is being committed.

Demolition
That the landlord intends to demolish or reconstruct the property (or a building of which it is part) and needs possession to do so.

In the following two cases the landlord must show *both* that it is reasonable to make an order for possession *and* that suitable alternative accommodation is available.

Special features or people with special needs
Where the property has special features designed for occupation by physically handicapped people and the present tenant is not so handicapped: the landlord must prove that the property is required for occupation by a handicapped person.

The same rule applies to properties let to people with special needs where those needs are met by a nearby social service or facility. This might cover the provision of housing for old people and the existence of a social centre within the block of flats or near by.

Under-occupation
Where the tenant succeeded to the tenancy on the death of the previous tenant (but not as a husband or wife of the tenant) and the property is more extensive than the tenant reasonably needs: notice to quit on this ground must be given between six and twelve months of the previous tenant's death.

This ground seems rather unfair because under-occupation is prevalent in the private housing sector – notably amongst owner occupiers. In practice public sector landlords may not be able to rely upon it because the general shortage of housing and the effect of sales of public sector property may severely reduce the amount of alternative accommodation available. Moreover it may be possible to argue that it is not reasonable to make an order for possession because so many properties in the private sector are either empty or under-occupied.

Getting public sector housing

Apart from duties owed to some homeless or displaced people (see page 212) a local authority or other public sector landlord has no obligation to house anyone. Moreover in deciding how to allocate its housing each landlord may establish whatever scheme it chooses. Most local authorities have a complex 'points' system which gives weight to such factors as length of time on the housing list, existing housing conditions, size of family and the likelihood of being able to obtain accommodation in the private sector. Some authorities place restrictions on entry to the housing list. It may be necessary to live in the locality for a particular time before an application can even be considered. If it is felt that a particular scheme is being operated unfairly there may be grounds for complaining to the Commissioner for Local Administration.

The scheme itself is usually beyond criticism – only its application can be attacked. Full details of allocation policies must now be published by each public sector landlord.

Tenancies not fully protected

Some public sector tenants cannot claim the full protection described above. Broadly just as the new security given to such tenants is modelled on that given to private tenants under the Rent Act 1977 so the exceptions also derive from that Act. For example, the tenancy of a property occupied by an employee of a public sector authority is not protected where the employee has the tenancy as part of the job. Also in this category are certain short-term tenancies of property intended for redevelopment or let to a person temporarily while he or she finds permanent housing having already found local employment. Students who are given tenancies in order to follow a course of study are not protected. But the important point to notice is that the vast majority of local authority tenants now have security of tenure.

Housing associations

These bodies have increased in number in recent years and represent a halfway house between private and public landlords. The type of property they offer may vary considerably. Some simply rent flats (not usually houses) while others offer more complex schemes. In these the tenant pays a deposit of about £500 and then pays a rent. On leaving after about four years or more a proportion of the increase in value of the property is paid to the tenant. The association itself buys the property in question (often a block of flats or a conversion in a large, older house) with the aid of a mortgage from public funds and the tax relief it obtains is reflected in the rent paid by each tenant.

As the possible forms of ownership vary so much it is essential to obtain advice if such a form of housing is being considered. It can be said here that the 'right to buy' which, as we saw, is a feature of public sector tenancies does not apply to housing association tenancies where the association is a charity (as most are). Tenants of housing associations are, however, *secure tenants* (as described on page 180), so they have a considerable degree of security of tenure.

18 Buying a public sector property

Before 1980 it was sometimes possible to buy, as a sitting tenant, the council home in which one lived. But some authorities would not sell and the overall possibility of buying varied from time to time. Central government could prevent or ease sales as a matter of general policy. But since the Housing Act 1980 the law has been simplified. The general rule can be stated quite simply. A secure tenant has the right to buy or obtain a long lease on the house in which he or she lives.

The landlord must provide a mortgage if the tenant requires one and certain discounts on the purchase price can be obtained. Of course, there are further restrictions and conditions which we will now look at in more detail.

The right to buy

This arises only when a secure tenant has been in occupation for three years or more. If a husband or wife succeeds to the tenancy on the death of his or her partner who was a tenant (see page 180) then the previous tenant's occupancy can be counted towards this period. But there are exceptional cases where the right to buy does not exist at all. These are:

- where the property is not part of a local authority's general housing stock (which will not be very common);
- where the property is specially designed for occupation by disabled people;
- where the property is let to old people and social or other facilities are provided near by for these people;
- more generally, where the property is specially designed for occupation by old people and the landlord applies to the government for an exemption which it must then grant;
- where the tenant has already had an order for possession made against him or has become bankrupt.

How to exercise the right to buy

The tenant writes to the landlord claiming the right to buy. A special form is needed. The landlord must reply within four weeks either admitting the right to buy or saying why in its opinion the tenant does not have that right. If the tenancy is joint, e.g. to a husband and wife, either or both can claim the right. Up to three members of a family living in a property who are not tenants can join in the claim.

Fixing the price

The price is taken as the market value disregarding any work carried out by the tenant or by a previous tenant, but also disregarding the failure of a tenant to carry out internal repairs. (The landlord will, in secure tenancies, have been responsible for exterior and structural repairs as in the case of a private landlord.) So the tenant does not have to pay twice for his own work but, equally, cannot claim a reduction because of his or her own neglect.

One very important point arises here. If the tenant is buying a house then the duty to repair and to insure will immediately fall on him or her. Even if the tenant has lived in the property for many years structural defects may have arisen which cannot easily be seen. A survey should always be carried out before claiming the right to buy. If major works are needed the landlord should be required to do these *before* the tenant goes ahead with the purchase so as to minimize the cost of future works. Once the purchase has gone through it will be too late to force the landlord to do the work. (This is not the case if a flat is being bought – the landlord will remain responsible for major repairs but may be able to charge the cost of these to the tenant.)

Discounting the price

Generous discounts are allowed off the market price. These are:

- if the tenant has been in occupation for 4 years or less – 33%;
- for each year *above* 4 years' occupation – 1%, subject to a maximum of 50%.

Suppose the market value of a house is £20,000 the price will be calculated as follows:

(a)	Tenant in occupation for 4 years	£20,000
	less 33%	£ 6,600
		£13,400

(b)	Tenant in occupation for 10 years	£20,000
	less 39%	£ 7,800
		£12,200
(c)	Tenant in occupation for 20 years	£20,000
	less 50%	£10,000
		£10,000

So the maximum discount is only achieved after 20 years' occupation.

Repaying the discount

In order to discourage tenants from buying at a discount and then immediately reselling at a profit, the tenant who does buy sometimes has to repay the discount. This occurs if the tenant sells within five years of buying. The amount to be repaid is the discount given less twenty per cent of that discount for each complete year after buying. So taking the above examples we see the calculations as follows:

- tenant sells immediately – repays £6,000;
- tenant sells after 2 years – repays £7,800 less 40% £3,120 = £4,600;
- tenant sells after 4 years – repays £10,000 less 80% £8,000 = £2,000.

The duty to repay is ensured by the landlord taking out a charge on the property which will become known to later purchasers.

Disputes about the price

The landlord must notify the tenant of the price it proposes to charge taking into account any discount to which the tenant is entitled. If the tenant thinks the price is too high then he or she is entitled, within three months, to have the price reconsidered by the district valuer. (His functions are described in the section on compulsory purchase on page 209. Basically he is a government employee concerned with property matters.) He must act independently of both landlord and tenant and consider any views they may have on the matter.

Finance

The tenant is entitled to a mortgage to cover the whole cost of the purchase (taking account of any discount permitted) together with the costs of the mortgage itself (on a fixed scale). But the tenant's income must first be assessed in accordance with rules. The limit for a mortgage will be about 2½ times annual income taking into account the incomes of all those who exercise the right to buy.

If the amount produced by this calculation is insufficient then the tenant does not lose the right to buy. Instead he or she can freeze the price for up to two years by notifying the landlord and paying a deposit of £100. During this time he or she can save towards the price or obtain a larger mortgage if his or her income has gone up in the mean time.

The right to a mortgage is not automatic, but must be claimed within three months of the price being fixed (see below for details of this).

Completing the purchase

Once the price has been fixed and a mortgage arranged the tenant must complete the purchase. If he or she fails to do so (unless completion has been deferred as explained above) then the landlord can require completion to take place within one month. If the tenant still fails to complete then the sale does not go ahead and the tenant must wait another twelve months to serve a fresh notice.

General advice on the right to buy

Two points are worth mentioning here. First, the prospect of buying at an attractive discount seems too good not to take it up. But there may be problems. How much will the mortgage cost taking into account tax relief? What is the state of the property? These questions have to be balanced against the acquisition of a large capital asset. Second, much of what was said earlier about buying properties and the importance of taking legal advice applies here (see page 154). A solicitor may be needed to advise on the terms of the purchase deed as the landlord can include any terms that are 'reasonable'. If a dispute arises it can be resolved by the county court.

19 Repairs to rented properties

Nothing creates more problems between landlord and tenant than the failure (usually by the landlord) to carry out repairs. The law here is complicated and gives the tenant a variety or remedies. Some are available against the landlord directly whilst others require the assistance of the local authority.

First, it is important to know what repairing duties the landlord and tenant will have. To begin, we shall consider those duties imposed by law.

The landlord's responsibility

Most short-term tenants can look to the landlord to repair the main structure of the property. In any letting of a house or flat for less than seven years then the landlord must:

- keep in repair the structure and exterior of the property, including drains, gutters and outside pipes; and
- keep in proper working order sinks, baths, toilets, electricity, water and gas supplies and radiators or other space- or water-heaters.

This obligation applies even where the tenancy has lasted for more than seven years provided it was initially a tenancy on a short-term basis such as a weekly, monthly or quarterly letting. Most lettings of homes are of a short-term nature to begin with so this duty placed on the landlord is very important in practice.

The facts of each case will decide exactly what is the 'structure and exterior'. In one case steps leading to a house were included in the definition because they were an essential means of access to the property. In another decision of the courts paving stones in a yard at the rear of a property were not part of the 'structure and exterior' when the usual means of access was via the front of the property. Also it is only the *installations* for the supply of services which are the landlord's responsibility and not the *appliances*, e.g. cooker, refrigerator, which are run from those installations.

These duties to repair placed on the landlord cannot be excluded by the lease unless the agreement of the county court is obtained before the letting begins. In practice this is very rarely asked for.

Notice to landlord

The courts have decided that before the landlord can be made liable for failure to repair he (or at least his agent who may collect the rent) must be told about the defect of which the tenant is complaining. It is not sufficient for this purpose to say that the landlord ought to have known of the defect or even that he deliberately stayed away so as not to discover what was wrong. Unfortunately notice must still be given even if the defect is a hidden one. Notice can be given by word of mouth but it is better to send the landlord a letter keeping a copy in case the notice has to be proved if the matter goes to court.

Any term in the tenancy which tries to place the above duties (or any part of them) on the tenant is of no effect. But every tenant has a duty to use the property 'in a tenant-like manner' and the landlord is excused from liability where the lack of repair is caused by the tenant's failure to do this. This means that the tenant must take proper care of the property and not damage it. The landlord is given the right to enter the property and inspect its state on giving twenty-four hours' written notice. Also the landlord is not liable where the property has been damaged by fire, flood or some other inevitable accident.

There are also implied conditions as to fitness in certain tenancies at very low rents but these are of little practical importance today. In furnished lettings there is an implied condition that the property is fit for human habitation at the start of the letting but not that the landlord must keep it in that state. Also if the landlord and the tenant share facilities, e.g. a bathroom, none of the above points will apply because the shared room or rooms will not be part of the property actually let. But the landlord has a general duty not to allow the rented property to become less useful to the tenant than it was intended to be. So the landlord must ensure that such facilities do not become unfit through a failure to repair.

The landlord's liability to people other than the tenant

All the above terms benefit the tenant alone. Only he or she can enforce those duties which the landlord has. But the landlord may have further duties to third parties on the property. First, the landlord may be the 'occupier' in law of common parts such as staircases, halls, corridors. (Obviously the tenant will be the occupier of the property that is actually let to him or her.) If those common parts are defective and either the tenant or other people (the tenant's visitors) are lawfully using them and are injured then they will be able to sue the landlord.

Even if the landlord is not the occupier of the common parts he may still be liable to third parties. If the landlord has a repairing obligation owed to the tenant (as set out above, for example) then the landlord has a further duty to all those who might be affected by defects in the state of the premises. That duty is to keep those people (which will include, but not be limited to, the tenant) and their property reasonably safe from personal injury or damage. For these purposes the landlord need not have been told of the defect. If the landlord does not know expressly of the defect it is enough that he ought to have known about it. Also the landlord will owe this duty not only where he is under an obligation to repair but also where he merely has the right to come on to the property and carry out any works which are the tenant's responsibility, but which the tenant has not done or not done properly.

What to do if the landlord won't repair

- The tenant can go to the county court if the works will cost less than £5,000 or otherwise to the High Court and sue the landlord for damages – the cost of the work. Also the court now has the power to order the landlord to carry out the work required (technically, this is known as an order of specific performance). If the tenant (or, in the cases mentioned above, a third party) is injured then the damages would include a claim for compensation for those injuries.
- The tenant can pay for the work himself or herself and then recover the amount spent by deducting it from the rent. What the tenant is not allowed to do is simply stop paying the rent because the property is in disrepair. Nor can the tenant save up the money needed to do the repairs out of the rent. The safest course is to tell the landlord of the defect, pay for it in a lump sum (having also sent the landlord an estimate) and then recover the amount spent from the rent. Of course, if the tenant cannot afford to pay for the work in one sum this remedy may not be of any great help.
- By going to a rent officer or the rent tribunal it may be possible to have the rent reduced on account of the failure to repair. This is something of a last resort because it may mean that the tenant has abandoned any hope of getting the property properly repaired.

- The tenant can ask the local authority to exercise some of its various powers to require repairs to be carried out. These have grown up historically and are in a rather complex and confused state. But this course is often preferable to court action which may lead nowhere. (It is worth remembering that some of these powers can even be invoked against the local authority itself when it is a landlord.)

Powers of the local authority

The powers a local authority has derive from two sources – housing legislation and public health legislation. Each will be considered separately.

Powers under the Housing Acts
The first point to notice is that a local authority can only act when it is satisfied that a defective property is 'unfit for human habitation'. This can arise from a number of causes and in particular the authority must consider whether the house is 'unfit' because of damp, poor natural lighting or ventilation, poor water supply or drainage and poor cooking facilities. Although these terms are wide they do not include, for example, the absence of gas or electricity as such nor that there is no internal toilet. One defect such as a broken or leaking pipe or a damp wall may be enough in itself to make the property unfit even though a small amount of expenditure is needed to put matters right.

The authority must be asked to inspect the property, and the public health inspector will usually be the person who does so. The authority should be pressed to act and, if possible, a surveyor's report should first be obtained. If the authority does inspect but is not satisfied that the property is unfit all is not lost for the tenant. He or she can go before the local magistrates' court and complain that the property is unfit. The court has power to require the inspector to reinspect and report not to the court but to the authority itself. A council tenant could use such a procedure. If on receipt of the report the authority does nothing it may be possible to obtain an order from the High Court requiring it to act promptly. Legal advice would be needed for this purpose.

What can the authority do?
Everything depends on whether the property is capable of being made fit at reasonable expense. As property has increased greatly in

value during the last ten years it should not be too difficult to persuade an authority that the expense is reasonable because the test usually applied is to ask whether the property will remain fit for at least another five years. And the property is likely to appreciate if the work is done even though the cost of labour and materials is itself rather high. Once the authority is satisfied on this point it serves a repair notice on the landlord stating what works are needed and by what time they must be carried out. If, as often happens, the landlord does nothing then the authority can do the work itself and charge the cost to the landlord. It can also charge the tenant which is not as bad as it sounds because the tenant only has to pay by instalments and these can be deducted from the rent. But the weakness of all this is that although the authority has a power to do the work if the landlord defaults it cannot be forced to do it.

The landlord can appeal against the notice to the county court, which can make any order it thinks fit. If the court decides that the property cannot be made fit at reasonable expense the authority has power to buy the property compulsorily. The problem here is that, as will be seen, the tenant has the risk of being evicted, but will normally have a claim for rehousing as a homeless person (see page 212).

An unfit property which is beyond repair at reasonable cost

1 The authority must give the landlord notice of a time and place when he may be heard as to his proposals for the property. The tenant has no right to be present at such a hearing.
2 Having held a hearing if the authority still thinks the property is unfit and beyond repair at reasonable expense it has a number of powers:

- it can accept an undertaking from the landlord not to use the house for habitation until it has been made fit. This may lead to the tenant's eviction but the authority will normally have to rehouse him or her;
- it may order the vacation and demolition of the property. Again the tenant will normally qualify for rehousing;
- it may make a closing order which prevents the property (or part of it) from being used. Again the tenant will have a claim for rehousing;
- it can purchase the property and take over the landlord's position, but only as a temporary measure until closure or demolition.

So it can be seen that the tenant may be advised not to use this avenue if it seems that the property is in so bad a state that it cannot be economically repaired. The remedies are too drastic.

A property not unfit but needing repairs

The local authority has power to serve repair notices and here the expense does not matter. Again the authority may do the work itself and charge for it if the landlord does not comply with the notice. The powers of local authorities to act have recently been strengthened.

If a property lacks certain amenities such as a fixed bath or shower, a wash basin or a sink (each with hot and cold water supply) or a WC then the landlord can be forced to provide those that are missing. The authority is not under a duty to act and it can accept the landlord's undertaking to do the work or if the landlord cannot or will not carry it out the authority can do the work itself. The cost can be recovered from the landlord. There are complex requirements about serving notices on the landlord and rights of appeal exist.

Powers of the local authority under the Public Health Acts

There is a great overlap between the powers of a local authority under these laws and under the housing laws. From the tenant's point of view the main difference is that complaints under public health laws tend to involve the courts as well as the local authority. On the other hand the procedure can be quicker because an inspector can act on his own initiative without having to refer everything back to the council.

Statutory nuisances

If a property is in so bad a state that there is danger or the risk of danger to health then a local authority has certain powers. It can serve a notice requiring the landlord to put matters right. Most often this procedure is used for damp properties or those with crumbling walls or dangerous wiring.

If the landlord does not do what he should the authority can take him to the magistrates' court which will order the landlord to do the work within a set time. The landlord can also be fined and the house closed. Again the tenant will usually have a claim to be rehoused – assuming he or she has a 'priority' need (see page 212).

The law can be used against local authorities as well as by them. A council tenant can bring proceedings direct to the magistrates' court which can make orders against the council.

Local authorities have special powers to get landlords to repair defective drains, pipes or WCs and these powers can be used by tenants if the authority will not act.

Multiple occupation
Local authorities have special powers to act where houses are occupied by more than one family. These are very complicated and range from requiring the landlord to limit the number of households who can live in a house to taking over the property either permanently or as 'managers'. Taking over the property places a lot of duties on local authorities and the procedure is not used very often.

General advice

In any case where a tenant wants to persuade the local authority to use some of the wide powers set out above it is always better to get specialist advice from a housing advice centre or Shelter or a law centre. Also, if more than one tenant is affected, it is better if all can act together rather than as individuals. Not only may this be cheaper, but it carries more weight with local authorities and with the courts.

20 Improving your home

Many people spend all the money they've got on buying a home and only later, when they have earned more money or can borrow some, do they set about improving it. At that time there are four main problems that can arise:

- is there anything in the deeds of the property, such as a restrictive covenant, that prevents the work from being done?
- is planning permission needed?
- will the work interfere with neighbours' rights?
- is consent needed under the building regulations?

Each of these problems will now be discussed in turn.

Restrictions in the deeds

In many older properties (and some newer ones on estates) there will be restrictions contained in the deeds. These are known technically as 'restrictive covenants'. (In the case of leasehold properties the lease will usually impose restrictions.) Restrictions of both kinds will limit the uses to which the land can be put. For example, there may be a requirement that the land shall be used for one house only or that no business is to be carried on on the property. In more modern instances houses on an estate development may have more detailed restrictions in that rules may be laid down about not extending the house without the original developer's permission, or not using the house for any trade or professional purpose.

There are a number of technical rules about who can enforce restrictive covenants. The person who originally imposed them may have died or sold the land for the benefit of which the covenants were originally imposed. In practice it is usually the owner for the time being of that land – the land originally benefited by the covenants – who can enforce them. In the case of a building estate each owner can enforce the restrictions against each other owner.

Even if there is a doubt as to whether anyone can now enforce a restrictive covenant it is most unwise to ignore it. There are two reasons for this. An injunction can be obtained to prevent a breach. This is a court order forbidding the action in question and it can even be in terms requiring a building erected to be pulled down if it infringes the restriction. Second, an order for the payment of damages can be made without an accompanying injunction and the amount to be paid might be very high.

Getting a covenant cancelled

On the other hand many restrictive covenants, even if they can be enforced, are now very out of date. They may have been created before an area became developed or built up and may act as an impediment to perfectly reasonable alterations to properties. There is a mechanism for varying such covenants or even cancelling them. It involves making an application to the Lands Tribunal (which is a specialized court dealing in property) on the basis that one of the following grounds exists:

- the restriction is obsolete due to changes in the neighbourhood; or
- the person entitled to the benefit of the covenant would not be harmed by its cancellation or restriction; or

- the covenant prevents the property's being used for some public or private purpose.

Such applications are highly technical and expert help is required although legal aid is available.

Another answer is to insure against the consequences of a breach of covenant. This will not prevent injunction proceedings being brought but it will meet any claim for damages. A single premium is paid and each case has to be looked at individually but the cost will usually be half a per cent of the amount insured. The policy can be passed on when a sale occurs but the amount insured for will need to be increased from time to time. However, the risk of proceedings to enforce the covenant will diminish as time goes by.

Planning permission

Since 1947 a succession of Acts has been passed which affect the rights of property. The principles involved are simple but the details can be very complicated. The general rule is that permission is needed from the local authority to do any work to a property or to make any change of use in it. As it would be absurd to apply for permission each time a person put a nail into a wall a series of exceptions have been created which benefit house or flat owners. The most important ones are as follows:

No permission required

1 Interior maintenance or alterations that do not materially affect the external appearance of a building.
2 Use of land within the boundaries of a house and garden or surrounding land for a purpose related to the occupation of the house; for example, a tennis court can be built in a garden.
3 External works (including extensions) where the size of the house is not increased by more than 15 per cent or 75 cubic metres whichever is the greater provided that the total extension is not more than 115 cubic metres.

Also an extension must not go above the original height of the house nor be built nearer the roadway than the original house. The 15-per-cent limit is fixed once and for all so that an extension five years ago that took up 12 per cent of the original area only allows another three per cent extension without permission. The size is taken as at 1948 – when the present planning laws first came into force – or when the house was built if that was later.

4 Building a garage, car port, greenhouse, garden shed or other outbuilding used in relation to the house. Again the 15 per cent rule applies.
5 Putting up fences, walls or other means of enclosure not more than two metres high or one metre on a boundary next to a public road.
6 Painting the exterior of a house or flat.
7 Paving a garden as a hardstanding area for vehicles.

In any other case planning permission is required.

Planning permission needed

Dividing a house into flats or dividing a large flat into two smaller ones requires permission even though no outward sign of the changes is made. Application is made by filling in a form which can be obtained from the local planning authority (there are proposals to introduce a fee for this 'service'). There must also be submitted two copies of a plan. If the application is refused or granted subject to conditions the owner does not like or even if nothing happens for eight weeks an appeal to the Secretary of State for the Environment can be made. This requires expert advice.

Enforcement by the local authority

If development takes place without planning permission having been obtained in a case where it should have been, then the planning authority can take steps to stop the unauthorized works or change of use. In the latter case there is no time limit for enforcement procedures, but in the case of building works the authority must act within four years.

The authority can serve an 'enforcement notice' on the owner setting out the breach of the planning laws in question and requiring it to stop within, say, twenty-eight days (it cannot be less than this period). In an urgent case it can also serve a 'stop notice' which requires the breach to cease within four days failing which a fine can be imposed by the magistrates' court. These are relatively uncommon because the authority must pay compensation if it has served a stop notice when it had no right to do so. In the case of an enforcement notice the owner can appeal (again to the Secretary of State for the Environment) by obtaining a form from that department. The appeal can be dealt with on paper or, if either party so wishes, an inspector can be appointed to hold a local inquiry. At that time the owner can contest the enforcement order in a number of ways:

- the facts alleged by the authority can be disputed; or
- it can be argued that permission is not needed or has been granted; or
- it can be argued that, even if there has been a break, the authority ought to grant planning permission. In other words the appeal will be treated as an application for permission.

The advantage of appealing is that provided this is done within the time limit set by the enforcement notice the notice cannot take effect until the appeal is heard. This may take many months. As with appeals against a refusal of planning permission specialist advice should be obtained.

Neighbours' rights

Neighbours, as we have seen, may have rights over a person's property. Building an extension cannot impede the use of these rights. In particular one right may develop in a way which is not readily apparent. This is the right to light. If an adjoining property has a window or windows in it then once a right of light to those windows has been enjoyed for twenty years or more the right becomes a legally enforceable one. A right to light will not become legally enforceable, however, if it is enjoyed by permission or it was expressly stated in the deeds that the neighbours could not object to any extension built even if it cut down their right to light. Of course, such a rule works both ways. Once an extension has been built it too will acquire a right to light – which must be through windows and not to a bare wall – after twenty years unless the above exception applies. The degree of light a neighbour is entitled to has to be measured by what is reasonable and will not necessarily be the amount previously enjoyed.

Building regulations

Even if planning permission has been obtained (or is not needed) the local authority may still need to give consent under the building regulations. These lay down in great detail how certain works should be carried out. They cover both matters of safety, e.g. adequate ventilation in bathrooms and matters of practicality. A builder employed by you will usually apply on your behalf or else an architect can be employed to prepare plans and supervise the builder's work. He will usually charge a percentage of the cost of the works. The question of bad work and service is discussed in general terms in the part of this book on *Goods and services* (see page 298).

It is important to check any mortgage you may have to see if the lender's permission is needed for alterations. Also the insurance company should be told and any additional premium due on the increased value should be paid.

Financing the work

Unless the owner is paying in cash some form of loan will be needed. One way of paying for alterations is to obtain a second mortgage. This tends to be expensive as the second lender usually wants the money paid back over a short period and at a higher interest rate than a first lender will charge. This is because the risk is higher and the second lender can only be paid in the event of a forced sale by the first lender after that prior debt is paid off.

It is often tempting to borrow money on a second mortgage particularly when a property has been owned for some time and the repayments on the first mortgage are now fairly low compared with the value of the property. Care should be taken because legal advice is needed as to the meaning of the various terms in the second mortgage document. These may be very harsh.

If at all possible it is more sensible to obtain a further advance from the first lender. A building society, for example, will often be able to make a further loan to an existing borrower even if funds are not readily available for new borrowers. The formalities needed to achieve this will usually be less than if a second mortgage is taken out.

Improvement grants

Grants can sometimes be obtained from the local authority. The law relating to this has been changed by the Housing Act 1980 and is extremely complicated. In essence the authority must provide a grant to carry out basic improvements such as providing a bath, sanitary facilities or other standard items. In other cases a grant may be made to improve older properties but the local authority has a wide discretion as to the amount of the payment and the conditions to be imposed – for example, repayment of the amount if the property is sold within two years.

Tenants can now obtain such grants but they may have to show that their intention is to sublet the property for at least five years. This could be on a 'shorthold' tenancy (see page 171).

21 The duties of a householder

The law imposes many obligations on those who own houses or flats. These fall under a number of headings.

Rates

Rates are charged by local authorities for the purpose of local expenditure although central government now meets a greater part of such spending than do local ratepayers. The system is that each property is given a rateable value. The work of valuing the property is done by the Inland Revenue and not by the local authority. The amount charged as rates each year is so many pence for each £ of the rateable value. (The amount is fixed each year by the local council.) The calculation of the rateable value is complicated. First, a 'gross value' has to be found. This represents the amount the property could be let for on a yearly basis with the landlord doing all repairs. This is then reduced by an amount that the notional tenant might have to spend on repairs if he or she were responsible for them. This is made on a fixed scale and bears no relationship to the actual state of repair. Revaluations should take place every five years but there has not been one since 1973 and it is not certain when the next one will take place.

It is possible to appeal against an assessment if either there have been changes in the locality which reduce the overall value of the property or if the value as fixed is very much out of line with comparable properties near by. The question is very technical and the appeal is made to a local valuation court (which is not a court in the real sense of the word); an appeal costs very little.

The person who must pay the rates is the occupier and not the owner. However, if the owner does pay he will often be entitled, under the terms of a lease, to pass on this payment to tenants. The penalty for not paying rates is that the local authority can obtain a 'distress warrant' from the local magistrates' court. This entitles them to seize any goods in the house in question and sell them to recover the money due. However, rate rebates are available on a means-tested basis, for those on small incomes.

Rates can be paid in a lump sum or by twice-yearly instalments or, in the case of home owners, by monthly instalments. This is advantageous as no interest is charged for this facility.

Empty houses
If a house or flat is empty no rates need be paid for the first three months. In most areas half-rates are then charged, but in some areas none are charged at all. The house must have no furniture in it at all to take advantage of these provisions.

Water rates
Water rates are now charged separately from the general rates and are usually paid half-yearly. The charge again is so many pence in the £ of the rateable value, but the amount paid is usually comparatively small. In most areas an extra amount must be paid for a garden hose (even if it is only used for car cleaning) or for a garden sprinkler. This law is often ignored but there are criminal penalties for doing so.

Road charges

These are now quite uncommon. If a road is a private one (which will be revealed by the searches made at the local authority when the property is acquired) the local authority may decide to take it over ('adopt' it, to use the technical phrase) and charge the house owners for the work involved in bringing it up to a suitable standard.

It is possible to appeal against either the whole scheme or the way in which the charges have been made. In the case of new estates the builder will usually enter into an agreement with the local authority to build the roads to a given standard and the authority will then take them over. The performance of the agreement is usually guaranteed by a bank or insurance company so that no liability will fall on individual house owners.

Nuisance

One person's neighbours may be reasonable people. Another's may not and may be noisy, inconsiderate and generally unhelpful. Although the law has a lot to say about the obligations neighbours have to each other it is worth saying that legal remedies in these instances are rarely worth invoking. Neighbours have to live with each other and the law should only be used as a last resort.

The general rule about neighbours' behaviour to each other is a simple and common sense one. Each party must behave reasonably. To bring an action in nuisance a neighbour must show two things. First, that the other person is interfering with the use and enjoyment of his or her land. Second, that the conduct in question is unreasonable in all the circumstances.

Each case will turn on its own facts but some examples may show how the courts approach the question. In one case it was decided that although the noise of building works was capable of being a nuisance, provided that it was confined to reasonable times during the day (and not the night) it was not a nuisance on those particular facts. Again the area in question would make a great difference. What would be acceptable in an industrial estate would not be at all reasonable in a suburban environment.

In another case a shop used for selling fried fish was held to be a nuisance as was a go-kart track used every day creating fumes and noise. In each instance the location of the offending source of smell or noise was crucial. Both were sited in the wrong place. Also if a person is particularly sensitive to noise that, of itself, will not make a neighbour's activities a nuisance. For example, if a person plays the piano and records the performances that of itself would not make it a nuisance. For a neighbour to mow the lawn with an electric mower would not be a nuisance for this is a reasonable and normal use of land. In each case it is a question of balancing the rights of adjoining parties.

Enforcing a claim

If it appears that a nuisance is being committed (and very often experienced lawyers find it difficult to predict what a court will do in a given case) the question is whether to sue in the High Court or county court for an injunction or damages. Legal aid is available and an injunction can be obtained speedily. But there is another possible remedy. If the nuisance is caused by noise a complaint can be made to the local authority which has the power to serve an abatement notice and, if this is not complied with, the authority can bring proceedings in the magistrates' court which may result in criminal penalties being imposed. The problem here is that court action then passes out of the hands of those immediately affected by the nuisance and into the control of the local authority. But in some cases it may be a simpler and cheaper remedy.

Some authorities even have staff available to deal with complaints at night about noisy parties. It may be possible to have a notice served there and then.

Smoke control

In most built-up areas smoke control orders have been made. These prevent coal being burned in fires or boilers and only permit smokeless solid fuels to be used. If a new order is made then grants can be obtained from the local authority to meet part of the cost of converting fires to take such fuel. The existence of such an order will be shown on the answer to the search received when the property was purchased (see page 156). However, such an order does not prevent an owner from burning house and garden rubbish in a garden bonfire.

Pets

Unless the terms of a lease or tenancy agreement prevent it anyone may own a pet. A dog needs a licence which costs 37½p each year – the same fee as charged in 1880.

If domestic pets harm someone else – for example, a dog bites a neighbour – then the owner will not be liable unless it can be shown that the pet was known to be dangerous. If a wild creature is kept then a licence is needed from the local authority. If such an animal does harm then the owner is liable for whatever harm it does.

Fences and trees

Fences

These two matters can cause many problems between neighbours. First, to whom do fences belong so as to fix responsibility for repair? Sometimes the deeds of the property will give the answer or previous owners may have said which fences they regarded as their own. Alternatively it may be possible to come to a fresh agreement with all the neighbours.

If the deeds say nothing and agreement is not possible the law may assist by applying certain presumed rules. If a fence or wall has pillars or supports on one side it will be regarded as belonging to the owner on the side where the pillars are found. This is because pillars which stick out would, if on the opposite side to that of the owner, be on the neighbour's land and constitute a trespass. The law, therefore, assumes that everything has been done properly and no trespass committed. Therefore the above rule will apply.

Even if ownership of a fence can be established it does not mean that the owner has to repair it. Unless the deeds say so there is no general duty to repair unless danger would be caused to others.

Party walls

In the case of semi-detached or terraced houses neighbours will share the dividing wall usually known as a *party wall*. The dividing line lies down the middle but that does not mean that one owner can demolish his or her half of the wall. There will be mutual rights of support which will effectively prevent any interference with the wall. Repairs are generally paid for jointly.

In parts of London (the inner-city boroughs) special arrangements apply to party walls under the London Building Acts. Formal notice has to be given if one owner wants to carry out work to the wall and there are provisions for disputes to be resolved by arbitration carried out by surveyors.

The encroaching fence

Finally, what happens if a fence is built in the wrong place and one owner's land is enclosed by a neighbour? This is a trespass but if the wrongful act continues for a long period (usually twelve years) then the true owner loses the right to recover the land. But in many cases the precise boundary will be difficult to discover (especially in country areas) and disputes of this sort can be very expensive to resolve before the courts. The evidence needed may come from the deeds or may come from what local residents know to be the position.

Trees

A fine leafy tree especially if it produces fruit may be an attractive feature of a garden, but there may be problems.

Overhanging trees

First, its natural growth may cause it to overhang or undermine neighbour's property. The law here is that the neighbour can cut off the branches or roots in question without asking permission to do so, but it is not always wise to insist on exercising such strict legal rights. In any event the wood belongs to the owner of the tree so it must be thrown or taken back. Second, and more seriously, tree roots can do considerable damage to adjoining property. The soil may dry out as a result of the roots' penetration towards sources of water. This causes subsidence or cracking to buildings and the owner of the tree will be liable in nuisance or trespass for the harm done. Such costs can be very substantial but are normally covered by standard insurance policies.

Obstructing light

Third, trees can obscure light from reaching a house. This problem was mentioned in relation to extensions and alterations to houses and it will be remembered that after a long period of enjoyment of light the right to it cannot be taken away (see page 202). So an overhanging tree may have to be cut down in such a case.

If a neighbour has recently opened up a window in a wall or builds an extension with a window in it, after twenty years that window will acquire a right to light which cannot be taken away. To prevent such a right arising it used to be necessary to erect a screen or hoarding to block the light. That was tedious, and in any event planning permission would now be needed to do so. Instead an owner can register a notice with the local authority which has the same effect. The Lands Tribunal has to consent to the notice being registered and the neighbour in question has to be informed.

Preservation orders

Finally, a tree may have had a preservation order made on it. This will prevent the owner from cutting it down or uprooting it. If the order was made before the owner bought the property it will have been notified to him or her on receiving the answer to the local search (see page 156).

Injuries to visitors

Homes are dangerous places. Many people are injured each year as a result of defects in properties. Injury or damage to goods is often sustained by visitors who in law include people like the newspaper delivery boy or postman who have good reason to come on to your property. The law is that the occupier of the property (who is usually the owner) owes a duty to anyone who is lawfully there to ensure that the premises are reasonably safe. How this duty is met will vary from case to case. In some instances the owner will have to make sure that dangerous defects – such as loose or defective paving stones in a front garden – are repaired promptly. In other cases it may be enough to put up a notice warning of the possibility of harm occurring. Obviously it would not be sufficient to put up a notice if small children frequent the property because they cannot read. On the other hand if a hidden defect caused someone harm then unless the owner could have been expected to know about it there would be no liability.

In most household insurance policies cover will be given for harm occurring to visitors. It is sensible to make sure that this is the case.

Trespassers

If the person injured is a trespasser then the above rules do not apply. The only duty owed to such a person is 'a common duty of humanity'. This means that an owner cannot set traps for such a person or have electrified fences around the property. The owner must not do any positive act to harm trespassers. But if it is known that children often come onto the property the rule is slightly different. They must be kept safe at all times or effectively excluded.

The only people who will be regarded as trespassers will be those who have no right at all to enter another person's property such as burglars or those specifically excluded by notice such as signs which say 'No canvassers or salesman'.

(The question of the liability of a landlord to his tenant or others for defects in common parts of premises is dealt with on page 190.)

22 The Englishman's castle

For many years now the law has strictly controlled what you can do in and around your own house. This chapter is about people who can come into your house against your will and people whom you can exclude or eject; it is also about being forced to sell your house to the council against your will and about forcing them to buy it when they don't want to.

Who can come in?

It is perhaps surprising that many people have power to enter property for some public purpose or other. A landlord can only do so if the lease gives him such a right or if he is coming to do repairs which are his responsibility. Here is a list of some other people who can also come in. Most of them need a warrant from a magistrates' court if you refuse to let them in voluntarily:

- policemen – to arrest someone or to search the property (with warrants in each case);
- gas, electricity, water officials – to read meters or attend to their installations;
- valuation officers – for rating purposes;
- local authority – under housing and public health powers;
- VAT officials – to examine business books and papers.

All such persons should carry some official identification and the owner should ask to see this.

Trespassers and squatters

In general, going on to someone else's property is not a crime. The sign 'Trespassers will be prosecuted' is nothing more than an idle threat. But trespass is a wrong under the civil law and a person on someone else's property without permission can be asked to leave. If he does not leave then reasonable force – no more than is necessary – can be used to evict him. A trespasser can be sued for damages, but only a tiny sum will be awarded unless some positive harm has been done.

In recent years large numbers of homeless people have taken to moving into empty properties. To some extent this is when the house or flat belongs to a local authority, which may try to reach some informal agreement with squatters until they can find somewhere else to go.

If squatters move into a privately owned property then the criminal law does have something to say. Such squatters will commit an offence if they refuse to go when the owner asks them to do so. Moreover there is a speedy procedure in the civil courts for getting possession back. Court officials will evict the squatters. Although the owner is entitled to use reasonable force to evict squatters it is usually wiser to put matters into the hands of the police or a solicitor, for otherwise violence may result.

Compulsory purchase

In this country great emphasis is placed on private property. On the other hand, public development – roads, airports, hospitals, and so on – are needed; an owner may stand in the way of redevelopment, and the public interest may require that person (or family) to move out and receive compensation for the loss of a home.

The procedure, however, is quite lengthy. There will usually be a public inquiry where the viability and desirability of the whole scheme can be considered and objections heard. Ultimately the scheme may be approved and the question then is – how much compensation does the owner receive?

Compensation

The general rule is that the market value of the home is what is paid. Obviously there is no such value because nobody would buy a property about to be compulsorily acquired. So the usual method is to look at the price of comparable properties currently on the market.

If a price cannot be agreed the Lands Tribunal will decide the matter. The district valuer is the person who will represent the body which is to acquire the home and he is very knowledgeable on property matters. Details of all house sales in the area are supplied to him by the government so it is sensible to employ a professional valuer as your representative. The fees and legal costs of your valuer are usually paid by the acquiring body.

The only occasion on which less than market value is paid is when slum properties are being bought. These are regarded by the law as having outlived their useful life and therefore worth only the site value. Exceptionally, some homes in a slum area may be in very good condition and the owners of these may be able to obtain extra compensation. Again professional advice is desirable.

If a part only of a property is taken – for example, a part of a garden to build a road – then compensation is not only for the land itself (which may be a rather small amount) but also for any permanent loss in value the rest of the property suffers.

Since 1973 it has been possible to claim compensation not only for land that is taken away, but also for the environmental effects of a development such as a road. These are: noise, vibration, smells, smoke fumes, and so on. Mere loss of privacy, however, cannot be compensated in this way. The measure of compensation is the drop in value by reason of the development. Also grants are available for soundproofing and double glazing where a new road is built which is noisy, or where an airport is extended.

An extra payment can be claimed by owners or tenants, known as a 'home loss payment', whenever a home is acquired compulsorily. This is really compensation for the trouble of moving rather than for the land. It is three times the rateable value of the property.

Local authorities must sometimes rehouse those – including caravan dwellers – whose homes are acquired compulsorily. However, most people who are already home owners prefer to buy somewhere else with the compensation. In most cases the availability of new accommodation on the market for such people will prevent a claim for rehousing being made.

Objecting to a neighbour's planning proposals

There is no general rule that neighbours have a right to be consulted when an application for planning permission is made. But in some cases publicity must be given to an application by means of an advertisement in a local newspaper and by a notice on the land itself. These are essentially cases where particular inconvenience or disturbance may be caused in the locality. Examples are the use of land for a cinema, theatre, bingo hall or a building over twenty metres high, or the use of land for disposal of refuse. Then there is an opportunity to write to the local authority commenting on the application. If planning permission is refused and the applicant appeals, then anyone who made representations can be heard at the appeal.

In practice, local authorities do inform neighbours when applications for development are made which may affect their properties, and account is taken of anything said in reply by those neighbours.

Forcing a sale

In some cases refusal of planning permission by a local authority will lead to hardship. For example, a building may have been destroyed by fire yet the local authority may refuse to allow the site to be redeveloped. Such events will rarely affect home owners, but if they do, it is useful to know that the local authority can usually be compelled to purchase the property. Specialist advice (lawyers, surveyors) should be obtained as soon as such a claim against the local authority is thought likely to arise.

Of more practical importance to the home owner is the possibility of 'planning blight'. This occurs where some planning proposal exists (often only in outline form such as a new road) and, as a result, nearby homes become difficult to sell.

An owner occupier whose home is threatened with compulsory

purchase because of such a proposal can require the local authority to buy that home. If a government department is likely to acquire a home for some redevelopment proposal it too can be forced to buy. But once again, specialist advice is needed at an early stage.

23 Homelessness

Until 1977 the rights of homeless people were very limited. In that year the Housing (Homeless Persons) Act was passed in order to do something about the problem. Strangely enough, in the last ten to fifteen years there has been an excess of homes in Britain above the number of households needing accommodation. The reason why homelessness exists is that homes cannot always be found in areas where there are jobs, or the other way round. Moreover many homes are in very poor condition and are barely inhabitable. Also some empty homes are an inevitable result of a market in housing which leads to people selling and perhaps having to move before their old home can be finally disposed of.

What the Act does is to impose certain duties on local housing authorities (usually district councils or London boroughs) to rehouse some, but not all, homeless people. The rules laid down in the Act are accompanied by a Code of Guidance issued by the Department of the Environment which explains how the Act should be operated.

Who is homeless?

A person is homeless if he or she has nowhere to live together with any other person who usually lives with him or her as a member of his or her family. This makes it clear that one of the purposes of the Act is to prevent families being split up just because some members have somewhere to live but others do not. Also 'family' includes non-married partners with stable relationships. Even if accommodation is physically available a person will still be regarded as homeless if the accommodation cannot be used without violence being shown towards the occupier (battered wives), or the landlord has locked the tenant out (which is, of course, illegal), or it is a caravan or boat but there is nowhere to keep it.

Who does the local authority have to house?

First, a person must be homeless or threatened with homelessness within twenty-eight days. Second, it is not every such person who has a claim. A *priority need* must exist. This means that one of the following applies:

- that the person has dependent children living with him or her or is a pregnant woman (married or single);
- that homelessness has arisen because of fire, flood or some other disaster;
- that the person or anyone else who lives with him or her is vulnerable because of old age, mental or physical illness or some other special reason.

Although these groups are quite widely defined they do omit some people. Apart from pregnant women, single homeless people will not qualify unless they can be said to be 'vulnerable because of some other special reason'. This will be difficult to show in most cases but if, for example, a single person was being treated violently at home or had no parents he or she might be able to bring a claim.

The Code of Guidance suggests that old age refers particularly to those above retirement age (60 for women, 65 for men) and that a wide view should be taken of mental or physical illness.

Duties of the local authority

If an application is made for housing the authority has a duty to investigate the claim fully and ascertain whether a person is *homeless* and has a *priority need* for housing. If it appears that no priority need exists then their only duty is the somewhat imprecise one of offering advice and assistance. No time limit is laid down for the authority to complete its inquiries, but it seems that these must be undertaken reasonably speedily; there is a clear duty laid down in the Act to provide a written statement of the authority's decision.

Intentional homelessness

Two other hurdles may also stand in the way of an applicant. First, even if homelessness and a priority need are established the homelessness must not have been *intentional*. This means that the applicant must not have deliberately done something or failed to do something which resulted in homelessness. So not paying the rent when it became due or failing to defend proceedings for possession brought by a landlord where there was a good defence would be examples of this. But it must have been reasonable to continue to occupy the previous property, so that if the reason for non-payment of rent was that a claimant had become unemployed or was a battered wife, that should not be regarded as intentionally making oneself homeless. Equally it is not intentional homelessness if a person is genuinely unaware of some step he or she ought to take in order to keep the property he or she had. For example, not knowing of the possibility of obtaining a rent rebate would fall into this category.

It is for the authority to satisfy itself that someone became homeless intentionally. It is not for the claimant to show that he or she did not do so. So the claimant can and must have the benefit of any doubt.

Connection with another area

The second hurdle is that the claimant must not have a *connection with another* housing authority's *area*. The purpose of this bar is to prevent claimants from being drawn to areas in which they may happen to be temporarily when they may have a connection with some other area. For example, it is designed to prevent someone who comes from and has lived in London from applying to the housing authority in Newcastle having worked there for a short period and having become homeless. In such a case the area from which the person originally came takes a transfer of the responsibility to rehouse that claimant. There are complicated provisions for appeals to a body appointed by local authority associations in the event of any dispute. Temporary accommodation must be provided in the mean time, as it must if the homelessness was intentional. In the latter case accommodation must be provided for as long as it takes to give the claimant a reasonable opportunity to obtain other housing.

What kind of housing?

In most cases council accommodation will be provided. The Code of Guidance says that it ought to be of a permanent nature and not merely 'hostel' or 'bed and breakfast' accommodation. But the authority can also meet its duty by ensuring that someone else provides accommodation or by, for example, ensuring that the claimant obtains a mortgage to enable him or her to buy a property in the open market.

An authority also has a duty to store or otherwise protect the furniture and other property of the claimant if it has a duty to rehouse him or her and if it appears that such furniture or property would otherwise be damaged or lost.

The role of the courts

There is no formal mechanism by which an appeal can be made against an adverse decision by a housing authority. However, a number of cases under the Act have come before the courts and it is clear that if an authority fails to rehouse someone when it should do so it can be ordered to do so by the courts and is liable to pay damages for its breach of duty. The Act has been held to apply to people coming to this country from abroad as permanent settlers, although that will be very rare because in most cases an immigrant must be able to support himself or herself without support from public funds. Moreover a person from abroad is subject to the 'intentionally homeless test', which is a further bar to qualifying.

At Work

24 The contract of employment

A business organization usually has two ways of getting its work done. One way is to engage a contractor to do the job. The other is to engage its own employees to perform the tasks required. In either case, the arrangement is called a contract, for it consists of a legally binding agreement between the parties concerned.

If an outsider is engaged, the contract is said to be a contract *for services*. Where the business engages its own employees, the contract is called a contract *of service*. At first sight, the terms 'contract for services' and 'contract of service' appear to be very much the same; but in fact the difference between these terms is very important.

The contract of service

In the past, lawyers used to call an employer a master, and an employee a servant. A contract of employment between those parties was referred to as a contract of service. Such a contract gave rise to the relationship of master and servant. Though the terms 'master' and 'servant' have practically gone out of use in everyday life – having been replaced by the terms 'employer' and 'employee' – the legal basis of the relationship still remains the same, and it continues to give rise to important rights and duties for the persons involved.

These rights and duties make it important to discover whether a person is or is not a servant (employee). This could be a crucial matter, for example in the case of an accident causing injury at work, for our law imposes upon every employer a duty to take reasonable care to ensure the personal safety of his employees; but an employer generally has no such duty towards any outside contractor who works under a contract for services.

Further, an employer will be held liable for the wrongs done to other people by his employees in the course of their employment; but he will generally speaking not be liable for the wrongful acts of outside contractors engaged by him. In addition, the rights and duties given or imposed by various statutes apply only in the case of persons who are parties to a contract of service.

It is therefore very necessary to look closely at the contract of service and the meaning of some of the terms used in this area of law.

Making the contract

Many people do not realize that their employment is based on a contract because they believe that a contract is some kind of special document bearing seals. It is true that some types of contract are made in the form of a sealed document, but sealed documents are rarely used in the field of employment. In this sphere all that is needed is what is called a 'simple contract', which is an agreement with five basic characteristics:

- there must be a genuine *agreement* (that is, an offer by one party and an acceptance by the other);
- each party must have the legal *capacity* to enter into a contract;
- both parties must have an *intention* to enter into a legal relationship;
- there must be *consideration* (that is, each party must give something to the other); and
- the purpose of the transaction must be a *lawful* one.

Let's look a little more closely at each of these characteristics.

(a) Offer and acceptance

The offer of employment may be made in writing or it may be made orally. It may even be made by conduct, though this is now unusual. The acceptance may also be made in any of these ways. Except in special cases, such as that of seamen on foreign-going ships, no formalities are required – although employers are now obliged to give the employee a written note of certain details of the contract (see page 222).

However, though there is no need of formalities, the terms of the offer must be precise. Vague or uncertain promises do not constitute an offer; for example, 'Drop in on Monday and we'll see what we can do for you' is not an offer of employment on that day or any other. Again, an 'offer' of engagement in a particular post 'at a salary to be agreed between us' is not good enough.

Once an offer is accepted, a contract comes into existence; it then cannot be varied by either party, except with the consent of the other party.

(b) Legal capacity of the parties

Not everyone has the capacity to enter into a legally binding contract. Persons of unsound mind cannot do so, and people under the age of eighteen years are not capable of making certain kinds of contract. However, lack of legal capacity rarely arises in the sphere of employment. Even a person under eighteen years of age will be bound by a contract of employment or of apprenticeship, provided that the contract is, on the whole, for his benefit – even though it may contain some terms which in themselves are not to his advantage. Such a person must take the rough with the smooth, unless the whole arrangement is manifestly unfair.

(c) Intention to create legal relations

The parties to a contract must intend to be legally bound. Where what is being done is a business transaction, rather than a mere social engagement, the law presumes that the parties to that transaction each have an intention to be legally bound. Employment is a business transaction, so the intention to enter into legally binding relations is presumed in any agreement to offer and accept employment. If there is no such intention, then the parties must make it absolutely clear in their agreement. This is most unlikely to be the case in any agreement concerning employment, since in this sphere 'business is business', and the parties to it will intend to acquire legally enforceable rights from their bargain.

(d) Consideration

Consideration is the 'price' that each party to a contract pays to the other. In employment the general rule is that 'the consideration for work is wages, and the consideration for wages is work'.

Sometimes, however, the rewards for work do not consist entirely of payment in the form of money. In a contract of apprenticeship or of training, the consideration consists of the training given. Even if the apprentice receives money payments as well, the contract will be broken if he is not given training. And the training must include an opportunity of doing the actual job, not merely of being given instructions about its theory.

Generally speaking, so long as an employer pays the wages that were agreed in the contract he fulfils his obligations. He is not also bound to find work for the employee. As one judge said: 'Provided I pay my cook regularly, she cannot complain if I choose to take all, or any, of my meals out. Employers are not bound to supply work to enable the employee "to keep his hand in".'

However, there are a few exceptions to this rule. One exception, as we have already seen, applies in the cases where the consideration takes the form of training, as in the case of apprentices. Another is where the remuneration consists only of payment by piecework or by commission. Where, for example, the remuneration of a salesman was agreed to be by commission only on sales, it was held by a court that the employer must give the salesman the opportunity of earning commission by allowing him to work. But it was quite different in another case, where a salesman was paid by salary as well as commission on sales. Here the employers had paid the salary, so they were not obliged to provide an opportunity to earn commission as well.

Other people who have the right to be given the work as well as the wages agreed are those who have an interest in the publicity attaching to their jobs; for example, actors. Here the payment of agreed salary will not be enough to fulfil the contract; the agreed role must also be provided.

(e) Legality

No valid contract can exist where the purpose of the agreement is to commit a crime or a civil wrong, or where the object of transaction is one forbidden by law.

Obviously an agreement to hire an assassin is not a valid contract; equally invalid would be the employment of 'call girls' or prostitutes.

Less obvious perhaps is the situation where the wages paid includes an amount which is paid tax-free in circumstances where, to the knowledge of both parties, tax ought to have been paid. Such an arrangement is illegal because it is a fraud upon the Inland Revenue. It can have disconcerting consequences for the participants, quite apart from the risk of prosecution.

Thus, in one case an employee had been wrongfully discharged without notice. He brought an action to recover salary in lieu of notice. The terms of his contract had provided a salary of £13 per week, plus £6 expenses. The evidence showed, however, that the expenses actually incurred did not exceed £1 per week, and that the figure of £6 had been inserted to avoid tax. The court held that the whole contract was void as being a fraud upon the Inland Revenue. As a result the employee had no right to bring any action for wrongful dismissal. He had himself been a party to the fraud.

A similar result was arrived at in a more recent case, involving a claim brought before an industrial tribunal in respect of unfair dismissal. Part of the employee's wages had, with her consent, been paid free of tax. Hence it was held that she lost any right she might otherwise have had to bring her case before the tribunal.

Beware, therefore, of entering into any such illegal arrangement, however tempting it may appear, for there will be no legal remedy if any dispute arises between you and your employer.

Needless to say, the harsh rule indicated above will not apply where one party is innocent and the illegality is on the side only of the other party. In such a case the innocent party will not lose his right to legal remedy.

Another kind of illegality which is relevant to employment is what is called an agreement in unreasonable restraint of trade. Any agreement which is in unreasonable restraint of trade is unenforceable in law; and this rule becomes of great significance in cases where an employer tries to restrain the freedom of an employee to seek employment with a competitor if and when the employment comes to an end (see page 231).

The contents of the contract

A contract of service will normally consist of a number of terms. Those terms which have explicitly been agreed by the parties, either orally or in writing, are called 'express terms'.

However, even where a contract has been put into writing, it is most unlikely that every contingency will have been provided for and set down. Hence not every term will have been expressly mentioned. This is likely to be still more the case where the contract is a wholly oral one.

Implied terms

Where a dispute arises as to the nature or extent of the obligations that were intended to be undertaken by either party to the contract, a court may be called upon to resolve the problem. Frequently the court is able to do this by discovering implied terms. An implied term is one which, as its name indicates, is not expressly mentioned, but which common sense shows that both parties must have intended when they entered into their agreement. Sometimes such implied terms arise from general custom or usage in the industry concerned, or in the district in which the business is carried on, and of which both parties can be deemed to be aware. Usages can also arise from the results of collective bargaining carried on between trade unions and employers' associations on such matters as wage rates and conditions of employment in the trade concerned. The results of collective bargains will usually become implied terms in individual contracts of employment.

Written statement of terms of employment

Because most contracts of employment are largely unwritten when they are made, there could be a great deal of argument about what exactly they contain. For this reason the Employment Protection (Consolidation) Act 1978 requires employers, not later than thirteen weeks after the beginning of employment, to give to the employee a written statement setting out the main terms of his employment. The particulars must include the following:

- details of the identity of the parties;
- the date the employment started;
- whether work with a previous employer is to be regarded as being continuous with the present employment;
- the rate of pay, or the method of calculating it;
- the intervals at which payment is to be made, i.e. weekly, monthly, or otherwise;
- the arrangements regulating hours of work to be done, including the normal hours of work;
- any terms and conditions relating to holidays and holiday pay, to absence through sickness, and sick pay, and to pension schemes (other than state schemes);
- the length of notice to be given by each side to terminate the employment;
- the title of the job that the employee is to do.

In addition to these details the following information must also be provided:

- particulars of any disciplinary rules that apply to the employee;
- the identity of a person to whom the employee can apply for redress of any grievance arising from the employment, or from disciplinary decisions;
- the machinery for pursuing and dealing with such matters, if there is any.

If, under any of these headings, no particulars are given, that fact must be stated. Thus, if there are no arrangements for providing payment during periods of sickness, this must be made clear by entering words like 'no arrangements for sick pay'. It is not permissible to leave a blank space on the form.

After the statement has been given to the employee, if there is any change in the terms of the employment, a further statement indicating the nature of the change must be given to the employee not later than one month after the change has taken place.

Other methods of providing written particulars of the contract
In order to avoid unnecessary duplication of effort, the Act provides that in two sets of circumstances the statement referred to above need not be given to each employee.

The first of these circumstances is where the whole contract has been put in writing and includes all the particulars mentioned in the points listed above. In such a case a copy of the contract must be made available to the employee.

The second set of circumstances is where details of all the required particulars are made reasonably available to the employee by means of some document which the employee has an opportunity of reading in the course of his employment, or which is made reasonably accessible to him in some other way.

In practice, such a document normally consists of a set of works rules or other publication issued by the employer. It can, however, equally be a copy of a collective agreement entered into by the employer and trade unions.

Very often it is by this means that the terms of a collective agreement become incorporated into the individual contracts of service of employees. The terms of those individual contracts are thus varied as and when the collective agreements are varied. Such changes most frequently occur when negotiations between unions and employers result in pay increases, though this does not mean that all changes have to be to the employee's advantage. In one case, unions had agreed with the employer that an additional Saturday-morning shift would be worked. An employee, who had hitherto worked under a contract providing for only five days of attendance each week, refused to work on Saturday morning. The court held that he was in breach of contract, since his contract had been varied by the collective agreement.

There are three other features of a statement of terms of employment which should be noted:

- A statement of terms of employment need not be given to any employee who works for less than 16 hours a week. Hence 'part-timers' need not be given a statement. There are exceptions to this rule, and these relate to part-timers who have worked 8 or more hours a week for five or more years, and to full-timers who worked more than 16 hours a week but whose contract has been changed to a work period of less than 16, but more than 8, hours a week. Such people will, for a period of 26 weeks following that change, be treated as though they were still working more than 16 hours per week so far as concerns the issuing of the statement required by the Act.

- Any complaint about a failure to give all or any of the required particulars, or any query concerning what particulars ought to be given, can be referred to an industrial tribunal. The tribunal has power to resolve the matter.
- The statement given is only a note of some of the contents of the contract of service; it is not the contract itself. The fact that the employee may have signed it will be taken to mean only that he has received and read it – unless words are used indicating that he has thereby agreed to the terms and conditions set out.

Normally the contract of service will have already come into being well before any statement is issued, and that contract will usually contain terms (either express or implied) which are additional to those set out in the statement.

25 The rights and duties of employer and employee

Having looked briefly in the previous chapter at the contract of service, we must now examine the legal rights and duties which it gives to, or imposes on, the parties concerned.

Duties of the employer

It is worth pointing out here that the employer may be an individual person, or the employer may be a corporate body. A corporate body is an organization of individuals which has been given legal personality by the law, e.g. a limited company like ICI, or a statutory corporation like British Rail.

If you work for a company, it is the company itself which is your employer – not its managing director, nor even its chief shareholder. Though a number of persons in that company may have varying degrees of managerial authority, so that one or more of them may commonly be referred to as 'the boss', they can give orders only on the authority of the company, and it alone is the employer. If the company is wound up, that terminates the contracts of employees; but if the controlling interest in the company is merely taken over by some other group of persons, that fact will not alter the legal relationship of the company to its employees, so long as the company remains in being.

Payment of wages; itemized pay statement

The first duty of the employer is to pay the wages agreed in the contract of service. Failure to do so will be a breach of a fundamental term of the contract. The Employment Protection (Consolidation) Act 1978 provides that each employee must be given an itemized pay statement in writing. Such a statement must contain particulars of: (a) the gross amount of wages or salary; (b) the amounts of deductions and the reasons for them; (c) the net amount of wages or salary payable; and, if different parts of that net amount are payable in different ways, (d) the amount and method of each part-payment.

If such an itemized pay statement is not provided by the employer, the employee may refer the matter to an industrial tribunal. The tribunal can order the employer to refund to the employee any unnotified deductions which have been made during the thirteen weeks immediately before the application to the tribunal. This will be so whether those deductions were in accordance with the contract of service or not.

Sickness

Temporary absence from work by an employee on account of accident or personal injury will not terminate the contract of service, though it will excuse the employee from performing his contract during the period of absence.

Sickness or accident which gives rise to an inability to perform the contract indefinitely may, however, bring the contract to an end, by what is known as 'frustration'. Frustration occurs where an external event, unforeseen by the parties and unintended by them, makes further performance of the contract impossible. Examples would be where a bus driver became blind, or where – as happened in one case – a young musician employed to play on six evenings a week suffered a nervous breakdown which made it impossible for him to play on more than three evenings.

Payment of wages during sickness

Since temporary absence through sickness or injury does not terminate the contract, the contract continues, and so in theory does the obligation of the employer to pay wages.

However, this obligation is usually modified by agreement, whether the agreement is expressly incorporated into the contract of service or whether it is implied there by reference to a collective bargain with unions or derived from a custom of the industry, locality, or the enterprise itself. Hence few employers are, in practice, under an obligation to provide wages during periods of sickness. If the employee has a right to receive pay during periods of sickness that right is normally to be found in the contract itself. So if the contract includes, for example, a requirement to produce a medical certificate of disability, then a failure to produce such a certificate may be a breach of contract, giving the employer the right to refuse payment or even to dismiss the employee.

Though the receiving of national insurance sick benefit or injury benefit does not automatically relieve an employer from the obligation to continue paying wages or salary, most employers now have agreements incorporated into the contract of service which take account of any sums received from national insurance in determining how much will be paid to the employee.

It is important to note that from April 1983 employers are responsible for paying 'statutory sickness pay' to their employees for the first eight weeks of absence through sickness or industrial injury. Those payments are not wages: they simply replace the existing state benefits and do not affect the contractual position described above.

Holidays and holiday pay

The law does not normally oblige an employer to give holidays or to provide holiday pay. Any such arrangements must be found in the contract of service and be part of the terms of the employment that have been agreed.

Interruptions to work from external causes
If work is prevented by external causes such as fire, adverse weather conditions or labour disputes elsewhere which interrupt supplies, the employer is normally under no obligation to continue paying his employees who are prevented from working. If such an obligation is to be imposed, it must arise from agreement. In some industries such agreements have been arrived at, providing for what is called a 'guaranteed wage', usually for a limited period, and subject to various conditions.

Normally, therefore, such matters must be determined by reference to the contents of the contract of service.

Guarantee payments
The Employment Protection (Consolidation) Act 1978 provides some relief from the somewhat restrictive rules of law set out above. Any employee with four or more weeks of continuous service is entitled to payment if his employer does not provide him with work for a full day on which he would normally be employed in accordance with his contract of service. The lack of work must be due to some occurrence affecting the normal working of the employer's business. This right to pay will be lost if the lack of work is caused by a strike, lockout or other industrial action involving the employees of the employer, or if the employee unreasonably refuses to do alternative work that is suitable for him.

The number of days covered by this statutory guarantee is not more than five in any period of three months; though this number, and the amount of the maximum daily payment required, may be varied by order of the Secretary of State from time to time.

Any provision of the contract of service which requires payment to be made for workless days will, of course, be taken into account as reducing, or even (where large enough) as superseding, this statutory obligation on the part of the employer.

It should be noted that there is no statutory obligation upon the employer to make any guarantee payment for a day on which the employee's contract of service does not require him to work.

A failure by the employer to make a guarantee payment may be referred to an industrial tribunal.

Duty to pay expenses
The second duty of the employer is to repay to the employee any expenses that the employee may have incurred on his employer's behalf in the course of the employment. This obligation clearly

covers, for example, the costs of travel in the course of work; but it does not cover the costs of getting from home to work unless there is some special agreement to that effect, for how the employee gets to work is normally of no concern to his employer.

(Certain other duties that are imposed upon the employer are dealt with on pages 233–43.)

Duties of the employee

Obedience to lawful and reasonable orders

The first and most important duty of the employee is that of obedience to the lawful and reasonable orders of the employer. A deliberate refusal to carry out such orders will be such a fundamental breach of the contract that it will justify an immediate termination of the employment.

Lawful

What orders are lawful is, of course, a matter of law. In one case, an airline pilot was instructed by his employers to fly in breach of certain legal regulations. He refused to do so and left the employment. His employers sued him for breach of contract. The court held that he was not in breach of contract. It was his employers who were in breach.

Reasonable

What orders are reasonable is a more difficult question, for it can be answered only after an examination of all the aspects of the individual case. One aspect of importance will be the extent and scope of the duties which the contract envisaged as being part of the job the employee was engaged to perform. In other words, the 'job description' applicable to the employee's work will furnish the chief test for deciding whether any order is reasonable in his case. Thus it was held by the courts in one case that an order to wind lace on to cards in company with factory operatives was not reasonable when given to a man who had been engaged to be a lace buyer. In another case, it was held to be reasonable for labourers engaged to clean out drains to be ordered to clean out boiler flues, since such work was reasonably similar to what they generally did. On their refusal to do the work ordered, these men had been justifiably dismissed.

Circumstances, however, alter cases. On the one hand, a gardener who had refused to do some work ordered by his employer and who had expressed that refusal in obscene language was held, by the Court of Appeal, to have been justifiably dismissed – not for the use of that language, but for the deliberate breach of instructions. On the other hand, a gardener who had stopped using an electric hedge-cutter because of the rain, but who had then used the time to sharpen his tools, was held to have been unjustifiably dismissed by his employer, even though the gardener had used obscene language in reply to that charge.

Wrongful dismissal

All these cases illustrate dismissal by the employer in breach of contract, which is called a *wrongful dismissal.* Any contract of service can be terminated, by either party, on the giving of appropriate notice; a wrongful dismissal occurs if the employer terminates the contract without giving proper notice. Only a breach of contract by the employee can justify dismissal without due notice.

Unfair dismissal

This rule must now be regarded as modified, in practice, by the provisions of the Employment Protection (Consolidation) Act 1978. Under this Act, every employee (with certain exceptions) is given the right not to be *unfairly dismissed* by his employer.

'Unfair' dismissal is a concept quite different from 'wrongful' dismissal. In the first place, unfair dismissal is determined by quite different tests, and not by the courts. And the remedies for *wrongful* and *unfair* dismissal are also different.

A dismissal, whether with or without notice, will be regarded as unfair unless (a) the reason for the dismissal was a reason listed in the Act, and (b) even if the reason was one of those listed, the dismissal was reasonable in all the circumstances of the case.

(Unfair dismissal is dealt with in detail on pages 249–53.)

Possession of reasonable skill

Every employee is considered to promise that he possesses such skill and aptitude as is reasonably customary in the occupation or trade in which he has accepted employment. A failure to reach or to maintain that reasonable standard will justify the dismissal of the employee. Where those standards change over a period of time, for example by the introduction of new and improved technology, the employee will be expected to keep reasonably abreast of those developments, though the employer also has a duty to ensure that his employees are kept reasonably well informed. So it has been held that where a task requires special skill, as does that of a factory doctor, such an employee must be judged by the standards appropriate to that skill. Such an employee is expected to give his employer advice on safety problems and to keep himself adequately informed of developments in that sphere.

So one of the reasons for dismissal permitted by the Employment Protection Act is one 'relating to the capacity or qualifications of the employee for performing the work he was required by his employer to do'.

Duty of loyalty or good faith

Whether expressly mentioned or not, there is implied in every contract of service a duty of good faith on the part of the employee towards the business interests of the employer. The extent of this duty will, of course, vary greatly. It will be more exacting upon a manager or a confidential secretary than upon an office boy or a labourer. But some duties are general – no bribes must be accepted, no conflicts of economic interest must be allowed to arise, and confidential matters must remain confidential.

This duty will exist so long as the contract lasts, and it will exist both during working hours and outside them. Though, generally speaking, a man may do whatever he wishes in his own free time, an employee may not use that time to assist his employer's competitors – still less to compete with him himself. This rule applies equally to ordinary workers and to managing directors.

So also an employee must not use his position to make a private profit from his employer's business by, for example, giving preferential treatment to customers who offer bribes – even though his employer's business suffers no direct loss as a result.

An employee is, however, not bound to keep confidence about any business activity of his employer which is illegal, for all citizens have a duty to uphold the law. Nor is an employee bound (unless his contract expressly so provides) to reveal to his employer all his own faults or omissions.

An employee must not use his employer's property or money for his own purposes, unless permission has been granted. This is so even if no dishonesty is intended by the employee. In one case a manager borrowed money from the shop till, into which he placed an IOU, and he replaced the cash on the following day. The Court of Appeal held that such borrowing was a breach of contract justifying the manager's dismissal.

An employee must take proper care of his employer's property that is in his custody, and he will be liable for any damage or loss that may occur as result of his carelessness. In one case a supervisor negligently allowed some vacuum cleaners to remain in a van parked outside his house. The cleaners were stolen from the van at night. The supervisor was held liable for their loss.

Restrictive covenants (see also page 221)
In some circumstances an employer may seek to strengthen or to widen the duty of good faith already implied in every contract of service by getting the employee to agree to a written contract (called a covenant) which expressly protects the interests of the employer even though the employment has ended.

Such a covenant will normally seek to restrict the employee from competing with his former employer in the employer's line of business.

In general the courts will not enforce such a restrictive covenant if its effect is too wide in extent or if its duration is unduly long; and, even where these requirements are met, the courts will not uphold such a covenant unless it is for the protection of some actual business interest of the employer's.

Much will depend upon the circumstances of each particular case, but it can be said that the courts will never enforce a covenant which prevents an employee from taking up any form of work at all, or which prevents him from using his natural aptitudes or acquired experience and skill in any given occupation. For a restrictive covenant to be enforced it must be shown that some legitimate business interest of the former employer is being infringed by the employee. Thus, in one case, a clerk/negotiator was employed by an estate agent who operated from two offices which were several miles apart. The contract of service contained a covenant by which it was agreed that on termination of the employment the clerk/negotiator would not set up in estate agency business within five miles of either office for a period of three years. He had at no time worked at one of the two offices, but on leaving the employment he did set up in business within five miles of the office at which he had worked. The court held that the restriction imposed was too wide as respects the office at which he never worked, but was effective as respects the office at which he had.

In another case a woman employed as a hairdresser was party to a covenant by which she undertook not to be employed in any capacity in the business of ladies' hairdresser within one half-mile of any premises of her employer. This restriction was to operate for a period of one year. Having been dismissed for good cause by her employer, she took employment with a rival hairdresser within 150 yards of her previous employer's premises. The Court of Appeal held that the restriction was valid, despite the fact that it had been drafted in wide terms ('not to be employed in any capacity'), for it was clear that what the parties had had in mind was employment only as a hairdresser.

From these cases it can be seen that the goodwill (i.e. the trade connection) of an employer's business is regarded as an interest that the courts will readily protect in cases where an employee could continue to exercise personal influence over his former employer's customers. Furthermore, the courts will interpret the restrictive covenant according to its common-sense meaning, rather than in accordance with the literal terms in which it was set down.

However, if the service of the employee is terminated by the employer other than for good cause, the restrictive covenant will no longer be binding upon the employee. A person who breaches a contract cannot also claim to have the benefit of it.

Duty to avoid misconduct

An employee has a duty not to commit such misconduct as may adversely affect his employer's business interests. Misconduct is a very wide term, so its significance will depend upon the circumstances of each case. Not every form of misconduct will constitute a breach of contract so fundamental as to justify dismissal by the employer, nor can misconduct be confined only to activities during working hours. The test is whether that conduct adversely affected the business, or could reasonably be thought to do so.

Thus, in one case, a woman office supervisor frequently regaled her office colleagues with stories of her somewhat colourful sex-life. This so irritated the other girls that they refused to work with her. Her employers in consequence dismissed her, and she then claimed that she had been unfairly dismissed. Her claim was rejected. What she did in her own time was her own affair and its morality was neither here nor there; but it could not be permitted to disrupt the work of her employers' office.

What may be serious misconduct on the part of one employee may not be serious on the part of another. Drunkenness on the part of a manager or of a headmaster will normally be more seriously regarded than drunkenness on the part of a labourer, whether it occurs on or off the employer's premises. What matters always is the degree to which it may affect the employer's business interests.

Those interests may include not only its profitability but its public standing or prestige.

26 Health and safety at work

An employer has a legal duty to ensure the safety of his employees. This duty is personal to the employer and although he may delegate the duty to managers and others he cannot escape the responsibility for seeing that it is carried out.

The law on this subject is contained in many decisions of the courts over the years and in various Acts of Parliament.

Duties of the employer – case law

It is clear from the decisions of the courts that the employer's duty is to take such care for the safety of his employees as a reasonable man would take in all the circumstances of the case. The House of Lords has held that this duty is three-fold:

- the duty to provide safe plant and machinery;
- the duty to provide a competent staff; and
- the duty to provide and maintain a safe system of work.

If the employer fails to take reasonable care and, as a result, an employee suffers an injury that should have been foreseen, that will be negligence and the employee will be able to sue for damages.

How much care?

The lawyer's answer to that question is the somewhat unsatisfactory one of 'reasonable care'. Translated into the field of employment this means, not that the employer must eliminate every conceivable danger, but that he must take such reasonable precautions as experience has shown to be necessary. The extent of these precautions will depend on three things:

- the *likelihood* that the harmful event will occur;

- the *gravity* of the resulting harm if it does occur; and
- the *cost* of taking precautions to prevent its occurrence.

So, for example:

- where a farm worker caught an almost unheard-of disease from the rats on the farm his employer was not negligent (it was extremely unlikely that he would catch the disease);
- but an employer who failed to provide goggles for a one-eyed worker, who lost the sight of his only eye in an accident, was negligent (the injury that in fact occurred was extremely grave);
- and an employer who had spread sawdust over the greater part of a factory floor which had been made slippery by a flood was not held to be negligent merely because an employee slipped and fell on an untreated section of that floor.

Foresight

In order to prove that his employer has been negligent an employee will have to prove not only that the employer failed to take reasonable care but also that he should have foreseen that the employee would be injured in the way that in fact he was. The law expects employers to keep abreast of new developments in safety procedures in their own industries but they cannot be expected to foresee things that are beyond the existing state of scientific knowledge.

So, for example, where a workman was injured in an explosion caused by a hitherto unknown chemical reaction between asbestos and sodium cyanide his employer was not negligent even though the two substances only came into contact because of the employer's lack of care.

Contributory negligence

Just as the employer has a duty to ensure the reasonable safety of his employees, so also each employee has a duty to take reasonable care for his own safety. An employee must perform his work with such degree of skill and care as can reasonably be expected of a person doing the work concerned.

If an accident which causes injury is partly the result of negligence by the employer and partly the result of negligence on the part of the employee, the employee will not lose his right to sue the employer, but the court will reduce the amount of damages (compensation) payable by the proportion to which the injured employee himself contributed to the damage suffered.

If an employee's own lack of care has contributed to the damage suffered he is said to be guilty of contributory negligence.

The compensation is reduced not by the extent to which the injured person contributed to *causing* the accident, but to the extent that he contributed to the *damage* suffered.

If, for example, helmets should be worn whilst doing any particular kind of work, a head injury which is partly the result of failure to wear a helmet may well bring a finding that the employee concerned was guilty of contributory negligence, even though the employer's negligence was the cause of the accident; and compensation will be reduced accordingly.

Where an employee's injury is solely due to his own fault, he will have no right at all to compensation from his employer. This was the case where two men engaged in unloading a truck in a scrapyard found what they thought was a live artillery shell. They tested it by striking it with a heavy hammer. It exploded, causing them injury. They sued their employer, claiming that he had been negligent in not providing a safe system of work. The court held that the employer was in no way to blame. The men had been the authors of their own misfortune.

Duties of the employer – statute

Several Acts of Parliament impose upon employers the duty of ensuring the personal safety of employees. Among these are the Factories Act 1964, the Mines and Quarries Act 1954, other legislation applying to particular industries, and the more recent Health and Safety at Work Act 1974 which applies to all forms of employment.

The extent of the duty imposed by these Acts differs from that imposed by the law relating to negligence (see page 233). The standard of care required by the law of negligence is that which would be taken by a reasonable man in all the circumstances of the case. The standard of care imposed by each Act is that set out in the actual words of the statute. Depending upon the words used this standard may be similar to that of the law of negligence or it may be much stricter, or even absolute.

The Factories Act 1961

Under this Act the duty of care is imposed upon the 'occupier' of any factory, i.e. upon the person or business organization which operates the factory. As its name implies, the Act applies only to factories, but the word 'factory' is defined as any premises in which articles are made or adapted for sale, in which work is done by persons engaged in manual labour for an employer who is carrying on the business for purposes of gain.

So, as can be seen, a factory is not defined by its size or appearance, but by what is being done there. Hence a prison workshop is not a factory, for the activity of prisoners is not employment for wages by an employer who is running a business for profit.

Safety provisions of the Act

In some instances the requirements of the Act are peremptory and absolute. Thus, Section 14 says: 'Every dangerous part of any machinery, other than prime movers and transmission machinery . . . shall be securely fenced, unless it is in such a position or of such construction as to be as safe to every person employed or working on the premises as it would be if securely guarded.'

This section is unqualified. This means that there is no excuse for the use of machinery which is dangerous if unguarded. No considerations of practicability or of profitability can be permitted to override the statute. If a machine cannot be used so as to comply with this section, then it cannot legally be used at all.

So also, Section 22 requires that 'Every hoist or lift shall be of good mechanical construction, sound material, and adequate strength, and shall be properly maintained.' In one case a lift had failed. It had fallen down the shaft and killed a passenger. The occupiers of the premises proved that they had employed engineers to examine the lift weekly and to maintain it in good condition, but the House of Lords held that as soon as the lift broke down it at once ceased to be 'properly maintained'. The failure of the lift was itself a breach of the statute and the occupiers were liable.

Less rigorous requirements

It is important to notice that certain expressions used elsewhere in the Act impose something less rigorous than the absolute duty of the kind mentioned above.

Thus, for example, the Woodworking Regulations call for the upper guard of any circular saw to be kept 'as low as practicable'. 'Practicable' is given its plain dictionary meaning, that is, capable of being carried out in action, or feasible. The fact that the precaution required is difficult, or inconvenient, or uneconomic, is no excuse whatever. What is practicable must, however, at least be within the limits of present technical knowledge.

An even less rigorous obligation is imposed where the words 'reasonably practicable' are used in the Act. This is so, for example, in Section 28 which requires 'all floors, steps, stairs, passages, and gangways to be of sound construction, properly maintained, and, so far as is reasonably practicable, to be kept free of any obstruction and from any substance likely to cause persons to slip'.

The use of the phrase 'reasonably practicable' means that in considering the use of any precaution, the costs involved can be taken into account (see page 234).

Enforcing the Factories Act

There are three ways of enforcing this Act. The first two ways – prosecutions in the magistrates' courts and improvement and stop notices – are in the hands of the Safety Inspectorate, whose powers are dealt with in detail on page 241.

The third method of enforcement is for the injured employee to bring a civil action for damages against his employer. This is called an action for breach of statutory duty.

Civil action for breach of statutory duty The injured employee will have to prove that his employer's breach of the Act was one of the causes of his injury, although he does not have to prove that it was the only one.

Any attempt by the employer to argue that the employee freely agreed to the breach of duty and accepted the risk of injury will not protect the employer from liability. Where an Act of Parliament imposes a duty this cannot be abolished by a private agreement.

Contributory negligence by the employee (see page 234) will be taken into account and the damages awarded reduced accordingly. Where, as in some cases, a statutory duty is imposed upon both employer and employee and an accident results from a breach, the employer will not be excused, but the employee's own breach of duty will be treated as though it were contributory negligence.

If, however, the statutory duty is imposed upon the employee alone, and not on the employer (not a very frequent case) then a breach which injures that employee will not give him any claim against the employer, for the employee is the author of his own misfortune.

Finally, it should be noted that the safeguards provided by the Factories Act cover not only the employees of the occupier of the factory, but also all persons working on the premises, that is, anyone who is present on business. This would include, for example, self-employed window-cleaners, or even visitors, so long as they are not trespassers.

The Health and Safety at Work Act 1974

Although, as can be seen from the last paragraph above, the Factories Act covers more persons than the employees of the factory, it applies only to premises designated as factories. So also the Mines and Quarries Act applies only to mines and quarries. In other words, most of such protective statutes apply only to specific places and to specific activities. As result of this, many fields of employment were not covered by any form of statutory protection. To remedy this situation Parliament passed the Health and Safety at Work Act 1974.

This Act covers all forms of employment. It sets out general rules and sets up two bodies to draw up more specific rules and to enforce the Act.

These bodies are the Health and Safety Commission, and the Health and Safety Executive.

Health and Safety Commission

This body has the duty of drawing up regulations giving effect to the objectives of the Act and covering specific industries and activities. Such regulations, when approved by the Secretary of State, have the force of law. They may provide for the repeal and replacement of any existing legislation concerning safety at work.

The Commission will also issue Codes of Practice indicating how certain forms of work should be carried on so as to ensure safety of persons doing that work or affected by it. Such codes will not have the force of law, but any failure to observe the code can be taken into account in any proceedings brought in consequence of a breach of the Act or of the regulations.

The Commission will also sponsor research into the avoidance of accidents, and it can hold inquiries into any accident which occurs.

The Health and Safety Executive

This is the body which enforces the Act. It controls the inspectors who actually carry out this activity, and who have power to bring prosecutions for any breach of the Act or of the regulations. It also has an Employment Medical Advisory Service to give advice on medical issues arising from employment, i.e. industrial diseases and the like.

General duties of the employer
The Act is what is called an 'enabling Act' because it only lays down general duties and gives to the bodies mentioned above the power to make more specific rules and to enforce them. However, the general duties are important. They are as follows:

- an employer must ensure, so far as is reasonably practicable, the health, safety and welfare of all his employees;
- he must provide and maintain plant and systems of work which are, so far as is reasonably practicable, safe and without risks to health;
- he must ensure, so far as is reasonably practicable, safety and the absence of health risks in the use, handling, storage and transport of articles and substances;
- he must provide instruction, training and supervision such as is necessary to ensure, so far as is reasonably practicable, the health and safety of employees;
- he must ensure that any workplace, and the access and exit to it, are kept, so far as is practicable, free from risk and maintained in a safe condition; and
- he must, so far as is practicable, provide for his employees a working environment that is safe and which provides adequate facilities for their welfare at work.

Other duties
Every employer must publish to all his employees a written statement of his general policy on health and safety at work and of the arrangements he is making to carry out that policy.

An employer must not make any charge to employees in respect of any protective clothing, or other gear, which is required by any Act or regulation.

Every employer, and every self-employed person, has a duty to conduct his business in such a way as to secure, so far as is reasonably practicable, that persons not in his employment who may be affected by it are not exposed to risks to their health or safety.

Duties of employees
It is the duty of every employee while at work to take reasonable care for the health and safety of himself and of any other person who may be affected by his acts or his omissions at work. In addition, every employee must cooperate with his employer, so far as is necessary, to enable the employer to conform with the requirements of any statute.

It is also the duty of everyone not to misuse or interfere with anything provided under the statute to ensure health, safety, or welfare.

Duties on others

Designers, manufacturers, importers, and suppliers of any article for use in work have a general duty to ensure, so far as is practicable, that the article is safe and without risks when properly used. A similar duty falls upon erectors and installers of articles for use at work.

Safety representatives

Since October 1978 employees have had the right to appoint safety representatives at their places of work. This right is given only to trade unions recognized by the employer, i.e. those unions with which he negotiates on matters concerning wage rates and conditions of employment. As far as possible such representatives must be persons who have been employed for two or more years, unless they have had experience as a representative in some other employment. The appointment must be notified to the employer in writing.

Duties and powers Safety representatives have the function of investigating potential hazards and dangerous occurrences at the workplace, of investigating complaints from employees concerning safety, and of making representations to the employer about these or any other matter relating to safety, health, or welfare at work. They are to represent the employees in any discussions with the inspectors of the Health and Safety Executive, and they have the right and duty to inspect the workplace at least once in every three months, or even more frequently if the employer agrees. Notice must be given to the employer of the intention to carry out an inspection, and he must give such facilities and assistance as are reasonably necessary.

If an accident has occurred the representatives have powers to carry out an immediate inspection, provided it is safe to do so.

Safety representatives have the right to inspect and take copies of any document relating to safety which the employer is required by law to keep. This will not be so, however, where the document relates to a matter of national security or to any individual.

The employer must permit safety representatives to take such time off, with pay, during working hours as is necessary to carry out their duties, or to undergo training in those duties. If the employer fails to provide these facilities a complaint may be taken to an industrial tribunal and the tribunal may make a declaration and award compensation.

Safety committees

Any two safety representatives may require the employer to establish a safety committee. Where such a request is made, the employer must consult with the representatives concerned and also with the trade unions which have members employed by him; and he must establish the committee within three months of being asked for it. The employer must then post up a notice, which can be seen by the employees, stating the composition of the committee and the workplaces covered by it.

The Health and Safety Executive have stated that the safety committee should consist of equal numbers of persons representing management and employee representatives.

Function of safety committees The function of the committees is to promote the cooperation of employer and employees in developing and carrying out measures to ensure the health and safety of employees, and to assist the employer in carrying out the objectives of the Act. The activity of the committee should be kept quite separate from that of other joint bodies, such as those which deal with wages and conditions of employment. Safety committees do not control the safety representatives (for these are appointed by trade unions), but safety representatives may be (and usually are) members of the committee.

Enforcement of the Health and Safety at Work Act

The criminal law Prosecutions may be brought against any person or body whose act or omission causes a contravention of any provision of the Act or of any regulation made under it. Such prosecutions are normally brought by the inspectors on behalf of the Health and Safety Executive, and they are brought in a magistrates' court, or (in more serious cases) before a crown court. Magistrates' courts have powers to impose a fine of up to £1,000. Where proceedings are brought, on indictment, to a crown court, that court has power to impose a fine (without upper limit) or imprisonment for up to two years, or both (see page 417 for more details of criminal courts).

Where an offence has been committed by a body corporate, e.g. a limited company, then any director, manager, or similiar officer of that body may also be liable to punishment if it is shown that the offence was due to his consent, connivance, or neglect of duty.

The civil law The Act forbids the bringing of any civil action for damages by a person who has been injured by reason of a breach of any of the general duties set out in the Act. But it provides that such a civil action may be brought in respect of a breach of any regulation made under the Act, unless that regulation provides otherwise.

Administrative action All the hitherto separate inspectorates are now brought together under the control of the Health and Safety Executive. Hence we no longer have separate Factory Inspectorates, Mines Inspectorates, Alkali Inspectorates, etc.

The inspectors have the duty of keeping a watchful eye on all workplaces, and an inspector may enter any such workplace at any reasonable time to examine it or anything in it, and to require any person to give him information. It is an offence to obstruct an inspector in carrying out his duties.

If an inspector believes that a contravention of the Act is taking place or is likely to take place, he may serve an 'improvement notice', requiring steps to be taken to remedy the contravention and giving details of the contravention and of the nature of the steps to be taken.

If the inspector believes that any activities in the workplace are likely to involve a risk of serious personal injury, he may serve (on the person in control of the premises) a 'prohibition notice'. This notice will give instructions that the activities referred to must be stopped until such action as the inspector requires has been carried out.

Appeals A person or body on whom a notice has been served has the right of appeal to an industrial tribunal. If the notice was an improvement notice its effect will be suspended until the tribunal gives its ruling. If the notice is a prohibition notice then it will remain in force until the tribunal gives its ruling. The tribunal may uphold a notice, or revoke it.

It will thus be seen that the administrative sanction under this Act is very much stronger than was the case under earlier legislation. This, in conjunction with the activities of employees' safety representatives, may well bring an era of greater safety at work.

27 Other protection at work

Several statutes protect the interests of employees at work, or in connection with their work.

The Truck Acts

The Truck Acts 1831–1941 provide that the wages of manual workers must be paid in cash, not in kind. Such wages must also be paid in full, without deduction of any kind – except for statutory deductions such as income tax, national insurance and the like. An employer who is owed a debt by an employee cannot deduct the amount of that debt from wages. No fines may be imposed in respect of bad workmanship or for disciplinary reasons, unless such right has been included in the employee's contract of service.

These rules, however, will not make it illegal for an employer to set aside amounts taken from wages at the employee's request for them to be paid to third parties, e.g. subscriptions to a trade union or to some other body.

The Truck Acts apply only to manual workers and shop assistants, but the legal requirement to pay wages in cash is sometimes found to be inconvenient for a variety of reasons, including those of security. Accordingly, the Payment of Wages Act 1960 has made it permissible to pay wages by cheque, banker's order, or money order, provided the employee agrees in writing, and provided that no additional charge is made for this service by the employer. Any manual worker may give four weeks' written notice to cancel this arrangement and thus to revert to cash payments.

Sex discrimination

The Sex Discrimination Act makes sex discrimination unlawful in employment, in education, in the provision of goods and services, and in the disposal and management of premises. The Act sets up a body called the Equal Opportunities Commission to enforce the legislation and to promote equality of opportunity between the sexes. It has a discretion to assist individuals who consider that they have been discriminated against. The address of the Commission is given at the end of this book (see page 448).

Cases involving discrimination in matters concerning employment may be taken to an industrial tribunal. Discrimination in other fields is dealt with by the county courts.

Direct sex discrimination occures where a person treats a woman, on grounds of her sex, less favourably than he would treat a man.

Indirect sex discrimination occurs where there is treatment which appears to be equal as between the sexes, but which is in fact discriminatory in its effect on one sex, i.e. where there is a condition to be complied with which applies to either sex, but which it is more difficult for women to comply with than it would be for men. An example would be where there is a condition of employment that all applicants must be six feet tall.

The Act forbids any discrimination against married persons in the field of employment. No married person must be treated less favourably than an unmarried person. No person may be discriminated against merely because he or she has asserted rights under this Act or under the Equal Pay Act.

It is unlawful for any employer to discriminate in relation to any employment by him in Great Britain, or in any recruitment of employees.

Exceptions are made from these rules in cases where there is a genuine occupational qualification for the job (not being a matter of physical strength or stamina). This would apply, for example, to employment in the dramatic profession, or employment as attendant in a changing-room or lavatory. Here, considerations of authenticity, or of decency, would be valid reasons for discrimination between the sexes.

Exemption from the provisions of this Act is made where there is employment in a private household or in a small firm employing not more than five persons in total.

The Act does not apply to any arrangements concerning special treatment of women in connection with pregnancy or childbirth; or to any arrangements relating to death, retirement, or pensions schemes.

Equal pay

The Equal Pay Act came into force at the same time as the Sex Discrimination Act, in 1975, and is to be read in conjunction with it. The Equal Opportunities Commission has the duty of overseeing the enforcement of both Acts, but anyone may take a complaint to an industrial tribunal without obtaining the consent of the Commission.

The purpose of this Act is to prevent discrimination between men and women in relation to the terms and conditions of employment.

Accordingly, every contract of service must provide for equality of treatment, and any contract which does not contain such a provision will now, by statute, be deemed to contain what is called an 'equality clause'.

This means that where a woman is employed on like work with a man in the same employment, her contract must be not less favourable than his. Any difference between the two contracts will be justified *only* if that difference is due to some cause other than the difference of sex.

If a woman is employed on work that is rated as *equivalent* (in terms of effort, skill, or decision) to work done by men, such a woman is to be regarded as being employed on *like* work: (a) if the work done is broadly of the same kind, so that the differences are not of practical importance, and (b) if the jobs concerned have been given an equal value (as regards effort, skill or decision) as a result of a work study carried out to evaluate the work of both sexes.

These rules of law are now supplemented by the provisions of Article 119 of the Treaty of Rome (the basic document of the European Common Market) which prevails over our own legislation in this field.

By Article 119 men and women must receive equal pay for doing equal work, whether they are doing the equal work at the same time or at any other time. Hence a woman does not have to point to a man currently doing equal work. If a former male employee got more pay for doing such work, and a woman currently is paid less than he was, she is being discriminated against, and can bring a case to the industrial tribunal.

By the Act, any collective agreement which regulates rates of wages must now contain an 'equality clause', and so must all pay-structures which fix terms and conditions of employment. Any dispute concerning such structures or collective agreements in this matter may be referred, by any of the parties to them, or by the Secretary of State, to the Central Arbitration Committee established under the Employment Protection Act 1975.

Racial discrimination

The Race Relations Act forbids discrimination on racial grounds. It sets up a Commission for Racial Equality to supervise the enforcement of the Act, and to give assistance to organizations working to promote race equality. (For the address of the Commission see the list on page 447.)

Complaints concerning discrimination on grounds of race may be taken to an industrial tribunal, provided that the discrimination relates to the field of employment. Race discrimination in other spheres goes to the courts.

Discrimination may be direct, or it may be indirect – these terms are defined on page 244. 'Racial grounds' means colour, race, nationality, or ethnical or national origins. It is thus a wide term.

The Act makes it unlawful for any employer to discriminate, on grounds of race, in offering employment or in the terms of employment – including any benefits, opportunities of training or of promotion, or in matters relating to dismissal or termination of employment.

There are some exceptions, but only in cases where membership of a particular race or racial group is required for authenticity, as in dramatic performances, or in the preparation of food for consumption in a particular setting (e.g. kosher meat).

Application of the Act to other bodies in employment field

The Act forbids racial discrimination by trade unions, vocational and professional bodies, or by employment agencies, in matters relating to admission to membership, provision of benefits, or giving of services.

Regulation of hours of work

In general the law does not regulate the hours of work of adult males. There are exceptions to this. For example the Mines and Quarries Act limits the number of hours that may be spent underground in any one day to not more than seven, and the Road Haulage Act limits the number of hours that any driver may be on duty in any one day.

In industrial employment the hours of work of women, young persons, and children are limited by several Acts.

Thus, for example, no woman or young person may be employed in any factory for more than 48 hours in any week, or for more than 5 hours continuously without a break of at least ten minutes, or for more than 9 hours in any one day. The number of hours of overtime is limited and even then it can generally be worked only with the approval of the Secretary of State. Women and young persons may not be employed on night shifts in factories. A young person is one under eighteen years of age, but over school age.

A few occupations are forbidden to women. Thus, they cannot be employed in underground coal-mining, nor in certain processes relating to the annealing of glass or handling of lead.

The employment of children is closely controlled by law. 'Children' means persons who are of compulsory school age. They must not work in any industrial establishment (mine, factory, or workshop). They may not be employed at all for more than two hours on any school day. Local authorities have power to make rules regulating the employment of children in their area and these have the force of law. Special regulations apply to the employment of children in the entertainment industry.

28 The ending of employment

Where a contract of employment is for a fixed period it will automatically come to an end at the expiry of that period. Where, as is usually the case, the contract is for an indeterminate period the employment is brought to an end by either party's giving the appropriate notice to the other.

This chapter is about the form and length of notice; the remedies for wrongful and unfair dismissal; and about other rights that may arise on the ending of employment.

Notice under the contract

The appropriate period of such notice will be the period which is specified in the contract itself. If the period is not specified in the contract, then it will be implied from custom or usage in the industry, trade or profession concerned. Thus, it was held in one case that a hairdresser's assistant who was paid by the week was entitled to one week's notice; whilst in another, a musician was held to be entitled to two weeks' notice; for such periods were customary in the occupations concerned.

Where there is neither an express term nor an implied term in the contract, the period of notice will be what is reasonable in the circumstances. Decisions of the courts indicate that in such cases the status of the employee will be important. Thus a newspaper reporter has been held entitled to one month's notice, a foreign correspondent to six months' notice, and an editor to twelve months' notice.

Unless the engagement is for a fixed period of time, there is no employment which cannot be brought to an end by the giving of notice by one party to the other. There is no such thing as 'permanent employment', as is sometimes fondly imagined to exist by employees who have become members of the employer's 'permanent staff' or have been admitted to membership of a pension scheme operated by the employer. All such employment can be terminated by the giving of appropriate notice, and without any obligation to give reasons for it, still less to justify it.

Notice under the Employment Protection Act

The above rules of the common law have, however, been modified by recent statutes, the provisions of which are now set out in the Employment Protection (Consolidation) Act 1978.

As we have already seen (page 222), this Act requires the employer to give to the employee a note outlining certain particulars applicable to the contract, including the length of notice to be given by either party. The Act also sets out certain minimum periods of notice to be given to terminate the employment.

The statutory minimum period of notice to be given by an employee is one week; but the minimum period of notice to be given by the employer will vary with the length of the employee's service. These periods are as follows:

- not less than one week's notice if the period of continuous employment is less than two years;
- not less than one week's notice for each year of employment if the period of continuous employment is two years or more but less than twelve years;
- not less than twelve weeks' notice if the period of continuous employment is twelve years or more.

None of these statutory minimum periods will come into effect, however, until the employment has lasted four weeks or more; but thereafter the minimum periods set out in the Act will prevail over any contrary provision in the contract of service, unless the contract provides that the employer must give a period of notice at least one week more than the minimum laid down in the Act.

It will be seen therefore that if, for example, a contract of service provides that one month's notice of termination is to be given by either party, the provisions of the contract will prevail over those of the Act until the employment has continued for five years so far as concerns the appropriate notice to be given by the employer, while the provisions of the contract will always prevail over those of the Act in respect of the notice to be given by the employee.

The Act's requirements concerning minimum length of notice do not affect any rights of either party to terminate the contract of service without notice where the other party has committed a serious breach of the contract.

Unfair dismissal

As we have already seen (page 247), at common law any contract of service could be terminated by proper notice given by one party to the other. No reason needed to be given. An employer could terminate the employment of the employee for good reason, bad reason, or no reason at all; all the law required was that appropriate notice should be given. Even where dismissal was wrongful it remained effective, for no court of law has power to order any person either to employ or to be employed. If, therefore, an employee was dismissed without notice in circumstances in which notice should have been given (i.e. where he was dismissed in breach of contract) the only remedy open to that employee was to sue for the amount of money which he would have earned during the appropriate period of notice he ought to have had. This was poor consolation indeed.

Statement of reasons

Now, under the provisions of the Employment Protection (Consolidation) Act 1978, every qualified employee is entitled on the termination of his employment to request from his employer a written statement of the reasons for his dismissal, whether the termination was with or without notice, or where (if the employment was for a fixed term) the term of employment expires without being renewed. This right arises after twenty-six weeks' continuous employment.

Right not to be unfairly dismissed

In addition, every qualified employee has the right not to be unfairly dismissed by his employer, whether that dismissal occurs with or without notice or by the expiry of a fixed-term contract without renewal, or even because of the employee's termination of the contract by reason of the employer's conduct.

This last form of termination is called 'constructive dismissal'. It occurs when the employee himself terminates the contract because of (and only because of) an employer's breach of contract.

The right not to be unfairly dismissed arises when the employee has completed fifty-two weeks of continuous service under a contract providing for not less than sixteen hours' employment per week. (There are some exceptions to this rule, for even if the contract of a qualified employee is changed to provide less than sixteen – but more than eight – hours a week, that employee's rights in this matter will be preserved for the six months following the change; and even a contract for eight or more – but less than sixteen – hours a week will suffice to give these rights where the employee concerned has been continuously employed for five years or more.)

Certain types of employment are excluded from the provisions set out above. Among these excluded types are employment wholly or mainly outside Great Britain, employment as a police constable, and employment as a registered dockworker. There are also certain exceptions in the case of small firms employing fewer than twenty employees (see page 261).

How unfairness of dismissal is determined

The jurisdiction in complaints of unfair dismissal has been placed by the statute into the hands of industrial tribunals. Such matters are not within the jurisdiction of the courts, except where there is an appeal on a point of law. (The procedure for appeals is dealt with on page 253.)

Any employee who believes that he has been unfairly dismissed may, provided he has the necessary period of qualifying service, make application to have his case considered by an industrial tribunal by sending the appropriate form to the Central Office of the Industrial Tribunals for England and Wales, at 93 Ebury Bridge Road, London SW1W 8RE. The application must be made within three months of the dismissal. That office will invite the employer concerned to submit his 'notice of appearance', indicating whether or not he proposes to contest the claim, and outlining his reasons for doing so. The Central Office will then arrange for the case to be heard at the most appropriate local centre at which sessions of the industrial tribunals take place.

The tribunal is composed of three poeple. The chairman is legally qualified; the other two members are people appointed by virtue of their industrial experience. Normally one of these members has a trade union background and the other a management background.

In determining whether the dismissal of the employee was fair or unfair, the employer must show:

- what was the principal reason for the dismissal; and
- that this reason was one of the reasons set out in the Act.

The reasons set out in the Act are reasons relating to:

- the capability or qualifications of the employee to do the work he was employed to do;
- the conduct of the employee;
- the redundancy of the employee;
- the inability of the employee to continue to work without giving rise to the contravention of some duty or restriction imposed by an Act of Parliament;
- some other substantial reason of a kind such as to justify the dismissal of an employee from the position which he held.

If the reason shown by the employer is not one or more of the kinds set out above then the dismissal will be held to be unfair.

Even where the reason is shown to be one or more of those set out above, the tribunal must then determine whether it is satisfied that, in all the circumstances of the case, the employer acted reasonably in treating that reason as sufficient to justify the dismissal.

The 1978 Act provided that the burden of showing that he acted reasonably rested upon the employer, but the Employment Act 1980 amended the 1978 Act in such a way as to remove this burden, leaving it to the tribunal to draw its own conclusion from the evidence given by the contending parties.

In reaching its decision the tribunal will not have regard to how its members would have handled the situation had they been in the position of the employer, but rather to whether the decision of the employer was within the range of actions which a reasonable employer might be expected to take in the circumstances. In considering these circumstances the tribunal will take into account the size and resources of the employer's business, and the general manner in which the dismissal was handled.

Unless the tribunal is satisfied that the dismissal was in all the circumstances reasonable, that dismissal will be held to be unfair. (Certain reasons for dismissal are automatically unfair; see pages 261–2.)

The remedies available for unfair dismissal

If the tribunal finds that the dismissal was fair it will make an order accordingly and dismiss the case. Normally no costs are awarded to either party. Each party must therefore pay his own costs for any legal or other representative he may have engaged. If, however, it is shown that any application for a hearing is frivolous or vexatious, the tribunal may impose costs upon the party concerned. However, a party will not be penalized merely because he held a mistaken, but sincere, belief in the justice of his complaint.

If the tribunal finds that the dismissal was unfair it will invite the applicant to indicate what remedy he desires. The remedies available are reinstatement, re-engagement, or compensation.

Reinstatement or re-engagement

In considering whether to make an order for reinstatement or for re-engagement the tribunal will take into consideration not only the wishes of the employee but also whether it is practicable for the employer to comply with such an order. The tribunal will also take into account the extent (if any) to which the employee contributed to the dismissal and, if he did so, whether it would be just to make such an order. In fact, orders for reinstatement or re-engagement are made in only a very small number of cases. Where, however, such an order is made and the employer unreasonably refuses to comply with it, then the tribunal will order the payment of an additional sum by way of compensation. The maximum amount of such additional sum is fixed by regulations which may be amended by the Secretary of State from time to time. As from 1 February 1982 this maximum is £7,000. It should, however, be noted that if the employer offers to reinstate the complainant and the complainant unreasonably refuses to accept that offer, the tribunal will reduce the amount of the basic award (see below) which would have been justified by the unfair dismissal. In practice few, if any, cases have resulted in such an award.

Compensation

The most common remedy for unfair dismissal is compensation, though here also the tribunal will have regard to the extent (if any) to which the employee's conduct contributed to or subsequently excused his dismissal, and will adjust its award accordingly.

The award will consist of a basic award (which is an amount dependent upon the length of the employment) and a compensatory award related to the loss incurred. The basic award ranges from a minimum of *nil* to a maximum amount of £4,050; and the compensatory award ranges from *nil* to a maximum amount of £7,000. As indicated above, these maxima are set by regulations that may be amended by the Secretary of State from time to time. The figures given here are those in force from 1 February 1982.

In practice the amounts awarded are quite modest, generally being only of a few hundred pounds. In 1978 the modal (i.e. the most common) award was in the range £300–£750; and less than one-tenth of one per cent of applicants received more than £6,000. Any idea that huge sums are regularly awarded by tribunals is clearly quite erroneous.

Appeals

From the decision of an industrial tribunal an appeal may be made by either party to the Employment Appeal Tribunal. Such an appeal must be on a question of law and must be lodged within six weeks of the date of receipt of the decision of the industrial tribunal. The Appeal Tribunal does not redetermine the facts of any case, but considers only the application of the law to those facts. The facts always remain as found by the industrial tribunal, though the conclusion to be drawn from those facts is always a matter of law. The Appeal Tribunal is made up of a High Court judge and two lay members. No costs are normally payable in respect of such appeals, though there is power to impose costs where the Appeal Tribunal finds that the conduct of a party is frivolous or vexatious.

From the Employment Appeal Tribunal a further appeal lies to the Court of Appeal, and from that court (by leave) to the House of Lords. In the Court of Appeal and in the House of Lords costs are payable in the normal way.

Other rights

Redundancy

Where an employee's service is terminated by his employer because of redundancy a qualified employee will become entitled to a redundancy payment from the employer. Such qualification will arise as soon as the employee has completed a minimum period of 104 weeks of continuous employment.

The amount of the payment depends upon the length of continuous service and upon the age of the employee. No service will count unless the employee was at least 18 years of age, and no account will be taken of any service given by any employee who, if a man, has attained the age of 65 or, if a woman, has attained the age of 60.

Within these age limits, the right to redundancy payment is as follows: for service between the ages of 18 and 22, half a week's pay for each year of continuous employment; for service between the ages of 22 and 41, one week's pay for each such year; and for service between the ages of 41 and 64 (59 in the case of a woman), one and half weeks' pay for each such year.

Not more than twenty years of service may be taken into account, and the maximum weekly wage allowable is £135 (though that amount may be varied by order of the Secretary of State from time to time).

It can thus be seen that the maximum sum receivable is made up of payment in respect of twenty years' service after the age of 41 at the rate of £135 per week, i.e. £4,050.

Where a man becomes redundant after the age of 64 but before he is 65, or where a woman does so after the age of 59 but before she is 60, the amount receivable will be diminished by one-twelfth for every month which has passed since that 64th (or 59th) birthday. As has been indicated above, redundancy which occurs after a man has passed the age of 65, or a woman has passed 60, will attract no payment at all.

Definition of redundancy

Redundancy is defined in the Employment Protection (Consolidation) Act 1978. A person is to be taken as having been dismissed by reason of redundancy if his dismissal is attributable to:

- the fact that his employer has ceased, or intends to cease, to carry on the business for which the employee was employed, or has ceased or intends to cease carrying on that business in the place where the employee is employed; or
- the fact that the requirements of that business for employees to carry out work of a particular kind, or in a particular place, have ceased, or diminished, or are expected to cease or diminish.

Dismissal is defined in the same manner as in the section dealing with unfair dismissal, above.

Transfer of the business

It is a principle of the common law that the contract of service is a personal relationship, and that such a contract cannot be transferred by either party to someone else. Hence if an employer ceases to employ, the contract of service automatically comes to an end, so that any employee who is otherwise qualified would be eligible to claim redundancy payment.

The 1978 Act, however, deals with this matter by making provision to ensure that where a business is transferred as a going concern to a new owner and that new owner offers to renew the employee's contract of service on the same terms as before, or upon new terms which constitute an offer of suitable employment, then the employee will lose any right to redundancy payment if he unreasonably refuses that offer.

Redundancy payment is similarly denied to a redundant employee if at the time of his dismissal, or within four weeks of it, his former employer makes an offer such as is mentioned above and it is unreasonably refused by the employee. Until recently, however, if a business was transferred to new owners its employees had little employment protection (other than a contractual period of notice and rights, if any, to redundancy payments) unless the new owners offered to keep them on. Now, by the provisions of the Transfer of Undertakings (Protection of Employment) Regulations 1981, where a business is sold to new owners all the employees will be transferred (under their existing conditions of service) to the new owners along with the business, and any existing collective agreements with trade unions will be transferred also.

It can be seen that these rules abrogate the principle of the common law that contracts of service are not assignable.

The new Regulations make special provision for the situation in which the assets of a company which is in liquidation are transferred to a subsidiary that is then sold off to a new owner. These provisions are designed to prevent the occurrence of a situation which sometimes occurred in such circumstances, in that the former employing company no longer had any assets from which to meet the cost of redundancy payments, so that these eventually had to be paid by the Secretary of State, i.e. by the taxpayers at large. Now the new owner will take over such portion of the workforce as he wishes to retain, whilst the remainder will be deemed to have been made redundant immediately before the company's assets are transferred to him.

Any dispute as to qualification for redundancy payment, or as to its amount, may be taken to an industrial tribunal, which has powers to determine the matter.

There are two other points to bear in mind: first, an employer who has given an employee notice of termination of employment may require that employee to work out his period of notice. If the employee wishes to leave earlier than the date of expiry of the notice, he must advise the employer in writing of his intention to leave earlier, and the employer may then require the employee to withdraw that notice, and advise him that he (the employer) will contest the right to redundancy payment. If the employee does not comply with the employer's requirements the employee will lose any right to redundancy payment unless an industrial tribunal determines otherwise.

The second point is that no right to redundancy payment will arise where an employee is dismissed (whether with or without notice) because of conduct which constitutes a breach of contract by the employee.

Lay-off and short-time working

Neither party to a contract of service has the right to suspend the contract unless the contract provides for it. Any lay-off or suspension will therefore constitute a repudiation of the contract so as to terminate it, and any qualified employee thus laid off or suspended could claim redundancy payment. The 1978 Act, however, provides that where an employee's remuneration depends upon work done and he is given no work to do in any week, or where because of lack of work he earns in any week less than half a normal week's pay, such an employee may give written notice to his employer of his intention to claim redundancy payment. To be effective, the lay-off or short-time working must have lasted for four weeks up to the date of the notice or for a series of six weeks or more within the last thirteen weeks.

The employee must also give notice to terminate the employment, such notice being that required by his contract, provided it is not less than one week's notice.

Thereafter, the contract will be regarded as having terminated by reason of lay-off or of short-time working, and the employee will be eligible to receive redundancy payment.

However, this right will be lost if at the date of service of the notice of intention to claim payment there was a reasonable probability that within four weeks of that time there would ensue a period of full employment lasting not less than thirteen weeks. It is for the employer to show this reasonable probability, and he will not be able to do this unless within seven days of the service of notice to claim payment he gives the employee written notice of his intention to contest that claim. Even where the employer has served such a counter-notice he will not be able to contest the claim if the lay-off or short-time working continues for the next four weeks following the service of the notice of intention to claim.

Change of place of work

As can be seen, redundancy will occur if there is a cessation of work for the employee at the place where he is employed, but this will not be so if the contract of service contains an express (or an implied) term that the employer may require the employee to work elsewhere. Hence whether an employee will, or will not, be eligible to receive redundancy payment will depend upon the construction of the contract. If under the contract the employee can be required to work in some other place and he does not do so, then he will not be eligible to receive redundancy payment, for he will be regarded as having left his employment voluntarily and in breach of contract.

No redundancy payment is available for persons who leave their employment voluntarily, unless that leaving is as a result of 'constructive' dismissal, i.e. as a result of a breach of contract on the part of the employer.

Who pays?

The burden of making redundancy payments falls upon the employer. Where an employer is insolvent and the whole or part of the payment remains unpaid the employee may claim against the Secretary of State who has power to pay the requisite amount out of the Redundancy Fund. The Secretary of State has the duty also of making refunds to employers who have made payments, provided that those payments were made in accordance with the provisions of the Act. There will be no refund where any payment was not obligatory under the Act. This is to ensure that there can be no collusion, at the expense of the state, in an employer's payment to a redundant employee of more than is provided in the Act. If an employer gives what is sometimes called a 'golden handshake' he must do so at his own expense.

29 Enforcing rights at work

If you have a grievance at work there are many different ways of trying to get it put right. Some of them are set out in this chapter.

Grievance procedure

Every employer is obliged by law to inform employees of the name of the person to whom grievances relating to employment may be referred, and the nature of the method of procedure. If you do not have a copy of this information, ask for it, and then act in accordance with its instructions.

Trade union help

If a trade union operates and is recognized at your place of work, it will usually have a shop steward or other representative there. His/her duty on behalf of members is to represent them in any discussion or difference with the management. Usually the best thing is to raise your problem with your immediate supervisor; and them, if agreement is not reached, to call in the shop steward even though you intend to use the grievance procedure, so that the shop steward is conversant with the issue and can accompany you or represent you if the procedure so allows.

The full-time union official

If you are a member of a trade union, you or the shop steward may refer any issue to its attention. Any such reference or request for assistance should preferably be sent in writing to the official at the union's local office. The address of that local office will be found in the telephone directory. Though it may be possible to phone the official, you should remember that a busy official may well be out of his office dealing with other cases like yours, and that a letter makes a more permanent record of your request.

The union official should in any case be always advised if your grievance is one that is shared by other members of the union.

Industrial tribunals

Application for a matter to be dealt with by an industrial tribunal must be made on the proper form. Such a form of application can be obtained from any government Jobcentre in your locality, or from the Central Office of the Industrial Tribunals, 93 Ebury Bridge Road, London SW1W 8RE. The instructions on the form are quite simple.

If you decide to take your case to a tribunal, make sure that your case is submitted in time and that it is worthy of attention. Costs may be awarded against applicants whose cases are frivolous or vexatious. One way of ensuring that your case has merit, and of obtaining professional representation, is to ask your union to handle it for you. If the union refuses to do so, you will not lose the right to press your case, but the refusal may indicate that your claim is not as well founded as you thought. It goes without saying that only members of a union normally can expect to be represented by it.

Before any case is heard by a tribunal, conciliation between the parties is usually undertaken by a conciliation officer of ACAS. No report of what happens during conciliation is given to the industrial tribunal, for such matters are confidential to the parties. If, however, an offer is made to you by your employer in the course of conciliation, give careful attention to it – even though you are not obliged to accept any offer and may insist on your case being heard by the tribunal. Many a person has refused an offer in conciliation and then has found that the tribunal awards less, or even dismisses the case. This, of course, is not always so; but it is worth remembering.

Pre-hearing assessment

You should note that a tribunal has power to hold a preliminary inquiry to consider whether a case is likely to be successful. This is called a pre-hearing assessment, and if it takes place the parties concerned will be notified of it and invited to give their views. If the tribunal considers that the case of the complainant, or the contention of the other party, has no reasonable prospect of success then the tribunal will advise the person concerned that though he can still claim his right to a full hearing of the case he will run the risk of costs being awarded against him if his case is not successful. This rule of procedure came into effect on 1 October 1980.

Courts of law

Industrial tribunals do not deal with issues of contract, e.g. non-payment of wages due, or failure to give appropriate notice of termination, save in so far as such behaviour is evidence of unfairness of dismissal. Claims for payments due are matters for a county court, or the High Court.

Similarly industrial tribunals do not deal with claims for compensation for personal injury. These are matters for county courts or the High Court, depending upon the amount of compensation sought.

Though every litigant has a right to present his case in person, you would be well advised never to go to law without first obtaining professional advice and representation. Most trade unions maintain a legal department which gives legal advice and/or representation to members – though no union will undertake to litigate on every issue that may be presented to it. Most union members find, however, that legal advice and aid are among the greatest advantages of union membership. Application for such aid is normally made to the head office of the union, through the local branch secretary, who will usually provide you with the appropriate form.

If you wish to act independently of a union, you may consult any local solicitor. His name will be found in the Yellow Pages of your phone directory. He can also advise you of the Law Society's legal aid scheme (and see page 422).

Claims for benefit

If you are absent from work though industrial injury or disease, or are out of work altogether, you may (if properly qualified) have a right to national insurance industrial injury benefit, or to unemployment benefit. Inquiry should first be made of your local Jobcentre, which will then direct you to the appropriate office of the Department of Health and Social Security, by whom such payments are made.

If you are dissatisfied with their ruling on the matter, you may appeal to a Social Insurance Local Appeal Tribunal (*note*: not an industrial tribunal). If you are in a union, it will advise and represent you there.

Qualifying periods for complaint

1 Redundancy payments (see page 253)

There must have been not less than two years (104 weeks) of continuous employment in the service of the same employer, or of that employer and an associated employer, or of his successor in the same business organization.

2 Claims in respect of unfair dismissal (see page 249)
There must have been not less than one year of continuous employment, in circumstances similar to those required for redundancy.

There is an exception in the case of small firms which employ twenty or fewer employees. Here, any new employee engaged after 1 October 1980 will require to have completed two years of employment in order to bring a claim concerning unfair dismissal. This exception will, however, cease if during that employment the employer's total workforce at any time exceeds twenty employees. The normal period of one year will then apply.

3 Dismissals which are automatically unfair
No minimum period of employment is necessary to bring a claim for unfair dismissal where the dismissal is automatically unfair. Under the Employment Act 1982 a dismissal is automatically unfair if it is for any of the following causes:

- because the employee was, or proposed to become, a member of an independent union;
- because he had taken part, or proposed to take part, in the activities of an independent union at an appropriate time; or
- because he was not a member of any union, or any particular union or one of such unions, or refused to become or remain a member.

The dismissal will be fair where the employee concerned refuses to become or to remain, a member of a union, or of a specified union, where by agreement or practice the employer operates a 'closed shop' (called in the Act 'a union membership agreement'). Even where there is a closed shop the dismissal will still be unfair if:

- the employee objects on grounds of conscience or other deeply held convictions to membership of any, or any particular, union;
- he was in the employment before the closed shop came into effect and remained a non-unionist;
- the union membership agreement has not been approved by a secret ballot of the employees involved within a period of five years prior to the dismissal.

The new Act provides that such ballots must be taken every five years if the union membership agreement (closed shop) is to remain in force. In any first ballot on this matter taken on or after 15

August 1980 the agreement will be regarded as approved only if not less than 80 per cent of those to be covered by the agreement vote in favour of it. In any subsequent ballot, not less than 85 per cent of those who actually do vote must vote in favour, if approval is to be given. Such majorities are, in fact, remarkably high; and they are clearly designed to make it difficult to create or to maintain a closed shop.

The Employment Act 1982, which made the above provisions, also applies retrospectively, in that the government will compensate those employees who were dismissed between 1974 and 1980 for failing to comply with the provisions of a closed shop, where that dismissal would have been unfair under the terms of the 1980 Act. Application to the Secretary of State for such compensation must be made by 27 October 1983 (unless the Secretary of State extends the date), and claims will be determined by the Secretary of State – not, it will be noted, by an industrial tribunal.

Where dismissal takes place in any of the circumstances which make that dismissal automatically unfair, special provisions are made for compensation, which will be on a higher scale than that ordinarily available.

Thus the special minimum basic award (subject to reduction where the applicant's conduct contributed to his dismissal) will be £2,000; and there will be a compensatory award of up to £7,000. If the dismissed employee applies for an order of reinstatement but the tribunal does not make such an order, the special award will be 104 weeks' pay subject to a minimum of £10,000 and a maximum of £20,000. Where reinstatement is ordered, but the employer refuses to comply with it, the special award will be 156 weeks' pay subject to a maximum of £15,000; but such a higher award will not be made if the employer can show that reinstatement is not practicable.

It should be noted that, just as in all other cases of compensation, the tribunal may reduce an award because of the complainant's conduct; and that any award will be reduced by one-twelfth for each month that the complainant's service was after the normal statutory retirement age (fifty-nine for a woman, and sixty-five for a man).

A further point to be noted carefully is that where an employee has been dismissed because of a breach in the rules applicable to union membership agreements (i.e. where he was unfairly dismissed for failure or refusal to be a union member, or a member of a particular union) then he may 'join' as respondents to his complaint those persons or the union(s) that brought pressure upon the employer to discharge him. So also the employer may join such persons or union(s); and compensation may be ordered to be paid by them.

4 Claims relating to maternity

No specified period of employment is required in respect of a claim that an employer has refused to give time off with pay to a pregnant employee to enable her to attend an appointment for the purpose of receiving ante-natal care.

Two years of continuous employment (up to the beginning of the eleventh week before the expected week of confinement) are required for a woman to be able to claim (a) maternity pay; and (b) the right to return to work. A woman intending to exercise her right to return to work after the birth of her child must inform her employer in *writing*. This must be done at least 21 days before leaving, and she must give the expected date of the birth. Seven weeks after the expected birth, the employer may write to the woman asking her for written confirmation of her intention to return to work, warning her that she must reply within 14 days or will lose her right to return.

The woman must also give at least three weeks' written notice of the day she intends to return to work.

A dismissal merely because of pregnancy is automatically unfair. So is a refusal to re-employ a woman who has the right to return to work after her period of absence on account of maternity. To this there is an exception. This applies to small firms which employ five or fewer employees in any case where it is not reasonably practicable for that firm to offer the woman her old job back, or other suitable work on the same terms, on her return to employment. In such a case dismissal will not be unfair. So also, where any employer finds it not reasonably practical to give the woman her old job back, or where in such a situation he offers her other suitable work on reasonable terms, and the woman either takes the alternative job or unreasonably refuses it, dismissal from the old job will not be unfair.

30 Trade unions and trade disputes

Collective bargaining

Although the legal basis of the relationship between employer and employee is the contract of employment or service, few employees are in fact afforded the opportunity of negotiating the terms of that contract. All that happens in most cases is that the would-be employee is given the opportunity to accept, or reject, an offer of employment on the terms presented to him.

The actual contents of the contract and the manner in which it is to be carried out are usually determined by a process of collective bargaining carried on between the employer (or the employer's association) and trade unions representing the interests of workers. This is not always the case, for sometimes the employer alone decides what terms he will offer to applicants for employment, but joint collective bargaining is the rule in most sections of British industry.

Such collective bargaining may be carried on at national level, e.g. through joint national councils, or at regional level, or at local level, e.g. through negotiations in the workplace. These processes may be formal, or they may be quite informal.

Since the wages and the other conditions of employment in one job, trade or industry always have some relationship with those in other jobs, trades or industries (because of the relative demand for labour and capital), the effect of such collective bargaining extends far beyond the occupations in which organized collective bargaining is carried on.

Today a vast structure of bargaining bodies exists to promote and to carry on collective bargaining. These arrive at agreements which are then incorporated into, or used to determine, the contents of individual contracts of service.

The collective agreement or bargain is not itself a contract (unless the parties expressly declare it to be so – which is rare), so the agreement is not legally enforceable as between the parties to it. However, they tend to observe the terms agreed because of their interests in making such bargaining effective and avoiding industrial disputes.

Wages councils

In some sections of industry employers and unions are poorly organized and workers may tend to be badly paid. In such cases the Secretary of State may, on representations being made to him, set up a national bargaining body, called a wages council. Such a council is normally made up of representatives of employers and of employees, together with other persons appointed by the Minister. Those other persons are often in a position to influence the deliberations of the council in arriving at its decision.

Such a council has the function of determining the remuneration and terms of employment of workers in the industry concerned. Its decision is embodied in an order. That order obliges every employer in the industry to pay wages and to observe conditions of employment which are not less favourable than those set out in the order. If he does not do so, the matter can be taken to court and the court will enforce the order. Wages councils currently cover about three million workers in more than forty industries.

Wages councils thus consist of a machinery for the establishment of minimum rates of pay and conditions of service. However, it should be noted that there is in Britain no law or legal machinery for establishing general minimum rates of remuneration (as there is in some countries). Our courts of law do not have the function of deciding what is the right remuneration for any form of employment. In general in this country both employers and unions prefer free collective bargaining to any form of government wage regulation through the medium of statutory rules or courts of law – or even of wages councils.

This is not to say that the government does not have a great influence upon wages and conditions of service, for it can not only determine the political and economic climate, but can – if it thinks fit – make laws to restrain rises in pay or prices, or to increase them. This, however, is a matter of political judgment, about which reasonable people may reasonably differ.

Conciliation and arbitration

For over one hundred years governments have sought to provide means by which industrial disputes may be resolved through the medium of conciliation or arbitration. Conciliation occurs where the parties to a dispute are assisted in arriving at a settlement by the services of a conciliator. Arbitration occurs where the parties agree to let some third person determine the outcome of the dispute between them.

At present these functions are carried out, on request, by the independent Advisory, Conciliation and Arbitration Service (ACAS) set up under the provisions of the Employment Protection Act 1975.

There is no compulsion to make use of conciliation or of arbitration, but in some industries the normal machinery of negotiation includes an agreement to take unresolved differences to arbitration and to abide by the outcome.

Trade unions and employers' associations

Trade unions and employers' associations have long existed in this country and they have enjoyed legal status for more than one hundred years. The statute law relating to trade unions and employers' associations is now set out in the Trade Unions and Labour Relations Acts of 1974–6, as amended by the Employment Acts 1980 and 1982.

The 1974 Act defines the term 'trade union' in some detail, the substance of which is that a trade union consists of an organization of workers, a principal purpose of which is the regulation of relations between those workers and employers or employers' associations. A body which consists of affiliated trade unions is itself a trade union within the meaning of the Act.

An employers' association is similarly defined, as an organization of employers or individual proprietors a principal purpose of which is the regulation of relations between employers and workers. A body which consists of employers' associations is itself an employers' association within the meaning of the Act.

It should be noted that there is nothing to prevent trade unions having purposes in addition to the principal one set out above. The same applies to employers' associations. Such additional purposes must, however, be properly authorized in the rules of the organization concerned, otherwise the spending of money for purposes not authorized by the rules can be restrained by the courts upon the application of any member.

Political funds

Special provisions apply in the case of the spending of funds by trade unions for certain political purposes. These rules are set out in the Trade Union Act 1913.

Thus if funds are to be used to promote the candidature of persons seeking public office (e.g. as members of Parliament or of local authorities), or are to be used in maintaining such persons, then a special fund called a political fund must be established for that purpose. Members who object to contributing to that fund must be excused from paying it (on giving due notice) and those members who are excused in this way must not suffer any loss of their normal rights as members of the union, except in relationship to the control and use of the political fund.

Contract of membership

The rules of a trade union (which must be made available to every member either free or on payment of a reasonable sum) constitute a contract between that member and the trade union. The content of that contract can of course be amended from time to time, as and when the rules themselves are amended in a manner prescribed in the rules themselves. Every member will be deemed to assent to such amendments of rules as may be properly made.

No member of a trade union may be subjected to any disciplinary penalty or be expelled from membership other than in strict accordance with the provisions of the union rules and in accordance with the requirements of natural justice.

Natural justice requires that any complaint must be drawn to the attention of the member proceeded against, that the member must be afforded an opportunity of presenting his side of the case, and the proceedings must be conducted in good faith. If a member is disciplined or expelled otherwise than in accordance with the union rules and the requirements of natural justice, then the courts can intervene to rectify the matter. No provision in the rules can exclude the jurisdiction of the courts.

Unreasonable exclusion from membership of a trade union, or unreasonable refusal of admission to membership of it, may now be made the subject of a complaint to an industrial tribunal, in any case where membership of a trade union is a condition for continued employment, i.e. where a 'closed shop' is in operation. This right was given by the Employment Act 1980.

Trade union rights at the workplace

The Employment Act 1982 provides that every employee shall have the right not to be penalized by his employer because of being or becoming a member of an independent trade union, or for taking part in the activities of such a trade union at any appropriate time. Appropriate time means outside working hours, or within working hours if consent is given by the employer and the union is one recognized by the employer.

Any penalization of an employee by the employer contrary to these provisions may be made the subject of complaint to an industrial tribunal. Any dismissal which is made because of the exercise of the rights given above is automatically regarded as an unfair dismissal. Note that no qualifying period of employment is required to achieve these rights (see page 261).

Special provisions apply, however, where there is an agreement that employees shall, as a condition of employment, be required by the employer to be in membership of a specified union or of one of a specified group of unions which is, or are, recognized by that employer. Dismissal for refusing to be a union member may then be fair, subject, however, to certain exceptions.

(This topic is dealt with on page 261.)

Trade unions normally appoint, or elect, workplace representatives. These are commonly called 'shop stewards'. Such representatives are given additional rights by the 1978 Act, in circumstances where the union concerned is recognized by the employer for bargaining purposes. Thus they must be given reasonable time off (with pay at their normal rates) to enable them to carry out union duties related to the industrial relations between the employer and the employees, or to undergo training (of a kind approved by the union or by the Trades Union Congress) in relation to those union duties.

Any failure by the employer to afford such facilities (or any dismissal because of using them) may be made the subject of complaint to an industrial tribunal.

Trade disputes

A trade dispute is defined by the Trade Union and Labour Relations Acts as any dispute between workers and employers, or between workers and workers, which is related to terms and conditions of employment; to engagement, non-engagement, suspension or termination of employment; to allocation of work or matters of discipline; to membership or non-membership of unions by workers; to facilities for union officials; to recognition by employers of unions; or to matters concerning machinery for consultation or negotiation on any of these matters. The Employment Act 1982 narrows this definition by excluding disputes between workers and workers, and by preventing trade unions or employers' associations from themselves being parties to such disputes. This means that the dispute must be between workers and their own employer. Further, the dispute must 'relate wholly or mainly' to the issues set out above, and not merely be 'connected with' them.

A trade dispute is thus a dispute or difference that concerns issues arising out of employment and the terms on which it is carried out. A dispute on a purely political issue is not a trade dispute: this was the decision in a case where employees of the BBC threatened to take strike action in protest at the system of apartheid operating in South Africa. The 1982 Act now excludes matters occurring outside Great Britain from being within the definition of a trade dispute, unless the people taking the action are likely to be affected by the outcome of the dispute.

However, where the consent of a Minister of the Crown is required to resolve any issue involving the matters set out above (for example concerning the rates of pay in the teaching profession), a dispute between workers and the Minister about such matters is still a trade dispute, even if the Minister is not the employer of those workers.

Rights given to participants in a trade dispute

Persons engaged in a trade dispute may take a variety of actions to persuade the other party to the dispute to accept their point of view and to settle the dispute on their terms. Such a dispute may be settled by negotiation, or by conciliation or arbitration. Sometimes, however, one or both of the parties may take what is sometimes called 'dispute action' or 'industrial action'; the workers may go on strike (with or without the approval of their union), or the employers may impose a lock-out.

A strike is a concerted refusal to work on the part of employees in order to compel their employer to accede to their demands.

A lock-out is a refusal by an employer to continue to employ in order to compel workers to accede to the employer's demands.

As explained earlier, any unilateral suspension of a contract of employment without the consent of the other party is a breach of that contract; and it entitles that other party to repudiate the contract and to claim damages for its breach.

Hence every strike or lock-out is normally a breach of contract. So an employer has a legal right to dismiss employees who take strike action. However, the employer must not, at least to begin with, 'pick and choose'. If he dismisses one of the strikers he must dismiss them all; and, for a period of three months after the dismissals, if he offers re-employment to one he must offer it to all. Selection of some strikers only for dismissal or re-engagement will allow the others to bring a claim for unfair dismissal. But once the three-month period is up, the Employment Act 1982 allows the employer a free hand. If he offers re-engagement to some of the strikers and not others, those not chosen cannot claim unfair dismissal.

The employer retains his common-law right to sue the strikers for damages. In this country it is extremely rare for an employer to do this, for persons who litigate are unlikely ever to resume cooperative relationships, while experience shows that normally both parties to a trade dispute expect employment to be resumed at some time, though perhaps upon new terms.

Inducement of breach of contract, and conspiracy

It is an actionable wrong for anyone to induce a party to a contract to breach that contract. 'Inducement' means any form of effective persuasion. Hence, at common law, anyone (including any trade union) who induces employees to strike in breach of their contracts commits a tort (actionable wrong) and may be sued for damages by the other party to the contract.

Where two or more persons agree to perform any wrongful act, or to do a lawful act in an unlawful manner, their agreement constitutes a conspiracy. If the wrongful activity is a criminal one, the result of that agreement is criminal conspiracy; if the wrongful activity is a tort or civil wrong, the result of the agreement is civil conspiracy. A combination of two or more people which induces a breach of contract is thus a civil conspiracy, and if damage (loss) results from it the person suffering that damage can bring a civil action for damages in compensation of the loss sustained.

Since a trade union is, of its very nature, a combination, any union-induced or union-supported strike would render the union liable in damages for civil conspiracy at common law. Statute has intervened therefore to give legal protection against these common-law liabilities by granting statutory immunity.

Statutory immunity

The Trade Union and Labour Relations Acts (as amended) provide that a person who, in contemplation or furtherance of a trade dispute, induces some other person to break a contract, or who threatens that a contract will be interfered with or be broken, shall not be liable to any action in tort. The Acts also provided that any act done by a combination of two or more persons, in contemplation or furtherance of a trade dispute, should not be actionable in tort if that act would not be actionable when done without such combination.

Trade unions, as such, were given additional immunity. No action in tort could be brought against a union in respect of any act done by it or done on its behalf. The Employment Act 1982 reduces the extent of this immunity. Henceforth unions, as organizations, will enjoy only the same degree of immunity from action as is enjoyed by individuals who are acting in contemplation or furtherance of the trade dispute in which they are involved. The union will be liable, however, only where the wrongful act complained of was authorized or endorsed by its executive committee or by a union official having actual or implied authority to authorize or endorse such an act. The act will not be treated as authorized or endorsed if it has been repudiated by the union executive committee or by an official who regularly attends its meetings; but that repudiation must be made as soon as practicable after it has come to their (or his) knowledge, and the person(s) purporting to authorize or to endorse the act have at once been notified in writing of the repudiation.

Where damages are awarded against a trade union they will be subject to certain financial limits, except in those cases in which some breach of duty on the part of the union has caused personal injury, or where the breach relates to the union's ownership, control or use of its property, e.g. personal injury caused by the negligent driving of a union car.

In those cases where financial limits apply, the maximum permissible damages will be related to the size of the union, ranging from a maximum of £10,000 where a union has fewer than 5,000 members, to a maximum of £250,000 where a union has 1,000,000 or more members.

The immunity thus given to individuals or unions who, in contemplation or pursuance of a trade dispute, induce a breach of contract relates only to the wrong of procuring that breach. It does not cover any other form of tort, such as trespass or conversion.

'Conversion' is a wrongful domination of some other person's property or wrongful denial of his rights of control over his own property. In *Prudential Insurance Co.* v. *Lorenz and Others* (1971) there was a dispute between the insurance company and its employees. In order to put pressure upon the employers, Lorenz and others persuaded collectors of insurance premiums to hold on to them and not to forward them to the company, pending the settlement of the dispute. The court held that the union officials, Lorenz and others, were not protected by the statutes, for they had committed the tort of conversion.

Action in furtherance of a trade dispute

Though many forms of action may be resorted to in furtherance of a trade dispute, many of such activities are regulated or limited by the law. The Conspiracy and Protection of Property Act 1875 forbids the use of violence or of intimidation, the endangering of life or limb, and the destruction of valuable property. It also forbids the persistent following of persons from place to place, or their being followed through the streets in a disorderly manner by two or more other persons, if this is done to compel the person followed from doing what he has a right to do. It is doubtful whether this Act is more than a statutory declaration of the position at common law.

One very common form of action in furtherance of a trade dispute is picketing. Pickets are persons who attend at or near a place of employment to persuade people to work or (more commonly) not to work. The Trade Union and Labour Relations Acts 1974–5, as amended by the Employment Act 1980, forbid the picketing of any person's residence, and restrict picketing to the pickets' own place of employment. An exception is made where the workers normally work at more than one place or at some place which it is not practicable to picket. In such a case picketing may be done at the employer's headquarters or at the place from which the work is directed. A further exception applies to trade union officials. These, though not themselves employees participating in the dispute, may join in the picketing, but only provided that they were elected or appointed to represent some or all of the workers in dispute. It should be noted that ex-employees are permitted to picket the place of work, but only if their discharge was one of the causes of the trade dispute. This extension of the right to picket was given by the Employment Act 1982.

Code of Practice

A Code of Practice has been drawn up by the Secretary of State to give guidance on this and related matters. The Code is not the law, but it can be taken into account in any legal proceedings concerning alleged breaches of the law in this sphere.

The Code draws attention to the existing duty of the police to prevent obstruction of the highway and to prevent breaches of the peace. It also draws attention to the fact that pickets have only the right of peaceful persuasion; they have no right to compel vehicles to stop, or to prevent persons from going to work.

The Code regards mass picketing as a form of intimidation, and it suggests that the number of pickets at any entrance should not exceed six, all of whom should be clearly identified and be under the control of an authorized union official. The Code also suggests that everyone has the right to cross a picket line without suffering subsequent penalty or disciplinary action – though this suggestion may well cause problems in the interpretation of union rules where the union has made a dispute official and binding on its members.

Secondary action

The primary parties to a trade dispute are the employer and the workers (or their union) involved; but very often other parties are involved, by having pressure put upon them by one or other of the primary parties. There may, for example, be boycotting (or 'blacking') of supplies or services provided by some other party to one or other of the primary parties. Action of this kind is called 'secondary action' and the Employment Act 1980 now regulates this.

This Act makes it generally illegal to induce a breach of a contract of employment, or to threaten to induce such a breach, where the employer concerned is not a party to the trade dispute. To this general provision there are, however, exceptions and in such exceptional cases secondary action will not be illegal. These are where the purpose of the secondary action was to prevent or to disrupt the supply of goods or services between an employer who is a party to the dispute and an employer who is party to the contract of employment to which the secondary action is directed; or, where the purpose of the secondary action is to prevent or to disrupt the supply of goods and services between any person and an associated employer of the employer who is party to the dispute.

In either case it must be shown that the secondary action was likely to achieve its purpose – a provision which is likely to pose some knotty problems for the courts in time to come.

Boycotts and coercive recruitment

The Employment Act 1982 makes void any agreement for the supply of goods and services that has the effect of requiring work to be done only by persons who are, or who are not, members of a union or of a particular union. The Act also forbids any refusal to do business with another person where the grounds of that refusal are that anyone providing, or likely to provide, goods or services is not a member of a union or of a particular union.

The Act removes any immunity that a person may have in connection with acts done in contemplation or furtherance of a trade dispute if he induces, or seeks to induce, another person to act in a manner outlined in the paragraph above, or where he induces, or seeks to induce, another person to incorporate a discriminatory 'union labour (or non-union labour) only' clause into a contract. So also, there will be no immunity for persons who organize action by employees that interferes, or is likely to interfere, with the supply of goods and services on the grounds that the work is done (or likely to be done) by employees of *another employer* who are, or are not, members of a union or of a particular union.

The effect of these sections of the 1982 Act is that any person who suffers damage as a result of any of the activities referred to may now sue to recover compensation from the persons (or union) who carry on those unlawful activities.

It can be seen that the 1982 Act greatly reduces the range of industrial activity permitted to trade unions. How effective the legislation will prove is a matter only the future can reveal.

Goods and Services

31 Faulty goods: rights against the seller

Napoleon said that the English were a nation of shopkeepers. English law always used to assume that buyers had a sufficient freedom of choice to be able to look after themselves. So, although the law made business sellers generally liable for defects in goods, it did nothing to stop sellers from excluding their liability. They could do this by putting in the contract of sale an *exclusion clause*: a clause which said that the seller was not liable for defects. The rights that buyers and sellers have against each other are a question of contract, and until 1973 a seller could insist on an oppressive contract if he wished to. But now buyers, particularly if they are consumers, are given quite strong protection by the Unfair Contract Terms Act 1977.

This chapter is about the buyer's rights against the seller. But it must be said now that all the rights in the world will be no use to you if you cannot find the seller, or if he has no money. If that happens you will have to sue some other person – usually the manufacturer – and as you probably haven't got a contract with him, your position will not be a strong one. What you can do if you can't sue the seller is explained in Chapter 32. Your rights when you yourself are a seller are explained in Chapter 34.

One general warning: the law of sale of goods was codified by an Act of Parliament passed in 1893. That statute was re-enacted as the Sale of Goods Act 1979. There have been many decisions in the courts explaining and interpreting the 1893 Act (as amended), and since the 1979 Act is almost exactly the same, word for word, these decisions will still apply to it although they are not mentioned in the Act. This means that it is dangerous to read the 1979 Act in isolation without any knowledge of the cases decided since 1893.

Note that if you agree to swap goods rather than to sell them, under the Supply of Goods and Services Act 1982 this is treated in effect as if each person were selling to the other the goods he is exchanging.

Making the contract

Once you have agreed on the thing you are buying and the price you are to pay, your contract exists. A contract is an agreement, that's all. But it must be definite; and courts will not normally enforce agreements to agree. Sometimes, if it is clear that there was a definite sale, a court won't be worried that the price was unclear, and will imply a reasonable price. But this is exceptional; normally if you haven't agreed on a price your agreement won't be definite enough to create a binding contract.

Proving that there is a contract

An oral agreement is enough; a contract does not have to be in writing. But if it is just your word against the seller's, then you run the risk that the court will believe the seller if he says that you're mistaken. It is always best to get something in writing stating the price and the date for delivery if this is not on the spot. A sentence will do: 'Agreed: sale of my car XYZ 123A to J. Jones for £250 cash, delivery 10th Jan.' Make sure the seller either writes it himself or signs it; otherwise a court won't give it much weight. And of course make sure that when you pay you get a receipt.

The seller's duties

The Sale of Goods Act lays certain duties on the seller, and these are set out below. Remember that a seller may try to exclude his liability; whether this will be effective or not is explained on page 280. Generally, the main *remedy* you will have if a seller doesn't fulfil his duties is compensation in *damages*. The law will not generally force the seller to perform the contract, but of course he may well prefer to do this rather than pay out damages. This is explained on page 283. Finally, there are some things you can't complain of; they are dealt with on page 285.

Delivery of the goods

The seller need not deliver the goods in the normal sense of that term unless he has agreed to do so. The Act says he must deliver; but all that means is that he must make the goods available for collection by the buyer.

The time when the goods must be handed over

This depends firstly on what has been agreed, and secondly on the arrangements for payment. Payment is important because the Act says that unless the seller has agreed to take payment after delivery, then he is entitled to hold on to the goods until he has been paid. Subject to this, if a time has been agreed, then the goods must be handed over at that time. If no time has been agreed, then the court will impose a reasonable time. So either at the time agreed or after a reasonable time the buyer can demand the goods; but unless it has been agreed that the sale is to be on credit, he must be prepared to pay at that time as well.

Ownership of goods

This is crucial. If the seller doesn't own the goods, or isn't entitled to sell them, then the buyer will be in a poor position. The true owner will be entitled to claim the goods back from the buyer. There are some exceptions to this; they are explained in the section *What to do if someone else claims ownership* (see below).

The seller's obligation to provide good title

'Title' means ownership. The Act says that if the seller doesn't give you ownership you can sue him. Unfortunately sellers who give a bad title are all too often rogues, and they either disappear or, if you can find them, they're bankrupt and not worth suing. For what it is worth, your rights are very wide. You can complain if any other person has any right which interferes with your enjoyment of the goods. The other person's right need not be full ownership; for example, you can complain if someone has a trade mark or patent which stops you from using or selling the goods.

What to do if someone else claims ownership

First, demand some proof of this ownership. The maxim that 'possession is nine-tenths of the law' is one of common sense; a court will want strong proof that someone other than the person in possession of the goods is the owner of them. Second, notify the seller; it may even be best if you return the goods to him (see page 284). Third, in certain exceptional cases you can become the owner of the goods even though the person who sold them to you was not. In that case the former owner will have no rights against you. These exceptions are listed below, but if you need to rely on them it is essential to get legal advice, because they are rather complicated. And in order to take advantage of any of these exceptions you must have bought in good faith without notice of the true owner's rights.

Exception 1: Estoppel If the true owner leads you to believe that you are getting a good title from the seller, he cannot afterwards say that you did not; lawyers say he is *estopped*.

Exception 2: Mercantile agents The Factors Act 1889 provides that if you buy goods from an agent whose business it is to sell goods belonging to other people you can get a good title from him. This only applies, however, if the true owner consented to the agent's possession. It means that the owner can't complain to you if the agent sold the goods when he shouldn't have done so.

Exception 3: Special powers Certain people have power to sell goods which don't belong to them; for example, sheriffs, pawnbrokers and innkeepers.

Exception 4: Market overt If you buy in a market which was set up by charter or statute, or under ancient custom (called a market overt), you get a good title even if the seller didn't have one. (The whole of the City of London is a 'market overt'.) But you must buy in good faith according to the custom of the market, in the open and between sunrise and sunset.

Exception 5: Purchase of a voidable title If a person obtains ownership of goods by fraud, he has only what is called a voidable title. That means that ownership can be taken away from him if the true owner *rescinds* (i.e. cancels) the fraudulent purchase. However, if you buy the goods from the fraudulent rogue before the rogue's purchase is cancelled, then you do get a good title to them and the true owner has no rights against you. But if you buy after cancellation, the moment at which the rogue loses even his voidable title, then you do not become the owner of the goods and the true owner can recover them from you.

Exception 6: Sellers or buyers in possession Sometimes one of the parties to a contract of sale sells the goods to a third person when he's not entitled to. A buyer, for example, may resell goods before ownership has passed to him, or a seller may sell the goods a second time after ownership has already passed to the buyer. Strangely enough, if that does happen, and the person who should not have sold had possession of the goods with the consent of the other party to the original contract, then the third person gets a good title. Note that the third party will not get a good title where the original parties had agreed not on a sale, but on a hire purchase deal, or on a credit sale with payment by instalments, unless the goods concerned were a motorcar and the third party was a private buyer. This means that if you, as a private person, buy a car and later discover that the person who sold it to you didn't own it but had it on HP, you nevertheless get a good title to the car. But if it had been a washing machine, the true owner could claim it back.

Quality of the goods

The goods must conform to their description

This really is about the identity, the nature, of the goods. You are entitled to have exactly what you were promised. It doesn't matter that what you get may be similar; it must be the same. So a 1965 Ford won't do for a 1966 one, a black jacket is no substitute for a blue one, etc.

The goods must be of merchantable quality

But only if the seller sells them 'in the course of a business'. So if you buy from a private person, you can't complain if the goods are worthless (as long as they fit their description). The courts haven't yet had to decide if a businessman who sells an article which he uses in his business but doesn't normally sell (e.g. an office typewriter) in law sells 'in the course of a business'. Most lawyers think that he does. Assuming there is a business sale, then the requirement of merchantability means that the goods must be of a reasonable quality. Obviously this will depend on the circumstances. Goods described as seconds may be flawed, and sale goods probably needn't be perfect. A new car shouldn't be scratched, but a second-hand car need only be roadworthy. Of course you can't complain of a defect that has been pointed out to you; and if you examine the goods, you can't complain of a defect which you should have noticed.

The goods must be reasonably fit for their purpose

Again, this only applies if the seller sells 'in the course of a business'. If the purpose for which the goods are required is not an ordinary one then you must tell the seller what you want them for. A shopkeeper selling washing-up liquid need not ordinarily ensure that it is safe for fine china, but if you tell him that is what you want it for then you can complain if it takes the enamel off your Dresden shepherdess. The seller will not owe you this duty unless you rely, or it would be reasonable for you to rely, on his skill or judgment.

Where both parties have equal skill the courts have held the buyer entitled to rely on the seller (who may well have information about the particular goods which the buyer won't have). If, however, the buyer is an expert it is probably unreasonable for him to rely on a non-expert seller.

Quantity of the goods

You need only take the quantity that you ordered. You can refuse to take less and there is no obligation to accept delivery by instalments. You can also refuse to take more and it is up to you whether you return the excess over what you ordered, or you return the lot, which the Act entitles you to do.

Can the seller exclude his liability?

Crafty sellers often claim that their contracts of sale excuse them from liability for defects in the goods they sell. Nowadays *every attempt* in ordinary consumer contracts to exclude liability is subject to a test of reasonableness under the Unfair Contract Terms Act 1977. Moreover in some cases exclusion clauses are absolutely null and void. This depends on the liability the seller is trying to exclude, and whether the sale is a 'consumer sale'.

The definition of a consumer sale

The seller must sell in the course of a business

This is the same test as was explained earlier on page 279. So a private sale is *not* a consumer sale, even if the buyer is also a private person.

The buyer must not buy in the course of a business

Somebody who makes a business of buying and selling the goods in question will not be a consumer. The difficult case is again the businessman who buys a typewriter for his office (see page 279). If the sale of that typewriter was 'in the course of a business', then presumably the earlier purchase was as well.

The goods

They must be of a kind ordinarily bought for private use or consumption. This will exclude things like machinery or computers.

The type of liability excluded

Description

The seller, whether he is a private person or in business, cannot exclude his liability to sell goods which correspond to their description.

Quality

In a consumer sale the seller cannot exclude his liability to supply goods that are of merchantable quality and are fit for their purpose. In a non-consumer sale, the seller must prove that any clause excluding these liabilities is reasonable.

Title

The Act says liability for bad title cannot be excluded at all, but there is provision enabling the parties to agree that the seller is only giving such title as he may have. So a blanket exclusion clause (e.g. 'Seller undertakes no liability as to title') will be void, but a carefully drafted clause agreeing that the sale is of a limited title may be effective. Unless there is such a clause a buyer will always be entitled to complain of any defect in title.

Negligence

Negligence is a failure to take reasonable care to avoid damage to others. Normally it is not important in sale of goods because a seller is liable for defects whether he took reasonable care or not. But it does have an effect on exclusion clauses. If death or personal injury is caused by negligence committed in the course of a business, no clause in the contract of sale can exclude liability. If other loss or damage is caused by negligence, the seller must prove that any exclusion clause is reasonable.

Other types of liability

If the buyer is a consumer, the seller must prove that the exclusion of liability is reasonable. This is also true if the buyer, even though not a consumer, buys subject to the seller's written standard terms of business. Otherwise the seller is free to exclude his liability, but it is worth remembering that the exclusion clause must be part of the contract. If it is on a document that you have signed, then it is part of the contract. But if it is written somewhere else (e.g. on another document or on a notice) it is only part of the contract if you saw it or should reasonably have seen it *before* the sale was agreed.

When is an exclusion clause reasonable?

The Unfair Contract Terms Act

This Act lists a number of factors that must be considered when deciding whether a clause is reasonable.

- *bargaining power* – could the seller insist on his own terms, or could the buyer readily find less oppressive terms somewhere else?
- *inducements* – did the customer get a lower price because he agreed to the exclusion? Could he have paid more and insisted on the seller undertaking full liability?
- *knowledge of the exclusion* – did the buyer know what he was agreeing to? Ought he to have known?
- *conditional exclusions* – if the buyer has to do some act (e.g. notify the seller within one month of sale) before he can insist on his strict legal rights, is the act required reasonable?
- *special orders* – was this something out of the ordinary which required special manufacture?

It is still guesswork to say how the courts will interpret these guidelines. It is clear that they will interact; mere knowledge of the exclusion might not make it reasonable, but if the buyer had the bargaining power to insist on it being removed, and didn't, then it might be reasonable. The courts might also have regard to the extent of the exclusion. It might be reasonable in some cases to undertake liability only for negligence. To some extent this uncertainty gives buyers bargaining power once a dispute has arisen; for a seller will be reluctant to have a court declare his exclusion clause unreasonable, and this may make him more willing to settle a claim.

When does the buyer become the owner?

The whole idea of a sale is that the buyer should become the owner of the goods. It is described in the Act as the passing of property. The Act makes a distinction between the sale of what are called *specific* goods – things that you can put your finger on and identify such as that Morris 1000 motorcar ABC456, and the sale of something which is *generic*, where a description only is given (say, two dozen tins of tomato soup), and it will be up to the seller to select the goods that he will supply under the contract. So a second-hand car will normally be specific, but a new car will be generic. With specific goods, once the sale is agreed they're yours – even though they are not to be paid for or delivered until much later. Generic goods do not become yours until they are unconditionally appropriated, which will usually be on delivery.

These are general rules which apply when the parties themselves have said nothing in their agreement about when property is to pass. It is, however, always possible for the parties to make an express provision of the passing of property in identifiable goods and this will override the general rules.

Property as a means of security

The most important aspect of ownership is that it can operate to protect a buyer or seller from the disastrous consequences of the other party's bankruptcy. This area of law is very complicated, but it is generally true to say that a buyer who has paid the price should insist that property passes to him from that moment. This means that if the seller goes bankrupt the seller's trustee in bankruptcy will not be allowed to sell the goods (which he otherwise could do for the benefit of the other creditors), but will be made instead to hand them over to the buyer. Similarly, a wise seller will provide that property is not to pass until the goods are paid for (this is known as reservation of title).

Buyer's remedies

Even though a seller may be guilty of the most flagrant breach of contract, a court will almost never order him to hand over the goods to the buyer. It will, however, force the seller to compensate the buyer in *damages* for any complaint that he may be entitled to make. In cases of serious breach, the court may allow the buyer, if he acts promptly, to *reject the goods* and sometimes to *cancel the contract.*

Damages

If you buy, or agree to buy, goods from a seller who then breaks the contract, he will be ordered to put you in the financial position you would have been in if he had fulfilled his contract. If the defective goods have a value, then he should pay you the difference between the value of what he promised and the value of what you got. (If the defective article doesn't even have scrap value, you can claim the cost of repair or replacement.) Often the value of what the seller promised will be the price you paid, but it need not be; you may have paid more or less than its true value, or the value may have increased or decreased by the time of the lawsuit.

Example: Suppose you have bought what is described as an oak table for £150. It turns out to be stained pine. A real oak table would be worth £200, and the pine table is worth £120. You can claim £80 damages (and not just the £30 difference between the price you paid and actual value).

Rejection of the goods

What is rejection?

It is your right to refuse to accept goods which are seriously defective. If you haven't received them, you refuse to take them; if you've got them, you return them. The practical advantage of rejection is that it saves you the bother of bringing a claim for damages. On the other hand, as long as he is still within the delivery time (see page 276), the seller can try again, and if he offers you goods with no serious defects within that time you must accept them.

A defect must be serious to justify rejection

If you can complain of any defect in title or quality (see pages 277–9), you are entitled to reject. The same applies if the seller supplies the wrong quantity (see page 280) or is late in making the goods available to you (see page 276). In these cases you need only prove a breach by the seller of the duty which he was bound to fulfil. In other cases, however, the right to reject is not automatic; you will have to show that the effect of the seller's breach is to make the purchase almost worthless. In these cases, unless your claim is very strong, you can only guess whether a court will agree that the defect was serious enough, and it may be wise not to reject.

A word of caution

The Act says you cannot reject once you have 'accepted' the goods. Before you are considered to have accepted the goods you must have had a reasonable chance to examine them. Once that time has passed, you accept the goods either by expressly saying so, or by doing something which denies the seller's ownership (e.g. giving the goods to someone else), or simply by holding on to the goods for longer than is reasonable. So if you want to reject, you must act promptly, and take care not to prejudice your position.

A second word of caution

If you reject when you are not entitled to, then you are in breach of your contract. If you are wrong about the seller's duty, or about the existence or seriousness of the defect, or if you have 'accepted' the goods, you cannot reject. If you do reject when you shouldn't, the seller may be entitled to cancel the contract, and you will have to compensate him for any loss he may suffer.

Cancellation of the contract

When can a buyer cancel the contract?

The buyer can cancel if a seller refuses to acknowledge his contractual obligations (for the most part, those set out on pages 276–80). Usually, cancellation will be a final rejection: a rejection of the goods at a stage when the seller can't or won't provide proper goods within the required time (see page 284). Once you have cancelled, you can refuse to pay for the goods; and if you have paid, you can demand your money back.

What are the advantages of cancellation?

It is safer to refuse to pay than to try to claim damages later. Even if you have paid, it is easier to claim your money back than to try to prove your loss when you come to claim damages. Cancellation is the most effective way of washing your hands of a deal which has gone wrong. But take care: the seller's refusal to carry out the contract must be definitive. If it is not, you will be liable to him.

When the buyer cannot complain

You can't complain about everything that goes wrong. You must be sure that the seller is in breach of a duty. If there has been accidental damage to the goods you may have to bear the loss. And if you commit a serious breach of your obligations, the seller can cancel the contract, and you will lose your rights. Finally, if more than six years have passed since you bought the goods, your claim is probably too late.

The seller must be in breach of a duty

Some problems aren't the duty of the seller at all

If you change your mind about the goods, or you buy them for a friend who doesn't need them, that's your problem. The same is true if you think you paid too much for them, unless the difference in price is so exorbitant as to make the goods unmerchantable. This is unlikely (see page 279). If you're worried about this sort of thing, you can ask the seller for a sale 'on approval', but you won't find many sellers who will agree to this (mail order sales are an exception, see page 291).

Other problems may or may not be the seller's duty
If he has made specific promises he is bound; if not go back and check the list on pages 276–80. Title and description are always a seller's responsibility, but a seller is only responsible for merchantability if he sells in the course of a business. And read through your contract, looking for exemption clauses. Check whether they are valid (see page 280). If they are valid, then the seller is not liable.

The risk of accidental damage
What is risk?
The Act says that once risk passes to the buyer, he cannot claim for any accidental damage that may occur to the goods. There are two exceptions: firstly, a seller is liable for damage due to an already existing defect, or to his own negligence; and secondly, any party who wrongfully delays delivery must pay for accidental damage caused by the delay.

What do I do if there has been accidental damage?
Check whether property has passed (see page 282); the Act says that risk generally passes with property. But it is open to the parties to agree when risk is to pass, so read your contract carefully. If you anticipate any accidental damage, make sure you insure.

The seller's right to refuse to perform his obligations
Just as you can cancel if the seller definitively refuses to carry out his obligations, so the seller can refuse to carry out his obligations if you refuse to carry out yours. This is explained in detail in Chapter 34, which looks at sale from a seller's point of view. The two most important duties which you may be in breach of are the duty to accept the goods, and the duty to pay. Again you must read your contract carefully. The Act says that you need not pay until the seller makes proper goods available to you – provided of course that your contract does not say otherwise.

32 Faulty goods: rights against the manufacturer

Manufacturers are under a general duty to consumers: they must take reasonable care to make sure that the goods they manufacture will not cause harm to consumers. There is no need for there to be any contract; this duty is part of the law of 'tort', the area of law which deals with the duties that citizens (and companies) owe to each other.

This general duty – which gives rise to what is called liability in 'negligence' – is one that manufacturers cannot get out of. The way it works is explained on page 289. It is possible that the manufacturer has made a contract with the consumer, and if he has, he may undertake a greater liability than negligence. This potentially greater liability is explained immediately below; the liability in negligence is one which every manufacturer undertakes and is explained afterwards.

Manufacturer's liability in contract

Is there a contract?

Ordinarily, of course, you'll have a contract with the seller. (Sometimes the manufacturer sells to you direct, in which case you have all the rights set out in Chapter 31.) But the fact that you have a contract with the seller doesn't stop you having one with the manufacturer as well.

The theory of it is that if the manufacturer has made a promise to you, and as a result of that promise you have bought the goods he manufactured, then his promise is a legally binding contract. What generally happens is that the goods have displayed with them, or are described as including, a manufacturer's 'guarantee' (sometimes called a 'warranty'), which contains an undertaking, a promise, given by the manufacturer to buyers of the goods.

Beware: always read the guarantee or promise with great care. Often something described as a guarantee contains no real promise at all, in which case it may well be worthless. On the other hand, you may find the promise quite separately made, e.g. in an advertisement. So long as there is a promise, and on the faith of it you buy the goods, the promise is legally binding.

What liability does the manufacturer undertake?
The only liability he undertakes (apart from the general liability in negligence) is what he has in fact promised to do. The Office of Fair Trading has suggested that if a manufacturer gives a guarantee he should undertake to repair or replace any defective parts within a specified time period free of charge. However, there is no obligation on a manufacturer to provide a guarantee in those terms or at all.

Read the guarantee or promise carefully. Often it will require you to send off a registration card, or to keep a receipt from the seller. Sometimes it will impose quite harsh conditions; for example, it may provide that the manufacturer's opinion of the defectiveness or otherwise of the goods is to be conclusive, or that the goods must have been purchased from a certain dealer, or that the buyer must certify that the goods have been properly installed. As a matter of contract, you must comply with the conditions. (Although if they were entirely unexpected you might stand a chance of having them declared void under the Unfair Contract Terms Act. The relevant section is one relating to contracts generally and not to sale of goods, but the criteria would be similar to those set out on page 282.)

Sometimes a manufacturer or a seller writes a clause into a guarantee saying that the guarantee is the *only* right of action the consumer has. This attempt to take away the consumer's rights is made void with regard to the seller's liabilities (see Chapter 37) by Section 6 of the Unfair Contract Terms Act 1977. Such attempts are also made void with regard to the manufacturer's liability in negligence by Section 5 of that Act, provided that the goods are of a type ordinarily supplied for private use or consumption, and that the defect complained of arises during 'consumer use' (i.e. so long as they are not being used for business purposes only).

Who can claim?
The manufacturer's obligation is only to the person with whom he made the contract. So if you give away the goods you've bought, or you resell them, the person to whom you gave or sold them has no direct claim; the manufacturer made no contract with him. But there is a way you can normally pass on the benefit of your contract: by giving the manufacturer a notice of assignment. All that you, as holder of the guarantee, need do is write – and sign – a letter to the manufacturer saying that you assign your rights under the guarantee to the person you're giving or selling the goods to, setting out his full name and address, and all the details of your right to the guarantee or promise (e.g. date and place where you bought the

goods, the number of any registration card, etc.). So if you're buying, or being given, goods from someone who has a manufacturer's guarantee, get him to sign a notice of assignment giving all those details – you can send it off yourself.

One possible obstacle: sometimes the guarantee or promise prohibits any assignment. It is possible that such a prohibition might be ineffective under the Unfair Contract Terms Act; but if it is effective, then only the original buyer can claim.

Manufacturer's liability for negligence

Whether or not there is a contract with the manufacturer, he is liable in tort for negligence if that negligence results in harm to the consumer or his property. The burden of proof is on the consumer: he must show that the manufacturer failed to take reasonable care in all the circumstances.

How much care must the manufacturer take?

He has to take reasonable steps to prevent any harm which he can foresee. Thus, if an electric iron overheats it could burn clothing and a manufacturer must therefore take reasonable precautions to prevent it overheating. A manufacturer of chemicals which have dangerous properties must take reasonable steps to warn consumers of those dangers. It is a general principle that manufacturers ought to foresee that consumers may be negligent. So they are still liable if consumers are negligent, although the consumer will have his damages reduced to the extent that he was at fault. Thus someone who carried on eating contaminated food after he should have realized it was bad might get his damages reduced by, say, fifty per cent. In one case it was held that a man who put his foot into the grass-ejection hole of a lawnmower had done something so silly that he got no damages at all.

At one time it was said that where the consumer was able to inspect the goods the manufacturer would not be liable for a defect which was apparent on inspection. Most lawyers now think that the manufacturer would still be liable, subject to a reduction in the damages to the extent that the injured person was negligent.

How do I prove my claim?

Any consumer can make a claim in negligence. But it may well be a difficult claim to make; the consumer, who usually has no expertise, has to prove that the manufacturer failed to act reasonably in his operations. The manufacturer's manager will swear in court that they have an efficient system of inspection and have done all that can be reasonably expected of them.

In practice the consumer's difficulties can be mitigated by two factors. Firstly, if the consumer can prove that nothing other than a defect in manufacture is likely to be responsible for the injury then it looks as if the manufacturer's inspection system wasn't as efficient as he thought. Secondly, manufacturers are liable for negligence by an employee. If that efficient system of inspection has allowed a defect to slip through, it may well be because an employee failed to take as much care as he should have. In a recent case a judge held that where a packing-case collapsed, and the manufacturer proved he had an efficient inspection system, the injured person had shown it was more likely than not that an employee had put too few nails into the case. The manufacturer was liable for the employee's negligence.

Nevertheless there are still accidents which are nobody's fault. In these cases, the manufacturer will not be liable for negligence.

Who to sue? Seller or manufacturer?

If you can sue the seller, your rights against him are much stronger than your rights against the manufacturer. The reason is that a business seller is liable whether or not he is at fault. But remember that only a buyer can sue the seller, also that the seller may not be worth suing. If you weren't the buyer, or if the seller is bankrupt, you are left with a much weaker claim against the manufacturer. Many people think this haphazard and unfair, for in the ordinary course the seller could pass the buyer's claim on to the manufacturer, because the seller himself bought from the manufacturer. The Pearson Commission recommended in 1978 that manufacturers should be liable for defects without the need to prove fault. That recommendation has not been implemented, and the law remains that unless a manufacturer has undertaken some greater contractual duty, he is only liable if he is proved to have failed to take reasonable care.

Other people who may be liable for negligence

The general rule is that everyone dealing with goods which he knows are going to be sold ought to take reasonable care to prevent damage which he could foresee if something went wrong. This is most likely to involve (apart from the manufacturer) a distributor, or some other person, who ought to know of a defect in the goods (e.g. because he inspects them, or ought to inspect them, or for some other reason).

But the need to prove that he was in fact negligent, and the difficulty of doing that, remains the same, whoever you are suing in negligence.

33 Unsolicited goods and mail order sales

This chapter is about two methods of trading in which buyer and seller never meet. In one case the seller sends goods that have not been asked for; in the other the buyer orders unseen goods on the strength of a picture in a catalogue.

Unsolicited goods

It has always been the law that no one can force you to buy something which you never agreed to buy. If goods arrive unrequested through the post, you are at perfect liberty to put them on one side and ignore all letters for payment – though you ought to keep the goods safely and let the sender come and take them back. On the other hand, if you choose to make use of the goods, then by doing so you may be presumed to have agreed to buy them.

The Unsolicited Goods and Services Act 1971 (as amended) gives a private citizen who has goods sent to him, which he didn't ask for, the right eventually to keep them as his own and for free. The right arises in two ways:

- the consumer can give the sender thirty days' notice to come and get the goods. If he doesn't, at the end of thirty days the goods belong to the consumer just as if he had bought them;
- alternatively, the consumer can sit tight for six months. So long as he hasn't unreasonably refused to let the sender collect the goods, they become his at the end of the six months.

Note: the Act only applies to private individuals and not to goods sent in relation to the receiver's trade or business. There the receiver cannot become owner under the Act, but of course he is not obliged to buy the goods at all.

Mail order

Buying by post is often convenient, but there are dangers. You may not know the financial status of the seller; you're not able to see the goods before they're delivered; and you usually have to pay in advance. You can minimize the risks by choosing a seller belonging to these trading associations:

The Mail Order Trading Association represents mail order houses with catalogues from which you select goods. They undertake to give two weeks 'on approval' for goods that are ordered, during which time you can change your mind about them and send them back. They also undertake to give a firm delivery date, after which you are entitled to cancel the sale if the goods haven't arrived.

The Association of Mail Order Publishers do not give such liberal terms, but undertake clear and accurate advertising and the right to cancel long-term contracts after twelve months, or if prices rise more than was expected. They deal mainly in advertisements of particular products such as books and records.

Also, many newspapers will operate a scheme to give you back money sent to a bankrupt trader who has advertised with them; but the scheme is rather complicated, and you should inquire of the newspaper before relying on it.

34 Selling goods: rights against the buyer

The most important right is of course the right to be paid. But sellers have another right, a right to have the buyer accept the goods. These two rights are considered first. There are a number of reasons why a buyer might be entitled to refuse to accept, and they are considered in the next section of this chapter on page 294. Finally, we consider how you can enforce your rights (see page 295).

The right to be paid

If the buyer refuses to pay, first consider whether he might be entitled to refuse performance (see page 294). Then, if none of those reasons is applicable, consider whether the time for payment has arrived.

- Have you and the buyer agreed on a time for payment? If you have, then payment will only be due at that time. If you haven't, then a court will say that payment is to be made at a reasonable time; normally that will be at the time agreed for delivery.
- Have you 'delivered' the goods to the buyer? (Remember that unless you agree to transport the goods, 'delivery' means simply making the goods available, see page 276.) The Sale of Goods Act says that a buyer can refuse to pay until the goods are 'delivered'. So you can only demand payment before the goods are available for the buyer if he agreed to this as part of the contract.

The right to insist on acceptance

It can be a nuisance to be stuck with goods that you've sold. Again, consider if any of the grounds on which a buyer can refuse to perform might apply. Then you must consider when the buyer's duty to accept (i.e. take delivery) arises, because the right won't be available till then. If you've agreed a time, then it is straightforward. If you haven't agreed a time, a court will allow the buyer a reasonable time; that will depend on the circumstances. If the seller knew that there were difficulties (e.g. transport) preventing the buyer taking the goods quickly, a court would normally allow the buyer a reasonable period to overcome these difficulties.

Grounds on which a buyer can refuse to accept

First, is there a binding contract? When a contract exists, and how you can prove it, are explained on page 276. If the buyer has taken delivery of the goods or paid for them, then a court will normally assume that a contract has been made. But if the buyer has done neither of these things, and denies that he agreed to buy, it is for you to prove that a contract was made. To prevent it being just your word against his, make sure you have something in writing (see page 276).

Second, you owe a number of duties to the buyer. They are set out on pages 276–80. (Remember that if you are a private seller you owe no duties in respect of merchantable quality and fitness for purpose.) If you are in breach of an applicable duty the buyer will have the right to reject (unless he has accepted the goods), and if your breach is very serious he may have the right to cancel. In order to know whether the buyer has these rights read pages 284–5. If you want to carry on with the contract and you don't think he has got such a right, tell him so. Point out to him that not every breach gives a buyer a right to cancel, and that you are obliged to pay him damages if he has any real grounds for complaint.

Excluding liability

Firstly, you can point out any defects that you know of. A court is unlikely to allow a buyer to complain of a defect he was told about.

Secondly, if you're worried that you might not be the complete owner of the goods you're selling, Section 12(2) of the Sale of Goods Act allows you to agree with the buyer that you are selling only such 'title' as you may possess. You must do this very carefully (see page 281).

Thirdly, you can attempt to exclude your liability for breach of any duty. But if you're a business seller selling to a consumer then you can't escape those duties. If you're not a business seller, or you're selling to a businessman, the Unfair Contract Terms Act, Section 6, says you can exempt yourself from liability if that is reasonable:

- The exemption must be part of the contract. You must make it clear at the time of the contract – orally will do, but you ought to have it put in writing to be on the safe side – what it is that you are not undertaking liability for.

- It must be reasonable. When an exclusion clause is reasonable is explained on page 282.

Enforcing rights

The right to payment
There are three ways you can enforce your right to payment:

(1) *By holding on to the goods*
The Sale of Goods Act gives you a lien on the goods. That means that you can hold on to them until you receive payment. However, your lien will be lost if you have expressly agreed to hand over the goods before payment. And it will also be lost if you give possession of the goods to the buyer.

(2) *By suing for the price*
This remedy is relatively simple. You hold the goods available for the buyer (if you haven't given them to him already) and claim the full amount that he agreed to buy them for. In effect you are forcing the buyer to perform. But it is not always available. You can sue for the price if:

- the property in the goods has passed to the buyer (so that he is the owner of them); or
- the buyer agreed to pay the price on a certain day (and he has not done so).

The passing of property is explained on page 282. Often it won't be clear whether property has passed, especially if you still have the goods (and even if the buyer has the goods it doesn't necessarily follow that the property has passed). Whether it has or not, if you're agreed on a day for payment, then you can sue directly for the price.

(3) *By claiming damages*
You can claim damages for any failure by the buyer to pay, but the amount will depend on the circumstances:

- if the buyer is holding on to the goods and won't give them back to you, then your damages are the full amount of the price he had agreed to pay;
- if the buyer is just late in paying, and hasn't got the goods the

damages will be very small: at best the interest on the period you are out of your money. This won't be worth suing for unless the delay is substantial;

- if the buyer absolutely refuses to pay, and you still have the goods, you can terminate the contract, and sell the goods to someone else. If you can't get as good a price as the buyer had agreed to pay, you can sue him for the difference.
  Example: Andrew agrees to buy your car for £1,000. A week later, when he ought to take delivery of the car, he refuses to do so, because he has been posted to Hong Kong. You resell the car to Bert for £800.
  You can claim £200 damages from Andrew; for if he had fulfilled his promise you would have received £200 more than you got from Bert. But if Andrew can prove that a used-car dealer would have given you £1,000 or more for the car, you can claim nothing from him. The reason is that you could have got just as much as Andrew promised elsewhere, so his failure to fulfil his promise should have caused you no loss.
  Take care: just because the buyer is late in paying, it doesn't entitle you to resell. You must still have the goods and it must be absolutely clear that he is refusing to pay. If you are in any doubt about this, the Act provides that you can give reasonable notice to the buyer of your intention to resell. If he doesn't pay on that date – whether he is refusing to pay, or whether he says he will pay later – you can resell.

The right to have the buyer take delivery

There is no specific right in the Sale of Goods Act to enable you to force the buyer to take delivery. But there is a special right to make a charge for looking after the goods. It only arises after you have requested the buyer to take delivery (and, of course, you can only do that if the time for delivery has arrived, see page 293). If the buyer doesn't take delivery within a reasonable time of the request, the Act says you can make a reasonable charge for the care and custody of the goods.

The Act says you can also claim damages for any loss you suffer from his failing to take delivery, for example if you have to pay someone to store the goods.

If the buyer, as well as refusing to take delivery, refuses to pay, you have all the rights set out above. If he has paid, the long-term position is unclear. In the short term, you can claim damages or a storage charge. But in the long term you would be unwise to resell the goods unless you had the written authority of the buyer to do so. This is because the buyer may well be the owner of the goods and anyone you sell to might not get a good title. Probably the best way to bring matters to a head would be to sue, claiming firstly the reasonable storage charge mentioned above, and secondly a court order that the buyer's refusal is a repudiation of the contract, entitling you to sell the goods.

What to do if a buyer complains

- First, if you think there may be any substance in the complaint, notify the person you bought from. You may have a right of action against him. If it is possible that the six-year period of limitation (see page 285) will run out in respect of the person you bought from, consider issuing a writ or county court plaint against him.

  Note: if the buyer says he is claiming for personal injury, get legal advice immediately. Personal injury claims are complex and can involve enormous amounts of money; it is not worth attempting to handle them on your own.
- Second, check to see if it is something the buyer has the right to complain of (see page 285).
- Third, if it is, check to see what remedies the buyer has (see pages 283–5). It doesn't automatically follow that because you are in breach the buyer can cancel: it may be that you can remedy the defect within the contract time.
- Fourth, if you want to go on with the contract, and you think the buyer might not have the right to cancel, tell him so. Point out that if he cancels wrongfully you will have to resell the goods, and hold him responsible for any loss you suffer.

  If the buyer agrees that the sale should go through and that claims should be dealt with later, see if the dispute can be resolved amicably. Make sure, though, that if you agree to do any repairs you don't admit your liability unless it is absolutely clear. Make any offer expressly 'without prejudice'.

  If the buyer insists on cancelling, assess your position. If he has good ground for cancelling, it is futile to carry on a dispute about it. But if you think he didn't have the right to cancel, either because the defect is not a real one or because it was one which in law does not give the right to cancel, then you will probably have to sue. The grounds on which you can sue have been explained above (pages 293–4).

35 Hire of goods and provision of services

Your rights and obligations when someone else is providing a service for you are now governed by the Supply of Goods and Services Act 1982. The Act says that where goods are *hired* to you the supplier has similar duties to those of a seller of goods. But under the Act a supplier of services does not have such strict duties; his only obligation is to carry out the service with reasonable care and skill. Where the supplier of services also supplies a finished product such as a double-glazed window, the courts have held that he is under an absolute duty to ensure that the product is reasonably fit for its purpose unless the contract says otherwise. It seems likely that the Act has not altered this position.

Rights

First, your rights depend on there being a contract. It needn't be in writing, but writing always helps if there's a dispute (see page 276).

Second, they depend on the terms of that contract. You are entitled to whatever the other party has agreed to do. Again, if there is a dispute it helps to have written evidence; if something is particularly important to you, put it in writing (e.g. in a letter) and keep a copy.

If there is nothing in the agreement as to the quality of the service, you are entitled to have the other party take all reasonable care to provide a satisfactory service. Moreover if he is producing goods (e.g. by constructing a desk, or cooking a meal) then he will incur the sort of liabilities explained in Chapter 31, provided he is supplying his own basic material. And in some cases the courts have held repairers, and other people who (even though they are not selling goods) are providing work and materials, strictly liable to provide something which is reasonably fit for its purpose (see page 279). Apart from these areas, however, it will usually be up to you to prove that the contractor has been negligent.

The contractor is entitled to a reasonable time to perform the service. Check to see whether you have agreed to give him a specific time. If you think he is taking longer than the time agreed, or longer than a reasonable time, and there is nothing to excuse the delay in the contract, then you can give him a period of notice. If he exceeds the notice, you may be within your rights to cancel the contract. But remember that to justify cancellation you must be prepared to persuade a court that the contractor's failure was really serious (see page 285).

Sometimes a contractor's standard terms will say that he is not liable for failure to provide a proper service. These are exemption (or exclusion) clauses, and their validity depends on considerations similar to those in sale of goods (see page 280). First, the contractor can't rely on them unless he brought them to your attention at or before the time the agreement was made. Second, he can't exclude his liability for death or personal injury caused by negligence at all. Third, other exclusion clauses must be reasonable (see the discussion of reasonableness on page 282).

Obligations

You must allow the contractor to perform the service. If you cancel the contract unjustifiably, the contractor can sue for any loss he suffers as a result. But in order to prove a loss he will have to show that there was no other equally profitable work available to fill the gap created by your cancellation, or that he has incurred expenditure that has been wasted.

You must also pay for the services. If the amount of payment was not agreed upon, you must pay a reasonable sum. The time for payment, unless otherwise agreed, would normally be on completion of the services. Moreover in a contract for building or repair work (again, unless otherwise agreed) you are entitled to refuse to pay if there is any substantial defect. In any event if you take the view that the contractor has not complied with his obligations (see page 298), you would be wise to pay any disputed amounts only after the dispute has been settled.

Example: A contractor agrees to transport your furniture from London to York for £500. When the furniture arrives, a vase worth £80 is broken. If you think the contractor or his employees have failed to take reasonable care of the vase (and the fact that it is broken is some evidence of this) and there is no valid exemption clause, pay only £420. You are entitled to 'set off' the £80 damage against the agreed price of £500.

If the contractor has still got your property when payment is due, he may claim to retain it until he receives payment (this is called ‘claiming a lien’). If there is a dispute, you can pay the money into court, or your solicitor can given an undertaking to pay the disputed amount if judgment is given against you, and the contractor should then release your property.

Some examples

Building and repair work

The work must be reasonably fit for its purpose. Disputes tend to be about specifications, time taken doing the work, and price. You can rely on oral agreement as to all these things, but you’re more likely to avoid disputes if you’ve got a contract in writing. If you’re concerned about delay, set a deadline at the time you make the agreement. As to price, the contractor will usually have given an estimate beforehand. If you are to hold him to that, you must show that it was more than an estimate, and was in fact a true quotation. Even then, you may find that his standard terms say that quoted prices can be increased for certain reasons, e.g. for increased material costs. He can only rely on this if his standard terms are part of the contract (see above).

Carriers

Carriers will almost always contract on standard terms. These will often say that they exclude liability even for negligence; such exclusion clauses will be subject to the test of reasonableness (see page 282). International carriage is governed by special conventions: road and air carriers are strictly liable for loss, but sea carriers are largely exempted. Insurance to cover carriage is comparatively cheap and you would ordinarily be wise to take it out; make sure it covers you door to door. If you are concerned about delay, make your concern and the reason for it known to the carrier and insurer at the time of making the agreement. Otherwise your losses (e.g. of profit) might be said to be unforeseeable and so not recoverable.

Accommodation and travel

Check the small print of any brochures before you sign. You will often find that the contract makes your deposit irrecoverable if you cancel. If you can show that the amount of the deposit is not a genuine estimate of the loss that cancellation will cause, you could in theory attempt to recover it; but you run the risk that the hotelier/carrier/tour-operator might prove that he suffered an even greater loss. As to exemption clauses, in travel the standard terms will almost always be thrust at you. In hotels, however, unless there has been earlier correspondence you are unlikely to be shown standard terms before you book. In that case they are not binding. In any event remember that you are entitled to insist that any exemption clause (within the UK) is reasonable (see page 282). If you're dealing with travel agents, it is wise to stick to those who are members of the professional association, ABTA.

Insurance
You will usually be asked to fill in a proposal form with a number of questions on it. Take great care with this, for the form will often contain a clause under which you warrant the truth of every answer. If any answer is incorrect, even though you had no reason to suppose that it might be, the insurer can refuse to pay up. If there is a question to which you think your answer could possibly be wrong, write beside it 'to the best of my knowledge' or some other words to show that you are not guaranteeing the truth of your answer.

Moreover the questions on the proposal form are not the end of the matter. The insurer can refuse to pay if there was anything at all that you did not tell him about which might have influenced a prudent insurer's assessment of the risk. This will include moral factors, e.g. any convictions for dishonesty. Make sure you disclose absolutely everything, and put it in writing.

Professional services
Doctors, dentists, lawyers, accountants, and architects are only liable if you can show that they were negligent (and lawyers are not liable for court work at all). The House of Lords has recently emphasized that an error of judgment is not negligent if it is an error which a competent professional man acting with ordinary care might have made.

In the case in question it was held that a surgeon's pulling 'too long and too hard' was not of itself negligence. Professionals, further, will generally be held to be entitled to adopt a course of action which is endorsed by a reasonable body of professional opinion. (See page 441 onwards for complaints about professionals.)

Action against a contractor

As well as – or instead of – bringing a civil action for damages against a negligent contractor you can also pursue your complaint in the following ways:

- for misleading advertising, complain to the Advertising Standards Authority, Brook House, 2–16 Torrington Place, London WC1;
- for conduct which you consider contrary to professional or trading standards, complain to a professional body or to a trade association; useful addresses are given on page 446;
- for contravention of the Trade Descriptions Act, and other legislation relating to consumer services, report the matter to the local trading standards officer whom you can contact through the local council. The Trade Descriptions Act makes it an offence to make a false statement about various aspects of goods or services which are offered. Prosecutions can only be brought by the trading standards officer. If a prosecution is brought, the criminal court has power to make an order to compensate you (the consumer) for loss you have suffered, but it will only do so if it is absolutely sure of the validity of your claim;
- for complaints about unsatisfactory repairs to cars or electrical goods it is worthwhile sending a copy of any complaint that you make to anyone else to the Director-General of Fair Trading as well. He is not only responsible for advising the government about general changes and improvements in consumer law but he can also take powerful action against individual firms about which he receives a lot of complaints. His address is: Office of Fair Trading, Field House, Breams Buildings, London EC4.

36 Money

This chapter deals with some of the common problems that people have over money: payments made by mistake; how cheques work; your rights when you use credit either just as a loan or for buying goods (e.g. on hire purchase).

Paying money by mistake

If you've paid money by mistake, then you're generally entitled to get it back. For example, at the supermarket cash desk the cashier taps out £1.50 instead of 50p. Even if you don't notice at the time, you can claim back the extra £1. The same is true if you get the wrong change. For example, your bill is £7.50 and you give the cashier a £10 note. The cashier gives you only £1.50 and you don't notice. You have paid the cashier £8.50 because of a mistake about the change, and you are entitled to your £1 that was missing. Notices on cash registers which say 'mistakes cannot be rectified' are almost certainly invalid under the Unfair Contract Terms Act; it is difficult to see that in ordinary circumstances they could ever be reasonable.

But there are two cases where a mistake won't help you. Firstly, you can only get your money back if you paid under a mistake of *fact*. If you're paying for goods or services then your obligation to pay depends on the contract you make (see Chapter 31), and once you've agreed on a price, that's it. It is too late to say, 'You're charging me too much', and it is no use saying that you thought you were bound to pay the price that was asked, for that is a mistake of law and not of fact.

The second case is where the person who receives the money relies on that fact and fritters it away. This is unlikely to happen with a shopkeeper, but it can happen between individuals. For example, you give a tip to a lad who you think is your newspaper boy; in fact you've mistaken his brother for him. If he spends it on sweets (or anything else that is not a permanent asset) then it is too late to complain.

Cheques

What you can do if you are given a cheque

The cheque is a direction to a bank to pay money. The person giving the direction is the signer on the cheque and is called, in legal language, the *drawer*. The bank who is to pay is called the *drawee* (because the cheque is said to be *drawn on* the bank). If you are named as the person to be paid, you are called the *payee*.

If a cheque is not crossed, then you can ask the bank to pay the amount of the cheque in cash. Most cheques are crossed, which means that the bank can only pay to another bank account. If you don't have a bank account, you will have to pay it into the account of a friend; to do that, you *endorse* the cheque to him by writing 'Pay (his name)' on the back and signing your name below.

Remember that the cheque won't ordinarily give you any rights against the bank. (The exception of course is where you have noted down a cheque card number on the back of the cheque, and the cheque is within the card limit.) The only advantage of an ordinary cheque is that it gives you the right to sue the drawer (who signed it). Unless he can show that you deceived him, or that you gave no value for the cheque (in which case he can 'stop' the cheque), he is liable. But if he gave the cheque as payment under a contract, and can show that he was entitled to cancel that contract (see page 285), then he can say that you gave no value.

Note: never accept a cheque made out to 'cash'. Banks accept them as a matter of practice, but they are not really cheques. A proper cheque must be made out to a named person, or to 'bearer'. A cheque made out to 'cash' will not give you a direct right of action against the drawer.

How to safeguard your position when you write cheques

A cheque is a valuable asset. In general, any person (and not just the payee) who has given value for it in good faith can sue you directly for the amount of the cheque. And if your bank has paid out in good faith on a cheque you wrote, they are entitled (provided that there were no suspicious circumstances) to debit your account, even if the person who presented the cheque was a rogue. (The bank is not ordinarily entitled to pay out on a forgery of your signature. If they do, they must reimburse you.)

You can protect your position to some extent:

- Always cross your cheques; then at least you can find out whose bank account they were paid into.
- If you think there is a real risk of a cheque being lost or stolen, you can write 'Not negotiable – account payee only' in between the crossed lines. The words 'not negotiable' mean that if the rogue passes on the cheque to someone else, that person gets no more right than the rogue had. The direction 'account payee only' means that if a bank pays the cheque into an account of anyone but the person named on the cheque as payee then they (the bank) will be liable for any loss.

When can I stop cheques?

The only circumstances when you can stop a cheque are set out above (and they may not apply if you used a banker's card or the payee has endorsed the cheque). Only do so if you are sure of your ground; otherwise you may find yourself being sued, and justifiably so. Moreover, never buy goods with the intention of stopping your cheque straight away; this is a criminal offence under the Theft Acts.

Credit

Credit often causes legal headaches, usually because the repayment terms prove to be more difficult in practice than they seemed at first.

The Consumer Credit Act 1974 (which extends the protection given by earlier Moneylenders Acts and Hire Purchase Acts) gives you a degree of protection against harsh repayment terms and it also gives you certain safeguards when you buy goods on credit; for example, by HP (hire purchase).

Credit is a very complicated area of law and the following discussion has to be fairly general. If you are in trouble with someone who has lent you money, or given you credit to buy goods, get legal advice right away. There are three reasons for this. First, although the Consumer Credit Act was passed in 1974 not all of its provisions are in force at the time of writing. Your rights may depend on what provisions are in force when you are in difficulty. Second, many of the rights you have involve an application to the court and it is easier to have a lawyer do this for you. Third, it is important not to go wrong when dealing with creditors. When you need credit in the future, potential creditors will check your name with credit reference agencies; if you have defaulted on an earlier agreement, that fact will be on their lists. (If you want to see the records that your creditor is checking with, you can do so for a charge of 25p; but although you can complain if an entry is wrong, you can't do much about it if they've got the facts correct.)

Harsh repayment terms

You have two safeguards. Firstly, in every case you can complain if there is an 'extortionate credit bargain'. That's defined by the Act as being one where the repayment terms are 'grossly exorbitant' or 'grossly contravene ordinary principles of fair dealing'. The courts will take into account factors like the degree of risk involved to the creditor, the amount of any security offered, the experience and need of the parties. But the tests above use strong words, and an agreement would have to be very much out of the ordinary for a court to strike it down.

There is a second safeguard, which requires agreements to comply with certain formalities. But this doesn't apply in every case. The amount of credit involved must be between £50 and £5,000. Certain organizations (e.g. banks and insurance companies) are often exempt. Where the safeguards about formalities do apply, they mean that the agreement must be in writing, and you must be sent a second copy of it. It must show the true rate of interest, taking into account the fact that the principal is being paid off bit by bit.

A failure by the creditor to comply with the formalities will not give you an automatic right to cancel. The court will look to see whether it has led you to do something you might not otherwise have done. If you knew what you were doing all along, it will probably enforce the agreement.

Cancellation

A special right to cancel may be given to you if you sign the agreement at a place which is not trade premises (e.g. at home). You have a cooling-off period of four days from the time you receive your second copy, and at any stage during that time you can write to the creditor and cancel. But this is a special right – it only applies where an agent has spoken to you and told you about the deal, and you have not signed the forms at business premises. (The period for cooling off will be increased to five days if and when that part of the Consumer Credit Act 1974 comes into force.)

Difficulty in paying

If you are finding the payments difficult, and you think you won't be able to keep them up, it may well be worth writing to the creditor. It is no use to him to be continually having trouble with your loan. If you can show that you will be able to repay by extending the total period of payment and decreasing the amount of each instalment, the creditor is likely to agree to this, rather than have the trouble of going to court.

If the creditor takes out court proceedings, get legal advice right away. (You can do this under the 'green form' scheme, see page 428). The court has power to order that judgment be suspended, or that money be paid by instalments; but it won't make such an order unless you or your legal representative is present.

Where a creditor has got a judgment against you in your absence, you can apply to have a new hearing, or for time to pay. Again, get legal advice.

Buying goods on credit (including HP)

If you are buying goods on credit all of the above explanation applies just as it would to any loan.

But often the creditor will retain the ownership of the goods until he has been paid in full. This can be done by a hire purchase (HP) agreement (i.e. one where you only get *a right to buy* when you have paid the instalments) or by a 'conditional sale' (where there is a sale right away, but you don't become the owner of the goods until you have paid the full price).

The advantage this gives to the creditor is that, until the price is paid, he can take back the goods. Because this advantage was used unscrupulously, the Consumer Credit Act 1974 and other legislation protects you in cases where you are paying off by instalments, and the total amount lent is less than £5,000.

Before reclaiming the goods, the creditor must serve a 'default notice', and this must state how any default can be remedied. When the full provisions of the Consumer Credit Act are in force, the default notice will entitle you to ask the court for more time, and also to vary the arrangements for payment. If you receive a default notice, *act on it*. Either pay the money claimed, or get legal advice. If you don't act, the creditor may be entitled to repossess the goods. (In general, he will have to go to court to do so if you have paid one third or more of the total price.)

The consumer credit legislation also gives you a right to return the goods when you have paid half the total purchase price, and thus bring the agreement to an end. But apart from this case, it can be very dangerous to return the goods. Creditors often state that a minimum payment has to be made on doing so. That usually won't be enforceable, but again, get legal advice.

Note: when you buy goods on credit you often find that the person who is selling to you is not the person you are dealing with. If the credit is being provided by a finance company, it is common practice for the retailer to give you some forms in which you make a contract with the finance company. At the same time, he fills in a form in which he sells the goods to them. This does not prejudice your legal rights in respect of the goods (see Chapter 31). If you have any complaint about the goods, you can act against whoever is the seller under your agreement, whether it be the retailer or the finance company. If it is the finance company, they are bound by any promises or representations made by the retailer.

You and Your Car

37 Preparing your car for the road

Having obtained your car, you cannot of course just get into it and drive away. There are a number of formalities which must be attended to, which may be summarized as follows:

- the car must be registered and licensed, and the name of the owner (or new owner if it is a second-hand car) must be entered in the log book;
- you must be in possession of a valid driving licence;
- you must take out a third-party insurance policy covering the use of the car which satisfies at least the minimum requirements of the law;
- except in the case of a car which was first registered less than three years previously, you must be in possession of a valid MOT test certificate relating to the car (this is still known as a Ministry of Transport test certificate although the Ministry has now become the Department of Transport and is headed by a Secretary of State).

Registration and licensing

Registration

The registration and licensing of motor vehicles is now the responsibility of the Driver and Vehicle Licensing Centre, Swansea, which operates through local vehicle licensing offices. Motor vehicles must be both registered and licensed before they can be driven on the road. If you buy a second-hand car, it will of course be already registered, but you should check whether the excise licence is still valid and if it is not you should apply for a new one. If the car is both registered and licensed then all you need to do is to register the change of ownership by sending the registration book (popularly known as the log book) to the Registration and Licensing Centre for amendment. If you buy a new car you should check that it is both registered and licensed before you take it out on the road.

When the vehicle is first registered it is the duty of the Minister to issue a registration book and to allot the vehicle a registration number. The registration book contains the name and address of the registered owner and should be kept by him. If the car is sold it is the duty of the seller to notify the change of ownership and of the buyer to fill in his own name and address in the registration book and send it in, in order that the change may be registered. Even when the owner of the vehicle merely changes his address he must fill in his new address in the log book and send it in for registration (something that can very easily be overlooked). The registration number must be displayed on plates at both the front and the rear of the vehicle. The plates must conform in size and colour to certain legal requirements and it is an offence to allow them to become so obscured by mud, etc. that they become illegible.

Licensing

Application for an excise licence should be made not more than fourteen days before the date on which the licence is required to take effect and should be accompanied by the registration book, the appropriate certificate of insurance, the MOT test certificate (if applicable), and of course a cheque for the duty payable. The rate of duty depends on the use to which the vehicle is to be put; it is an offence to use a vehicle for any purpose for which the correct rate of duty has not been paid. The current rate of duty for a private car is £85 per annum. A private car can however be used for the carriage of goods, even goods in connection with a trade or business, without incurring any higher duty, provided it is not adapted for the purpose. If it is so adapted, it becomes a goods vehicle and a higher rate of duty must be paid, as long as it is used for the carriage of goods.

Excise licences may be issued for any period of six or twelve months and the licence itself must be displayed on the windscreen of the car in such a position that it can be easily seen. It is an offence to keep or use a car on a public road unless it is licensed. It is not necessary that it should be driven. Even if the owner has no intention of driving it the car must still be licensed if it is kept on a public road.

Contrary to popular belief, no days of grace are allowed in the renewal of an excise licence and application for renewal should be made a week or two before the current licence expires.

Driving licences

Obtaining your licence

It is an offence to drive a motor vehicle on a road if the driver does not hold a valid driving licence authorizing him to drive vehicles of the class in question. Except in the case of those persons who, at some time in the ten years immediately preceding the date of the application, have held a full driving licence, such a licence will only be issued to persons who produce evidence that they have passed the test of competence to drive (the driving test). Furthermore, the applicant for a driving licence must satisfy the Minister on the following points:

- that he is old enough to drive (the minimum age for driving a motorcar is seventeen);
- that he is not disqualified from driving;
- that he is able to read in good daylight (with the aid of glasses if worn) a number plate at a distance of 75 feet if the letters and figures are 3½ inches high and 67 feet if they are only 3⅛ inches high;
- that he is not suffering from a relevant disability. Relevant disabilities include epilepsy, severe subnormality, mental deficiency and sudden attacks of disabling giddiness or fainting. If the applicant is suffering from a relevant disability the Minister may refuse to grant a licence at all or may grant it for a limited period only or subject to such conditions as to the type of vehicle to be driven as he thinks fit. In making this decision the Minister has the right to consult the applicant's medical advisers and also any report that may have been made on his performance by the examiner who conducted his driving test. The applicant must declare on his application form any disability whether relevant or not which might affect his fitness as a driver either now or in the future. He must also inform the Minister should any such disability develop after the licence has been issued, and failure to do either of these things is an offence.

Provisional licences

Unless the applicant has held a full driving licence or has passed the driving test at some time during the preceding ten years the first licence issued to him will be a provisional licence which is valid for one year only but may be renewed. The holder of a provisional licence may drive a car on the road but only subject to the following conditions:

- he must display 'L' plates at the front and rear of the vehicle;
- he may drive only when accompanied by a supervisor. The supervisor does not have to be a registered driving instructor, but he must be the holder of a full driving licence authorizing him to drive vehicles of the class in question;
- he may not draw a trailer nor drive on a motorway.

When the holder of a provisional licence has passed his driving test he will be given a certificate of having passed the test of competence to drive and will be treated as if he were the holder of a full licence. He may exchange his provisional licence for a full licence immediately if he wishes. Alternatively he may wait until his provisional licence expires and exchange it then. Full driving licences are now issued to last until the holder reaches the age of seventy. A driver whose licence expires when he reaches the age of seventy is of course entitled to have it renewed but may be subject to further medical checks. The current fee for a full licence and for a provisional licence is £10.

Classification of driving licences

For the purpose of licensing drivers, motor vehicles are divided into groups. Persons who have held driving licences for many years may find that they are authorized to drive vehicles of any group, but for a long time it has been the practice to issue licences which authorize the holder only to drive vehicles in a specified group or groups. Should such a person wish to be qualified to drive vehicles of a different group it will usually be necessary for him to take an additional test, although for this purpose he will not normally need to take out a provisional licence – his full licence will usually serve as a provisional one.

Production of driving licence

When the licence has been issued it should be signed by the holder in ink (failure to do so is an offence) and should normally be carried around by the holder whenever he is driving. Any police constable may stop any vehicle that is being driven on a road at any time and demand production of the driving licence, but only for the purpose of ascertaining the name and address of the holder, the date of issue, and the authority by which it is issued. He is not entitled to look at any endorsements which may be on it. If the driver does not have his licence with him he does not commit an offence provided he produces it within five days at any police station named by him.

Unlike a certificate of insurance however (see below), he must produce it in person. He cannot send it by post.

Third-party insurance

Why we must have third-party insurance

The law relating to third-party insurance is complex and requires careful explanation. The basic principle is that if a person drives a motor vehicle on a road, he is liable for any personal injury or damage to property which that vehicle may cause, provided – and only provided – his own negligence was responsible for such damage or injury. He is not liable for damage or injury which is the result of a pure accident; for example, a crash caused by the fact that the driver has been stung by a passing wasp.

A motorcar can be a lethal weapon, and thc most trifling act of negligence can sometimes cause untold harm. The civil law does not measure degrees of negligence and if the driver has been in any way at fault he is liable for the total consequences of his actions. The average motorist is not usually able to meet the heavy claims that may be made against him, and even before third-party insurance was made compulsory in 1930, many motorists did insure on a voluntary basis against the risk of such actions being brought against them. Since 1930 it has been an offence for any person to use or to cause or permit any other person to use a motor vehicle on a road unless the use of that vehicle is covered by a third-party insurance policy which satisfies the minimum standards laid down by the Road Traffic Act. Since 1971 a passenger carried in the vehicle is treated as a third party for this purpose and it is now necessary to be insured against possible claims that may be made by him.

Minimum cover

Three important points now need to be stressed. The first is that the object of third-party insurance is to protect the third party, not the motorist, i.e. it is to ensure that the person who has been injured by the motorist's negligence shall not go uncompensated as a result of the inability of the motorist to meet the claim.

The second point is that the minimum cover required by the law is confined to actions for causing death or bodily injury and also to claims for the payment of such sums as the motorist might be liable for in respect of any emergency treatment which might be necessary if he is involved in an accident. A motorist is not required to insure against the risk of causing damage to property, although in practice most do.

The final point is that it is the *use* of the vehicle that must be covered by insurance, not the *vehicle* itself or the *driver*. A man may have a policy which covers himself while driving any vehicle, or he may have a policy which covers his car either when it is driven by himself (this is called a 'named-driver' policy) or when it is being driven by any licensed driver. In either case the law is satisfied, for it means that there will always be an insurance company willing to accept financial responsibility.

Types of policy

The insurance policy must be issued by an authorized insurer, who is defined as a person or body of persons carrying on motor insurance business in Great Britain. A wide variety of policies is available. The most important categories are as follows, although there are many subdivisions of each:

- policies which satisfy only the minimum requirements of the law, i.e. actions for causing death or bodily injury. These policies are of course the cheapest and are sometimes known as Road Traffic Act policies;
- policies which, in addition to the minimum cover required by law, protect the motorist against the risk of actions brought in respect of damage to property. The property is usually another vehicle but it may be a wall, gatepost, or shop window, etc. Although it is not legally necessary, the vast majority of motorists do in fact have this protection;
- policies which, in addition to all the above, provide cover for the driver himself and his vehicle. These are known as comprehensive policies and may be confined to damage, fire or theft in respect of the insured's own vehicle or may be extended to give full personal cover to the driver himself and even his family if he wishes. These policies are the most expensive but where the car is being bought on hire purchase it is probable that the finance company, for its own protection, will insist on such a policy being taken out. Even a comprehensive policy, however, seldom covers all forms of consequential loss, such as loss of earnings if the driver is injured, or the hire of a replacement car. These can of course be made the subject of a separate insurance policy if required.

Insurance companies vary in the premium they demand. Often their premiums vary according to the circumstances of the applicant. Young people frequently have to pay more than older persons, for the accident rate is higher among the young; applicants in a poor state of health or with a bad driving record must not be surprised if they find they have to pay more in consequence. It is usually a good plan to take out your policy through an insurance broker, who because of his greater experience of the market can often secure terms more suitable to the applicant's circumstances than if he attempts to do the job himself.

No-claims bonuses

Most companies offer 'no-claims bonuses', i.e. a reduction in the premium for each year of accident-free motoring. It is important to remember, however, that a no-claims bonus means what it says. It is not a no-fault bonus. Most insurance companies have agreements among themselves for the mutual settlement of small claims irrespective of fault (known as knock-for-knock agreements), and a company which has had to pay out under one of these agreements may well reduce the motorist's no-claims bonus even though the motorist may have been in no way to blame.

Contractual nature of third-party insurance

A third-party insurance policy is in essence no more than a contract between the insurance company and the insured motorist, under which the company agrees to meet any financial claims that may be made against the motorist as a result of his driving his car on the road.

There is one respect in which an insurance policy differs from nearly all other types of contract. It is what lawyers call a contract of the utmost good faith. This means that both parties must disclose to the other all relevant facts, i.e. all facts which might make the other party hesitate before concluding the bargain. This does not apply to most contracts. When two people make a contract, the law does not usually require them to reveal facts which might be detrimental to their interests. They must not lie or cheat, and if they are asked questions they must answer them truthfully. But they do not have to volunteer information if they do not wish to do so. This does not apply to insurance policies. It is difficult to see what information the company could have which would be of interest to the motorist, but the motorist is in a very different position. He alone knows his own personal circumstances and it is obvious that these may have a very direct bearing on the willingness of the company to accept the insurance. Failure on the motorist's part to disclose this information will entitle the company to repudiate the policy.

This principle, incidentally, applies to all forms of insurance but it is perhaps most important of all in third-party insurance, where the applicant's driving record, his previous convictions if any, the state of his health, the use he makes of his car, etc. are all facts which should be fully revealed.

Repudiation of liability

A contract can be made subject to conditions, provided that both parties agree to them and if either party breaks a condition the other party may be entitled to repudiate the contract. Insurance companies almost invariably insert conditions in their policies. Typical examples are that the motorist shall not admit liability if he is involved in an accident and that he shall report the accident immediately to the insurance company.

If the motorist were to break any of these conditions this might entitle the company to repudiate their liability on the contract. But if this happened the person who would suffer would be the unfortunate third party, who might find himself deprived of the compensation which he would otherwise have expected to receive. He could of course, as we have already seen, bring an action against the motorist but the motorist might not have the necessary funds to meet the claim.

Since the whole purpose of insurance is to protect the third party, the law has made special provisions for this. The rules are complicated but their effect is as follows. In most cases where the company repudiates liability for breach of a condition, having the legal right to do so, it must still pay the third party's claim. The company can then recover the amount from the motorist if it can get it. Unfortunately this protection applies only to the minimum cover required by the law, that is actions for causing death or bodily injury. If, therefore, the third party's claim is for damage to his property only, he may well get nothing if the insurance company repudiates the policy for breach of condition.

If the motorist is bankrupt

One would have thought that with so many rules the position of the third party would be foolproof, but it is not. There are still several loopholes not all of which have been effectively plugged by the law. The first problem arises when the insured motorist is bankrupt.

A person is said to be bankrupt when his liabilities exceed his assets. In such a case, since he cannot pay his debts in full he is permitted, on certain conditions, to clear himself by paying each creditor a percentage of what he owes him. Obviously a bankrupt cannot be permitted to pay any one of his creditors in full, since to do so would reduce the available assets and amount to a fraud on the other creditors. According to the provisions of a third-party insurance policy, the obligation of the company (except in those exceptional cases where, as we have seen, the third party is entitled to take direct action against the company) is to pay the insured motorist, who must then use the money to satisfy the third party's claim. But if the motorist is bankrupt the third party's claim will be only one of his debts, possessing no priority, and there is a danger that the third party will get only a proportion of what is due to him. In such circumstances the law again directs that the motorist's claim on his insurance company shall be transferred to the third party, who may then enforce it direct.

The Motor Insurers' Bureau

There remain only the problems of the uninsured driver and the hit-and-run driver. To drive a motor vehicle on a road without adequate insurance cover is a serious offence, but this would be small consolation to the injured third party who may find that his only remedy is a rather dubious claim against the motorist himself. And if, as in a hit-and-run case, the motorist cannot be traced, he will not even have that consolation. To meet this problem the insurance companies themselves have set up and financed a body known as the Motor Insurers' Bureau. Although originally a voluntary body, this is now semi-official and operates under the terms of various agreements that it has made with the Department of Transport. The method of operation is as follows.

Where the motorist is uninsured the third party must first bring proceedings against the offender himself, notifying the Bureau either before or not later than seven days after the start of the proceedings. If a judgment is obtained, but not satisfied in full, the Bureau will then pay to the third party any balance which remains outstanding. Where the offending motorist cannot be traced at all the Bureau will usually meet the claim, provided application is made to it not later than three years from the date of the event which gave rise to the claim.

Finally it must be confessed that there are occasions when even the Motor Insurers' Bureau can prove to be a broken reed. In the first place the protection it affords applies only to those risks which are required by law to be covered by compulsory insurance, i.e. death or bodily injury. The person whose property or vehicle is damaged by an uninsured driver will receive no help from the Bureau, and if the driver cannot be traced he is literally without any remedy at all. In the second place no protection is given where the plaintiff has been injured by deliberate running-down. Lastly the Bureau accepts no responsibility where the vehicle in question is owned by or is in the possession of the Crown.

Certificate of insurance

When the insurance has been effected the company will issue a certificate of insurance, which the motorist should carry around with him. Since the policy may take some time to prepare most companies will issue immediately a cover-note, which has the same effect as a certificate of insurance. The procedure to be followed if you are involved in an accident is described in Chapter 41, but it is worth stressing here that any police constable has the right to stop any motor vehicle that is being driven on the road and demand production of the insurance certificate. If the driver does not have the certificate with him, no offence is committed provided it is produced within five days at any police station named by him. In this case however (unlike the case of the driving licence) it does not have to be produced in person. It can be sent by post.

Exemptions from third-party insurance

The following classes of vehicle are not required to be covered by third-party insurance:

- vehicles owned by a person who has been able to set aside the sum of £15,000 to meet any possible claims that may be made against him. It is remarkable that this sum has not been increased in fifty years in spite of the ravages of inflation. Probably this is because so few people take advantage of this provision;
- Crown vehicles;
- vehicles owned by certain public bodies such as local councils, the police, and area health authorities;
- invalid carriages.

You will have seen by now that the law relating to compulsory third-party insurance is very complicated, and you may perhaps think that much of it will not apply to you. In all probability you are right. The trouble is you can't be sure. Hit-and-run accidents occur every day. The man who knocks you down in his Jaguar may turn out to be a businessman teetering on the verge of bankruptcy, and the courts are full of actions brought by disappointed third parties who find their legitimate expectations defeated by circumstances arising out of the relationship between the motorist and his insurance company of which they knew nothing. It is as well therefore to be prepared. You cannot be too careful.

MOT test certificate

Construction and Use Regulations

The Minister of Transport has always had power under the Road Traffic Acts to prescribe by regulation the construction, weight and equipment of motor vehicles and the manner in which they may be used on the roads. This power he has exercised by issuing the Motor Vehicles (Construction and Use) Regulations. These regulations are frequently amended, and it is the practice of the Department to issue a new and completely revised edition every three or four years. The current edition is dated 1978.

Motor vehicles are classified into recognized types in the Road Traffic Act, and no motor vehicle may be used on a road unless it conforms to one or other of the recognized types. Where, however, it is necessary to design a special type of vehicle for a particular job (e.g. the carriage of an abnormal load) the Minister has power to authorize the use of such vehicles by making what is called a Motor Vehicles (Authorization of Special Types) Order.

Part II of the Construction and Use Regulations lays down rules governing the overall length and width of each type of vehicle. It also prescribes detailed requirements relating to such matters as brakes, tyres, springs, seat belts, speedometers, petrol tanks, mirrors, windscreen wipers and washers, horns, silencers, lighting equipment, and even such unlikely items as closets and urinals fitted to a motor vehicle. Part III deals with the maintenance of such equipment and the manner in which a vehicle may be driven on a road. Most of the regulations concern goods vehicles but there is much that affects the private motorist.

The requirements are very complex and to set them all out in detail would require a book several times the size of this one. If the reader is in doubt regarding the equipment on his vehicle or the manner in which it is being maintained he would be well advised to seek help from a police station (or perhaps a local garage), since it is an offence to use a motor vehicle on a road in contravention of the Construction and Use Regulations.

The testing of motor vehicles

The law has always controlled the construction and maintenance of motor vehicles but it is only in the past twenty years or so that the rules have become as detailed as they are today. This reflects the increased number of vehicles on the road and the increased efficiency of the law-enforcement machinery. The more detailed the rules are, the greater is the likelihood that they will be broken, and the more necessary it is to ensure that this does not happen. The powers of the police and vehicle examiners to impose spot checks on vehicles will be dealt with in a later part of this book (Chapter 42), but something must be said here of the arrangements for the periodical testing of motor vehicles.

Heavy goods vehicles must be tested annually from the moment they are first used on the road. Light goods vehicles and private cars must be first tested not later than three years from the date of first registration and thereafter annually. In the case of private cars, tests are usually carried out at garages specially approved for the purpose by the Department of Transport. The statutory requirements of the test include the following items: brakes, steering gear, lighting equipment and reflectors, stop lamps, tyres, seat belts and seat anchorages, direction indicators, windscreen wipers and washers, horns, and the condition and bodywork of the vehicle in so far as this may affect the vehicle's braking or steering. If the vehicle passes the test the owner will be given a certificate to that effect. If the vehicle fails the test the owner will also be given a certificate to that effect specifying the reasons for the failure. It is possible to appeal to the Minister of Transport against the refusal of a test certificate but it is not advisable to do so unless you are very sure of your ground. A vehicle that has failed the test may of course be resubmitted for a further test as soon as the defects have been remedied.

A police constable is empowered to stop any motor vehicle on the road at any time and demand production of the MOT test certificate where relevant. If the driver does not have the test certificate with him he may produce it at any police station named by him within five days. In no circumstances should you wait until your existing certificate expires before resubmitting your car for testing. The test certificate is valid for one year but where the vehicle is retested not more than a month before the existing certificate expires, the new certificate will commence to run on the day the old certificate expires.

It is an offence to use on a road a motor vehicle subject to testing if a valid MOT test certificate is not in force. It is not, however, an offence to do so if the vehicle is being driven in any of the following circumstances:

- on its way to or from a place where by previous arrangement the test is to be carried out;
- for the purpose of the test itself;
- where a test certificate is refused, on its way to or from a place where by previous arrangement the defect is to be remedied;
- where it is being towed on its way to a place where it is to be broken up.

It will be noted that the first of those exemptions applies only where arrangements for the test have been previously made. There is some doubt about the legal position when the vehicle is taken to a garage which offers to test vehicles without previous arrangement and it is suggested that, unless the vehicle already has a valid test certificate, you should not take it to a garage for testing without a prior appointment if you wish to be sure of avoiding prosecution.

Offences

(See page 405 for proposed increases in maximum fines.)

Offence	*Maximum penalty*	*Endorsement*	*Disqualification*
Driving without a licence	£100	Obligatory if accused is not entitled to hold a licence, but not if he has merely forgotten to renew it.	Discretionary, but only where endorsement is obligatory
Failing to comply with conditions prescribed for a provisional licence	£100	Obligatory	Discretionary
Driving with defective eyesight	£100	Obligatory	Discretionary
Obtaining a driving licence while disqualified	£100	—	—

Offence	*Maximum penalty*	*Endorsement*	*Disqualification*
Driving while disqualified	(a) summarily – 6 months and/or £1,000 (b) on indictment – 12 months and/or a fine	Obligatory	Discretionary
Failing to produce a licence in court	£100	—	—
Failing to sign a driving licence	£50	—	—
Failing to produce driving licence, insurance certificate or test certificate when lawfully required to do so	£50	—	—
Using a motor vehicle while uninsured	£200	Obligatory	Discretionary
Failing to comply with Construction and Use Regulations	£100, or in certain serious cases involving danger £400*	No, except where disqualification may be ordered when it is obligatory	Only in certain serious cases involving danger when it is discretionary
Using a vehicle subject to testing without a test certificate	£100	—	—

*The Transport Act 1982 proposes to increase these penalties to £500 and £1,000 respectively.

38 Driving your car on the road

This chapter is about the highway itself and the ways in which the various users of it are controlled by means of signs, lights, and other devices. It also deals with the legal requirements about lights on motor vehicles.

Highways and highway authorities

What is a public highway?

Roads are such a common feature of the English countryside that it is not easy to appreciate the complicated legislation that surrounds them. Many centuries ago when most of the land in England was privately owned, it was realized that it was necessary to give the public the right to travel. To facilitate this, landowners would 'dedicate' a part of their land to the public for their use. The land so dedicated was known as a public highway and the cost of maintaining it fell upon the inhabitants at large, which usually meant the parish. The right to use the highway was however confined to a right to 'pass and re-pass' only. Strictly speaking this is still the law today, and neither pedestrians nor motorists have the right to congregate on a public highway. It is true that the courts have recognized the right of a pedestrian to stand still for such innocent purposes as tying his shoelace or looking in a shop window, and the motorist who stops his car in order to buy a newspaper is unlikely to fear police harassment; but the police do have the right to 'move on' both pedestrians and motorists – a right which they exercise very sparingly and only when circumstances make it absolutely necessary.

The expression 'public highway' means therefore simply a place where the public have a right to go. It is not synonymous with road and includes all public places such as squares, cul-de-sacs, and even footpaths. It should be contrasted with a private road which is the property (and also the responsibility) of the owner. It often happens that the public are permitted to use private roads, but when they do so, they use them by leave only and not by legal right. A public right of way over private land can only arise when the public have made uninterrupted use of the land for a considerable number of years without their right to do so ever having been effectively challenged, and landowners sometimes prevent this from happening by exhibiting a notice to the effect that the public use the land by leave only. Alternatively they sometimes close the land for one day in the year. Both methods are effective by showing either that the public do not use the land by right or that their use of the land has not been uninterrupted. When a new housing estate is built it sometimes happens that the roads on it are private roads until such time as the local highway authority is prepared to take over the responsibility of maintaining them. This process is known as 'adoption' and one may still see the notice 'Not adopted' at the entrance to streets in urban areas.

Highway authorities

The old process of dedicating a highway is now a thing of the past. Modern highways are created by the highway authority which is usually the local county council (in London it is often the council of a London borough) or, in the case of national trunk roads, the Department of Transport. The highway authority is responsible for building and maintaining the highways (for which purpose it receives a grant from central government funds), and a person who has suffered injury or damage as a result of the defective state of the highway may well have an action against the highway authority if he can show that it was their negligence that caused his loss.

The advent of the motor vehicle did little to change the law on public highways, except that it became customary to regard a road as divided into two parts – the carriageway for the use of vehicles and the footpath or verge for the use of pedestrians. However, whereas the pedestrian has an unrestricted right to use the carriageway whenever he chooses, the right of the motorist to use the footpath is restricted by law. The growing practice of parking cars on pavements and footpaths is one of dubious legality. There is a section in the Road Traffic Act 1974 which prohibits this, but this section has not yet been brought into force although the government has been threatening to do so for some time. In some areas the practice is forbidden by by-laws.

It is an offence to drive a motor vehicle off the road altogether except only when it is driven not more than fifteen yards from the road and solely for the purpose of parking.

Motorways

One serious disadvantage of the old system of dedicating highways and making them the financial responsibility of the parish concerned was that roads tended very much to be local affairs. The inconvenience of this became more obvious when the growing mobility of the population created a demand for roads that would enable people to travel from one part of the country to another in the shortest possible space of time. The classification of roads into 'A' and 'B' categories by the Ministry of Transport in the nineteen-twenties had little significance in law, but in 1936 Parliament by the Trunk Roads Acts transformed many of the major 'A' roads into trunk roads. These were taken out of the hands of the local authorities and made the direct responsibility of the Ministry of Transport. Unfortunately these roads were simply the old roads added together, and they faithfully reproduced the squiggles and turns which had not mattered so much in earlier times when the Queen's Highway was intended to be used by man and beast alone. Although many attempts were made to straighten and improve these roads, the need for straight purpose-built roads became more obvious. In this respect England lagged sadly behind the Continent, and it was not until 1949 that Parliament authorized the building of special roads – motorways – and even later than that before the necessary finance was made available.

Motorways are special roads in more senses than one. They have their own special regulations which do not apply to ordinary roads. They have their own system of traffic signs and their own speed limits. They may be used only by certain classes of vehicle (pedestrians, pedal-cycles, light motorcycles, and learner drivers are all banned). Above all, parking and the making of U-turns are strictly forbidden, and so is stopping for any purpose except in a serious emergency, when ordered to do so by a police officer, or as a result of mechanical breakdown. Detailed guidance on motorway rules and the manner in which motorways may be used will be found in the Highway Code.

The Highway Code

One of the problems which face the people who draft road traffic law is the immense amount of detail which the subject-matter necessitates. If all this detail were made law there is a danger that the law might become top-heavy and unenforceable. There is also a danger that injustice might be done; for, while there are many things that a good driver should not normally do, there may well be exceptional circumstances – far too wide and varied in nature to specify in legislation – which may make it absolutely essential for him to do them. To meet this problem Parliament has authorized the issue of the Highway Code.

The Highway Code is a statutory document issued on the authority of the Road Traffic Act, and a detailed knowledge of its provisions is essential for everyone who wishes to pass the test of competence to drive. But the Highway Code is not itself law in the sense that a breach of its provisions will automatically expose you to a criminal prosecution. It is rather a code of practice – a collection of common-sense rules with which you are expected to comply. If you do not comply with these rules the court may well consider you have been driving carelessly or even recklessly, unless there is a very good reason for your failure to do so.

What the Road Traffic Act actually says is the following:

> A failure on the part of a person to observe a provision of the Highway Code shall not of itself render that person liable to criminal proceedings of any kind but any such failure may in any proceedings (whether civil or criminal . . .) be relied upon by any party to the proceedings as tending to establish or to negative any liability which is in question in those proceedings.

What this means is that where a court has to decide whether or not a person has behaved in a reasonable manner in a given set of circumstances, the question of whether or not he has complied with the provisions of the Code may be a very relevant factor. For the average motorist therefore the Highway Code is probably more important than the Road Traffic Act itself. His own safety as well as the safety of others will probably depend on his observance of it.

Traffic signs

Classification of traffic signs

One cannot travel far on an English road without seeing a traffic sign. They come in all shapes, sizes and colours, and a generous selection will be found in the Highway Code, although the list given there is by no means exhaustive. One advantage of the trend towards Europeanization is that most traffic signs are now common throughout Europe, so that the driver who takes his car abroad will at least be in familiar surroundings.

It is sometimes said that traffic signs can be classified according to their shape. The rectangular ones give information, e.g. they tell you how many miles you are from the nearest town. Triangular ones give warnings, usually of hazards ahead, while the circular ones are mandatory – you comply with them or else. Although this is roughly true there are of course exceptions.

A more scientific classification is between those traffic signs which are authorized under Section 22 of the Road Traffic Act 1972 and those which depend for their validity on local traffic regulation orders. This requires a little explanation. Signs authorized under Section 22 are known as 'statutory prohibitions, restrictions or requirements'. The Minister of Transport has power to determine them, and the current list is as follows:

- Stop (at junction of major road)
- Give way (at junction of major road)
- Stop (road works ahead)
- Straight arrow indicating that traffic is to proceed in a given direction
- Diagonal arrows meaning 'Keep left' or 'Keep right'
- Red traffic lights (including flashing red signals on motorways)
- Double white lines painted on the road
- Round red sign with a white band meaning 'No entry'
- Temporary signs erected by the police such as 'No waiting' cones.

Traffic regulation orders

The regulation of traffic in local areas, however, is very much a matter for the local authority. Only they can know their own district. Any local authority which is also a highway authority can therefore make a traffic regulation order dealing with such matters as the direction in which traffic may proceed, restrictions on waiting and on the loading and unloading of vehicles. Once these orders are approved by the Minister of Transport they have the force of law. Hence signs such as 'No right turn' or 'One-way street' are usually authorized under local traffic regulation orders.

If you disobey a traffic sign which conveys a positive requirement or restriction (it is difficult to see how you can disobey a traffic sign which merely warns you that the road narrows or informs you that you are ten miles from Bristol), you commit an offence; it does not make much difference whether the traffic sign is authorized under Section 22 or a local traffic regulation order – the maximum penalty is the same. It is true that offences against local traffic regulation orders are not disqualifiable, while offences against the traffic signs authorized under Section 22 usually are, but there is not much comfort in this. If you swing across a line of traffic in defiance of a 'No right turn' sign, or drive in the wrong direction along a one-way street, it is extremely probable that the police will add on a charge of careless driving as well – and that is disqualifiable.

Section 22 offences

Section 22 creates two separate offences, which are as follows:

- disobeying a signal given by a police constable who is for the time being engaged in the regulation of traffic in a road;
- failing to comply with a traffic sign which indicates a statutory prohibition, restriction, or requirement.

The expression 'traffic sign' is defined as including not only traffic signs in the conventional sense (whether fixed or portable), but also lines or marks painted on the surface of a road, and the red light shown on traffic signals. Something must be said about the latter. If the traffic lights are showing red or red-with-amber this is an absolute order to stop in all circumstances. Contrary to popular belief there is no right to jump the traffic lights where they are showing red-with-amber. The only exception is where a horizontal green arrow is also illuminated indicating that it is permissible to 'filter' to the left despite the red light. On motorways and at places such as level-crossings a flashing red light is sometimes used instead. What is the position if the traffic lights (as sometimes happens) are stuck at red? There is no law on this subject but a judge once expressed the opinion that provided the motorist has waited a reasonable time to make sure that the lights are not working properly, he commits no offence if he proceeds, provided he does so with great caution. The amber light alone is also an order to stop but in this case only if you can do so in safety. If you cannot safely stop, bearing in mind the traffic behind you, you may cross the lights. The green light is of course an indication that you may proceed but it is not a licence to commit mayhem or manslaughter. You are still bound by the general law which requires you to drive carefully in all cases, and if some silly idiot has jumped the light ahead of you you cannot ram him simply because the lights were in your favour.

Ignoring the signals of a police officer who is for the time being engaged in the regulation of traffic in a road is also an offence, and to this has now been added signals by a police officer to pull up or proceed in a certain direction for the purpose of taking part in a traffic survey. Traffic wardens are sometimes specially authorized to regulate traffic, and where this is the case it is an offence to ignore their signals too. It is also an offence for a pedestrian to disobey the signals of a police officer who is regulating traffic, although prosecutions for this are rarely brought.

Police officers have no power generally to order a motorist to break the law, although this is something that needs to be interpreted with a good deal of common sense, since police officers do have a general duty to protect life and property which can sometimes override the law. In one case a serious accident occurred in a one-way street. In order to clear the street for the speedy arrival of the ambulance a police officer ordered a motorist to reverse his vehicle in the wrong direction. This he refused to do and he was later convicted, not for disobeying the instruction (which was technically illegal), but for obstructing a police officer in the execution of his duty.

Defences

Assuming that you have been charged with disobeying a policeman's signal or failing to comply with a traffic sign, what defences are available to you? Firstly it must be said that these are offences to which the 'notice of intended prosecution' procedure applies (see Chapter 42, page 386), and if you have been neither warned nor notified of the intention to prosecute within fourteen days then no prosecution can be brought. It is not a defence that the accused did not see the traffic sign, since the law will say, not unreasonably, that if he had been keeping a proper look-out he would have seen it. The position in relation to a police signal is less certain. If the circumstances were such that the motorist could not possibly see the signal, then he probably has a defence but they would have to be extreme. Presumably the policeman himself would be plainly visible and the motorist ought to anticipate the possibility that he might give signals. Where the contravention was due to circumstances in which the motorist was wholly blameless he will certainly have a good defence, e.g. a sudden mechanical breakdown (provided this was not caused by faulty maintenance), or the fact that he was run into from behind. A motorist can scarcely be expected to see a traffic sign painted on the road if the road is six inches deep in snow, but this argument might not apply to a conventional traffic sign. The law might argue that he could see the traffic sign anyway and it was his duty to stop and clear the snow away in order to see what it said. Traffic signs must conform in size, colour and type to specifications laid down by the Minister of Transport and if the sign is so defective as to be scarcely recognizable this might be a good defence. There is a presumption, however, that traffic signs do conform to the specifications and the burden of proof, which would be a heavy one, would be on the motorist.

Seat belts

The fitting of seat belts in the front seats of cars and most types of light vans and three-wheeled motor vehicles has been compulsory for many years and, since 31 January 1983 it has been an offence to drive such vehicles or to ride in the front seats unless such a seat belt is worn. The regulation applies only to persons who are over fourteen but it is the driver's responsibility to see that children under fourteen do not ride in the front unless they are wearing a seat belt or are in an approved type of child restraint.

Seat belts need not be worn by the following categories of persons:

- Persons holding a valid medical exemption certificate (see below for details);
- Persons who are making local delivery or collection rounds (whether goods or mail) and using a vehicle constructed or adapted for that purpose;
- Police officers while protecting or escorting persons;
- Firemen while on duty and wearing operational clothing or equipment;
- Taxi-drivers while plying for hire or carrying passengers for hire;
- Drivers of private hire vehicles while carrying passengers for hire;
- Persons riding on a vehicle being used under a trade licence for the purpose of investigating or remedying faults.

Apart from the above exempted categories the seat belt need not be worn in the following circumstances:

- When you are reversing or involved in a manoeuvre which includes reversing;
- By the supervisor of a learner-driver at any time while the learner-driver is carrying out a manoeuvre which involves reversing;
- By a person who is conducting a driving-test if the wearing of a seat belt would endanger himself or any other person;
- Where the seat belt has become defective on the journey in question, or even on a previous occasion provided steps have been taken to have it repaired or replaced.

Persons seeking exemption on medical grounds should in the first place consult their doctor. If a medical examination is necessary a fee will be payable and it would be advisable to ascertain how much this will be before the examination takes place. Persons in receipt of supplementary benefit or certain other welfare payments may be able to obtain a free examination on direct application to the Department of Transport. The exemption certificate, if granted, may be indefinite or for a limited period only. The certificate should be carried round by the holder and produced for inspection on demand by a police officer. If you do not have the certificate with you, however, you may produce it within five days at any police station specified by you.

Pedestrian crossings

Controlled and uncontrolled crossings

Pedestrians have the right to use any part of the carriageway whenever they choose to do so and may therefore cross it whenever and wherever they like. Where the traffic is heavy, this is obviously a dangerous thing to do and, to assist them, the law directs that in certain places a section of the carriageway shall be set aside for their use. These sections are known as pedestrian crossings and they may be controlled or uncontrolled.

A pedestrian crossing is said to be controlled when the flow of the traffic is regulated either by a policeman on point duty or by traffic lights. If there is a policeman on point duty, then both vehicles and pedestrians must obey his signals. If there are traffic lights, then vehicles must of course comply with them, but there is no legal requirement that pedestrians should do so. On the other hand, it is both stupid and dangerous for a pedestrian to cross against the lights; if he were knocked down and injured while doing so he would probably find it very difficult to make out a case against the motorist concerned. A crossing that is controlled neither by a policeman nor by traffic lights is said to be uncontrolled, and on these, neither vehicles nor pedestrians have priority unless the crossing is marked as a zebra crossing, in which case pedestrians have priority. A zebra crossing ceases to be uncontrolled if a policeman has for the time being taken over the regulation of traffic on it, and in this case pedestrians lose their priority and must comply with the signals given by the policeman.

Zebra crossings

A zebra crossing is marked out in alternate black and white stripes, and a flashing orange globe is positioned at each end of it, sometimes on a bracket but more usually on the top of a vertical black-and-white striped pole. If the crossing is divided by a central reservation, each half of the crossing is treated in law as if it were a separate crossing. This means that a motorist is under no duty to accord precedence to a pedestrian who is on the other half of the crossing. Sometimes flashing orange globes are placed on the central reservation also, but there is no legal requirement that this should be done. The edges of the crossing are marked by a row of metal studs known as the limits of the crossing. Parallel to these studs and about a metre away a broken white line is painted on the road known as the give-way line, and the area beyond this line on each side of the crossing is marked out by zigzag lines. These areas are known as the zebra-controlled areas.

A zebra crossing does not cease to be a zebra crossing merely because one of the orange globes is not flashing properly or because some of the studs are missing or the marks on the road defective, provided the whole is clearly recognizable as a zebra crossing. Where, however, none of the globes is illuminated then the crossing ceases to be a zebra crossing, and no prosecution could be brought in respect of it.

Offences on a zebra crossing

There are four offences which a motorist may commit in connection with a zebra crossing. These are as follows:

- failing to accord precedence to a pedestrian;
- halting on the crossing itself;
- halting in the zebra-controlled area;
- overtaking a moving or stationary vehicle in the zebra-controlled area.

It is also an offence for a pedestrian to loiter on a zebra crossing, although prosecutions are seldom brought for it. Let us examine each of those four offences in detail.

Failing to accord precedence The pedestrian is entitled to precedence only when he has actually set foot on the crossing. A pedestrian waiting at the kerbside has no precedence, although the High Court has ruled that a woman pushing a perambulator has precedence provided the perambulator or part of it is on the crossing even though the woman herself is not. A pedestrian who steps on to the crossing after the vehicle has crossed the limits of the crossing (i.e. the line of studs at the side of the black and white stripes) has no precedence. The legal position which arises when a motorist crosses behind a pedestrian who has not reached the other side is a little uncertain. The courts have held conflicting opinions on this, and if you wish to be absolutely safe you should avoid doing it.

It cannot be emphasized too strongly that the duty to stop and give precedence to a pedestrian is an absolute one – even when he darts suddenly across the road under the wheels of your vehicle – for the law will say in that case that you knew you were approaching a pedestrian crossing and you should have been travelling at such a speed that you could stop if necessary at a second's notice. The only possible defence might be that for reasons which were absolutely no fault of yours at all you had lost control of the vehicle.

Halting on the crossing or in the zebra-controlled area Whether you stop on the zebra crossing itself or in the zebra-controlled area, it is equally an offence, even if you have passed over the crossing and have halted in the zebra-controlled area beyond it. Unlike the duty to accord precedence to a pedestrian, however, this is not an offence of absolute liability and there are a number of defences. Obviously it is not an offence if you have halted in order to accord precedence to a pedestrian. Nor is it an offence if you have halted as a result of circumstances that were entirely beyond your control, or for the purpose of avoiding an accident or (temporarily) before turning right or left. Vehicles used for police, fire-brigade, and ambulance, etc. purposes may halt if it is necessary for them to do so, and so also may buses for the purpose of picking up or setting down passengers, but in the latter case only in the zebra-controlled area on the far side of the crossing. Even if a policeman on point duty is for the time being regulating traffic on the crossing, it is still an offence to halt – unless of course the policeman has signalled you to do so, in which case it would be an offence not to.

Overtaking a moving or stationary vehicle in the zebra-controlled area This is only an offence when the vehicle overtaken is on the near side of the crossing. It is not an offence to overtake a vehicle on the zebra-controlled area on the far side. Moreover the vehicle overtaken must be either the only one in the area or the one that is nearest the crossing. It is not an offence to overtake a line of vehicles provided you pull up before you draw parallel with the leading one.

Overtaking is defined as allowing any part of your vehicle to pass in front of any part of the other one. Thus if you overtake you commit an offence even though, realizing what you have done, you subsequently draw back.

Where, however, the vehicle is stationary, it is only an offence to overtake it if it is halted for the purpose of according precedence to a pedestrian. It is not an offence to overtake a vehicle which is halted for any other purpose whether legitimate or illegitimate. But where the vehicle is halted for this purpose, you should be very careful indeed, for the law can be very strict. We have already seen that a vehicle is under no duty to accord precedence to a pedestrian who has not yet set foot on the crossing, but if out of courtesy a vehicle has done this, it is an offence for you to overtake it. Moreover in one, admittedly rather extreme, case a van drew up level with a Mini which had halted in order to accord precedence to a pedestrian. Because of its quicker acceleration, the van drew ahead of the Mini and the driver was convicted of overtaking, even though at the time in question the pedestrian had crossed over and was safely on the other side.

Pelican crossings

It is now a common practice to site pedestrian crossings in places where the flow of traffic is already controlled by traffic signals and to give the pedestrian some measure of control over the signals by operating a push-button. Since 1971 these crossings are known as pelican crossings, although other types of push-button-controlled crossings are occasionally found which do not conform precisely to pelican requirements. The characteristic of a pelican crossing is that when the pedestrian presses the push-button a green light (sometimes accompanied by an audible signal) indicates that it is safe for him to cross. As far as the motorist is concerned the law is very similar to the law relating to a zebra crossing, except that the sequence of light signals is different. In place of the red-with-amber there is a flashing amber light. This means that it is permissible for the motorist to cross but that he must accord precedence to any pedestrian who may happen to be still on the crossing.

Street playgrounds and school crossings

Street playgrounds

A street playground is a section of the carriageway which has been reserved either exclusively or in part for the use of children as a playground. They are occasionally found in built-up areas where playing facilities are restricted. Where such an area is so designated, its use by vehicular traffic is either prohibited, or restricted at all times, or at certain times only. Local authorities which set up playgrounds usually control their use by means of by-laws, and it is an offence for a motorist to infringe these.

School crossings

A school crossing is rather like a pedestrian crossing but differs from it in the sense that its use is confined to schoolchildren. A local authority may set up a school crossing in any place where between the hours of 8 a.m. and 5.30 p.m. children are in the habit of crossing to and from school.

Sometimes the school crossing is sited on an existing pedestrian crossing, but it does not have to be, and there is no requirement that the crossing must be marked out in any particular way. It must be controlled by a patrolman who must wear a prescribed uniform (which must include a white coat or macintosh – but where a traffic warden is acting as a school crossing patrolman, it is sufficient if the warden is wearing a traffic warden's uniform), and carry a prescribed sign, i.e. a circular sign with the words 'Stop – children' on it on the top of a vertical pole. Whenever this sign is exhibited it is the duty of the motorist to stop in order to accord precedence to the children.

Once the sign is exhibited there are two offences which a motorist may commit in connection with a school crossing. These are:

- failing to stop before reaching the place where the children are crossing; and
- setting the vehicle in motion so as to reach the place where the children are crossing before the sign is lowered.

In connection with the second offence it is pointed out that since the motorist cannot know when the patrolman intends to lower the sign, it is better, to be absolutely safe, not to set the vehicle in motion until he has done so.

There are, however, a number of defences to these charges. In the first place there must be children crossing or seeking to cross on their way to or from school and between the prescribed hours. The expression 'school' is liberally interpreted and includes private schools, Sunday schools, and nursery schools, but some kind of school there must be. It is a defence if the children are playing truant at the time although this might be difficult to prove. The law does not apply to adults although it seems that it does apply to a mixed party of children and adults, and in one case a motorist was convicted for interfering with the progress of an adult although at the time the children under her care had safely crossed over. What if the patrolman exhibits the sign when no children are crossing or seeking to cross? One motorist was acquitted on this ground but the correctness of the decision has been doubted and it is much wiser to stop in all circumstances, once the sign is exhibited.

In the second place the patrolman must be wearing at least his white coat (fluorescent jerkins or sleeves are sometimes worn in addition, but these are optional) and the sign exhibited must be of the prescribed type. There is a presumption of law that both the uniform and the sign conform to the requirements of the law, and if your defence is based on the fact that they do not, the burden of proof will be on you.

Finally, although the duty to stop, as in the case of a pedestrian crossing, is an absolute one, it is almost certain that the accused would be acquitted if he could show that his failure to stop was due entirely to circumstances beyond his control and for which he was in no way to blame.

Lighting

The regulations that govern the lighting equipment that must be carried on motor vehicles are very complex indeed and there are many variations dependent on the type of vehicle and the manner in which it is being used. It is not practicable in a book of this nature to set out these regulations in detail, but something must be said of the offences that arise in connection with them. The three most important are as follows:

- The Road Traffic Act itself lays down the minimum requirements which every vehicle must possess and also the additional requirements which are necessary in the case of vehicles of certain types. The Road Vehicles Lighting Regulations specify in great detail the construction and design of front lamps, rear lamps, reversing lamps, reflectors, direction indicators, stop lamps, etc. It is an offence to cause or permit a vehicle to be on a road in contravention of these provisions. The only defence is where the accused can show that the contravention occurred as a result of the negligence or default of some other person whose duty it was to provide the equipment. This defence is clearly intended chiefly to benefit a person who is driving a vehicle in the course of his employment but it might benefit the private motorist, e.g. where he drives a borrowed car in ignorance of the fact that the lighting equipment is defective.

Liability under the Road Traffic Act is strict and it is no defence that the driver did not know that he was breaking the law. In one rather extreme case a stone smashed a rear lamp and the driver was convicted because he drove for some distance without knowing that the lamp was out. Admittedly this was a very old case and it is possible that if these facts occurred today the police might at their discretion decide not to prosecute, or if they did, that the court might grant an absolute discharge, but there is no guarantee of this.

- The Construction and Use Regulations require motor vehicles to be equipped at all times with such lighting equipment and reflectors as would enable them to be driven at night without breaking the law. The law does not apply, however, to vehicles such as racing-cars which are not provided with any lighting equipment at all because they are never intended to be driven at night.
- The Construction and Use Regulations also require that the lighting equipment previously referred to shall at all times be maintained in such a condition that the vehicle could be driven during the hours of darkness without breaking the law. In this case it is a good defence to show that the contravention was due to a defect in the equipment which had only just occurred or, where the defect had occurred some time previously, that steps had already been taken to have the defect remedied, provided of course in both cases that the vehicle was not at the time being driven during the hours of darkness. The hours of darkness are defined as the time between half an hour after sunset to half an hour before sunrise.

Certain other miscellaneous offences deserve mention. It is an offence to sell or to offer to sell a motor vehicle the lighting equipment of which does not comply with the requirements of the law. It is, however, a good defence if the seller can show that he had reasonable cause to believe that the vehicle would not be used on a road during the hours of darkness until the defects had been remedied. It is an offence to use a motor vehicle on a public road during the hours of darkness without having the rear number plate illuminated, except only when the vehicle is lawfully parked without lights. In this case liability is not strict and it is a good defence if the accused can show that he had taken all reasonable steps to prevent this happening. Finally it is an offence to park a car without lights on a road during the hours of darkness unless *all* of the following conditions are satisfied:

- the road must be one subject to a speed limit of 30 m.p.h. or less;
- the car must be parked with the left or near side as close as possible and parallel to the edge of the carriageway (in a one-way street the car may be parked on either side provided it is as close as possible to the edge of the carriageway);
- no part of the car must be less than fifteen yards from a road junction (irrespective of whether the junction is on the same side of the road as the car or on the opposite side);
- the car must not have a caravan or trailer attached.

A private car may also be parked without lights in a recognized parking-place. The use of parking-lights is now discontinued and a car which cannot satisfy all the above requirements must display all four lights front and rear.

Offences

(See page 405 for proposed increases in maximum fines.)

Offence	*Maximum penalty*	*Endorsement*	*Disqualification*
Driving a motor vehicle elsewhere than on a road	£20	—	—
Prohibited vehicle using motorway	£500	Compulsory	Discretionary
Offence against the Motorway Regulations committed in respect of a motor vehicle except the offence of stopping on the hard shoulder	£500	Compulsory	Discretionary
Stopping on the hard shoulder of a motorway	£500	—	—
Disregarding the signal of a policeman on point duty or failing to comply with a traffic sign which indicates a statutory prohibition, restriction or requirement*	£100	Obligatory	Discretionary

*Notice of Intended Prosecution procedure applies to this offence (see Chapter 42).

Offence	*Maximum penalty*	*Endorsement*	*Disqualification*
Failing to comply with a traffic sign under a local traffic regulation order	£100	—	—
Offences on a pedestrian crossing	£100	Obligatory	Discretionary
Contravening an order relating to a street playground	£100	Obligatory	Discretionary
Offences in connection with school crossings	£100	Obligatory	Discretionary
Offences against the Lighting Regulations or against the lighting provisions of the Road Traffic Act	£100	—	—
Lighting offences under the Construction and Use Regulations	£100	—	—
Using a car at night without having the rear number-plate illuminated	£20 (£50 for a second or subsequent conviction)	—	—

39 Various road traffic offences

This chapter describes most of the common driving offences – such as speeding, careless and reckless driving, taking and driving away, and obstruction. It also suggests some defences for each offence and lists the maximum penalties.

Speeding

The commonest of all road traffic offences. It is not usually thought of as particularly serious but it carries endorsement and, therefore, if repeated too often it can lead to compulsory disqualification.

There are five different kinds of speed limit, which may be summarized as follows:

- speed limits imposed on a restricted road;
- speed limits imposed on particular classes of vehicle;
- general speed limits on roads other than motorways;
- general speed limits on motorways;
- speed limits imposed in special places such as royal parks or the London docks.

There is also an offence of failing to comply with a minimum speed limit, although prosecutions for this are comparatively rare, and the offence, unlike speeding generally, does not carry endorsement. Let us examine each of the major types of speed limit in turn.

Speed limit imposed in a restricted road

A restricted road (the old term for this was a built-up area) is a road in which there is a system of street lighting by means of lamps placed not more than two hundred yards apart. A trunk or classified road is not, however, a restricted road for this purpose even if it has such a system of street lighting unless that system was provided before 1 July 1957. On such a road a general speed limit of thirty m.p.h. is usually imposed, although the Minister does have the power to increase or reduce this limit. He also has the power to impose such a limit on a road which does not have the prescribed system and to 'derestrict' a road which does. The existence of the restriction is indicated by the familiar traffic sign (a figure surrounded by a red circle) and the absence or end of such a restriction by a white circle with a diagonal black bar.

In the absence of derestriction signs it is wise to assume that any road which has the prescribed system of street lighting is a restricted road. Where the road does not have the prescribed system and is restricted only by virtue of a direction given by the Minister then the absence of restriction signs is a complete defence to a prosecution.

Note: the exception relating to trunk and classified roads where a system of street lighting was installed before 1 July 1957 will be repealed when the relevant provisions of the Transport Act 1982 comes into force. For details see page 404.

Speed limits imposed on particular classes of vehicle

For certain special types of vehicle there is an overall speed limit which must be observed wherever it may be, except on a motorway, in which case the motorway speed limits will apply. Such a vehicle may therefore be subject to two speed limits – one in respect of the vehicle and one in respect of the road on which it is travelling. In such a case it must of course comply with whichever limit is the lower unless it is on a motorway. There is no special speed limit for private cars and the private motorist need therefore only concern himself with general speed limits.

General speed limits on motorways and elsewhere

On roads other than motorways there is a general speed limit of seventy m.p.h. on dual carriageways and sixty m.p.h. on other roads. These limits were introduced as a temporary measure in 1977 and are still with us. Since they are general speed limits they do not have to be indicated in any way by signs. The Minister does however have power to impose lower limits on particular sections of these roads, and where this is done the fact must be indicated in the usual way.

On motorways there is a general speed limit of seventy m.p.h., which is slightly reduced in the case of heavy goods vehicles or certain vehicles drawing trailers or caravans. Vehicles for which a particular speed limit is prescribed are exempt from this when travelling on a motorway provided of course they comply with the general limits imposed on all motorway traffic.

Proof of speeding

The fact that a person was exceeding the speed limit is for obvious reasons difficult to prove; the law is that no one can be convicted of speeding solely on the opinion-evidence of a single witness. This means that to secure a conviction the prosecution must produce either at least two witnesses, or alternatively a single witness provided his evidence is corroborated by a mechanical device such as a speedometer, stop watch, radar, or vascar. Where two witnesses are used it is essential that their evidence should relate to the same moment of time. If for example the two witnesses are a hundred yards apart, it is obvious that neither can corroborate the evidence of the other. For this and other reasons the police prefer to rely on the evidence of mechanical devices. It is possible to challenge the accuracy of such devices but it is not wise to do so unless there are reasons for believing that the device is wildly inaccurate, or perhaps where it is alleged that the accused has only slightly exceeded the limit.

When a motorist is charged with speeding, the prosecution should indicate within fairly narrow limits the place where the offence is alleged to have taken place. This makes it virtually impossible to secure a conviction where the only evidence available to the prosecution is that the motorist must have exceeded the speed limit in view of the time he had taken to cover the distance in question (such information is often available from written records), but such evidence can certainly be used in corroboration. Finally, although the law directs that a motorist should not be convicted on the opinion-evidence of a single witness it does not make such evidence inadmissible. Where for example a policeman swore that the motorist flashed past him at sixty miles an hour on a restricted road, the court accepted this as proof that he was breaking the speed limit, although they could not accept the witness's opinion as to the actual speed at which he was travelling.

Exemptions and defences

Vehicles that are being used for fire-brigade, ambulance or police purposes are exempt from speed limits but only if the observance of the limit would hinder them in the purpose for which they were being used on that occasion. Police vehicles are not normally exempt, but would be if for example they were chasing a criminal. A fire engine is exempt when it is going to a fire but not when it is returning home after having put it out. A doctor carrying a dying patient to hospital in his private car would probably be exempt on the grounds that his car was being used for ambulance purposes, but not a doctor who was hurrying to the scene of an accident. In the latter case, however, it is likely that even if the doctor were convicted the court would hold that there were special reasons for not endorsing his licence.

Speeding is an offence to which the 'notice of intended prosecution' procedure (see page 386) is applicable. This means that the motorist cannot be prosecuted at all unless he was warned at the time of the offence that proceedings might be instituted against him or he received such a warning or notice within fourteen days. The offence is committed if the motorist exceeds the speed limit even for the briefest interval of time but it is a common practice for magistrates to adjust the fine according to the gravity of the offence.

Obstruction

Meaning of obstruction

We have already seen (page 323) that the right of both pedestrians and motorists to use a public highway is a right to pass and re-pass only and the police are empowered to 'move on' any person or vehicle. The fact that the police have the right to move you on, however, does not make it a criminal offence to stand still. Indeed except where the obstruction was so serious as to constitute a public nuisance it does not appear that the law concerned itself with the criminal aspects of obstruction until the invention of the motor vehicle.

The capacity of a motor vehicle for obstructing the flow of traffic is so much greater that legislation was seen to be necessary. There are now two statutory provisions dealing with this matter – Section 121 of the Highways Act 1959 makes it an offence *wilfully to obstruct the free passage of a highway* and Regulation 122 of the Construction and Use Regulations 1978 makes it an offence to *cause or permit a motor vehicle or trailer to stand on a road so as to cause any unnecessary obstruction thereof.*

There are important differences between these two provisions. The Act includes pedestrians as well as all classes of vehicle and covers the whole of the highway including the footpath. The shop-keeper who spreads his goods on the pavement is therefore in danger of prosecution under the Act. The regulation refers to *motor vehicles and trailers* standing on a road. The definition of a road is probably wide enough to include the footpath but there is a separate provision making it an offence to park a vehicle on a footpath or grass verge. At the time of writing, this provision has not yet been brought into force, although it is possible that in some areas this may be an offence under the local by-laws. Where motor vehicles are concerned the police usually prefer to use the regulation rather than the Act – if only because the penalties are greater.

There is no legal definition of obstruction and in the early days magistrates tended to take the attitude that to constitute the offence it was necessary for the prosecution to show either actual or potential obstruction. The enormous increase in the volume of traffic on the roads has necessitated a more flexible interpretation, and nowadays the courts tend to regard obstruction as the same as unreasonable use of the highway. Actual obstruction will almost always result in a conviction. This would cover the motorist who blocks the highway with his vehicle or holds up traffic on a busy road by performing a U-turn. But a conviction can also be recorded where there is no actual obstruction if the magistrates consider that the motorist has behaved in a selfish or unreasonable manner. It is impossible to be more definite. Much depends on the amount of space taken up, the length of time the car was allowed to stand and even the driver's motives in leaving it there, and magistrates are entitled to use their knowledge of the local geography and the prevailing traffic conditions in deciding whether or not there was an obstruction. It is not an obstruction if the car has broken down provided the driver has done everything that was reasonably possible to remove it as quickly as possible.

Related offences

Where a road has been designated a clearway (the fact will be indicated by the appropriate traffic signs) it is an offence to stop at all, except with police permission, or where the driver has stopped to avoid an accident or through circumstances beyond his control. There is also an exemption for vehicles used in the public service such as fire brigade, police, ambulances and vehicles used for collecting and delivering mail. Local traffic regulation orders sometimes declare streets to be 'no waiting' streets but allow exemptions for the purpose of loading and unloading goods. The exemption is not necessarily confined to goods vehicles but the putting in and taking out of small parcels in a private car would not be covered by it.

It is an offence to abandon a vehicle or part of a vehicle on any public land, and local authorities have the power to remove and dispose of such vehicles, charging the cost to the owner – if he can be found. Further powers of removal are conferred on the police and on local authorities in the case of vehicles which appear to have been abandoned or to have been left in such a position as to constitute an obstruction or danger or in contravention of parking restrictions. A police officer may require the owner to remove the vehicle, and if necessary have it removed himself. The cost is chargeable to the owner. Abandoned vehicles may be disposed of but not until every effort has been made to trace the owner.

Parking

The increase in the volume of traffic on the roads and the increasing pressure on parking-space has forced Parliament to empower local authorities to provide both off-street and on-street parking-places. On-street parking-places are often controlled by parking meters. There are no national laws governing parking meters. The conditions on which a parking meter may be used are laid down in the relevant local order and since these may vary from one area to another the motorist who wishes to familiarize himself with them would be well advised to write to the local authority concerned or to consult the local police. A typical order might make the following provisions. Insertion of a coin into the meter entitles the motorist to park for a certain period. If that period is exceeded an excess charge must be paid. If the vehicle is there for more than a given period (usually four hours) an offence is committed and the motorist cannot buy off this offence by a further payment. As a rule he is permitted to go to another parking-place once his time is up but not to return to his original one until a prescribed period has elapsed. In some cases exemptions and periods of grace are allowed but not always. In one case a motorist was fined for leaving his car for no more than a minute while he went to get change for the meter but it is not suggested that this is typical.

The suspension of the parking meter for any reason whatsoever (usually indicated by placing a bag over it) would make it difficult for a successful prosecution to be brought. In effect the suspension of the parking meter means that the ordinary law is revived, i.e. the position is the same as it would have been if the parking meter had never been erected. In one case a motorist was fined for leaving his car in a space where the operation of the parking meter was suspended, but the High Court ordered his conviction to be quashed on the grounds that even without the parking meter he would have been allowed to park for thirty minutes. *Note:* the Transport Act 1982 provides for immobilization devices to be attached to vehicles that are unlawfully parked. For details see page 404.

Fixed penalty procedure

Parking meter offences are now controlled by the fixed penalty procedure. This means that when such an offence is committed a police constable or traffic warden may serve a notice in the prescribed form on the culprit requiring him to pay the prescribed penalty within a certain period of time which must be not less than twenty-one days. If he does so no proceedings in court can be taken. If he does not do so or if he wishes to dispute liability the matter can be settled in the court in the usual way. Because of the difficulty in establishing the identity of the culprit the notice may now be served on the registered owner who will be held responsible unless he can show either that he was not the owner of the vehicle at the relevant time or that although he was the owner the car was at the time in the possession of some other person without his consent. If appropriate the notice may be left affixed to the vehicle and it is an offence for any person other than the driver or owner to remove it.

Careless and reckless driving

Meaning of 'careless' and 'reckless'

Although these two offences are quite separate and distinct they are taken together in the same section because of their obvious similarity.

Careless driving is defined in the Road Traffic Act; a person is guilty of careless driving if he drives a motor vehicle on a road either:

- without due care and attention; or
- without reasonable consideration for other persons using the road.

Reckless driving means just what it says – that is driving recklessly and it is now clear that this implies at least some degree of knowledge and fault on the part of the driver.

The difference between careless and reckless driving can best be illustrated by a few examples. The following would probably be held to be *careless* only:

- mounting the pavement;
- turning left after signalling a right-turn and without taking precautions;
- turning into a main road without making sure the way was clear;
- failing to comply with a traffic sign;
- splashing a pedestrian by driving through a puddle;
- failing to dip headlights at night in the face of oncoming traffic.

The following would probably be held to constitute *reckless* driving:

- crossing the traffic lights at red;
- driving at an excessive speed in a restricted area;
- overtaking at speed on a dangerous bend or in the face of oncoming traffic;
- deliberately swerving from left to right while driving.

The above examples are no more than guidelines. In deciding whether the accused's driving was careless, reckless or neither, the court will take all the factors into consideration including weather conditions and the nature and volume of the traffic which may be on the road at the time. Thus an act which might be considered careless if committed in conditions of poor visibility might well be considered not careless if committed when the visibility is good. To make a U-turn on a motorway would almost certainly be held to be reckless driving (as well as an offence against the Motorway Regulations) but to do the same thing on an open country road with no traffic in sight would probably be held to be not even careless. We have seen (page 325) that the Highway Code does not have the force of law but that a breach of its provisions may be accepted by the court as evidence that the accused was driving carelessly or recklessly, but even here this is not conclusive. If the conditions are such that no possible harm could result it may well be that a motorist could break the provisions of the code without committing any criminal offence at all.

Defences and exemptions

There are not many possible defences to a charge of careless or reckless driving apart from the obvious one of denying the facts, but one defence which the courts have consistently allowed occurs when the accused can show that the act complained of resulted from his losing control of the vehicle for reasons which were entirely beyond his control. The driver who has been stung by a wasp for example can scarcely be expected to maintain the standard of care which the law normally demands. Another example is mechanical breakdown although in this case it is essential to show that the cause of the breakdown could not have been reasonably anticipated. If a man takes a car out on the road knowing that the steering is defective or the tyres badly worn he must not expect to be acquitted of careless driving if an accident happens as a result of the defect. There is no exemption in favour of the drivers of police, ambulance and fire-brigade vehicles, although where the offence is committed in the course of duty and the circumstances justify it, it is probable that a lighter penalty will be imposed.

Mode of trial

Careless driving is a summary offence whereas reckless driving can be tried either summarily or on indictment (see page 417 for an explanation of terms). Both are endorsable and for this reason the police sometimes add a charge of careless driving to a less serious charge, e.g. disobeying a traffic sign. In such cases the court ought not to convict of both offences unless there is evidence of carelessness independently of the less serious offence; the accused should beware of pleading guilty to both charges especially when the less serious offence (unlike careless driving) is not endorsable.

Under English law it is an almost invariable rule that a man can only be convicted of the offence with which he has been charged.

There are some very rare statutory exceptions to this rule, however, and one of these is to be found in the case of reckless and careless driving. If a man is charged with reckless driving and the court is of the opinion that that charge is not proved it may at any time during the trial or immediately thereafter direct that a charge of careless driving may be substituted in its place subject to the right of the accused to demand the recall of witnesses for further cross-examination or to ask for an adjournment if it should be necessary to do so. Both reckless and careless driving are subject to 'notice of intended prosecution' procedure (see page 386). This means that the police cannot bring either charge unless the accused was warned at the time of the offence or received written notice within fourteen days of the intention to bring proceedings. The right of the court to substitute a charge of careless driving for one of reckless driving is not apparently affected by the fact that the original notice of intended prosecution referred only to the major charge.

Causing death by reckless driving

This offence must not be confused with manslaughter. To cause the death of a human being by an act of gross and culpable negligence is manslaughter and this is a very serious crime indeed, punishable with life imprisonment. The natural reluctance of juries to convict motorists of such a serious crime, except perhaps in the most extreme cases, resulted in the introduction in 1956 of a new offence – that of causing death by reckless driving, punishable by a maximum of five years' imprisonment.

It is clear that the difference between manslaughter and causing death by reckless driving lies in the degree of negligence involved, this being less in the case of the second offence. It does not follow, however, that a man cannot be convicted of causing death if the manner of his driving would not have justified a conviction for reckless driving if he had not killed anyone. We have seen in the previous section that the difference between reckless and careless driving may well depend on external factors, and it may well transpire that a man may be convicted of causing death, even though his manner of driving in the abstract would have been no more than careless. Obviously his carelessness must be a contributory factor in causing death but it need not be the only or indeed a substantial factor.

In one case the accused was driving at eighty m.p.h. along a restricted road when he crashed into a car which was straddling the road, killing the lady driver. The jury was of the opinion that she was more to blame than he was since she had emerged from a side-road without taking precautions. Nevertheless it was held that he was rightly convicted of causing death by reckless driving.

Contrary to the general rule that a man can only be convicted of the offence with which he is charged, the court may, on a charge of causing death, convict the accused of reckless driving if they think that the evidence justifies it. One curious result emerges from this. 'Notice of intended prosecution' is necessary on a charge of reckless driving but not on a charge of causing death. Nevertheless the absence of a notice of intended prosecution does not bar the court from substituting a conviction for reckless driving in the aforementioned circumstances.

As in all cases of homicide under English law, death must take place within a year and a day. Causing death by reckless driving does not mean that the motorist is no longer in danger of a charge of manslaughter. The motorist who drives at eighty m.p.h. in a restricted area while blind drunk and kills somebody is certainly in danger of prosecution for the more serious charge.

Causing bodily harm by furious driving

This is a very old offence dating back to 1861 – long before the petrol engine was invented. It is committed by any person in charge of a carriage or vehicle who causes bodily harm to another person.

It is still used occasionally today for several reasons. First, unlike the offences previously discussed, the vehicle does not have to be a motor vehicle. The charge can be brought against the driver of a horse-drawn vehicle or even a pedal cyclist. Second, again unlike the previous offences, it can be committed anywhere and not only on a road. Third, no 'notice of intended prosecution' is necessary. The police have been known to use this charge when a charge of reckless driving was impossible because, as a result of a slip-up, the necessary notice of intended prosecution had not been sent.

From the point of view of the motorist the charge has the advantage that neither endorsement nor disqualification can be ordered in respect of it.

Taking a conveyance

Taking a conveyance is not stealing

Under English law a man cannot be convicted of stealing unless he intended permanently to keep the article which he is accused of having stolen. The illegal borrowing of a motor vehicle, however detestable a practice it may be, is not stealing since the borrower, even if he has no intention of returning the vehicle to its rightful owner, very rarely intends to keep it for himself.

The practice of borrowing someone else's car for a joy ride and of ultimately abandoning it, perhaps in a damaged condition, is unfortunately so common nowadays that it has been necessary for the law to make it a separate offence in its own right. This offence is known as 'taking a conveyance' and is committed by any person who takes a conveyance for his own or another's use without the consent of the owner or other lawful authority. (The bailiff who takes your car in satisfaction of a judgment debt does not commit this offence, because although he may well be taking it without your consent he has lawful authority to do so.) It is also an offence if any person, knowing that a conveyance has been so taken, either drives it or allows himself to be driven in or on it.

What then is meant by taking a conveyance? Before it can be said that a person has taken a conveyance it must be shown that he has taken possession or control of the conveyance without the owner's permission and that the conveyance has moved albeit to a slight degree. Moreover the vehicle must have been used as a conveyance, which means that he must have been carried inside it. Merely pushing a vehicle does not therefore constitute this offence. Also the act must have been deliberate. A person who accidentally touches the accelerator of an automatic drive car while the engine is running, thereby propelling it forward, is in no danger of conviction.

Defences

It is of course essential that the conveyance should have been taken without the owner's permission; this defence is extended to cover the case of the person who honestly but mistakenly believes he has such permission and even to cover the case of the person who knows that he has not got the owner's permission but believes that he would have got it if he had asked for it. The son who 'borrows' his father's car without permission would not be convicted of this offence – unless of course his father had expressly forbidden him to do so. In one case a man borrowed his friend's car in the belief that his friend would have given permission if he had been asked. His friend admitted that normally this would have been true but not in this particular case, as at the time the car had no fan-belt. As the accused did not know this he was acquitted.

Everyone has the right to remove a vehicle which is obstructing his lawful right of way. If, therefore, you find that the exit from your garage is blocked by a parked vehicle you are entitled to remove it. As a rule it is better first to find the owner and ask him to remove it, but if you cannot find the owner or if you can and he refuses to remove it, you are certainly entitled to move it yourself. These circumstances would of course constitute a perfect defence if you were subsequently charged with taking a conveyance.

It will be noted that we have used the term 'conveyance' and not 'vehicle'. This is deliberate. Although in this book we are concerned only with the problems of the motor vehicle, this crime is in fact wide enough to cover any kind of conveyance, i.e. anything that is designed or adapted for the carriage of persons by land, water or air. It does not even have to be power-driven.

Originally an indictable crime only, this offence is now triable either summarily or on indictment (see page 417).

Tampering with motor vehicles

This offence is committed by a person who gets on to a motor vehicle or who tampers with any part of the machinery without lawful authority or reasonable cause. It is less serious than the preceding offence and it may happen that a person who really intended to take the vehicle away, but who was stopped before the vehicle was moved, can be charged with this offence instead. The vehicle must be on a road or in a parking-place provided by a local authority. The offence is not committed if the vehicle is on private land or in a car park provided by, say, a nationalized undertaking.

It is also an offence for a person to get into or to take hold of a motor vehicle while it is in motion on a road, without lawful authority or reasonable cause either for the purpose of being carried in the vehicle or for the purpose of being drawn by it.

Vehicle interference

This is a new crime created by the Criminal Attempts Act 1981. Prior to the passing of that act the police could arrest any person if they had reasonable cause to believe that he was loitering with intent to commit a felony. This so-called 'sus-law' was deeply resented and was in fact repealed by the aforementioned statute. However, in recent years it had become obvious that the offence was most frequently committed by persons who had criminal intentions in relation to motor vehicles and so it was replaced by a new crime which is known as 'vehicle interference'.

The offence is committed by any person who interferes with a motor vehicle or with anything carried in or on it with the intention either of stealing the vehicle or anything carried in or on it or of taking and driving away the vehicle without the owner's consent.

Before a man can be convicted of this offence the court must be satisfied that he intended to commit one of these crimes, although it is not necessary to prove which one it was.

Criminal damage

A person who damages the property of another whether deliberately or by negligence is liable to be sued in a civil action for compensation by the person whose property he has damaged. In all probability he has committed a criminal offence too, for the Criminal Damage Act 1971 makes it an offence deliberately or by recklessness to damage or destroy the property of another and an even more serious offence if human life is endangered in consequence.

The motor vehicle is particularly vulnerable in this respect. The man who 'borrows' a motor vehicle may well damage it in addition either by reckless driving or by breaking the lock in order to get in. Nor is the damage confined to the vehicle itself. The man who by reckless driving knocks down a brick wall may face a charge for this offence even though the vehicle itself is unhurt. In these circumstances, however, he is more likely to be charged with reckless driving unless the incident took place other than on a road, for reckless driving is an offence that can only be committed on a road while offences under the Criminal Damage Act can be committed anywhere.

When a person is convicted of an offence under the Criminal Damage Act the court has the power, if it chooses to exercise it, of ordering the accused to pay compensation of any amount up to a maximum of £1,000 to the person whose property he has damaged. This is in addition to any fine or other penalty imposed in respect of the offence itself.

Offences

(See page 405 for proposed increases in maximum fines.)

Offence	*Maximum penalty*	*Endorsement*	*Disqualification*
Failing to observe a minimum speed limit*	£50	—	—
Exceeding the speed limit other than on a motorway*	£100	Obligatory	Discretionary
Exceeding the speed limit on a motorway* (private cars only)	£500	Obligatory	Discretionary
Obstruction under Highways Act 1959	£50	—	—
Obstruction under Construction and Use Regulations	£100	—	—
Stopping on clearway or in breach of local traffic regulation order	£100	—	—
Offences in connection with parking meters	£20	—	—
Abandoning a vehicle or part of a vehicle	£100 on first conviction. £200 and/or 3 months on second or subsequent conviction	—	—
Careless driving*	£500	Obligatory	Discretionary
Reckless driving*	Summarily – £1,000 and/or 6 months. On indictment – unlimited fine and/or 2 years	Obligatory	Discretionary but obligatory for a second offence committed within 3 years
Causing death by reckless driving	5 years	Obligatory	Obligatory
Causing bodily harm by furious driving	2 years	—	—
Taking a conveyance, etc.	Summarily – £1,000 and/or 6 months. On indictment – unlimited fine or 3 years	Obligatory	Discretionary
Tampering with a motor vehicle	£100	—	—

*'Notice of intended prosecution' procedure applies (see Chapter 42).

Offence	*Maximum penalty*	*Endorsement*	*Disqualification*
Vehicle interference	£500 and/or 3 months	—	—
Getting into or holding on to a motor vehicle in motion	£20	—	—
Criminal damage (value of damage not above £200)	£1,000 and/or 6 months	—	—
Criminal damage (value of damage exceeding £200)	Summarily – £1,000 and/or 6 months. On indictment – unlimited fine and/or 10 years	—	—
Criminal damage with reckless disregard for human life	Life imprisonment	—	—

40 Drink-driving offences

This chapter is mainly about the two principal offences which involve drink and driving: being unfit to drive through drink and driving with an excess of alcohol in the blood. The chapter also examines in detail the procedure for administering the breath test and looks briefly at other offences connected with drink and driving. Important changes in the law are proposed and may be in force by the time this book appears. See page 370. Offences committed before the new law comes into force will still be tried under the existing law.

'Unfit to drive'

It has for many years been a serious offence under English law to drive or to attempt to drive on a road or other public place a motor vehicle while unfit to drive through drink or drugs. It is also a serious offence to be in charge of a motor vehicle in the same condition, and until 1967 when the breathalyser was introduced these were in fact the only offences that could be committed in this connection.

In order to explain why the law was changed it is necessary first to examine the law as it was before 1967, and to highlight the difficulties it presented both to the police who had to administer it and to the courts who had to interpret it. Perhaps the greatest difficulty of all was to decide what the law meant by 'unfit to drive'. Alcohol affects people in different ways. It is even possible for *A* with alcohol in his body to be still a better driver than *B* who has none and the imprecise nature of the expression 'unfit to drive' made it difficult to apply any objective standards by which the fitness could be measured. In 1962 Parliament attempted to define the expression 'unfit to drive' by saying that a motorist is unfit to drive through drink or drugs if his ability to drive properly is for the time being impaired, a definition which didn't help very much, for most drivers whether good or bad would find their driving impaired if they had drink inside them.

Clearly a relevant factor in deciding whether or not a man is fit to drive is the amount of alcohol in his body. At that time the only way in which this could be ascertained was by taking a sample of his blood or urine and subjecting it to chemical analysis, and persons accused of drink-driving offences were invariably invited to offer such a specimen voluntarily. They could not, however, be compelled to do so, and if they refused there was nothing the police could do about it. The reason for this extraordinary law was that English criminal law had never taken kindly to a situation in which a man could be compelled to give evidence which might be used against him. This law could of course be changed but Parliament shrank from the extreme step of taking someone – who might turn out to be wholly innocent of the charge against him – to the police station and submitting him to the indignity of such a test, for it will be appreciated that there was no way in which such a test could be carried out at the roadside.

The breathalyser

Nevertheless the clamour for a more objective and precisely determinable test became louder until in 1967 there was produced a device known as the Alcotest 80 which consisted of a bag fitted with a mouthpiece and containing crystals which would turn green in colour on coming into contact with the prescribed amount of alcohol. The breathalyser (as it has become almost universally known, although the word occurs nowhere in the Road Traffic Acts) is easily portable and the test can therefore be administered at the roadside by any policeman who has reason to believe that a motorist may have alcohol in his body. The maximum level of alcohol permitted by the law is 80 milligrams per 100 millilitres of blood (or 107 milligrams per 100 millilitres of urine) and if the test shows a level exceeding this amount the driver can be arrested and taken to the police station where he can be required compulsorily to provide a specimen of blood or urine for a laboratory test. Failure to take the breath test and failure to provide a specimen of blood or urine when lawfully required to do so are also offences in themselves unless there is a reasonable excuse. Thus the teetotaller who knows that he is innocent is still in danger of conviction if he refuses to blow into the bag.

In 1967 therefore three new crimes were added to the calendar – those of *driving*, *attempting to drive* and *being in charge of* a motor vehicle with *excess alcohol in the blood*. These crimes have nothing whatsoever to do with the motorist's fitness to drive. If the alcohol in his body exceeds the prescribed limit he is guilty; if it does not he is not guilty. It is as simple as that. With the introduction of the new law it might have been expected that Parliament would have repealed the old but this was not so. The old unfitness to drive law was retained so that there are now not three but six offences which a motorist might commit in connection with drunken driving. One reason for this was that the old unfitness to drive law applied to drugs as well as to drink while the breathalyser offences are not appropriate to drugs.

How are these offences committed?

With this explanation in mind, we can examine the offences in detail. Certain preliminary points must first be clarified. Unfitness to drive offences are charged under Section 5 of the Road Traffic Act 1972 and excess alcohol offences under Section 6 of the same Act. For the sake of brevity and convenience these offences can be referred to as Section 5 and Section 6 offences respectively throughout the rest of this chapter. Both Section 5 and Section 6 offences can only be committed while the motorist is driving, attempting to drive or is in charge of a motor vehicle, and in all cases the motor vehicle must be on a road or other public place. As all these expressions have at various times caused the courts considerable problems of interpretation a more detailed explanation is necessary.

What is a road?

The word 'road' needs no definition although it must be remembered that for the purpose of most road traffic offences it includes private roads as well, provided the public have access to them, i.e. provided there is evidence that the general public use them even though they have have no legal right to do so. The expression 'public place' is more difficult. Whether a place is public or not is largely a matter of degree depending on the use made of it by the general public and different courts may well have different views on the matter. A car park belonging to a private club is clearly not a public place but a car park belonging to a public house may well be deemed to be so since it is a known fact that these places are often used by people who are not customers of the public house. Not long ago a man put his car into such a place and then entered the pub, where he remained drinking until closing time. An hour after the pub was closed he was found in his car paralytic drunk. A prosecution for being in charge of a motor vehicle with excess alcohol was dismissed. The magistrates considered that while the car park might have been a public place during opening hours it was most unlikely that the landlord would have tolerated the presence of intruders an hour after closing-time and the car park had therefore ceased to be a public place. He was very lucky.

When are you driving?

The meaning of the expression 'driving' has been the subject of many decisions in the courts. In 1973 the High Court attempted to clarify the matter by laying down guidelines for the assistance of the police and the motoring fraternity. These guidelines may be summarized in the following propositions:

- the motorist is driving while the car is in motion;
- he is also driving for the brief interval of time after the vehicle has stopped and he is switching off the ignition and applying the handbrake;
- if he stops before completing his journey it is a question of fact depending on the reason why he has stopped and the duration of the stop as to whether he is driving or not;
- he is still driving if his car is halted at the traffic lights.

When he has completed his journey he is no longer driving subject to the brief interval of time previously referred to; if he is prevented from driving, whether by the police or by his friends, he is no longer driving.

A man who is not actually *driving* when the offence was allegedly committed may still be charged with *attempting to drive* if he was doing something with the obvious intention of setting the vehicle in motion, e.g. switching on the ignition or turning the starting-handle. Mere fiddling with the controls without any intention of setting the vehicle in motion is not attempting to drive but if the accused clearly intended to start the engine it is no defence that the car was incapable of being driven anyway.

Meaning of 'in charge'

It is not necessary that the accused should be either driving or attempting to drive. He can still be prosecuted for being in charge of a motor vehicle while unfit to drive or with excess alcohol. Whether he is actually in charge is a question of fact which is often very difficult to determine.

The English courts consider that a man remains in charge of his vehicle as long as it is on the road until he either abandons it or hands it over to someone else. In one case a drunk left his car on a garage forecourt and walked home. He was half a mile away when he was arrested but he was still held to be in charge, as also was a bus driver who left his bus at the side of the road and went home to his tea. We shall see later, however, that the harshness of the English law is mitigated by a special defence which is available to the accused in certain circumstances.

What is a motor vehicle?

The expression 'motor vehicle' is not difficult to understand. It means any mechanically propelled vehicle (including those driven by steam or electricity) intended or adapted for use on roads. It includes therefore motor-bicycles, auto-assisted cycles and mopeds, but not pedal cycles. (There is a separate offence of riding a pedal cycle while unfit to ride through drink or drugs.)

Having made these matters clear we will now examine these offences in detail. Let us begin with the three Section 5 offences.

Section 5 offences (unfit to drive)

Subsection 1: *driving* or *attempting to drive* a motor vehicle on a road or other public place while unfit to drive through drink or drugs.

Subsection 2: *being in charge* of a motor vehicle which is on a road or other public place while unfit to drive through drink or drugs.

Section 5 has the disadvantage from the point of view of the police in that in order to obtain a conviction it is necessary to show that the accused was unfit to drive, which, for the reasons we have explained previously, is sometimes difficult to do. Evidence that the accused was driving erratically, that he could not stand upright or that his speech was slurred have all been accepted at various times as evidence from which the accused's unfitness to drive may be inferred, provided also of course that there is evidence that he had been drinking.

On the other hand Section 5 has two advantages again from the police's point of view. The first is that a police constable may arrest any person on a reasonable suspicion of having committed a Section 5 offence and the second is that no roadside breath test is necessary in these cases.

The procedure is as follows. A police constable may arrest without warrant any person if he has reasonable grounds for suspecting that he has committed any Section 5 offence. No roadside breath test is necessary and the accused may be taken directly to the police station.

At the police station the procedure will depend on whether the accused is suspected of having drink or drugs inside him.

Drink

If the offence is concerned with alcohol the accused must first be given the opportunity of undergoing a breath test. He has nothing to gain by refusing to take the test since refusal without reasonable cause is itself an offence. If he takes the test and the result is negative, i.e. the crystals do not turn green, it is possible that the police may drop the charge (but not inevitable since the charge concerns unfitness to drive rather than excess alcohol). If the result is positive the police will then require him to provide a specimen of blood or urine for the purpose of a laboratory analysis. The procedure by which this is done must be strictly complied with and is described in detail in the section dealing with Section 6 offences below (see page 360). Again, refusal to provide a specimen without reasonable cause is an offence in itself. The results of the analysis may then be used at the subsequent trial as evidence that the accused was unfit to drive.

Drugs

If the charge is concerned with drugs then the following procedure must be followed. In this case, oddly enough, the police have no power to demand a specimen for laboratory analysis. The reason for this is that it is a precondition of the police's power to demand a specimen for laboratory analysis that the accused should be offered the opportunity of first undergoing a breath test, and as we have already said the breath test is incapable of detecting the presence of drugs. However, he may be invited on a voluntary basis to provide such a specimen and his refusal to do so without reasonable cause may be used with devastating effect against him at his trial.

Defence

Where the offence is concerned with being in charge of a motor vehicle while unfit to drive there is a special defence of which the accused may be able to avail himself. If he can prove that there was no likelihood that he would drive as long as he remained unfit, he cannot be convicted. The same defence is available where the charge is under Section 6 (2) – being in charge of a motor vehicle with excess alcohol – but there is a curious difference between the two defences. Where the vehicle is so badly damaged or the accused is so badly injured that driving would be impossible anyway this factor may be taken into consideration and the defence allowed where the charge is under Section 5 (2), but not where the charge is under Section 6 (2).

Section 6 offences (excess alcohol)

Subsection 1: *driving* or *attempting to drive* a motor vehicle on a road or other public place having consumed alcohol in such a quantity that the proportion thereof in his blood as ascertained from a laboratory test for which he subsequently provides a specimen exceeds the proscribed limit.

Subsection 2: *being in charge* of a motor vehicle on a road or other public place having consumed alcohol in the circumstances laid down in subsection 1.

Prosecutions under Section 6 are much commoner than prosecutions under Section 5, for in this case there is no need to prove unfitness to drive. They have the disadvantage (from the police's point of view) that the roadside breath test is mandatory (insofar as charges of driving or attempting to drive are concerned) and (unlike Section 5 offences) there is no power to arrest unless the driver has either failed to provide a specimen of breath, or has done so and the result has proved positive. Where the charge is being in charge of a motor vehicle with excess alcohol there is no power to administer a breath test at all and therefore no possibility of arrest unless the driver has been involved in an accident, in which case a breath test can always be administered (see page 363).

The breath test

When it can be administered

The breath test can only be administered by a police constable in uniform and only then if he or she has reasonable cause to believe either that:

- the driver has alcohol in his body;
- the driver has committed a traffic offence while the vehicle was in motion; or
- the driver was driving or attempting to drive the vehicle at a time when it was involved in an accident.

In this connection it is as well to remind the reader that the expression 'police constable' includes all police officers irrespective of rank.

At the moment, the police have no power to impose random breath tests. They do of course have the power to stop any vehicle they like on the road and for any reason – or indeed for no reason at all if they choose – but, having stopped the vehicle they have no power to impose a breath test unless one or other of the above three conditions is satisfied.

The Blennerhasset Report of 1976 recommended that the police be given greater powers to impose a breath test at will, but no government has so far shown much enthusiasm for implementing this report.

When the breath test was first introduced in 1967 the courts tended to interpret the law very literally indeed. The procedural steps which the police are required to observe in administering the breath test and in taking a specimen for laboratory analysis are very complicated, and in addition the manufacturers of the breathalyser contributed to the muddle by requiring the following conditions to be observed before the breathalyser could be relied on to function properly:

- at least twenty minutes must elapse between the last drink and the taking of the test;
- the accused may not smoke shortly before or during the taking of the test;

- the bag must be filled by a single breath in not less than ten nor more than twenty seconds.

In the early days of the breathalyser all the above requirements had to be strictly observed and many obviously guilty persons were acquitted on what must have seemed to the general public very technical points indeed. In 1970, however, the House of Lords ruled that the manufacturers' instructions did not have to be slavishly complied with and that a breach of them need not necessarily invalidate the test. Nor is the constable under a duty to ask the accused when he last had a drink or a smoke, provided he acts in good faith. If the constable knows the driver has had a drink or a smoke recently then he ought to wait. If he does not know and has no reason to suspect it the test is not made invalid thereby. The reason for the twenty-minute rule is that when a man has a drink the alcohol concentration in his mouth may remain for anything up to twenty minutes before it is dissipated and may therefore give a falsely high reading. The ban on smoking is due to the fact that tobacco smoke on the breath can cause the crystals to turn brown and so make any reading impossible, although it is understood that the effect of tobacco smoke on the test is likely to be of much shorter duration than that of alcohol in the mouth.

The breath test is no more than a screening device. If it proves positive it merely authorizes the police to arrest the driver and take him to the police station for a laboratory test and it is on this test that his subsequent innocence or guilt will be decided.

Driving with alcohol in the body

The first circumstance in which the breath test can be administered is where a police constable has reasonable cause to suspect the driver of driving or attempting to drive with alcohol in his body.

The suspicion must be a reasonable one. It is unlikely that a single act of careless driving would suffice. But it would certainly be sufficient if the driver were driving erratically or recklessly. It is essential that the driver should still be driving or attempting to drive when the suspicion of alcohol arises, but it is not essential that he should still be driving, etc. when the breath test is administered provided the administration of the test forms a link in a continuous chain of events. For example, a policeman sees a driver driving recklessly and weaving from side to side of the road; he gives chase but by the time he catches up with him the driver has reached the safety of his home and put his car away: the driver may still be breathalysed even though he is no longer driving, for in this case the suspicion of alcohol arose while he was on the road.

Exceptionally it is possible for the suspicion of alcohol to arise before the man has commenced driving. In one case a policeman saw a man who was clearly paralytically drunk. Half an hour later the policeman saw the same man driving a car. The court held that in these circumstances he was entitled to breathalyse him.

The breath test must be administered 'there or near by'. The expression has been interpreted by the courts with some common sense but clearly if the policeman has no breath bag with him he cannot take the motorist to a police station for the test since this would not be 'there or near by'.

Driver has committed a moving traffic offence

The second set of circumstances occurs when a police constable has reasonable cause to suspect that the driver has committed a *moving traffic offence*. A parking offence would not be sufficient. In practice, although the police have power to do so, they rarely breathalyse a motorist simply because he has committed an offence unless there are other factors present which give rise to a suspicion of alcohol. It is important to remember that both in this case and in the previous one (suspicion of alcohol) it is not essential that the policeman's suspicions are justified. The law only requires that he should have reasonable cause. The lifelong abstainer who indignantly refuses to take a breath test is still guilty of an offence provided the policeman's suspicions were reasonably justified.

Where the breath test is administered on this ground it must be administered as soon as is reasonably practicable after the commission of the offence. If the constable has no breath bag with him he may send for one and if the motorist refuses to wait it is probable that the court will consider this as tantamount to a failure to provide a specimen of breath.

Vehicle involved in an accident

The third circumstance arises when an accident occurs owing to the presence of a motor vehicle cn a road or other public place. A constable in uniform may breathalyse any person who he has reasonable cause to believe was driving or attempting to drive the vehicle at the time of the accident. It is not necessary that another vehicle should be involved. It is still an accident if your car comes into collision with a human being, an animal or a stationary object. For the purpose of this law the word 'accident' has its normal popular meaning and is not confined to the rather stricter definition of an accident which is laid down for the purpose of the offence of failing to stop after an accident (see Chapter 41, page 372).

Where the breath test is administered following an accident there is no requirement that it should be administered as soon as is reasonably practicable, but because any analysis of blood or urine obtained as a result of the breath test must relate to the alcohol level at the time of the accident excessive delay may be fatal to the prosecution.

Where the accused is injured and in hospital the breath test may be administered at the hospital but only with the knowledge and consent of the medical officer in charge of the patient. An ambulance is not a hospital for this purpose and it has been held that the police are entitled to breathalyse a person who is in an ambulance and on his way to hospital. Once the ambulance reaches the hospital the person becomes a hospital patient and the consent of a medical officer must be obtained even though the patient has not yet been seen by a doctor. A person who is receiving outpatient treatment is regarded as a hospital patient as long as he is on the hospital premises and the treatment is still uncompleted. A patient in a hospital cannot be arrested but, provided the breath test proves positive, the police do have the right to demand a specimen of blood or urine for analysis, again provided the medical officer in charge is informed and consents to the request being made.

Procedure following the administration of the breath test

We will assume that the police have made a valid request for a breath test in one of the sets of circumstances outlined above. If the result of the test is positive, that is if the crystals turn green, the policeman will arrest the accused and take him to the police station. There is no point in refusing the breath test since refusal or even failure to inflate the bag (see below) will usually justify the constable in arresting him anyway. There are many ways in which the accused can frustrate the test – he may refuse to wait until the equipment arrives or he may snatch a quick drink before the test is administered – but they are all useless. Apart from the fact that the court may construe the accused's behaviour as a refusal to take the test there is also the possibility that a charge of obstructing a police officer in the execution of his duty or of perverting the course of justice may be preferred.

At the police station
Once at the police station the procedure which the police are required to follow is extremely complex and consists of the following stages:

- The accused must be offered a second opportunity of undergoing a breath test. There is no obligation on him to do so but he has nothing to gain by refusing. If the result is negative the police may well drop the charges and if it is positive he is in a no worse position than if he refuses for in both cases the police are justified in proceeding to the next stage.
- The next stage is for the police to request a specimen of blood or urine. The request must be made in the following manner:
  (a) it must be made by a constable;
  (b) the constable must warn the accused that failure to provide a specimen may make him liable to imprisonment, a fine and disqualification;
  (c) the initial request is for a specimen of blood. If the accused refuses he must be asked to provide two specimens of urine within an hour. If he fails or refuses to do this he must again be asked to supply a specimen of blood;
  (d) if a specimen of blood or urine is provided the constable must offer the accused a similar specimen in a suitable container for his own analysis if he wishes to have one and, if he does so wish, the specimen must be provided.

If the above stages are not carried out in the correct order this may result in an acquittal. We say *may* because the court has a discretion in the matter, a discretion which they will certainly exercise in favour of the accused if it can be shown that he has been prejudiced by the failure. Thus where an accused is charged with failing to provide a specimen, he will certainly not be convicted if it can be shown that he has never been warned of the legal consequences of his failure. However, where the accused has actually supplied the specimen the precise order in which the requests were made is irrelevant. Once the accused has provided a valid specimen he cannot be asked to provide another one. In one case a constable accidentally threw away a sample of urine. It was held that he was not permitted to request another one. Once the specimen of blood or urine has been provided the police have power to detain the accused further until he is able to provide a breath test which is no longer positive.

Analysis of blood or urine

As soon as the specimen of blood or urine has been taken it will be analysed and it is on the result of this analysis that the question of whether the accused had excess alcohol in his blood will be determined. The analyst does not have to give his evidence in person provided a copy of his certificate is served on the accused seven clear days before the trial and provided the accused does not serve notice on the prosecutor at least three days before the trial requiring the analyst to be present in person. Where the specimen is one of blood a copy of the medical practitioner's certificate to the effect that he took the specimen of blood from the accused with his consent should be similarly served at least seven days before the trial. Again the accused has the right to demand the doctor's personal attendance but there is no point in demanding the attendance of either analyst or doctor unless the defence intends to challenge the accuracy of the analysis. To do so merely to inconvenience the prosecution would do the accused no good and may well prejudice the court against him.

Failing to take the breath test or to supply a specimen

The offences of driving, attempting to drive or being in charge of a motor vehicle while unfit to drive through drink or drugs or with excess alcohol in the body are not the only crimes that can be committed in connection with drunken driving. It is an offence for the accused without reasonable excuse to fail to supply a specimen of breath when lawfully requested to do so, and it is also an offence to fail without reasonable excuse to provide a specimen of blood or urine when lawfully requested to do so. These two offences are now examined in greater detail.

Failing to take the breath test

The first thing to notice is that the law uses the word 'fail' not 'refuse'. Obviously if the motorist refuses point blank to comply then he fails to provide a specimen of breath but he may fail to provide a specimen in circumstances which fall far short of refusal.

This is where the 'reasonable excuse' comes in although the burden of proving this is on the motorist. It is not a reasonable excuse that the motorist is well aware that he has not been drinking provided the policeman had reasonable cause to suspect that he had. The policeman's suspicions do not have to be correct. But it would be a reasonable excuse if the motorist, although willing to comply, was prevented from doing so by circumstances beyond his control – as in the case of the motorist whose bag burst as soon as he blew into it. A medical condition making it dangerous for him to blow hard would also be a reasonable excuse. Where a reasonable excuse is established this will be a good defence to a charge of failing to provide a specimen of breath but it will not save the motorist from being arrested, for the same section empowers the policeman to arrest him and take him to the police station in all cases where he has not provided a breath specimen whether he had a reasonable excuse or not, provided the policeman has reasonable cause to suspect that he has alcohol in his body.

Failing to supply a specimen

The taking of a specimen of blood or urine for laboratory analysis is a more formidable affair and the scope of reasonable excuse is perhaps in this case wider. It has already been pointed out that a prosecution for failing to provide such a specimen cannot be brought unless the procedural steps outlined in the previous section have been strictly complied with. But provided they have been complied with and the arrest was lawful in that the constable had reasonable cause to suspect the presence of alcohol, it is no defence that the accused has in fact committed no offence at all. He must still provide the specimen.

It is not easy to say what constitutes a reasonable excuse since there are no general principles and guidance can only be obtained from the decided cases. The following have been held at various times *not* to be reasonable excuses:

- a genuine religious objection to the shedding of blood;
- a refusal to supply a specimen unless a solicitor is present;
- in the case of a lady motorist, a refusal to supply urine because no policewoman was present (the court held in this case that she should have provided a specimen of blood);
- the fact that the accused had been assaulted by a police officer (the assault in this case was a very minor one: a serious assault might well be held to be a reasonable excuse);
- where the accused agreed to provide a specimen of blood but only on the condition that it was taken from his big toe (it appears that the motorist has no right to select the portion of his anatomy from which the blood is to be taken. This is a matter for the doctor's discretion).

In the following cases it was held that the accused *did* have a reasonable excuse:

- where the accused having already supplied a specimen of urine which had been accidentally thrown away refused to supply a further specimen of blood;
- where the accused was so afraid of the needle as to be physically incapable of submitting to it (this was supported by medical evidence);
- that the accused was concussed at the time.

Once the motorist has provided a specimen he cannot be charged if he refuses to provide a second one. In one case a motorist who had provided a specimen of urine took it away with him, unnoticed by the police, when he left the station. It was held he could not be charged with failing to provide a specimen because he had in fact done so – but that he could be charged with theft.

Alternative offence

Section 12 of the Licensing Act 1872 makes it an offence for a person to be in charge of any carriage horse or cattle on any highway or other public place when drunk. The penalty is a £10 fine or one month's imprisonment. This charge, which is older than the petrol engine, is little used nowadays, particularly since it cannot be used against any person who is liable to be charged under Sections 5, 6 or 9 of the Road Traffic Act. It might be used in cases where for some technical reason a charge under the more modern statute cannot be brought.

Offences

The Criminal Law Act 1977 has now made all drink-driving offences punishable summarily only – (see page 417). The act has, however, increased the maximum penalties. Furthermore the reference to obligatory disqualification means disqualification for a *minimum* period of twelve months. The Court of Appeal and the Magistrates' Association have repeatedly urged magistrates to impose longer periods of disqualification particularly where the alcohol level in the blood greatly exceeds the permitted legal maximum.

Offences

(See page 405 for proposed increases in maximum fines.)

Offence	*Maximum penalty*	*Endorsement*	*Disqualification*
Driving or attempting to drive while unfit through drink or drugs	Six months and/or £1,000 fine	Obligatory	Obligatory
Being in charge of a motor vehicle while unfit through drink or drugs	Three months and/or £500 fine	Obligatory	Discretionary
Driving or attempting to drive with excess alcohol	Six months and/or £1,000 fine	Obligatory	Obligatory
Being in charge of a motor vehicle with excess alcohol	Three months and/or £500 fine	Obligatory	Discretionary
Failing to provide a specimen of breath*	£50 fine	—	—
Failing to provide a specimen for laboratory analysis	(a) If at the relevant time the driver was driving or attempting to drive – six months and/or £1,000 fine.	Obligatory	Obligatory
	(b) If at the relevant time the driver was in charge of a motor vehicle – three months and/or £500 fine	Obligatory	Discretionary

Note: in the case of those offences which carry obligatory disqualification the minimum period is increased from twelve months to three years if the accused has been convicted of a similar offence at any time within the ten years immediately preceding the offence in question.

*When the relevant provisions of the Transport Act 1981 are in force, this offence will carry discretionary disqualification.

Proposed changes in the law

When the first edition of this book appeared, mention was made of the fact that there was at that time a bill before Parliament one of the purposes of which was to make considerable changes in various aspects of road traffic law.

That bill has now been passed and is now the Transport Act 1981. The new provisions concerning the compulsory wearing of seat belts and the new system of penalty points have been described in the appropriate chapters of this book. Unfortunately there is still no indication as to when the government proposes to implement the new provisions relating to drunken driving.

It is possible that these laws may be in force by the time this second edition is in print and for that reason a brief summary of the changes appears below:

- Although preliminary screening by means of a breathalyser will take place as before, the formal testing at the police station will now be carried out by means of a new breath machine which is capable of measuring the proportion of alcohol in the breath with a much higher degree of accuracy. Nevertheless blood or urine tests can still be demanded in the following cases: (a) where the charge involves the use of drugs, (b) where the accused is incapable for medical reasons of blowing into the machine, and (c) where no breath machine is available at the police station, or where it is not practicable to use it.

  The prescribed limit on the new breath machine is 35 microgrammes of alcohol in 100 millilitres of breath. Two specimens of breath shall be demanded and the operative level shall be the lower of the two. Where, however, this lower level does not exceed 50 microgrammes the accused shall have the right to demand that a specimen of blood or urine be taken and, if this is done, neither specimen of breath shall be used. As under the present law the Secretary of State will have the power to vary this level by order.
- The new act will give a policeman power to breathalyse a motorist who is merely in charge of a motor vehicle, if he has reasonable cause to suspect that he has alcohol in his body. At the moment the police have no power to breathalyse a person who is merely in charge.
- Perhaps the most important change in the law is that, in future, a police officer will have power to breathalyse a person if he has reasonable cause to suspect (a) that he has been driving or

attempting to drive or been in charge of a motor vehicle on a road with alcohol in his body, or (b) that he has been driving or attempting to drive or been in charge of a motor vehicle on a road and has committed a traffic offence while the vehicle was in motion.

The importance of this change lies in the fact that it will no longer be necessary that the motorist should be still driving, etc., when the suspicion of alcohol arises. Thus many of the hair-splitting decisions as to whether a motorist is driving or not will become superfluous.

- A change that is nearly as important is that the new act gives the police the right to enter, if necessary by force, any premises where the accused is or where they have reasonable cause to expect him to be, for the purpose of (a) administering a breath test if they have reasonable cause to suspect that the accused was driving a motor vehicle on a road at a time when it was involved in an accident resulting in injury to some other person, or (b) arresting a person who is suspected of having driven while unfit to drive or, where the charge involves excess alcohol and the accused has either failed to provide a specimen of breath or has provided one and the result of that test is positive.

  It should be added that these new provisions will not apply in Scotland.
- Where a specimen of blood or urine is demanded the choice will in future be left to the police except where medical advice is against the taking of a sample of blood. At the moment the choice lies with the accused.
- The offence of failing to provide a specimen of breath for the purpose of a breathalyser test when lawfully required to do so will in future carry discretionary disqualification.
- The anomaly referred to on page 360 has been removed by the new act. When a man is in charge of a motor vehicle, irrespective of whether the charge involves unfitness to drive or excess alcohol, the court is directed to ignore the condition of the driver and the state of the vehicle in assessing the likelihood of his driving the vehicle.
- The new law will make it impossible for the driver to evade the consequences of his actions by 'snatching a quick drink'. At the moment if a driver is able to take a drink just before the test is made, this will invalidate the result of the test because it will be impossible to show that the level of alcohol indicated by the test was the level in his body at the time the offence was committed.

The new act prevents this by directing that the level of alcohol indicated by the test shall be presumed to be the level that was in his body at the time the offence was committed and the accused can upset this presumption only by showing that he had consumed alcohol after he had ceased to drive, etc., and that, if he had not done so, the level of alcohol in his body would not have rendered him unfit to drive or exceeded the prescribed limit, as the case may be. In practice, of course, this would be virtually impossible to do.

- One slight relaxation in favour of the driver is that where he is detained at the police station the police must release him if they are satisfied that, although he is still under the influence of alcohol, there is no likelihood of his driving a motor vehicle while still in that condition. At the moment they are entitled to detain him as long as the level of alcohol in his body exceeds the prescribed limit.

41 What to do if an accident happens

Statistics show that there is a high degree of probability that every motorist on the road will be involved in an accident sooner or later, even if it is only a minor bump or scrape. However, accidents are not usually anticipated and when they do occur the motorist's personal qualities are apt to be put to a very severe test. He will be bewildered – perhaps even in a state of shock; but if he can keep his head and remember certain basic rules he may be able to save himself from a great deal of inconvenience later on. So it is worth while to be prepared and to have a clear picture of what is to be done – you never know, your accident might happen tomorrow.

What is an accident?

For the purpose of the offences of failing to stop after an accident and of failing to report an accident, the Road Traffic Act lays down a very clear definition indeed, a definition which is worth quoting in full:

If in any case, owing to the presence of a motor vehicle on a road, an accident occurs whereby personal injury is caused to a person other than the driver of that motor vehicle or damage is caused to a vehicle other than that motor vehicle or a trailer drawn thereby or to an animal other than an animal in or on that motor vehicle or a trailer drawn thereby or to any other property constructed on, fixed to, growing in or otherwise forming part of the land on which the road in question is situated or land adjacent thereto . . .

It is clear that the above definition envisages damage or injury of some sort but there is more to it than that. If injury is caused to a human being it must be to someone other than the driver of the car which caused it. In ordinary speech if a man injures himself he may say that he has had an accident but he has not had an accident for the purposes of the Road Traffic Act. It is sufficient, however, if he injures a passenger carried in his own vehicle. If injury is caused to an animal it must be a horse, cattle, ass, mule, sheep, pig, goat or dog. It is an accident if you run over a dog but not if you run over a cat or a hen, nor presumably if you collide with an elephant. If it is a vehicle that is damaged it must be a vehicle other than your own or a trailer drawn by your vehicle. Finally it is also an accident if you damage a fixed object such as a signpost, wall, gate, lamp standard, provided this is constructed on, fixed to, growing in, or forming part of, the land. Thus it is not an accident for this purpose of the law if you collide with a portable news-stand or a packing-case left in the road, but it is if you collide with a stationary bicycle for a bicycle has been judicially declared to be a vehicle. In all cases the accident must have been caused owing to the presence of a motor vehicle on a road. It is not a reportable accident therefore if the incident takes place in a field or on private land. But the law does not say that your vehicle must have caused the accident. It is still an accident and you will have the same legal obligations even if you are totally innocent of blame.

What you must do

Here we must distinguish between two entirely separate and distinct courses of action. The Road Traffic Act lays down a procedure which you must rigorously observe. At the same time it is very probable that your insurance policy will oblige you to do or to refrain from doing certain things; for instance, it is probably a condition that if you are involved in an accident you must not make an admission of liability and you may be required to do your best to get the names and addresses of possible witnesses. The insurance company will almost certainly require you to report the accident to them within a certain period of time.

These requirements are not backed by the law and you commit no offence if you do not comply with them but they are terms in your contract with the insurance company; if you break them you may find your legal rights against the company adversely affected. Since different companies have different requirements it is impossible to generalize. The golden rule is to be absolutely clear in your mind what your insurance policy requires you to do if you are involved in an accident.

Let us now turn to the requirements of the law.

Duty to stop

The Road Traffic Act says that if you are involved in an accident, as defined above, you must in all cases stop.

The duty to stop is a strict one – you must in all circumstances stop, and 'stop' means long enough to enable any interested party to demand your name and address if he wishes to. No use stopping for a couple of seconds and then driving hastily on. In one case a motorist who had been involved in such an accident drove on for a quarter of a mile, then changed his mind, turned round and went back. It was held that he was rightly convicted of failing to stop after an accident. However, it is a defence to this charge if the driver did not know that an accident had happened, but it is a defence that should be used with caution. In a perfectly genuine case the court will accept it but it is difficult to imagine how a driver could be involved in an accident, except perhaps the most trivial, without knowing it, and since every driver is likely to try this defence in default of any other you must not be surprised if the court views it with suspicion.

Having stopped, it is then your duty to give particulars as to your name and address, the name and address of the owner of the vehicle and the vehicle's identification marks to any person having reasonable grounds for demanding them. This means any person who is involved in some way in the accident. Although the law is somewhat uncertain on this point it is probably an offence if you refuse.

The duty to give this information is personal and cannot be delegated. A business executive who was involved in an accident left his secretary behind to give the necessary details because he was in a hurry. He was later convicted of failing to stop and give particulars. Of course no offence is committed if no one asks you for the information, or indeed if there is no one there to ask you, but in this case you must report the accident to the police.

Duty to report the accident
If you give the information described above it is not necessary for you to report the accident to the police. If you do not give the information you must report the accident to the police. Reporting to the police means reporting the accident to any police constable or at any police station. The reporting must be done in person – you cannot just telephone in the particulars. Note also that the law says 'as soon as is reasonably practicable and in any case within twenty-four hours'. It does not say simply 'within twenty-four hours'. In one case a motorist was convicted even though he did report the accident within twenty-four hours because the court was of the opinion that he could have easily reported it sooner if he had chosen to do so.

Accidents involving personal injury

The previous section outlines the procedure which must be followed in all cases where an accident, as defined in the Act, occurs owing to the presence of a motor vehicle on a road. Where personal injury is involved there are certain additional requirements. The injury must be to some person other than the driver of the vehicle concerned, although a passenger in his vehicle would be included. In this case the driver must produce his certificate of insurance either to the police or to any person who has reasonable grounds for seeing it; if he does not do so, he must report the accident to the police as soon as possible and in any case within twenty-four hours and produce his insurance certificate, except that if it is not possible for him to produce the certificate immediately he may do so at any police station specified by him within five days of the accident. In this case he does not have to produce the certificate in person – he may send it by post if he wishes. This is in addition to the requirement that he should give his name and address, etc. to an interested party, although failure to produce the certificate at the time of the accident is not an offence provided it is subsequently produced in the manner laid down by the law.

The object of producing the certificate is to enable the party concerned to see that the certificate is a valid one and to note the name of the company. If the certificate is produced in a manner which does not allow this to be done, this is not a valid production to satisfy the law.

Emergency treatment

Members of the medical profession can scarcely withhold their services, when needed, on the grounds that they may not be paid for them. For this reason the law affords them a special protection. When a member of the medical profession renders first aid in an emergency to someone who has been injured in a road accident, the driver of the vehicle involved in the accident must pay to him a sum which is now fixed at £6.75 plus a mileage allowance if the doctor has been forced to travel a long distance. The obligation to pay this is a strict one, i.e. it does not matter whether the driver caused the accident or not. Even in an obvious 'suicide' case where the victim runs in front of your car without warning, it is still you who must pay the doctor's bill, although in this case you would have the right to recover the amount by means of a civil action from the person whose negligence caused the accident – if you can get it and if you think it is worth it.

Where the victim has received hospital treatment the hospital has the right to recover the cost but in this case the cost can in general only be recovered from the person responsible for the accident or, more probably, his insurance company. What the law says is that where payment has been made by an authorized insurer under the provisions of a third-party insurance policy, or by the owner of the vehicle concerned in those rare cases when he has taken out a security or made a deposit as an alternative to third-party insurance, then the person making the payment, irrespective of whether the payment has been accompanied by an admission of liability or not, shall be liable to pay to the hospital their normal charge for treatment provided this does not exceed £125 in the case of an outpatient and £1,225 in the case of an in-patient.

Offences

Offence	*Maximum penalty*	*Endorsement*	*Disqualification*
Failing to stop after an accident	£1,000	Obligatory	Discretionary
Failing to report an accident	£1,000	Obligatory	Discretionary

42 The motorist and the police

In England the police are not above the law. Even where the law gives them special powers these must always be exercised within the strict parameters which the law lays down, and if the policeman exceeds these powers he is just as much answerable to the law as is the ordinary motorist.

The criminal process

Bringing the accused before the court

When a man is accused of having committed a crime there must be some way in which he can be brought before the court which will be responsible for trying it. In England there are two such ways – *summons* and *arrest*. It is sometimes said that the difference between these two methods lies in the fact that a summons is used for less serious offences and arrest for the more serious; this is no more than broadly true. The real distinction is that a summons is used where there is little reason to fear that the accused will not appear voluntarily to answer the charge and arrest where the charge is of such a nature that there is good reason to fear that he may not. This explains why the majority of road traffic offences are dealt with by means of a summons.

The decision whether or not to prosecute is not normally taken by the policeman who investigates the incident. What usually happens is this. The policeman who believes that a road traffic offence has been committed is entitled to stop the offending motorist and to demand his name and address and the production of his driving licence. In certain cases he is required by law to warn the motorist that he may be prosecuted (or to send a written notice to that effect within fourteen days – see page 386 under *Notice of intended prosecution*) but in the majority of cases he is not. He will certainly make a report on the incident, and the decision whether or not to take proceedings will usually be taken by a senior police officer. Only in very serious cases will the matter be referred to the Director of Public Prosecutions. If it is decided that proceedings shall be taken, a summons will normally be issued.

Summons

A summons is usually issued whenever information has been laid (either by the police or by a private person) that a crime has been committed and it has been decided to take proceedings. It will inform the motorist of the precise charge which he is to meet and the section of the statute in which it is laid down. It will specify the time and place of the hearing and it will give him sufficient supporting detail so as to enable him to identify the incident in question.

Arrest

The process known as arrest is rather more serious. When a man is arrested he is deprived of his liberty and taken to a police cell. The police cannot hold him indefinitely. They must either bring him as soon as is practicable before a magistrate who will decide what is to be done with him – he may for example order his release, commit him for trial or remand him on bail or in custody – or they must release him on police bail.

The principle behind arrest is that if a man is to be arrested, a warrant for his arrest should be issued. This is a document issued by a magistrate and it must identify by name the person to be arrested as well as the charge against him. Once the warrant is issued the accused may be arrested by any constable at sight. The constable does not have to have the warrant in his possession at the time although the accused is entitled to know the reason for the arrest and should be shown the warrant as soon as possible if he asks to see it.

Arrest without warrant

If a man could be arrested only with a warrant a great many criminals would go scot free. The burglar caught in the act is not likely to wait around while the policeman obtains a warrant. For this reason the police have always enjoyed extensive powers of arrest without warrant. A policeman may arrest without warrant any person who commits a serious crime in his presence or even any person whom he reasonably suspects of having committed a serious crime. In recent years the list of these 'arrestable' offences has tended to lengthen and has even penetrated the field of road traffic law. We have seen in an earlier chapter that a policeman may arrest any man who is driving or attempting to drive a motor vehicle on a road while unfit to drive through drink or drugs. He may also arrest a man who refuses to submit to a breath test when lawfully requested to do so or, where the breath test has been administered, in cases where it has proved positive. He may also arrest a man for the charge of taking a conveyance contrary to Section 12 of the Theft Act. However, such examples are comparatively rare. In the majority of cases the policeman can only stop the offender, take his name and address and make a report with a view to the issue of a summons if it is decided to take proceedings.

Wrongful arrest

When a man has been arrested on a charge of which he is later proved to be totally innocent, it is only natural that he should feel considerable resentment and perhaps wish to sue the police for wrongful arrest. If he does, it is unlikely that he will be successful. When a policeman arrests a man he cannot in many cases know for certain that the man is guilty. Provided he has acted on a reasonable suspicion this is as much as can be expected. Wrongful arrest means an arrest that is contrary to law, such as arresting a man for an offence, e.g. speeding, for which the law does not permit him to be arrested, or possibly arresting him in circumstances in which the policeman could not possibly have had any reasonable suspicion of his guilt.

Police questioning

Apart from using the process of arrest the police have no power to require any person to go to the police station. They frequently endeavour to do so by using excuses such as 'helping them with their inquiries' or saying 'you would prefer to answer questions at the police station rather than at your front door with the neighbours watching'. You can refuse to submit to these blandishments if you wish and insist on your right not to go to the police station except under arrest, in which case the policeman must tell you the charge on which he is arresting you, but it is not always wise to do so. If you are innocent it is your duty to help the police, and if you are guilty there is a danger that your refusal might just tip the scales in the policeman's mind in favour of arresting you after all.

The question of whether or not you should answer a policeman's questions raises another issue of the greatest importance. It is the duty of the police to prevent crime and to discover criminals; in furtherance of this duty they are entitled to put any questions they choose to members of the general public. But there is no corresponding duty on the public to answer them except only in those specific cases where the law says they must. The Road Traffic Act for example empowers a policeman to stop any vehicle on the road and demand to know the driver's name and address and also the name and address of the owner of the vehicle; failure to give this information is an offence in itself.

The matter is further complicated by the fact that English law will not compel a person to answer questions or to make statements if the information thus provided is likely to incriminate him of some offence, unless there is a positive rule of law requiring him to do so. It was this that delayed the introduction of the breathalyser – until its use was made compulsory a motorist could not be compelled against his will to provide specimens of blood or urine which might later be used to show that he had been guilty of a drink-driving offence. This meant that a policeman ought not to interrogate a person if he believed that person to be guilty of an offence, since by doing so it might be argued that he was seeking to obtain evidence which might later be used to that person's disadvantage. This principle conflicted, however, with his other duty to ask questions in order to find out who the offender was. The dilemma was solved many years ago by the judges of the High Court who issued a series of rules known as the Judges' Rules in order to guide the police in the interrogation of suspected persons.

The Judges' Rules

The Judges' Rules do not have the force of law in the sense that a breach of them is an offence in itself, but a trial judge can rule that evidence that has been obtained contrary to the spirit of the Judges' Rules is inadmissible.

The rules themselves are complicated but their general effect is easily explained. If in the course of interrogating a person a policeman forms the opinion that he may be guilty of an offence then he must caution him to the effect that he is not required to say anything and that anything he does say will be taken down in writing and may be used in evidence. Once the caution is administered the man knows that he makes further statements at his peril, and if he is wise he will say nothing more. After he has been arrested and charged he must be cautioned a second time. After charging, the police may not put any further questions to him at all, but he has the right to make a statement if he wishes. The statement, if he makes one, must be taken down in accordance with a complicated procedure laid down in the Judges' Rules the purpose of which is to protect the police as much as to protect the accused, for it often happens that persons who have made a statement quite voluntarily may afterwards wish to retract it and will therefore argue that the statement was wrung from them by threats or inducements. If the procedure laid down in the Judges' Rules is followed this would be very difficult to establish.

In practice it is almost always better to say nothing once a caution is administered. It is most unlikely indeed that anything you say will cause the police to drop the charges against you and there is a very real danger that you may seriously handicap your legal advisers who will have the ultimate task of planning your defence and who must bear in mind that the statements you made can be submitted to the court in evidence. Even outraged protestations of innocence can be dangerous. There is usually more than one line to take in planning a defence and a statement which may be consistent with one line may be wholly incompatible with another. The golden rule is – once you are cautioned keep your mouth shut and say nothing until you have had legal advice.

(The Police and Criminal Evidence Bill, which could become law in the summer of 1983, proposes to replace the Judges' Rules with a Code of Practice issued by the Home Secretary.)

Various police powers

Mention has been made more than once in this book of the specific powers with which the law invests the police, e.g. the power to administer a breath test or the power to remove an abandoned vehicle. The list that follows is by no means exhaustive – no list in road traffic law ever is – but it does include the most important police powers that the motorist is likely to come up against and it includes a number that have not been mentioned before.

Power to regulate traffic

A policeman on point duty is a formidable person. On his skill and judgment the avoidance of accidents depends and it is only reasonable that he should be entitled to expect immediate compliance with his signals, which take priority over everything else; for example, the traffic lights ahead may be green but if the policeman signals you to stop, stop you must. His powers extend to pedestrians too as long as the latter are on the carriageway, and he may now require a motorist to stop and take part in a traffic survey. A more detailed discussion of the law on this topic will be found in Chapter 38, page 328 onwards.

Power to test condition of vehicles

An authorized examiner may test any motor vehicle on a road in order to ensure that the requirements of the law are being complied with in respect of brakes, silencer, steering-gear, tyres, emission of smoke or fumes, lighting equipment, reflectors and noise. Authorized examiners are often civilians appointed for the purpose but a police constable may act as authorized examiner provided he has been specially empowered to do so, in which case he must carry his authority with him and produce it on demand. A civilian examiner cannot order a vehicle to stop for the purpose of undergoing the test; this can only be done by a police constable in uniform.

If the driver is in a hurry he has the right to request that the test be postponed unless the constable is of the opinion that the condition of the vehicle is so defective that it ought not to be allowed to proceed, or that the test should be carried out immediately by reason of an accident having occurred. In the latter case where the policeman is not himself to carry out the test he can insist that the vehicle is not moved until the test has been completed. Tests of this nature can be carried out at any time provided the vehicle is on a road, and should not be confused with the periodical testing of motor vehicles (see Chapter 37) which is a preliminary to the issue of an MOT certificate.

Under the Construction and Use Regulations a police constable in uniform or an authorized examiner is empowered to test the brakes, silencers, steering-gear, tyres, lighting equipment and reflectors of any motor vehicle on any premises where the vehicle may happen to be. In this case, however, unless the owner of the premises consents to the test being carried out, it is necessary for the examiner to give previous notice of his intention unless the vehicle has been involved in an accident within the previous forty-eight hours, in which case neither consent nor notice is necessary.

Power to stop vehicles

A police constable in uniform may require any person driving a motor vehicle on a road to stop. It must be stressed that this power is an absolute one, i.e. the policeman does not have to have a reason for stopping you. It is not of course suggested that the police are likely to stop vehicles for the fun of it, but if you fail to stop when ordered to do so, an offence is committed whether the policeman had a reason or not. When the policeman stops a vehicle he has the right to demand certain information and the production of certain documents (see the next two sections).

Power to demand production of driving licence

A police constable has the right in the case of the following persons –

- any person driving a motor vehicle on a road;
- any person whom he has reasonable cause to believe was the driver of a motor vehicle at a time when it was involved in an accident on a road;
- any person whom he has reasonable cause to believe has committed a traffic offence;
- the supervisor of a learner driver who is driving a motor vehicle on a road, or any person whom the constable has reasonable cause to believe was the supervisor of a learner driver at a time when the vehicle was involved in an accident

– to demand production of the person's driving licence in order to discover the name and address of the holder, the date of issue and the authority by which it was issued. However, he has no right to look at any endorsement that may be on it. Failure to produce the licence is not an offence provided the person in question produces the licence in person at any police station specified by him within five days.

When a policeman demands production of a driving licence he may also require the motorist to state his date of birth in the following circumstances:

- when no driving licence is produced (in this case the motorist must state his date of birth even though he subsequently produces the licence within the stipulated five days);
- where the licence is one issued by a local authority;
- where the constable has reason to suspect that the licence produced is not the motorist's own, or that it has been forged or altered in some way.

A traffic warden has the right to demand a motorist's name and address but (unlike a policeman) he has no right to demand production of your driving licence.

Power to obtain name and address and demand production of insurance certificate

A police constable also has the right in the case of the following persons –

- any person driving a motor vehicle on a road;
- any person whom he has reasonable cause to believe was the

driver of a motor vehicle at a time when it was involved in an accident on a road;
- any person whom he has reasonable cause to believe has committed a traffic offence

– to demand the person's name and address, the name and address of the owner of the vehicle and production of the relevant certificate of insurance and MOT test certificate (provided of course the vehicle is subject to annual testing). Failure to produce these documents is not an offence provided they are produced at any specified police station within five days. In this case (unlike a driving licence) they do not have to be produced in person. They can be sent by messenger or by post.

The supervisor of a learner driver and any person whom a police constable has reasonable cause to believe was the supervisor of a learner driver at a time when the vehicle in question was involved in an accident on a road may also be required to give his name and address as well as the name and address of the owner of the vehicle but he cannot be asked to produce the insurance certificate and MOT test certificate since these are the responsibility of the driver.

Power to have vehicles weighed
Authorized persons have the right to require any person who is in charge of a motor vehicle on a road to allow it to be weighed and for that purpose to proceed to the nearest public weighbridge. The term 'authorized person' includes police constables who have been specially authorized to do this and who must produce their authority if asked to do so. This power is mainly intended to prevent the overloading of goods vehicles and it is very unlikely that such a request would be made to the driver of a private car.

Power to demand pedestrian's name and address
We have already seen that a pedestrian who is on the carriageway must comply with any signal given to him by a police constable who is engaged in the regulation of traffic. If he fails to do so the policeman has the right to demand his name and address.

Power to operate the fixed penalty system
In order to prevent the courts from getting cluttered up with too many trivial cases the law has devised a system that is known colloquially as the fixed penalty system. The system now applies in the whole of England and Wales and normally covers the following offences:

- parking on a road at night without lights where these are required by law;
- obstructing a road (but not other forms of obstruction), waiting, being left or parked or loaded or unloaded in a road contrary to law;
- non-payment of parking meter charges;
- using a vehicle in contravention of a traffic regulation order;
- using a vehicle in contravention of certain Construction and Use regulations (but excluding all offences which carry discretionary disqualification);
- using a vehicle on a public road without a vehicle excise licence.

The system operates as follows. Where an offence has been committed a police constable or traffic warden may serve a fixed penalty notice on the offender or, if he cannot be found, may fix it to the vehicle. The notice informs the offender that if he pays the fixed penalty (at the time of writing this is £10) no further proceedings will be taken. The advantage of paying the fixed penalty from the motorist's point of view is that the amount is less than the fine he may have to pay if proceedings are taken, and also that if he pays the fixed penalty no conviction will be recorded against him.

If the fixed penalty or excess meter charge is not paid within the prescribed period (usually twenty-one days) the police or local authority concerned may then serve a statutory notice on the registered owner of the vehicle. This requires the registered owner either to pay the penalty within the prescribed period (usually fourteen days) or to serve a statement of ownership on the authority who issued the notice. If the owner can show in this statement that he was not the registered owner at the time the offence was committed he can escape liability although he is required in this case, if he is able to do so, to give the police the name and address of the person from whom he bought it or to whom he sold it and the date of the purchase or sale as the case may be. He may also, if he chooses, serve with the statement of ownership a statement of facts giving the name and address of the driver (if it was not himself) at the time the offence was committed. In this case the police will then proceed to prosecute the driver, although if for any reason the driver cannot be convicted, the original owner will remain liable. The registered owner can also escape liability if he can show that although he was the registered owner at the relevant time the vehicle was being driven by some other person without his consent.

Note: the Transport Act 1982 provides for a number of important changes to be made in the fixed penalty procedure. For details see page 404.

Power to remove vehicles
This power was discussed in Chapter 39, page 344.

Power to question people
See under *Police questioning*, page 379.

Notice of intended prosecution

In certain cases the law imposes restrictions on the right of the police to prosecute. The offences concerned are:

- reckless driving;
- careless driving;
- exceeding a speed limit;
- disobeying traffic signs and police signals;
- leaving a vehicle in a dangerous position;
- aiding and abetting the committing of any of the above offences.

In the case of all the above offences the police cannot prosecute unless:

- the motorist was warned at the time of the offence that he might be prosecuted (an oral warning is sufficient); or
- he receives a summons within fourteen days of the offence; or
- a notice of the possibility of prosecution is sent within fourteen days of the offence either to the driver or to the registered keeper of the vehicle.

It will be noted that the above requirements are alternative so that if the accused is orally warned at the time no notice of intended prosecution need be sent and even if he was not warned a prosecution can still be brought provided a summons or a warning notice is sent within fourteen days. If the accused wishes to rely on this defence he must himself prove that he was not warned at the time and that no warning notice was sent to him or to the registered keeper of the vehicle.

The oral warning should be given 'at the time' of the occurrence but this is loosely interpreted. A warning given as near to the time of the event as possible will do and it does not have to be in any precise terms provided its meaning is clear. If, however, the accused is unconscious at the time or perhaps too drunk to understand what was being said, then a written notice should be sent in addition. Where a written notice is sent there is no requirement that it should have been received by the accused provided it was sent in such a manner and at such a time that it would in the normal course of events have been received by him. An error in spelling the motorist's name is not likely to invalidate the procedure provided it is clear for whom the notice was intended; in one case where the police had only the registration number of the vehicle and were misinformed by the licensing authorities as to the owner's name, it was held that this did not prevent a prosecution from being brought.

An important change in the law has now directed that the above procedure need not be complied with if the vehicle in question has been involved in an accident. Before the law was altered the police were faced with a particular difficulty in this respect. When an accident occurred, especially if a number of vehicles was involved, the police had often no means of knowing at the time which drivers were to blame, and so to cover themselves were forced to send notices of intended prosecution to all the drivers concerned, some of whom were probably wholly innocent. To prevent the alarm and despondency which inevitably resulted, accident cases were taken out of the scope of the notice of intended prosecution procedure. Since the law merely referred to 'an accident', however, it seems that the procedure does not now apply even when only a single vehicle is involved.

Offences

(See page 405 for proposed increases in maximum fines.)

Offence	*Maximum penalty*	*Endorsement*	*Disqualification*
Failing to produce driving licence in court when convicted	£100	—	—
Obstructing the testing of a vehicle by an examiner on a road	£50	—	—
Failing to stop when ordered by a policeman to do so	£100	—	—
Failing to produce driving licence or state date of birth	£50	—	—
Failing to give name and address or to produce insurance and MOT certificate	£50	—	—

Offence	*Maximum penalty*	*Endorsement*	*Disqualification*
Removing or interfering with fixed penalty ticket	£20	—	—
Failing to pay a fixed penalty, etc. or to serve a statutory statement of ownership	£100	—	—
Making a false declaration in a statutory statement of ownership	£400	—	—

43 The motorist and the courts

This chapter is about certain court procedures and criminal penalties of special interest to motorists. In particular it deals with pleading guilty by post, endorsement and disqualification.

Procedure

In English law all criminal offences are classified by the way in which they are tried; they may be triable summarily only, triable on indictment only or triable either way (see page 417 for an explanation of these terms).

The vast majority of motoring offences are triable summarily only; those that are triable either way include reckless driving, criminal damage (where this exceeds £200), theft and the taking of a conveyance, and driving while disqualified. Manslaughter and causing death by reckless driving are triable on indictment only.

Summary trial in the magistrates' court

A summary trial in a motoring case will normally start with a police officer laying information that an offence has been committed. If it is decided to go ahead with the case the next step is the issue of a summons.

Pleading guilty by letter

Where the motorist receives a summons he will be advised in many cases of his right to plead guilty by letter. If he decides to do this it will not be be necessary for him to appear in court at all and he will be informed in due course of the penalty which the court has decided to impose. He must remember to send in his driving licence if the offence is an endorsable one and he is also invited to submit a 'plea in mitigation'. He would be well advised to take full advantage of this and to consider carefully how it is to be worded. Contrary to popular belief magistrates take pleas in mitigation very seriously and although they cannot secure you an acquittal (you have already pleaded guilty) they may well result in a lighter penalty. If for example you are charged with speeding and your excuse was that you had received a message to the effect that your wife had been taken seriously ill, this could mean a very light penalty indeed. You cannot incidentally be disqualified from driving in your absence, and if the offence with which you are charged is a disqualifiable one and the magistrates are considering disqualifying you they must warn you of this and give you an opportunity to appear in person.

Conducting your own case

The question of whether or not you are legally represented at the trial must depend on the length of your purse and the gravity of the charge. If the case is a fairly straightforward one and you know you are guilty it is generally better to plead guilty. However, if the case is a tricky one, above all if it is a disqualifiable offence, then it would be wiser to seek a solicitor's help. If you feel you need professional help and cannot afford to employ a solicitor it is possible to apply to the magistrates' court for legal aid (see page 432), although this is very difficult to obtain and is likely to be granted only in exceptional cases. If you are a member of the AA or the RAC you should contact them. If the offence with which you are charged is endorsable then you must do one of three things in connection with your driving licence. You must either

- have it delivered to the clerk of the court not later than the day before the day appointed for the hearing; or
- post it by either registered post or recorded delivery service in a letter addressed to the clerk of the court so that in the ordinary course of post it would reach him by that day; or
- have it with you at the trial.

If you are convicted and you have done none of these things, that is an offence in itself. If you are acquitted then of course there is no offence for in that case the court will have no power to demand your licence for endorsement.

Penalties

The penalties which a magistrates' court can impose include the following: absolute discharge; conditional discharge; fine; imprisonment; endorsement; disqualification. A magistrates' court can also make a probation order but this is not often done in the case of road traffic offences.

Unlike some Continental systems, English criminal law works on the principle of fixing maximum penalties which are usually rather high, and leaving the court a considerable latitude in imposing a penalty which will be fair, taking all the circumstances of the case into consideration. This has the advantage of enabling the magistrates to make the punishment fit the crime, but it also has the disadvantage of resulting in wide variations in the penalties imposed according to the different ideas which different magistrates may have of the seriousness of the offence. To get round this difficulty the Magistrates' Association has published a list of suggested penalties to assist the courts. These suggested penalties are of course no more than guidelines. The magistrates may, if they see fit to do so, impose any penalty up to the maximum laid down by the law. The fines mentioned in the tables which will be found at the end of some chapters in this book are of course maximum fines. The fines suggested by the Magistrates' Association for a first conviction average out at roughly a quarter of the maximum.

Discharge

An absolute discharge is in effect no punishment at all. It is granted when the accused although convicted of an offence is not considered by the court to have behaved in such a way as to merit punishment. A conditional discharge is similar except that in this case if the accused is convicted of a second offence within the prescribed period – usually twelve months – he will be punished for both offences. Where the offence is an endorsable one the fact that the motorist has been granted a discharge does not mean that his licence must not be endorsed as well – unless the court considers at its discretion that the same circumstances which justified their granting a discharge constitute a special reason for not endorsing.

Fines

Nowadays in deciding the amount of a fine, a court will take into consideration not only the circumstances of the case but also the offender's means and his ability to pay. If necessary fines can be paid by instalments and application can always be made to the court to have the instalments adjusted if the offender's means alter – for example he may lose his job. The maximum fine which a court of summary jurisdiction can impose for any one offence is £1,000. For most road traffic offences the maximum fine is usually much lower than this.

Imprisonment

Not many road traffic offences are punishable with imprisonment, and even in the case of those that are, it is unlikely to be imposed on first conviction except in very bad cases. Even then it may be suspended for a period of not less than one nor more than two years. This means that provided the accused does not commit a further offence punishable by imprisonment during the period covered by the suspension he will not be required to serve the original sentence.

Where the maximum penalty for an offence is shown as a fine or imprisonment the courts may impose either but not both. Where the maximum penalty is shown as a fine and/or imprisonment the court may impose either or both together if it chooses. The maximum length of imprisonment for any one offence which a court of summary jurisdiction can impose is six months. In the case of those offences which are triable either way, the accused must be warned if he agrees to summary trial that if on conviction the court is of the opinion that he deserves a punishment more severe than the summary court has power to impose, he can be committed to the Crown Court for sentence.

Endorsement

Road traffic offences are either endorsable (in which case the court must endorse the offender's licence if he is convicted unless it considers there are special reasons for not doing so – more about this later) or they are offences in respect of which endorsement cannot be ordered. There is no such thing as discretionary endorsement in the sense that there is discretionary disqualification. Construction and Use offences are not endorsable with the exception of those dealing with brakes, steering-gear, tyres, weight or generally with using a vehicle in a dangerous manner. Even in these cases the motorist may escape endorsement if he can show that he did not know and could not in the circumstances reasonably have known that an offence was being committed. It is clear therefore that although in road traffic law there are many 'technical' offences it is not possible for a motorist's licence to be endorsed for an offence unless he was conscious of the fact that he had been to some extent at least at fault.

With the advent of computerization endorsements are now recorded in accordance with a rather complicated code. Two initial letters indicate the category of the offence (D R = a drink-driving offence, P C = an offence in connection with a pedestrian crossing, etc.). This is followed by two digits the first of which indicates the particular offence that has been committed within that category and the second whether the accused was convicted of the offence itself, or of aiding, abetting, counselling, procuring, causing, permitting or inciting the commission of the offence. The sentence imposed is then indicated by a further and equally complicated code.

We have already seen that in order that the endorsement may be entered on the licence the accused must have it with him or send it to reach the court a day before the hearing. But what if the accused has no licence? He might for example have been charged with driving without a licence. Or he may be driving on an international driving permit, a foreign licence or a Northern Ireland licence, none of which can be endorsed by an English court. The explanation is as follows: what counts is not whether the licence has been actually endorsed but whether the court has made an order for endorsement, and this the court can always do even if the driver has no licence or only a licence which the court has no power to endorse. If such an order has been made but no licence has been endorsed the driver must reveal this fact if and when he applies for an English driving licence; he commits an offence if he does not do so, unless the order for endorsement was made so long ago that he is now entitled to a 'clean' licence. Endorsements do not last for ever. A motorist is entitled to apply for the removal of an endorsement after four years (eleven years in the case of a drink-driving offence).

It has been said already that although there is no such thing as discretionary endorsement, a court does nevertheless have the power not to make an order for endorsement, if it considers that there are special reasons for not doing so. Special reasons are not statutorily defined but it is clear from a long list of judicial cases that they must refer to the offence and not to the offender. Thus it would not be considered a special reason that the accused was of good character or had a long and clean driving record. Nor would his personal circumstances be taken into consideration. There are some people such as doctors and lorry drivers who are dependent on their driving licence for their livelihood and to endorse their licence might bring them nearer to compulsory disqualification. But none of these factors would be accepted as a valid reason for not endorsing since none of them relate to the offence itself. It is not easy to say what would be a special reason since there are so many different courts each of which may have its own ideas on the subject. The fact that the offence was a very trivial one, or that the accused had been tricked into committing it by a third party or had committed it in an emergency or from some worthwhile motive have all in the past been accepted as special reasons, and probably would be again. A motorist accused of a drink-driving offence was able to show that he exceeded the limit only because a friend had, unknown to him, laced his beer with spirits. He was convicted but his licence was not endorsed. Similarly an ambulance driver, carrying a dying patient to hospital, who went through the traffic lights at red also escaped endorsement.

Disqualification

Unlike endorsement, disqualification can be discretionary or obligatory. Thus road traffic offences, as far as disqualification is concerned, fall into three categories: those in respect of which disqualification cannot be ordered, those in respect of which disqualification may, at the discretion of the court, be ordered, and those in respect of which it must be ordered. Where disqualification is discretionary the court may disqualify for any period it thinks fit – periods as short as a week have been known. Where disqualification is obligatory the court must disqualify for a minimum period of twelve months unless it considers that there are special reasons for disqualifying for a shorter period or for not disqualifying at all. In certain cases the minimum period of obligatory disqualification is extended. For example, a second conviction for a drink-driving offence in ten years will carry a minimum period of three years' obligatory disqualification. In the case of reckless driving disqualification is discretionary but it becomes obligatory in the case of a second conviction in three years.

The peculiarities of the English criminal process are such that a motorist sometimes finds that what he considered to be a single act of bad driving has been multiplied by police ingenuity into a series of offences, but this does not produce the hardship which at first it might be thought to cause. It is true that if a man is convicted, say, of three offences all arising out of the same incident then three convictions will be recorded against him. But the court, although it is obliged to impose a penalty in respect of each conviction, will always take care to see that the total penalty is not out of proportion to the gravity of the offence as a whole. If each offence is endorsable then three endorsements will be recorded, but only one of these will count for the purpose of the penalty points system (see next section). In the case of disqualification the same object is achieved by the rule that says that all periods of disqualification imposed must run concurrently. This means that although the accused may be disqualified in respect of all three offences he will in effect serve only whichever period is the longest.

As in the case of endorsement the court may decide not to disqualify or to disqualify for a shorter period than the minimum imposed by law if it considers that there are special reasons for doing so, and the test as to whether there are special reasons or not is exactly the same as in the case of endorsement (see previous section). It goes without saying that if the court decides that there are special reasons for not endorsing then they cannot disqualify – even though disqualification may normally be obligatory for this offence.

We have already seen that although a court cannot endorse a foreign driving licence or an international driving licence it can still make an order for endorsement which amounts to pretty much the same thing. It can also disqualify a person who holds such a licence. This does not affect the validity of the licence in any way but it does mean that the holder of the licence is banned from driving on the roads in this country and from applying for or holding a British driving licence for as long as the period of disqualification lasts. In the case of an ordinary British driving licence, the effect of disqualification is to revoke the licence altogether. This means that when the period of disqualification runs out the offender cannot just resume driving. He must apply for a new licence all over again.

A person who has been disqualified by a magistrates' court may appeal against the disqualification provided notice of appeal is given within twenty-one days. Even where the disqualification is obligatory it is still possible to appeal on the grounds that the magistrates ought to have found that there were special reasons for not disqualifying. When notice of appeal is given the magistrates may, at their discretion, suspend the disqualification until the appeal is heard. It must not be forgotten, however, that the Crown Court has power to increase a sentence and if it considers the appeal frivolous and the length of the period of disqualification inadequate, it may well lengthen it.

Where a person has been disqualified from driving it is always possible for him to apply to have the disqualification lifted even before the period has run out. But there are time limits within which this right must be exercised. If the disqualification is for less than four years, application cannot be made until two years have elapsed. If the disqualification is for four years or more but for less than ten years he must wait until half the period of disqualification has elapsed. If the disqualification is for ten years or more he must wait five years. It is clear from these figures that no application for removal can be made if the disqualification is for two years or less, nor can any application at all be made to lift an order that the offender be disqualified from driving until he passes the driving test. Application for the removal of a disqualification must be made to the court which originally imposed it. If the application is refused it may be repeated an indefinite number of times provided a period of three months is allowed to elapse between each application.

Compulsory disqualification

In an attempt to deal with the habitual offender, English law has always imposed an additional penalty on persons who, because of the frequency of their road traffic offences, have collected a more than average number of endorsements on their driving licence. Until 1 November 1982, this was achieved by imposing an additional penalty of six months' disqualification on any person whose licence had been endorsed three times in a period of approximately three years.

The injustice of this method lay in the fact that all offences were treated equally. Thus three endorsements for speeding in three years would entail compulsory disqualification whereas two endorsements for reckless driving in the same period would not.

In order to remedy this state of affairs the Transport Act 1981 introduced a new system known colloquially as the 'points system', which came into force on 1 November 1982. Under this system, each endorsable road traffic offence carries a certain number of points graded according to the gravity of the offence (see table at the end of this chapter) and compulsory disqualification is imposed when the total points score reaches twelve. Thus four convictions for speeding (rated at three points) would be required, whereas only two convictions for serious offences (rated at six points or more) would suffice. For some offences a range of points is given, thereby allowing the court some discretion to adjust the penalty to the seriousness of the circumstances. The Secretary of State is empowered by the act to vary the number of points for each offence if he sees fit to do so.

Where the accused is convicted of more than one offence on the same occasion, the number of points to be added to his score is the highest number which any one of them would have earned. No points are added in respect of any offence for which the accused is disqualified anyway. This explains why the table of points does not include any offence carrying obligatory disqualification, although if the accused is convicted of such an offence and the court decides that there are special reasons for not disqualifying him, four points will be added to his score.

Points which were earned more than three years previously are not taken into account in assessing the total and where a person is disqualified for any offence the effect of such disqualification is to 'wipe the slate clean' and to enable him to start afresh with no points.

The principle of additional disqualification which was a feature of the old 'totting-up' system has now been replaced by the principle of minimum compulsory disqualification. Where, as a result of a conviction, the accused's points total reaches twelve or more, he must be sentenced to a minimum period of disqualification which is six months if he has no previous disqualifications, one year if he has one previous disqualification and two years if he has more than one. For this purpose, however, disqualifications that were imposed more than three years before the current offence are ignored.

As a transitional measure, endorsements which were imposed before the points system came into force carry a flat-rate penalty of three points unless they were earned more than three years previously or the accused had been disqualified for the offence in question or on any subsequent occasion.

The power of the court not to disqualify or to disqualify for a shorter period than the minimum imposed by the law is preserved, but the wording of the statute suggests that the criteria to be adopted are likely to be more severe than they were under the old totting-up rules.

Disqualification pending the taking of a driving test

When a person is convicted of an offence carrying obligatory or discretionary disqualification, the court may if it sees fit to do so make an order disqualifying him from driving until he has passed a driving test. This order may be made irrespective of whether he has previously passed a test or not. The effect of the order is that the driver must take out a provisional licence and drive as a learner driver until he has passed the test. If he takes out a provisional licence but does not comply with the regulations governing learner drivers (e.g. he does not drive under 'L' plates or under the supervision of a qualified driver) then he may be prosecuted for driving while disqualified rather than for the less serious offence of driving in contravention of the regulations governing provisional licences.

If the accused is sentenced to a period of substantive disqualification and in addition is ordered to be disqualified pending the taking of a driving test then he must serve the period of substantive disqualification first. If, for example, on 1 January *X* is convicted of reckless driving, sentenced to twelve months disqualification and in addition is ordered to be disqualified until he has passed the driving test, then this means that for twelve months he will not be able to drive at all. On the anniversary of his conviction he will then be entitled to take out a provisional licence and to drive as a learner driver until such time as he passes the test.

No application can be made for the removal of a disqualification imposed pending the taking of a driving test, but where the accused is sentenced to substantive disqualification, and in addition is ordered to be disqualified pending the taking of a driving test, then he may of course apply for the removal of the substantive disqualification provided he is able to comply with the time limits laid down.

An order for disqualification pending the taking of a driving test should not be imposed as a punishment and should only be made where there are genuine doubts as to the driver's competence to drive. If the court is of the opinion that because of disease, disability or infirmity the accused should not be driving at all, the correct procedure would be not to make an order of disqualification pending the taking of a driving test, but to apply to the Secretary of State for Transport for the revocation of his licence.

Table of penalty points

Description of offence	*Number of points*
Any offence carrying obligatory disqualification where the court decides there are special reasons for not disqualifying	4
Reckless driving	10

Description of offence	*Number of points*
Careless driving	2–5
Being in charge of motor vehicle when unfit through drink or drugs or with excess alcohol	10
Failing to provide specimen for breath test	4
Failing to provide specimen for analysis	10
Failing to comply with traffic directions	3
Leaving vehicle in dangerous position	3
Failing to stop after accident	5–9
Failing to give particulars or report accident	4–9
Contravention of Construction and Use regulations	3
Driving without licence	2
Failing to comply with conditions of licence	2
Driving with uncorrected defective eyesight	2
Refusing to submit to test of eyesight	2
Driving while disqualified as under age	2
Driving while disqualified by order of court	6
Using or causing or permitting use of motor vehicle without insurance cover against third party risks	4–8
Contravention of traffic regulations on motorways	3
Contravention of pedestrian crossing regulations	3
Failure to obey sign exhibited by school crossing patrol	3
Contravention of order prohibiting or restricting use of street playground by vehicles	2
Exceeding a speed limit	3
Stealing or attempting to steal motor vehicle	8
Taking or attempting to take conveyance without consent or lawful authority or driving or attempting to drive a motor vehicle so taken or allowing oneself to be carried in a motor vehicle so taken	8
Going equipped for stealing with reference to theft or taking of motor vehicle	8

Note:

- endorsements that were earned before the coming into force of the system of penalty points carry a flat rate penalty of 3 points unless the endorsement was earned more than three years before the date of the current offence or the accused was disqualified on that or on any subsequent occasion;

- the Transport Act 1982 proposes to add to the above table the offence of aiding, abetting, counselling, procuring or inciting an offence involving obligatory disqualification. The offence will carry 10 penalty points.

44 Taking your car abroad

The practice of taking one's car abroad for a continental holiday is increasing. This practice has been made easier in recent years by the standardization of road traffic signs; the same signs are now in common use in most parts of Europe, and English drivers have little difficulty in recognizing at least the majority of them. Against this, there are many serious problems which will almost certainly be encountered. Apart from obvious ones like language difficulties and driving on the right-hand side of the road, there are many pitfalls and snags that the would-be holiday maker is well advised to consider before he takes the risk of driving his car across the international frontiers.

Foreign law

The first point to remember is that the world consists of a large number of separate and independent states and that each state is entitled to make its own laws. You must not suppose therefore that the laws and customs with which you are familiar in this country will necessarily prevail when you are abroad.

It is true that the criminal codes of most civilized countries contain a great deal of material that is common to all of them. This is also true of road traffic law. Offences such as drunken driving, reckless driving, speeding and obstruction will be found to exist all over Europe, but even where the offences are the same the details are often different. The law on drunken driving for example is often much stricter on the Continent and more rigorously enforced than it is here. In some countries it is an offence to drive with any alcohol at all inside you, and in some countries drunken driving is often punished with imprisonment, even on a first conviction. Moreover even though the offences may be the same as, or very similar to, what they are in England, criminal procedure is usually very different. There are not many countries where the police are as effectively restricted by law in dealing with the general public as they are here, and if you get into trouble with the continental police you must not be surprised if they do things to you which would be considered outrageous in this country. The safest thing to do when you are abroad is to conduct yourself in such a way that you do not fall foul of the laws or the police in the country you are visiting.

Because the laws and practices differ greatly in different countries it is impossible to give more than generalized advice. However, one thing is vitally important. You must familiarize yourself with the conditions which you are likely to meet abroad, and you should do this before you leave this country. If you are a member of a motoring organization such as the AA or the RAC they will probably be able to help you. If not you may be able to get information from the country's embassy in London. The sections that follow do not purport to give you detailed information – that must clearly depend on where you are going. They should be regarded rather as guidelines to the sort of thing you should be thinking about and checking up on before you go abroad.

Things to think about

Driving licence

Although most European countries recognize a British driving licence and will permit you to drive on it during your holiday, it must be a full licence. You cannot drive abroad on a provisional licence. You would in any case be well advised to obtain an international driving permit – this can be quite easily done – and in some countries this may be obligatory. Even in those countries which do recognize a British licence, the minimum age for driving may be higher than it is here, so that a seventeen-year-old, even if he held a full licence, would not be able to drive there.

Insurance

The first point to remember is that it is most unlikely that your British insurance policy will cover you while you are driving abroad. Most companies can supply you with an International Motor Insurance Card – known popularly as a 'green card' – and you should certainly take one of these out; indeed, in some European countries it is obligatory. But this card will only supply the minimum cover required by law and it is unlikely to cover you against injury to yourself or damage to your vehicle. If you should be involved in a serious accident while you are abroad the cost could be calamitous. There is no national health service in Europe and although some countries supply free medical treatment on a reciprocal basis (information on this can be obtained from the Department of Health and Social Security) it would be unwise to rely on this since there are likely to be limitations and conditions which may take away much of its value. Continental garage bills are enormous, and if your car should be badly smashed up you may well be bankrupted irrespective of whether you have it repaired out there or whether you have it towed home.

All of these items can be covered by extra insurance, which can often be arranged for you either by your motoring organization or by a travel agent. Insurance is expensive but the motorist who travels abroad without covering himself against every possible contingency is playing a game of Russian roulette. The odds may be in his favour but if anything goes wrong the consequences could be catastrophic.

Speed limits

Remember that on the Continent speeds are measured in kilometres per hour, not miles. The speed limit sign that you see may be a familiar one but it represents a maximum speed that will be not much more than half the speed it would indicate in this country. To avoid having to make mathematical calculations in the head you can buy a transparent sticker (easily removable) to stick on your speedometer which will indicate your speed in kilometres. Or you can easily make one yourself.

Minimum speed limits are commoner on the Continent than they are here and most continental motorways have minimum speed limits. Speed limits both maximum and minimum are usually more rigorously enforced abroad and if you break one you must not suppose that the continental policeman will necessarily turn the same friendly blind eye that his British counterpart will sometimes do in this country.

Lights
If you intend to drive at night you will have to have your lights adjusted. In this country headlights dip to the left but in Europe traffic usually drives on the right and your lights should be altered accordingly. Check up on whether there are any additional lighting requirements in the countries you are proposing to visit.

What you should take with you
Your car will need a GB plate to indicate its country of origin. In all countries it is advisable and in some countries obligatory to take with you a warning device consisting of a red triangle sign to set up on the road in case you are involved in an accident.

In addition to your usual travel documents make sure you have the following with you: driving licence; insurance documents; MOT test certificate (you may not need this but it is as well to have it with you); log-book; and, not least important, an adequate supply of reliable maps covering the area you propose to visit. (Continental maps are not as good as British ones and you would be well advised to obtain these here.)

One useful tip: never, never leave your documents in a parked car. The chance that your car may be stolen while you are abroad is much greater than it is here, not because Continentals are less honest than the British – there is no evidence of that at all – but because British tourists abroad are both conspicuous and vulnerable and therefore more likely to attract the attention of such thieves as may be about. If your car is stolen you have a better chance of getting it back if the documents of title are still in your possession.

Getting into trouble with the law

On the Continent, police powers are more extensive than they are here and if you should be involved in an incident which brings you up before a foreign policeman you would do well to bear that in mind. Never lose your temper and never, never talk down to him, however convinced you may be of your total innocence. As a rule it is very unwise to try to argue with him in his own language. However well you speak it he will almost certainly speak it better and this will give him an advantage from the start. Check up on the procedure to be followed if you are involved in an accident. In some countries it is an offence to move a vehicle after an accident. In other countries it is an offence if you don't. In Spain the police are entitled to detain a motorist and his vehicle, if an accident has occurred, until he has paid a deposit large enough to cover any fines that may be imposed. Again it is possible to insure against this and travellers intending to visit that country are advised to take out a 'Spanish bail bond' to cover the risk.

For minor traffic offences greater use is made of on-the-spot fines than in this country, and if one of these is demanded it is usually better (and often cheaper) to pay rather than to argue the toss, since the alternative – court proceedings – may be disastrous for the tourist. If you are mixed up in something really serious it is advisable to demand the services of a British Consul, and to make no statement of any sort whatsoever until you have had his advice.

Motoring offences are not normally extraditable and if you can return to this country before proceedings are commenced against you there is no way in which you can be compelled to return in order to face trial. However, if you are convicted in your absence you may have to give up all hope of ever visiting that country again.

Should a claim for compensation be made against you while you are abroad, do not attempt to deal with it yourself. Pass it straight to your insurance company unanswered. If on the other hand it is you who wish to make the claim for compensation, then you are in trouble. Such a claim can only be made in the foreign court and in accordance with foreign law. Obviously you will not want to hang about until the action comes on, and although it is possible to employ a British solicitor in this country to act for you the trouble and expense involved will only too often make it a profitless enterprise. This is another good reason for seeing that all such contingencies are adequately covered by insurance.

Appendix 1: the Transport Act 1982

The Transport Act 1982 has now received the Royal Assent and contains a number of important changes in certain aspects of the laws that have been discussed in the preceding pages. Although the Act is now on the statute book its provisions will come into force only on such day or days as may be specified by the Secretary of

State in an order made for that purpose. At the time of writing no such orders have been made and it is therefore impossible to say when the following changes will become effective, although it is likely that some of them at least will be brought into force in the near future.

- The fixed penalty system has been extended to cover a wide range of offences including speeding, pedestrian-crossing and street-playground offences, failing to wear a seat belt, breach of construction-and-use regulations, lighting offences, driving without a licence, breach of provisional licence regulations and failing to stop when ordered to do so by a police constable. As before, payment of the fixed penalty will obviate proceedings but when the offence is an endorsable one the licence will still be endorsed with the appropriate number of penalty points even though no hearing has taken place. The fixed penalty for an endorsable offence is increased to £20.
- A new power is given to a police officer to attach an immobilization device to any vehicle which he finds unlawfully parked on a road or to remove the vehicle to another place where such a device can be fixed. At the same time a notice must be affixed to the vehicle warning the driver that the vehicle has been immobilized and advising him as to the steps he must take and the penalty he must pay in order to obtain its release.

  No device may be fixed to a vehicle which is displaying a current disabled person's badge at the time (provided the vehicle was being lawfully used under the provisions of the law relating to disabled persons) nor to a vehicle parked in a meter bay provided the proper charges have been paid.

  This law will come into force only in those areas specified by the Secretary of State. In the initial stages it is likely that experimental orders (which will last for a maximum period of two years) will be made.
- The table of penalty points (see page 397) has been extended by the inclusion of the offence of aiding, abetting, counselling, procuring or inciting an offence involving obligatory disqualification. This offence will in future earn 10 penalty points.
- Definition of a restricted road. At present a trunk or classified road is not a restricted road for the purpose of the 30 m.p.h. speed limit even though it is provided with a system of street lighting of the required density unless that system was installed before 1 July 1957 (see page 340). This qualification is now to be

removed. Thus when this provision is brought into force no trunk or classified road will be a restricted road for the purpose of this speed limit.

- The maximum fines for a breach of the construction-and-use regulations have been increased (see footnote on page 322).

Appendix 2: the Criminal Justice Act 1982

The Criminal Justice Act 1982 contains provisions for substantially increasing the maximum fines payable for summary offences. At the time of writing it is not known for certain when these new fines will come into force but it is believed that this will probably be in April 1983. Offences committed after the new fines have come into force will be subject to the new higher maxima. Offences committed before the new fines have come into force will be subject to the old maxima, details of which are set out in this book.

The new provisions for maximum fines are as follows. Where a summary offence carries a maximum penalty which is greater for a second or subsequent conviction than it is for a first, the maximum penalty that can be imposed for a first conviction will be increased to that which is available for a second or subsequent conviction. All maximum fines will be re-calculated and increased in accordance with the following formula. There will in future be five standard levels of maximum fines which shall be as follows:

£25
£50
£200
£500
£1,000

Existing maximum fines will be increased by raising them to the amount shown at the next level up on the scale. For example, if the present maximum fine is between £25 and £49, the new maximum fine will be £50. By way of an exception, however, where the present maximum fine is between £400 and £499 the new maximum fine will not be £500 but £1,000.

There are a few offences, however, for which the new maximum fine does not correspond to the above formula. The only such offences mentioned in this book are the following:

	Old maximum	*New maximum*
Offences in connection with parking meters	£20	£50
Removing or interfering with fixed penalty ticket	£20	£50
Driving a motor vehicle elsewhere than on a road	£20	£200

The Law and the Courts

45 How law is made

There are two main ways in which law is made: by legislation, and by decisions of the courts.

Legislation

The most direct and obvious way to make new law is for Parliament to pass an Act, sometimes called a Statute; for example, the Employment Act 1980, which lays down among other things that in future a pregnant woman shall be entitled to time off from work to keep an appointment for a medical examination.

The effect of this is to create a new legal rule where none existed before. It is law made from scratch. Of course Parliament does not just casually decide to pass a law about this or that and then simply go ahead and do it. New Acts of Parliament are, in theory at least, the result of a long process of discussion and negotiation with all kinds of interested people and organizations; the Acts then have to pass through five stages in the House of Commons, five more in the House of Lords and then receive the Royal Assent before they become law.

The quantity and complexity of legislation has increased enormously in recent years and the fact that the Conservative and Labour parties regularly succeed each other in government has also led to a great deal of chopping and changing. One political party, when in power with a majority in the House of Commons, puts through an Act that expresses some aspect of its election manifesto – usually claiming that it has a mandate from the people to legislate in this way. When that government falls from power the other party takes over and, once again claiming a mandate, passes another Act repealing or amending the one passed by the previous government. This confusing process has been particularly rife in the areas of employment and housing law over the last ten to fifteen years. (The law on picketing and the sale of council houses illustrates how the pendulum can swing.)

In the session of Parliament which ended in 1980, seventy Acts of Parliament were passed, many of them introducing major changes in the law. That might seem quite enough to be going on with. Even practising lawyers, never mind ordinary citizens whose daily lives are regulated by these new laws, clearly have a full-time job in keeping up with the changes. But that is by no means the end of the story.

Delegated legislation

It is now considered to be the job of governments to regulate even the smallest details of everyday life and for this purpose an Act of Parliament is a somewhat blunt instrument. The practice has therefore grown up of wording Acts in general terms and then giving power to a Minister to make detailed regulations to make the Act work. The regulations are published in what are called Statutory Instruments.

For example, Section 44 of the Consumer Credit Act 1974 (which deals with buying goods and services on credit) says:

> The Secretary of State shall make regulations as to the form and contents of advertisements . . . with a view to ensuring that . . . an advertisement conveys a fair and reasonably comprehensive indication of the nature of the credit facilities offered . . .

The regulations referred to were not in fact made until January 1980 – six years after the Act was passed – and even then they did not come into operation until October 1980, by which time they had already been amended once. The regulations cover such points as the size of lettering to be used in advertisements offering credit, and as amended they run to pages of small print.

Ministers are not the only people to whom Parliament delegates the power to make law. Local authorities have the power to make by-laws 'for the good rule and government' of their districts: 'It shall be an offence to allow a dog to foul the footpath', 'No musical instruments to be played in the park', and so on. Even bodies like British Rail and the British Airports Authority have the power to make by-laws which apply within their own fields of activity.

Law made in this way is known as delegated legislation. Statutory Instruments and by-laws are just as much law as the Acts of Parliament which authorize them, provided that they do not go beyond the limits laid down in their parent Acts.

The European Economic Community

Even Acts of Parliament and the various kinds of delegated legislation made under them are not the only forms of legislation which can create new law in the United Kingdom. On 1 January 1973 the United Kingdom became a member of the European Economic Community and since then the Council and Commission of the Community have had power to legislate directly or indirectly for the UK.

Legislation passed by the Community takes the form of regulations and directives.

Regulations

When a regulation is made by the European Council of Ministers, or by the Commission, it has immediate and direct effect in all member countries including the United Kingdom. That means that it is part of the law of this country without any action by Parliament – and indeed Parliament cannot pass any Act which conflicts with a European regulation.

Directives

A directive is not, in theory, immediately effective in the United Kingdom. It is a declaration of Community policy but it is left to each member state to give effect to the directive by means of internal legislation. In this country this is usually done by means of a Statutory Instrument (see page 408).

Decisions of the courts

A stock question in examinations for law students is: Do judges make law? The correct answer, dressed up a bit to make it look respectable, is 'yes and no'.

In strict theory only Parliament (and the institutions of the EEC) can make law. The function of a judge is simply to discover what the law is and then to apply it to the particular case before him. In practice things don't work out quite as simply as that. The first problem for the judge is to find out what the law is. Even if there is an Act of Parliament that seems to apply to the problem, the words of the Act may not be absolutely clear in their meaning or they may not at first sight exactly cover the case in hand. (Anyone who has tried to draw up even the simplest set of rules soon discovers that it is impossible to achieve absolute clarity and precision.) That means that the judge will have to interpret the words of the Act – he will have to decide what the words mean. He does not do this according to his own private opinions but by following a set of rules laid down for the interpretation of Acts of Parliament.

When the judge has decided what the words of the Act mean and then applied them to the problem before him to arrive at a solution, he has done two things. First, he has settled the dispute between the two parties present in court and, as far as they are immediately concerned, that is the end of the matter. One of them has lost and the other has won and that's what they came to court for. (Questions of appeal come later.) But the decision in this case also creates a precedent for the future. That means that the judge's decision on the meaning of these words in that Act of Parliament must be followed – or at least considered – by any judge who has to apply the same words in any future case.

The so-called doctrine of precedent is a vital and distinctive feature of English law. The rule is that a court must follow previous decisions on similar facts. Every decision is not, however, of equal weight; decisions of the House of Lords, for example, are binding on all lower courts while decisions of a single High Court judge are strictly speaking not binding on other High Court judges – although they will not be lightly ignored. Another limiting factor on the operation of the doctrine of precedent is that past decisions cannot be referred to unless they have been recorded. Some system of recording important decisions of the courts has been in operation for about six hundred years but it was not until 1867 that a really accurate and authoritative system of reporting cases was introduced.

These reported decisions are important not only when it comes to interpreting Acts of Parliament but also in those areas of law which are not covered by any form of legislation. And in spite of the constant stream of ever more detailed Acts and Statutory Instruments there is a surprising amount of law which was not created by Parliament at all.

The modern law of negligence – the legal duty to take reasonable care not to injure other people by your actions – is based on a decision of the House of Lords given in 1932 in a case involving a decomposed snail in a ginger beer bottle. This decision has been considered and followed in countless cases in the last fifty years and each decision, by applying the same rule to a new and slightly different set of facts, has added one more tiny brick to the towering edifice of the law. Negligence now embraces such things as losses suffered as a result of careless advice, the careless manufacture of goods and injuries caused by carelessness on the road and at work. The categories of negligence are never closed. They grow steadily simply through decisions of the courts without any help from Parliament at all.

Some judges openly enjoy this creative role and frankly use their power to nudge the law gently in the direction that they feel it should go; others, adopting a more traditional attitude, attempt to apply the law as they find it whether they approve of the result or not. If the law is wrong, they say, it is up to Parliament and not the courts to change it. But whatever view the judge adopts he cannot avoid being part of the process of gradual change.

It is perhaps a peculiarly English paradox that the law should advance by looking backwards to the past. It is almost as if the judges were embarrassed by change so that they can only achieve it by stealth, advancing with their backs to the future.

Thus law continues to grow. New laws are added openly and deliberately by Parliament, and imperceptibly and at random by the decisions of the courts. The one certainty is that the whole body of law never gets smaller – only larger. As a whole it is unknowable; reading this book will not tell you all there is to know, or even all you need to know, about the law. But it may provide a few signposts to guide you through some of the murkier parts of the maze.

46 Civil and criminal law

There are many possible ways of classifying the law; you could, for instance, divide it into law made by legislation and law made by judicial decision (see Chapter 45). But for practical purposes the most important distinction is that between the civil and the criminal law.

The essential difference between these two branches of law is that the civil law is concerned with compensation whereas the criminal law is concerned with punishment. Like all generalizations this is an oversimplification but it does contain the key to the matter, which is that since the aims of civil and criminal law are different, the procedures, results and even the terminology will also be different.

Civil cases

In a typical civil case – an action to claim compensation for faulty goods or for injuries received in a road accident – the person bringing the complaint is called the *plaintiff* and the person against whom it is brought the *defendant*. (The plaintiff *sues* the defendant.)

The result of the case will be either *judgment* for the defendant – which means that the plaintiff has failed to prove his case and so gets no compensation – or judgment for the plaintiff – which means that he has won and will be *awarded a remedy* against the defendant.

The main remedy in civil law is an award of damages, a sum of money, intended to compensate the plaintiff for any losses or injuries caused by the defendant, which the court orders the defendant to pay to the plaintiff.

Once an award of damages has been made it is then up to the plaintiff to collect the money from the defendant. It is not just a matter of going to some office in the court to collect your winnings. If the defendant fails to pay then the plaintiff will have to go back to court to get its assistance in enforcing the judgment. This might be by means of an 'attachment of earnings order' or a 'warrant of execution' (see page 440).

In civil matrimonial proceedings – a divorce case, for example – the terminology and procedure are different. Here the person bringing the case is called the *petitioner* and the person against whom it is brought the *respondent*. If the petitioner is successful the result will be that the court grants a decree nisi of divorce.

Criminal cases

In a criminal case – a prosecution for murder or theft, for example – a *prosecutor* (usually acting on behalf of the state) *prosecutes* an *accused*. (In some minor criminal cases the accused is called the defendant.) If the prosecutor fails to prove his case the result will be a verdict of *not guilty* and the accused goes free. If the prosecutor does prove his case then the result will be a verdict of *guilty* and the accused, having been *convicted*, will be *sentenced* to some form of *punishment* such as imprisonment or a fine. (In some cases a criminal court can award compensation to a person who has suffered loss or damage as a result of the crime but this does not alter the fact that the main purpose of criminal proceedings is the punishment of those who are found guilty.)

A familiarity with the different terms used in civil and criminal proceedings is extremely helpful in understanding how the law works in all the areas dealt with in this book. But the real importance of the distinction between civil and criminal law lies, not in the different procedures and terminology, but in the results of those proceedings – compensation for the successful plaintiff or punishment for the convicted accused.

After that it may seem somewhat confusing to discover that the same act can give rise to both civil and criminal proceedings, but in practice this does not present much difficulty. For example, if a motorist drives his car so carelessly that he knocks me down he may be prosecuted for the crime of careless driving and I may also sue him in the civil courts for damages.

The motorist at least will readily appreciate the difference between the two cases. If he is convicted by the criminal court he may be fined up to £1,000, his licence will be endorsed and he may even be disqualified from driving (see page 393). If I win in the civil case he will be ordered to pay me damages; in practice these should be paid by his insurance company.

Civil and criminal courts

Because civil and criminal cases require different procedures and have different consequences it would seem logical that there should be different courts to deal with each type of case. This is, in fact, basically true although several courts can try both civil and criminal cases. The magistrates' court, for example, deals with a great number of matrimonial and family cases.

The system of courts described below is that of England and Wales. The organization of courts in Scotland and Northern Ireland is different.

Civil courts

The county court

There are over four hundred county courts in England and Wales and you can find the address of your local county court in the telephone directory under 'Courts'.

County courts deal only with civil cases and their powers are limited in two ways. They can deal only with cases that arise within their own areas and also involve limited amounts of money. (The money limits vary according to the type of case but, for example, in complaints about faulty goods or in claims for personal injury the total claim must be less than £5,000.)

The most important matters covered in this book that may be dealt with by the county court include:

- cases involving the sale or supply of goods or services (money limit £5,000) (see Chapters 31 and 38);
- claims for personal injury arising from negligence (money limit £5,000);
- claims for the possession of land or houses (the rateable value must be less than £1,000) (see Chapter 16);
- undefended divorce cases (only certain county courts, all outside London, can deal with these) (see Chapter 10);
- adoption and guardianship (see Chapter 3);
- cases involving domestic violence (see Chapter 9).

The court is presided over by a county court judge who is assisted by a registrar. The registrar is legally qualified and not only organizes the court business, but may also act as a judge in cases involving less than £200.

Appeals from the county court go to the Court of Appeal and, very occasionally, from there to the House of Lords. (In some family matters there can be an appeal to the Family Division of the High Court – see page 415.)

Most cases that are dealt with in the county court could also be heard in the High Court although if they are within the county court money limits this is actively discouraged. There are, however, some cases under the Rent Acts and in the areas of race relations and domestic violence that can only be heard in the county court.

The High Court

The High Court is made up of three divisions – the Queen's Bench Division, the Chancery Division and the Family Division. There are over seventy High Court judges – over forty of them in the Queen's Bench Division. Civil cases are normally heard in all three divisions by a single judge sitting without a jury.

The court is based in London and most cases, wherever the dispute may have arisen, are heard there although it is possible for civil cases to be heard by a High Court judge in some large towns and cities in other parts of the country. There is no upper or lower money limit to the cases that the High Court can deal with, although cases which could be heard in the county court are in practice usually dealt with there.

The Queen's Bench Division This, the busiest division of the High

Court, deals with a vast range of cases including breaches of contract, claims for damages for personal injury, commercial disputes of all kinds and shipping cases. (Judges from this division also try the more serious criminal cases in crown courts around the country – see page 420.)

The Chancery Division This deals with cases involving trusts, mortgages, disputed wills, company matters and taxation cases.

The Family Division The main cases heard in this division are defended divorce cases and other matrimonial cases in which complicated matters of law are involved, applications about adoption, wardship and guardianship, disputes about the ownership of property between spouses, and cases involving the occupation of the matrimonial home.

Divisional courts

Each division of the High Court in addition to acting as a court of first instance – a court that gives the first hearing to a case – can also act as an appeal court in some cases. Appeals are heard by two or three judges of the division sitting together in what is confusingly called a divisional court.

The Divisional Court of the Queen's Bench Division is again the busiest of the three; the bulk of its work is not civil but criminal. It hears appeals on points of law from magistrates' courts (see page 418).

The court also plays a unique part in supervising lower courts and tribunals and various public bodies and officials through the writ of habeas corpus and the three prerogative orders of certiorari, mandamus and prohibition.

The writ of habeas corpus (literally: 'you have the body') is used to compel anyone who is detaining another person against his will to come to court to justify the detention. It can be used, for instance, against a prison governor, the director of a mental hospital or the immigration authorities.

The order of certiorari can be used where a lower court or tribunal has misused its powers or acted against the rules of natural justice. The effect of the order will be to quash the decision of the lower court.

The order of mandamus is used to compel a lower court or tribunal to try a case or to force a public body to carry out its legal duty.

An order of prohibition is used, as its name suggests, to stop a lower court or tribunal from exceeding its powers.

Appeals from single judges of any division of the High Court, and from the divisional courts, in civil cases go to the Court of Appeal (Civil Division), and from there to the House of Lords. In certain rare cases, where the parties agree and a point of law of general public importance is involved, an appeal may leap-frog the Court of Appeal and go straight to the House of Lords.

The Court of Appeal (Civil Division)

The Court of Appeal is staffed by sixteen senior judges known as Lords Justices of Appeal. (There is also a Criminal Division of the court, see page 421, which is served by the same judges.) To hear cases the judges sit in threes and decision is by a majority.

The court hears appeals from the county court, from single judges of the High Court and, in some cases, from the divisional courts of the High Court.

House of Lords

For most purposes this is the highest court of appeal in England, Wales and Northern Ireland. It also deals with civil appeals from Scotland. Since 1 January 1973, however, the European Court of Justice has been the highest court for all matters involving the interpretation of Community legislation (see below).

When the House of Lords sits as a court only specially appointed legally qualified life peers known as Lords of Appeal (and certain others such as the Lord Chancellor) are entitled to take part. There are eleven Lords of Appeal, usually drawn from senior judges in the Court of Appeal although one or two will always come from Scotland. Five judges normally sit to hear each case and the decision is by a majority.

The House of Lords hears civil appeals from the Court of Appeal (Civil Division) and, in rare cases under the 'leap-frog' rules, directly from the High Court (see above).

Decisions of the House of Lords, although few in number (about fifty a year), are extremely important in the development of the law through the doctrine of precedent (see page 410). Decisions of the House are binding on all lower courts, which means in effect that only Parliament can change the law once it has been stated by the House.

The European Court of Justice

The European Court is the final authority in any case which involves interpreting the Treaty of Rome (which is the basic document of the EEC) or any other Community legislation such as regulations or directives (see page 409). The European Court does not have any jurisdiction over cases which affect only England or the United Kingdom. For these cases the House of Lords remains the highest court of appeal.

There are nine judges in the court – one from each country of the Community. All nine usually sit to hear each case.

Cases that start in the UK may go to the European Court in two ways. First, any court can refer a problem involving the interpretation of Community legislation to the European Court for an opinion. Until the opinion is delivered the proceedings in the United Kingdom will be adjourned. The second way in which a case may go to the European Court is when it involves the interpretation of Community legislation and it has been through every appeal procedure in the UK. This means in practice that in Community matters there is now an appeal from a decision of the House of Lords.

The criminal courts

Criminal offences are divided into three classes:

- offences triable only on indictment;
- offences triable only summarily;
- offences triable either way.

The importance of this classification is that the method of trial differs in each case.

A trial on indictment (oddly pronounced in*dite*ment) takes place in the crown court before a judge and jury; a summary trial takes place in a magistrates' court without a jury. The third category, offences triable either way, is more complicated. The case first comes before a magistrates' court which can either decide that the case should be tried on indictment in the crown court (in which case the accused has no choice in the matter), or it can offer the accused a choice. If the accused chooses to be tried summarily he can still be sent to the crown court for sentence if he is convicted by the magistrates.

Offences triable only on indictment include murder, manslaughter, causing grievous bodily harm and rape.

Offences triable only summarily include a host of miscellaneous minor offences, but the great majority of them are road traffic cases, including all the offences connected with drinking and driving.

Offences triable either way include common assault, bigamy, perjury and most kinds of theft.

The magistrates' court

The formal name for these courts is courts of summary jurisdiction and they are sometimes called by their old name of petty sessions.

There are nine hundred magistrates' courts in England and Wales, and they are staffed by Justices of the Peace assisted by a legally qualified clerk. They deal only with cases from their own districts.

The great majority of justices (or magistrates) are not lawyers; they are unpaid part-time people of some local standing appointed by the Lord Chancellor on the recommendation of a local advisory committee. In some large towns where the work of the magistrates' court is very heavy full-time, legally qualified magistrates, known as stipendiaries, are appointed. There are about fifty stipendiaries in England and Wales.

At least two lay magistrates must sit together to conduct summary proceedings. A stipendiary magistrate sitting alone has the same powers.

Summary proceedings These account for well over ninety-five per cent of all criminal cases and magistrates convict over one million summary offenders every year. Most of the offences are minor ones and the maximum penalties that magistrates can impose are imprisonment for six months and a fine of £1,000. Where the offence is one 'triable either way' and the accused has agreed to be tried summarily the magistrates may, after conviction, send the accused to the crown court for sentence if they feel that he deserves a heavier punishment than they have power to impose.

Preliminary inquiries in trials on indictment (committal proceedings) A person charged with an indictable offence appears first before a magistrates' court which has to decide whether or not to commit him to the crown court for trial. A single magistrate, lay or stipendiary, has power to take committal proceedings.

The purpose of committal proceedings is to allow the accused to see the strength of the prosecution's evidence against him and, if the prosecution's case seems too weak to stand up in a full trial, to ask the magistrates to stop the case there and then, which they have power to do.

Committal proceedings may take two forms. First, if the accused is legally represented and agrees, the statements of any witnesses for the prosecution and the defence may be given to the court in writing. (Prosecution statements must be first shown to the defence.) The magistrates can then commit the accused for trial at the crown court without even considering the prosecution's case. Obviously the accused and his lawyers will not consent to this procedure unless they feel that there is no chance of having the case stopped at this stage. This form of committal was introduced in 1967 to save time and duplication of effort.

If, however, the defence wants to challenge any of the prosecution's evidence, or there is a chance that the case could be stopped by the magistrates, then the committal proceedings will take the more cumbersome old-fashioned form. Prosecution witnesses will be present in court and give oral evidence. This means that they can then be cross-examined by the defence to show up any weaknesses in the prosecution's case. And when the whole of the evidence for the prosecution has been presented the accused can ask the magistrates to stop the case by submitting that there is no case to answer.

If the magistrates refuse to stop the case at this stage the accused can present his own witnesses and make another attempt to destroy the prosecution's case, or he can simply 'reserve his defence', which means that he presents no evidence and thus tells the prosecution nothing about the nature and strength of his defence. In that case he will immediately be committed for trial in the crown court.

Committal proceedings are normally held in public but unless the accused agrees, no details of the case beyond bare facts such as the name of the accused and the offence with which he is charged can be published until the case has either been dismissed by the magistrates or been dealt with by the crown court.

Juvenile courts These courts deal with criminal offences, other than murder, committed by children under the age of seventeen, and with certain other matters involving young people.

The courts are composed of at least three lay magistrates, one of whom must be a woman, drawn from a special panel of local magistrates.

The idea of these courts is that young people should not be brought into contact with the criminal atmosphere of the ordinary magistrates' courts, and they therefore generally sit at different times and in different places from the ordinary courts. They sit in private.

Domestic courts (civil cases) These courts are again made up of magistrates drawn from a special panel. They sit in private and deal with such things as maintenance, custody and access, and problems arising from domestic violence (see page 60 for more details).

Appeals Appeals from magistrates' courts in summary cases can take several forms:

- The accused may appeal not against his conviction, but only against the sentence. This is dealt with by the crown court.
- The accused may appeal against his conviction, unless he pleaded guilty before the magistrates. This appeal again goes to the crown court where the case is re-heard as if for the first time. The prosecution must present the case all over again and witnesses will give evidence and be cross-examined.
- Both the prosecution and the accused can appeal on a point of law to the Divisional Court of the Queen's Bench Division (see page 415) by way of case stated. This means that the magistrates can be asked to put in writing the facts of the case and the points of law involved. The divisional court will then decide whether the magistrates applied the law correctly to the facts.

The crown courts

Strictly speaking the Crown Court is one court but in practice there are separate crown courts in all the major cities and towns in England and Wales. The crown court for London is the Central Criminal Court, commonly known as the Old Bailey.

Crown courts deal with those criminal cases that are 'triable on indictment only' and those cases 'triable either way' that are sent to the court by the magistrates or where the accused chooses to be tried there (see page 417). In other words the crown court deals with all the more serious criminal cases.

The courts are staffed by High Court judges who travel 'on circuit' from London; by recorders, who are senior lawyers acting as part-time judges; and by circuit judges, who are normally county court judges. Where the accused pleads not guilty the judge always sits with a jury.

The more serious cases, such as murder or treason, are always tried by the High Court judges; less serious cases, such as manslaughter or causing grievous bodily harm, may be tried by recorders or circuit judges. (Lay magistrates may also sit with recorders or circuit judges. If they do the decision is by majority with the legally qualified judge having a casting vote.)

Appeals from the crown court against conviction or sentence go to the Court of Appeal (Criminal Division) (see below).

The crown court itself deals with appeals against conviction from magistrates' courts. In these cases a further appeal, by way of case stated, can be made to the divisional court.

The Divisional Court of the Queen's Bench Division

(See page 415 for the composition of this court.) The Divisional Court deals with appeals by way of case stated from magistrates' courts and from crown courts.

The Court of Appeal (Criminal Division)

This court is staffed by the Lord Chief Justice, Lords Justices of Appeal and a number of selected High Court judges. Three judges sit together to hear appeals from the crown court against conviction or sentence.

The House of Lords

The House of Lords is the highest court of appeal in criminal cases. The judges are the same as those who preside in civil cases (see page 416). Appeals may come either from the Divisional Court or the Court of Appeal (Criminal Division), but they are not numerous – less than a dozen a year.

47 Advice and assistance

The trouble with problems is that they are untidy, messy things; they do not come neatly filed under the headings of 'medical', 'family', 'financial' or 'emotional'. All too often the first problem you're faced with in dealing with a problem is to decide exactly what the problem is, because until you've done that you can't begin to tackle it.

This book is about some of the legal problems that can arise in everyday life; this chapter is about recognizing and defining the problem and getting professional assistance in solving it.

Defining the problem

You can of course go straight to a solicitor every time you think you've got a legal problem, and tell him the whole story, but with solicitors charging anywhere between fifteen and fifty pounds an hour this can be a very expensive hobby. And there is in fact a great deal that you can do on your own before seeking professional advice. (In an emergency – if you are forcibly evicted by your landlord, arrested by the police or beaten up by your husband – then of course you should get hold of a lawyer straight away, if you can find one.)

Finding out for yourself

There is a great deal of information on legal problems of all kinds available in the form of free leaflets – the difficulty may be to find the one that fits your problem.

The best starting point whatever your problem is the local library. If there is nothing on display that seems to fit your case ask the librarian. You may be surprised at how eager they are to help and at the amount of information they can provide. If the library does not have anything suitable in stock they may be able to get it for you or tell you where to find it for yourself.

If you have a problem at work, try the local Jobcentre or employment exchange. They have free leaflets on a whole range of subjects including redundancy, unfair dismissal, health and safety, racial and sexual discrimination, and equal pay.

For housing problems you can try the local council. They should have leaflets covering security of tenure, fair rents, rate rebates, etc. If there is a housing advice centre in your area, go there.

The Post Office has information on pensions and other state benefits and allowances.

Expert advice

If you can get all the information you need from books and leaflets you may be able to deal with the problem yourself, but in many cases you will still want some form of expert advice and assistance. (The reason for finding out what you can on your own beforehand is to save time and trouble at that stage.)

There are plenty of places you can go for help. For particular problems, trade unions or organizations like the AA or the RAC will be useful, and in appropriate cases you may be able to enlist the help of national bodies like the National Council for Civil Liberties or the Equal Opportunities Commission. (A list of useful addresses is given at the end of the book.)

For practical local help – and the opportunity to discuss your problem with an expert – you can go to the Citizens' Advice Bureau, a legal advice centre, a law centre or a solicitor in private practice.

Citizens' Advice Bureau

Many CABs in addition to providing their usual advice service now use the services of a practising solicitor. The schemes vary from place to place. In some places the solicitor will just be in attendance to give advice; in others he may be able to take on a case for you although even then he is not likely to go as far as appearing for you in court. Telephone your local bureau to find out whether they operate a scheme.

Legal advice centres

These are staffed by volunteer lawyers and are usually open one or two evenings a week. They exist in most large towns throughout the country but they will not usually take up a case for you. They are in the business of giving preliminary advice.

Law centres

These are staffed by full-time salaried lawyers and among other things they provide, usually free, the same services as solicitors in private practice. However, in order to avoid being flooded with work most law centres only deal with certain categories of cases: housing problems, urgent matrimonial disputes, trouble with the police and employment problems, for example. Each centre will tend to specialize in those problems which are most common in its own area.

Fixed-fee interview

Many solicitors operate what is called the *£5 scheme*. This is a scheme under which anyone – however rich or poor – can have an interview, lasting for half an hour, for a fixed fee of £5. At the interview the solicitor will not take on your case, but it can be extremely useful – in order to find out roughly where you stand legally, whether there is anything that you can do yourself and whether you would qualify for legal aid if you decided to pursue the matter.

The addresses and telephone numbers of legal advice centres, law centres and solicitors operating the £5 scheme can be found in the Law Society's *List of Legal Aid Solicitors*, which should be available at your local library and at a Citizens' Advice Bureau. The list also indicates which areas of law a particular firm of solicitors specializes in. (For legal advice centres it usually gives opening times as well.) The list is published annually and includes a brief summary of the current legal aid rules and financial limits.

Solicitors in private practice

There are two obvious problems about consulting a solicitor: how to find one, and how to pay his bill.

Finding a solicitor

If you have already employed a solicitor – to buy your house, perhaps, or to make a will – then it is obviously a good idea to go to the same firm again if you have a new problem. The only snag is that not all solicitors handle all kinds of work and they may not be equally good at dealing with all the different kinds of work that they do handle. The solicitor who helped you to buy your house may not be an expert in divorce and he may be extremely reluctant to take a case of, say, dangerous driving.

If you do not want to use the same solicitor again – or he does not want to handle your case – or you simply don't know a solicitor, then you should look at the *List of Legal Aid Solicitors* in your library. This will at least give you a rough idea of which firms in the area deal with your kind of problem. But this can still be a bit like picking names out of a hat and it may be worth asking the CAB or a legal advice centre for help. They will probably not officially recommend a particular firm but because of their experience of local solicitors over the years they will be able to steer you in the direction of the most suitable firms in your kind of case.

Changing your solicitor

Once a solicitor has completed a particular piece of legal work for you and you have paid his bill then the relationship between you is over and you do not have to go back to the same firm next time if you don't want to.

If you are paying your solicitor with your own money you can change and go to another solicitor even in the middle of a case. You do not have to give any reasons, but until you have paid his bill up to date the old solicitor will not hand over any papers about the case to the new solicitor.

If you are on legal aid you will have to have a good reason for changing your solicitor in the middle of a case. (A good reason would be, for example, that you had moved to another area.) Your old solicitor hands over the papers straight away and his bill is paid by the Legal Aid Fund.

If you are dissatisfied with your solicitor then you should consider changing – but do not make a habit of it. Once is all right, particularly if you have a good reason, but frequent changes will create the impression that you are a difficult client and you will find it increasingly hard to find a new firm to take you on. And you run the risk that your original problem will become buried under a mass of disputes with the earlier solicitors about lost papers and unpaid bills.

Complaining about a solicitor's bill

If you are paying your solicitor out of your own pocket and he has done work for you which does not involve going to court – such as buying or selling a house, or drawing up a will – there are two ways in which you can object to his bill if you think it is unreasonably high. You can ask your solicitor to apply to the Law Society for a remuneration certificate and you can ask the High Court to tax the bill.

Remuneration certificate

If you ask for a remuneration certificate your solicitor must send his file of papers to the Law Society, who will decide whether his charges are fair and reasonable. They may approve the bill or reduce it but they cannot increase it. You cannot ask for a remuneration certificate if you have already paid your solicitor's bill before you decide that it was too large. But if you are unhappy about the Law Society's decision or if you have already paid the money you can ask for the bill to be taxed.

Taxing a bill

This means that your solicitor's bill is considered by a 'taxing master' of the High Court. This official has the power to approve the bill as it stands, reduce it or even increase it.

A word of warning: if the bill is approved, increased or reduced by less than one-fifth then you will have to pay the legal costs of the taxing hearing. If it is reduced by more than one-fifth then your solicitor will have to pay the costs of the hearing, and if the bill is reduced by more than one-half he will be reported by the court to the Law Society.

Legal aid bills

If you are legally aided then you will have little chance to object to your solicitor's bill. Your 'contribution' to the cost of legal aid or advice will have been fixed in advance and in many cases you will not even know how much your solicitor is paid by the legal aid fund. (For legal aid and advice see page 428.)

Paying your solicitor

Civil cases

If you are paying your solicitor out of your own pocket then you should expect to be charged anything from £20 to £50 (plus VAT) for each hour he has spent on your case. (The amount charged per hour will vary according to factors like whether the firm is in London or the provinces and whether your case is dealt with by a clerk or by the senior partner.) This charge is called the solicitor's profit costs. You will also have to pay back to the solicitor any money that he has had to pay out on your behalf. That would include stamp duty and search fees in a house purchase, and even postage. These payments by the solicitor are called disbursements.

All this sounds very expensive and it is. It is therefore worth while before deciding to employ a solicitor to get estimates from a number of different firms. Because it is never possible to predict precisely how much work will be involved in a case, you will not get an exact estimate; but at least you will have some idea of what to expect.

If your case goes to court and you win, then your opponent, the loser, will normally be ordered to pay your costs. But there is a snag. In preparing your case your solicitor to be on the safe side will almost certainly have done more than turns out to have been strictly necessary to win the case. He may, for example, have collected more expert evidence than was necessary or briefed an experienced QC when a more junior and cheaper barrister would have been quite capable of handling the case.

The loser will only have to pay your reasonable costs – those necessarily incurred for the attainment of justice. The exact amount will be decided either by agreement between your solicitor and the loser's, or if they cannot agree, by the court in which the case was heard. In either case the amount the loser pays (called party and party costs) will almost certainly be less than your solicitor's total bill and you will have to pay the balance, called solicitor and own client costs.

If your case goes to court and you lose then you will usually have to pay your own solicitor's costs and those of the other side.

In small claims for less than £500 in the county court you will not normally be able to claim the cost of employing a solicitor at the hearing if you win – and if you lose you will not have to pay for a solicitor employed by your opponent. You will still be able to claim for such expenses as an expert's report and a small amount for your own time and trouble in preparing the case if you really have done it yourself. This rule is intended to keep solicitors out of small claim proceedings. (For more information on bringing a small claim in the county court see page 433.)

Costs in criminal cases

If you are convicted of a criminal offence you will often be ordered to pay at least some part of the costs of the prosecution. But if you are acquitted you will not necessarily recover the costs of your defence from the prosecution.

In the crown court you will normally be awarded your costs if you are acquitted – unless the court feels that in some sense you were really guilty but got away with it on a technicality. In the magistrates' court you are far less likely to get your costs when you are acquitted. In fact you will probably not get anything unless the magistrates feel that the prosecution's case was so weak that it should never have been brought.

48 Legal aid

The term 'legal aid' is loosely used to cover three different schemes under which the state provides financial help for people with legal problems:

- legal *advice* and assistance;
- legal *aid* in civil cases; and
- legal *aid* in criminal cases.

Legal *advice* covers assistance from a solicitor in legal matters which do not involve a court hearing; legal *aid* covers both preliminary advice and appearance in court. The schemes for legal advice and for civil legal aid are administered by the Law Society; criminal legal aid is dealt with by the criminal courts themselves.

Legal advice and assistance

This form of financial help is sometimes called the 'green form scheme' because of the colour of the form filled in by the solicitor when claiming it. The scheme covers any kind of legal advice and assistance which stops short of court proceedings (except for proceedings in the magistrates' court about domestic violence). Your solicitor fills in the green form on the spot and if he decides that you qualify he can start work straight away.

He can do up to £40 worth of work under the scheme (£75 in matrimonial proceedings where he drafts a petition). When the first £40 or £75 has been used up your solicitor can apply for an extension.

To qualify for assistance you must satisfy two means tests; one covers capital and the other income.

Disposable income

If your disposable income was less than £44 in the week before you applied or you were receiving supplementary benefit or family incomes supplement, you qualify for free legal advice (your solicitor's bill will be paid by the Legal Aid Fund). If your weekly income was between £44 and £93 you will have to pay a graded contribution towards your solicitor's fees. If your income was more than £93 you will get nothing from the Legal Aid Fund. Disposable income is calculated as follows:

1 The incomes of husband and wife are added together unless they are separated or are in dispute with each other.
2 Add up your gross income from all sources and then deduct tax and national insurance.
3 You can then deduct the following sums for any dependants:

	£
Husband or wife	29.38
Each dependant aged:	
over 18	30.83
between 16 and 17	23.69
between 11 and 15	19.73
less than 11	13.13

The figure you are left with is your disposable income.

Remember that even if you qualify for assistance because your disposable income is within the limits you will get nothing if your capital is over the limit (see below).

Disposable capital

To calculate your disposable capital add up everything you own of value such as jewellery, furs and money in the bank or post office. (You do not have to include the value of your house, the furniture in it, your clothes, the tools of your trade and possibly your car.)

You can then deduct the following sums for any dependants: £200 for the first, £120 for the second, and £60 for every other dependant.

If your disposable capital, after making allowances for any dependants, is more than £655 you will not be entitled to any financial help, *however low your income*.

Legal aid: civil cases

If you want financial help and your problem cannot be dealt with under the green form scheme (see page 428) or is likely to involve court proceedings then you will have to apply for a 'civil legal aid certificate'. This is a complicated procedure and it will probably be two months before you know what help you will get, if any. You can apply for an 'emergency certificate'. This will be issued in a few days on the basis of a provisional assessment. (If it turns out when the full assessment has been made that you were outside the financial limits you will have to repay any money already paid to your solicitor from the Legal Aid Fund.)

As with the green form scheme you must satisfy a means tests involving both capital and income, and in addition you must satisfy the Law Society's Legal Aid Assessment Committee that you have a reasonable chance of winning your case. The financial assessment is done by the Department of Health and Social Security.

Disposable capital

If your disposable capital is less than £1,310 you will not have to pay a contribution. If it is between £1,310 and £2,725 you will have to pay a contribution. The amount of your contribution will probably be all the capital you have above £1,310. Thus if your disposable capital adds up to £1,610 your contribution will be £300. This sum will normally be payable in advance in one lump sum. If your disposable capital is more than £2,725 you will not qualify for any financial assistance unless your case is likely to be very expensive indeed.

Disposable income

Even if your disposable capital amounts to less than £2,725 you will still have to come within the income limits to qualify for any financial help at all.

For legal *aid* your disposable income is calculated on an estimate of what you expect to earn in the year after your application for legal aid. The actual assessment is made by the Department of Health and Social Security and you will have to attend an interview and produce evidence of your earnings and expenses.

To arrive at the correct figure you deduct from your gross income what you pay in tax, rent or mortgage repayments, rates and certain other expenses which are regarded by the DHSS as necessary. You can also deduct from your income an allowance for dependants. These allowances are the annual equivalent of the weekly rates given on page 428. For example, for a dependent husband or wife you can deduct £1,528 and for dependent children sums ranging from £683 to £1,603 according to their ages.

If after all deductions and allowances your disposable income for the year is less than £1,850 you will be entitled to free legal aid. If it is between £1,850 and £4,440 you will have to pay a contribution. If it is more than £4,440 you will get no financial help at all.

If you have to make a contribution the maximum sum will be one-quarter of the amount by which your disposable income exceeds £1,850. For example, if your disposable income is £2,650 your maximum contribution will be £200. This sum will usually be payable by twelve monthly instalments.

Remember: to qualify for legal *aid* in a civil case you must not only satisfy the Law Society's Legal Aid Assessment Committee that you stand a good chance of winning your case; you must also come within the financial limits for both *capital* and *income*.

The figures given above are those in force on 1 January 1983. They are increased from time to time. You should check.

Civil legal aid and costs

The purpose of giving financial help to people with little money but pressing legal problems is to put them in the same position as people with enough money to pay their own lawyers out of their own pockets.

It has already been pointed out that if you are paying your solicitor out of your own pocket and you win your case you will not necessarily get enough money from the loser to pay the whole of your solicitor's bill (see page 427). The same is true if you are receiving legal aid.

Suppose that you have been granted civil legal aid and your contribution is assessed at £200. You sue for £1,000 damages and you win. Your solicitor's bill comes to £500 and your opponent is ordered to pay £400 towards this. The final result depends on what your opponent actually pays:

1 If he pays the whole £1,000 damages and the £400 costs then all this money goes first to the Law Society. They will then pay your solicitor's bill of £500. For this purpose they will use the £400 received from your opponent and £100 of your contribution. They will then send the balance to you: the whole £1,000 damages and a refund of £100 from your contribution. The whole case will therefore have cost you £100 in solicitor's fees – the same as it would have done if you had paid your solicitor wholly out of your own pocket.
2 If your opponent pays the £1,000 damages but not the costs, the Law Society will still pay your solicitor £500. They will make this money up by using the whole of your contribution of £200 and by taking £300 from the damages received from your opponent. They will then send you £700. The case will therefore have cost you £500 – made up of £200 in hard cash and £300 in damages not recovered. Once again this is the same final result as if you had been paying all the bills yourself.
3 If your opponent pays nothing at all then the £500 paid to your solicitor will be made up of your contribution of £200 and a

further £300 from the Legal Aid Fund. This time although you will have paid out £200 you will at least be better off than someone not on legal aid. He would have to pay the whole bill of £500 out of his own pocket.

Legal aid: criminal cases

If you are charged with a criminal offence the case will begin in a magistrates' court and you should apply to that court for legal aid. There is a long form to fill in about your income and capital but the rules about contribution and financial limits are not so clearly defined as they are in civil cases. And in most cases the court relies on the statements about income and capital made by the applicant without conducting an inquiry into their accuracy, although there is power to do so.

The rule is that the accused should be granted legal aid if 'it is in the interests of justice' that he should be represented by a solicitor but he has not got enough money to pay for one out of his own pocket. It will be in the interests of justice for an accused to have a solicitor if, for example, the charge is a serious one and he is likely to be put in prison if he is convicted, or if the case involves complicated issues of law. This means that legal aid will usually be granted for cases heard in the crown court, but the practice in magistrates' courts varies widely; it is very hard to predict whether legal aid will be granted in a summary case without knowing in which magistrates' court it is to be tried.

As in civil cases the applicant may be required to pay a contribution either by instalments or in a lump sum. If the contribution is in the form of a lump sum it will usually have to be paid before the legal aid order is made.

Applying for legal aid in a criminal case

As suggested above, the first step is to apply to the magistrates' court where the case is first heard. This is so whether the case is a summary one or triable on indictment (see page 417).

The magistrates' clerk can grant legal aid but only a magistrate can refuse it. If legal aid is refused by a magistrate you can apply again to the court on the day of the hearing. If legal aid is refused at this stage there is no further appeal.

If the accused is committed to the crown court for trial or for sentence he can ask the magistrates for more legal aid to cover the proceedings there. If the magistrates refuse the applicant can reapply to the crown court itself. There is no appeal from a refusal by the crown court.

If you need help in applying for criminal legal aid you might be able to make use of the 'green form scheme' (see page 428). If you have no opportunity to consult a solicitor before you appear in the magistrates' court then you should ask to see the duty solicitor at the court. Not all courts, however, have duty solicitors and if you are unlucky enough to strike one that does not then you should ask the court to adjourn your case so that you can get legal advice. This request will almost always be granted and you should be released on bail unless your case is a very serious one.

Note: the rules on criminal legal aid are to be changed in the near future. There will be stricter income and capital limits and the required contributions will be greater. When this happens it will be even more important to get legal advice as soon as possible.

49 Small claims in the county court

There is in fact no such thing as a small claims court. There are, it is true, two private arbitration schemes, one in Manchester and one in London, which deal only with small consumer claims but they are not part of the official court system. However, there is a special procedure in the ordinary county courts for dealing with claims for less than £500. That is what this chapter is about.

The two distinctive features of the small claims procedure are that the case will normally be dealt with by arbitration, and that neither side can claim from the other the cost of employing a lawyer at the hearing. The problem of costs is dealt with in detail in Chapter 47, but we emphasize that to know in advance that even if you lose you will not have to pay for lawyers employed by your opponent is a great comfort.

Arbitration

The main differences between an arbitration and a full trial in the county court are as follows:

- A trial will take place in public in open court before a robed judge; an arbitration will take place in private before the registrar (a court official) and there will be no wigs and robes. The parties normally sit round a table.
- In a trial the formal rules of evidence and court procedure apply; in an arbitration, at the discretion of the registrar, those rules are usually greatly relaxed. The whole proceedings are much less formal and intimidating. The advantages of this for someone bringing a case on his own without a lawyer are obvious.

Although the arbitration hearing may be informal, the registrar's decision (called an award) will be just as legal and binding as the decision of a judge given in open court and may be enforced in exactly the same ways (see page 439).

Deciding to go to court

There is really no limit to the types of case that can be brought under the small claims procedure, but by far the largest number heard fall into the rather vague category of consumer cases. These might be complaints about faulty goods or services, claims by a private person or a shop for the price of goods sold and, less often, claims for damage to motor vehicles and so on.

This chapter is written from the point of view of the plaintiff (the person making the complaint) in a typical consumer case. Before examining the procedure in detail there are three important warnings that must be given.

The man of straw

When you have exhausted all the informal methods of trying to get your complaint dealt with, you will then have to decide whether or not to sue. Before you rush off to the county court and start issuing summonses in all directions stop and check whether the man or the firm you are going to sue has any money. It is a waste of time, trouble and money to sue what lawyers call a man of straw. All the judgments in the world won't help you if your opponent has no money or has gone bankrupt. The time to check this is before you issue the summons.

Principles cost money

To win a case in court it is not enough to feel that you have been treated unfairly and that as a matter of principle they shouldn't be allowed to get away with it. This can be a very bad basis for starting a legal action. The courts deal in law, not in morality and common sense, and the law is precise. To win your case you must be able to prove that you have a specific 'cause of action'. It is not enough to argue that the defendant, your opponent, behaved badly – you must prove that his behaviour added up to a breach of contract or legal negligence, for example. If you are not sure whether your sense of personal grievance can be translated into an actionable legal wrong, get some advice. There are plenty of places you can go for this advice without having to spend large sums of money (see Chapter 47, page 421).

Seeing your case as others see it

Another good reason for seeking independent expert advice before deciding to sue is that it is almost impossible to be objective about your own case. In turning your grievance over in your mind you tend to give most weight to those facts that are in your favour and to suppress or ignore those that are less favourable. If you tell your story to an experienced professional adviser he will not be satisfied with your shortened and edited version of the facts. He will ask uncomfortable questions in order to discover both sides of the story. This does not mean that he is unsympathetic or that he is working for the other side. He is just doing his job, which is to give you a realistic estimate of your chances of winning in court, which he can't do without having some idea of the strength of your opponent's case.

If after considering all these warnings you are still determined to go ahead and sue, the best thing to do is to write one final letter asking for whatever it is you want. If that gets no response, then read on.

Which court?

County courts can only hear cases from within their own area. You must therefore bring your case either in the court in whose area the case arose or in the court in whose area the defendant lives or carries on business. In some cases all these factors will exist in the same court district – for example, if you buy faulty goods in a shop and the owner lives above the shop – but if there is a choice pick the court that is most convenient for you.

The defendant's name and address

You must get this right. This may sound obvious but it is important for several reasons. You will need the right name so that the defendant cannot deny that he is the person in question, and you will need the right address so that you can choose the right court and the summons can be correctly served. You will have to find this out for yourself, the court will not do it for you.

If you are suing a private individual the name and address should not present much of a problem if you remember to give the full name, or as much of it as you can discover.

If you are suing a limited company the company's full name and the address of the registered office (which is the one you have to give) should be on their writing paper. If it is not, or they've never written to you, then you will have to make a search of Companies' House.

If you are suing a firm – a business that is not a limited company – then you can describe the defendant as either 'Slickfix Builders (a firm)' or as 'Frederick Smith trading as Slickfix Builders'.

Particulars of claim

When you have worked out who you are going to sue and in which court, the next thing that you must do is to prepare a short statement of the main facts of your case. This document is your 'particulars of claim'.

You can write this on an ordinary piece of paper but it must be set out in the correct way. (For certain common types of small claim there are standard forms available from the court which can make the task a bit simpler.) The particulars of claim must name the plaintiff and defendant, set out the facts of the case in numbered paragraphs, summarize the legal basis of the claim, and state what remedy the plaintiff is claiming.

A simple particulars of claim might look like this:

IN THE ....COUNTY COURT

BETWEEN		Plaint No. ....
	Albert Stokes	Plaintiff
	and	
	Slickfix Building Supplies (a firm)	Defendant

Particulars of claim

1 On 10 January 1983 the Plaintiff bought a wheelbarrow for £65 from the Defendant's shop at 12 High Street, Bunbridge, Sussex.

2 Within one week the wheel fell off and one of the handles broke.

3 After several visits to the Defendant's shop asking for the barrow to be replaced the Plaintiff wrote to the Defendant on 30 January 1983 asking for a refund of the purchase price. The Defendant has refused to replace the barrow or refund the price.
4 The wheelbarrow is not fit for its purpose and is not of merchantable quality in breach of the conditions implied by the Sale of Goods Act 1979.
5 The Plaintiff therefore claims £65, the price paid for the wheelbarrow, and costs.
Dated: 10 February 1983
Signed: Albert Stokes
of 2 The Cottages,
Bunbridge, Sussex,
the Plaintiff.

You will need at least three copies of your particulars of claim, one for the court, one for the defendant and one for yourself.

Issuing a summons

The next step is to take your particulars of claim to the court in which you wish to issue the summons. When you get there you will be asked to fill in a 'request form'. This is a fairly straightforward form which asks the court to issue the appropriate form of summons.

There are two kinds of summons: a fixed date summons and a default summons. A fixed date summons is issued when you are claiming something other than money, such as possession of property or the return of goods. A default summons is issued when you are claiming money, whether it is a fixed sum or a claim for an uncertain amount of damages which will have to be assessed by the court.

The advantage of a default summons is that if the defendant does not put in a defence within fourteen days you can go back to court and ask for judgment straight away. If you are claiming a fixed sum the court will order the defendant to pay in full at once or by instalments. If you are claiming damages, for personal injuries, for example, the court will give judgment in your favour but you will have to make an appointment to see the registrar for him to fix the amount.

If you are uncertain which kind of summons is right for your case the court officials will help you. They are encouraged to help people suing in person with filling in all court forms although they are not allowed to give you legal advice – that is to say, advice about the merits of your case and how to prove it.

You will then be asked to pay the fee for issuing the summons. If your claim is for less than £250 the fee is 10p for every £1 that you are claiming with a minimum fee of £4. This fee will have to be paid in cash – the courts do not accept cheques.

When you have paid the fee you will be given a 'plaint note'. This is a receipt for your fee and it will also tell you the date for the pre-trial review if you have issued a fixed date summons. In a default action the date for the pre-trial review will be fixed later. The most important thing on the plaint note, however, is the plaint number. The courts do not file papers alphabetically but only under plaint numbers so you must quote this number every time you have dealings with the court and on every document connected with your case.

There is one more thing to do at this stage and that is to decide how you want the summons to be served on the defendant. If the defendant is a limited company then it can be served by post but in every other case the most sensible thing to do is to get the summons served by the court bailiff. This is the safest method of ensuring that the defendant really gets the summons – but it will cost you another £4.

Pre-trial review

The purpose of the pre-trial review, which will be held by the registrar in private, is to decide how the case should be disposed of. The proceedings are very informal and the registrar will first decide whether to allow the defendant more time to put in a defence if he has not already done so. If asked he will usually give the defendant another fourteen days.

The registrar will also consider any application for the case to be tried in open court rather than by arbitration. This will not normally be granted where the claim is for less than £500 unless the case raises difficult points of law, there are allegations of fraud, or both parties agree to it.

There are two other important matters that the registrar will also decide: first, whether either side should provide more details of the claim or defence; and second, whether either side ought to disclose to the other any relevant documents in their possession. It is therefore worth thinking in advance whether you want more details of any defence that has been put in or if you would like to see any documents that you think the defendant may have.

The last thing the registrar will decide is the date of the final hearing. He will probably not give you an exact date for this but should be able to give you a rough indication of when it will take place.

The hearing

If your case is being dealt with by arbitration this will be likely to take place in the same room as the pre-trial review and before the same registrar. As already pointed out, the proceedings will be informal and the strict rules that apply in open court will not usually be enforced. However, there must be some shape to the proceedings and the usual order of events will be as follows:

1 The plaintiff will speak first giving a brief summary of the case. After that the plaintiff will call any witnesses that he may have. It is in fact usual for the plaintiff to give evidence on his own behalf as the first witness.
  After each witness has given evidence he may be cross-examined by the defendant.
2 The defendant will then call his evidence and any witnesses may again be cross-examined.
3 The plaintiff will then summarize his case and then the defendant will have a chance for the last word.
4 The registrar will then make his award.

This is only a brief summary of the proceedings involved in bringing a small claim in the county court. For a much fuller account you should get a copy of a booklet issued free by all county courts entitled *Small Claims in the County Court*.

Enforcing a judgment

Unfortunately even if you get judgment in the county court this does not mean that you will automatically get your money. It is not simply a question of going to an office in the court and collecting your winnings; if the defendant does not pay up then you will have to go back to court and ask for their help in making him. This is called enforcing a judgment.

There are a number of ways of enforcing judgments and the two simplest are by means of a warrant of execution or by an order for attachment of earnings.

Warrant of execution

If you apply to the court for a warrant of execution the court bailiff will seize the defendant's goods and then sell them to raise the money to pay the amount that you are claiming.

This sounds fairly simple but there are two things to beware of. First, before you apply for a warrant make sure that the defendant has enough goods to cover the amount of your claim. Modern household furniture does not fetch very much at auction and much of it is on hire purchase and so cannot be seized in execution anyway. This method of enforcing a judgment is most useful against a shopkeeper who has trade goods that can be seized.

The second thing to take into account is that the process is not cheap. It will cost you 15p for every £1 that you are claiming and you will have to pay this fee whether the bailiff finds enough goods on the defendant's premises or not. (The maximum fee you can be charged is £25).

Attachment of earnings

An attachment of earnings order instructs the defendant's employer to deduct regular sums of money from his wages and pay them into court to meet your claim. This method of enforcement is obviously only useful if the defendant is in regular employment.

There are other methods of enforcing judgments such as garnishee orders, charging orders, and the appointment of a receiver, but these are somewhat complicated and you should get legal advice before attempting to use them.

If you are not sure which form of enforcement would be most suitable in your case it is possible to ask the court to summon the defendant so that he can be examined as to his means. There will be a hearing in court and you will be able to question the defendant about all his sources of income, which will be very helpful in deciding how to enforce a judgment.

For more details on how to enforce a judgment there is a booklet obtainable free from any county court called *Enforcing Money Judgments in the County Courts*.

Offers of settlement

It often happens that as soon as you have issued your summons the defendant, realizing that you mean business, makes you an offer. He will not usually offer the full amount that you are claiming but you should think very seriously before rejecting any offer out of hand. You can of course try to bargain him up a bit but it may well be worth saving yourself the time, trouble and worry of going on with the action by accepting a bit less than you originally hoped for.

If your claim is for more than £500, which means that you can be liable to pay the costs of the other side's solicitor, you should consider even more carefully before rejecting any offer. If the defendant pays money into court in part settlement of your claim then unless you are in the end awarded more than this part payment you will have to pay the costs of his solicitor from the date of the payment in.

50 Making a complaint

This chapter deals with making complaints against solicitors, doctors, dentists, the police, public corporations and central and local government.

Complaints against solicitors

If you think that your solicitor has been negligent in handling your problem then you will probably have to go to another solicitor if you want to take your complaint any further. A solicitor can be sued like anyone else but you should not be surprised if you find it a bit difficult to find another who is eager to take the case on.

Negligence means a failure by your solicitor to take such care in the handling of your affairs as a reasonable solicitor would. You can't sue him just because you lose the case he has been handling for you. You must be able to prove that you have suffered some loss because he has done something like failing to take a necessary step in a court action, or losing a vital document. If you do sue a solicitor for negligence and win, you can at least be sure of being paid since all solicitors must be well insured against negligence.

You can also complain about a solicitor to the Law Society but they will not deal with cases where you could sue for negligence in the ordinary courts. They only deal with breaches of the solicitors' code of professional conduct. This could include misusing a client's money, disclosing confidential information or even undue delay in answering letters. The Law Society will investigate your complaint and may deal with the matter by simply warning the solicitor. But if your complaint is found to be serious then it will be dealt with by an independent disciplinary tribunal which can fine the solicitor or even strike him off the roll of solicitors.

As the person bringing the complaint you will not be awarded any compensation.

If you are not satisfied with the Law Society's decision you can ask for the case to be reviewed by the Lay Observer, a non lawyer appointed by the Lord Chancellor. If the Lay Observer agrees with you he will ask the Law Society to reconsider their decision.

(For complaints about a solicitor's bill see page 425.)

Complaints against the police

The two most common ways of making a complaint against the police are by using the official complaints procedure or by taking civil action in the courts.

Official complaints procedure

This procedure should be used for serious complaints such as allegations that the police failed to observe the Judges' Rules, or that they manufactured evidence.

You should send your complaint in writing to the Chief Officer of Police in your area; you can get his address from any local police station, which should also have a leaflet explaining the complaints procedure.

Your complaint will be investigated by a senior police officer, usually from another force, and the results of the investigation will be sent to the independent Police Complaints Board, which has power to ask for further action if it is not satisfied.

If your complaint is upheld the police officers in question may either be prosecuted or be subject to internal police disciplinary measures.

Civil action in the courts

If a policeman assaults you or wrongfully arrests you it is possible to bring a civil action against him in the ordinary courts. You should get legal advice before deciding to do this because the police will defend the case vigorously. If you do win, however, you may get substantial damages.

Other things you can do

You can of course write to the press or to your MP and it is worth while contacting the National Council for Civil Liberties, 21 Tabard Street, London SE1, if you have any problems.

Complaints against doctors and dentists

If you have suffered injury because of your doctor's or dentist's negligence then you can sue in the civil courts for damages. These cases are usually quite complicated and can take a long time, and you will need legal advice.

Family Practitioner Committee

If your complaint is that your doctor failed to visit you, or that your dentist has charged you for treatment that should have been free or something of that kind, then you can complain to the local Family Practitioner Committee. The committee deals with almost all doctors, dentists, chemists and opticians working within the National Health Service and you will find the address in the local phone book.

If the complaint is considered serious then there may be a hearing at which you will be entitled to be present. If your complaint is upheld then the doctor may be cautioned or have money withheld from him.

Professional bodies

These bodies, such as the General Medical Council for doctors or the General Dental Council for dentists, deal with unprofessional conduct such as making improper sexual advances or breaching a patient's confidence.

The Health Service Commissioner

See page 445.

Complaints about gas and electricity

The first step is to complain at the local showroom. If that doesn't work then you should write to the local Gas Consumers Council or the Electricity Consultative Council. You will find the addresses of these bodies on the back of your last bills and in the telephone directory.

Complaints against central or local government

As the power of government has grown and its involvement in everyday life has increased so, almost inevitably, has the possibility of the individual being dissatisfied with the treatment he or she has received. For example, the Inland Revenue may have been very slow in dealing with a claim for a tax refund, or a social security benefit thought to be due may have been refused. A local authority may have failed to repair a road or provide some service it has a duty to provide. What can be done about it?

The first point to make is that there is no one simple solution to all such problems. There is a major distinction between a complaint where a legal remedy is provided and one where it is not. For example, if unemployment benefit is refused, an appeal may be made to a local tribunal. It is no good taking action via an MP before using this opportunity to have the case fully ventilated. But in many cases there is no direct remedy, particularly where a discretionary power exists in, say, a local authority but it has not been exercised. For example, a council decides not to give a student a grant where it has a discretion whether to give one or not. No reasons for its decision may have been given and no appeal exists. Only some action via a councillor, or just possibly in the courts, will achieve the desired result.

(For complaints about schools see page 55.)

Some possible steps

If the complaint is against *central* government and no appeal exists then one of the following steps could be taken.

1 *Letter to an MP*

He or she will then write to the appropriate Minister, and within about a month a full reply will be received often going far beyond any explanation previously given. This may show that the complaint is ill founded. Alternatively the MP might be persuaded to take the matter up again and perhaps raise the issue in Parliament.

2 *The Parliamentary Commissioner for Administration*

This is a rather long-winded title for an official, independent of the government, who can investigate grievances against central government. He is sometimes known as the Ombudsman, which is a Danish word for 'grievance-man'. This institution began in Scandinavia and was adopted here in 1976.

He can investigate 'maladministration'. That means that he cannot question government policy but only its application or implementation. He can look into such matters as delay, bias, neglect, corruption or incompetence. He has no power to award compensation or to order the government to do some particular act but he reports fully on each case and invariably his view is accepted. If his report is in favour of the individual, a remedy will be provided.

An initial approach to him must be made through an MP but, if he receives a direct complaint, he will himself send it to the local MP and ask if he has any objection to an investigation being made. Also if the complaint relates to the National Health Service he can consider it without any intervention by an MP. He cannot consider complaints about nationalized industries, e.g. British Rail or Post Office, but most such bodies have independent users' councils to whom complaints can be made.

3 *Action in the courts*

This involves a challenge to the legality of the government's act. It may mean showing that the department in question had no power to act as it did, that it failed to follow a correct procedure, or that it applied the wrong test when making the decision complained of. There is a vast body of law laying down when such challenges are possible, and legal actions of this kind are on the increase. Expert legal advice should be taken if it is desired to bring such a case.

If the complaint is against a *local authority* then, whilst an MP may be able to help, the first approach should be to a councillor for the ward in question. If that proves unsatisfactory then a complaint may be made to a local government Commissioner for Administration who operates on similar lines to the Parliamentary Commissioner of Administration.

District auditor

If the complaint is that a local authority has exceeded its powers then complaint may be made to the district auditor. He is an official whose duty it is to check a local authority's accounts and expenditure. If he agrees that powers have been exceeded he can order any councillor or officer who was party to the wrongful act to repay any unlawful expenditure. There are complex rules about hearings if such questions are in dispute.

Organizations and addresses

Advertising Standards Authority
Brook House, 2–16 Torrington Place, London WC1 (01-580 5555)

Advisory Centre for Education (ACE)
32 Trumpington Street, Cambridge (0223 51456)

Advisory, Conciliation and Arbitration Service (ACAS)
11 St James's Square, London SW1 (01-214 6000)
for regional offices see the local telephone directory

Airlines
see Civil Aviation Authority below

Association of British Adoption Agencies
4 Southampton Row, London WC1 (01-836 1373)

Association of British Travel Agents Ltd (ABTA)
55 Newman Street, London W1 (01-637 2444)

Automobile Association
Fanum House, Basing View, Basingstoke, Hampshire (0256–20123)

British Gas Corporation
59 Bryanston Street, London W1 (01-723 7030)

British Insurance Association
Aldermary House, Queen Street, London EC4 (01-248 4477)

British Pregnancy Advisory Service
Guildhall Buildings, Navigation Street, Birmingham 2
initial contact should be made by letter

British Railways Board
222 Marylebone Road, London NW1 (01-262 3232)

British Standards Institute
2 Park Street, London W1 (01-629 9000)

Capital Taxes Office
Lynwood Road, Thames Ditton, Surrey (01-398 4242)
for inquiries about capital transfers during life
and:
Rockley Road, London W14 (01-603 4622)
for inquiries about capital transfers on death

Child Poverty Action Group (CPAG)
1 Macklin Street, London WC2
initial contact should be made by letter

Citizens' Advice Bureau
see local telephone directory

Civil Aviation Authority
Room T502 Space House, 43–59 Kingsway, London WC2
(01-379 7311)

Commission for Racial Equality (CRE)
Elliot House, 10–12 Allington Street, London SW1 (01-828 7022)

Companies' Registry
55 City Road, London EC1 (01-253 9393)
also at:
Crown Way, Maindy, Cardiff, Gwent
initial contact should be made by letter or personal call

Consumers' Association
14 Buckingham Street, London WC2
publishers of *Which?* magazine;
initial contact should be made by letter

County courts and magistrates' courts
see local telephone directory under 'Courts'

Criminal Injuries Compensation Board
Russell Square House, Russell Square, London WC1 (01-636 4201)

Department of Health and Social Security (DHSS)
Alexander Fleming House, Elephant and Castle, London SE1
(01-407 5522)
for local offices see telephone directory

Divorce county courts
see local telephone directory under 'Courts'

Divorce Registry
Somerset House, Strand, London WC2
initial contact should be made by letter

Electricity Consultative Council
address obtainable from the local Electricity Board shop or from the telephone directory

Equal Opportunities Commission
Overseas House, Quay Street, Manchester (061-833 9244)

Fair Trading (Office of)
Field House, Breams Buildings, London EC4
initial contact should be made by letter

Family Planning Association
27 Mortimer Street, London W1 (01-636 7866)

Gas
see under British Gas Corporation above

General Dental Council
37 Wimpole Street, London W1 (01-486 2171)

General Medical Council
44 Hallam Street, London W1 (01-580 7642)

Health and Safety Executive
Regina House, Old Marylebone Road, London NW1 (01-229 3456)
for local offices see telephone directory under 'Factory Inspectors'

Health Service Ombudsman
see under Ombudsman below

Incorporated Society of Valuers and Auctioneers
3 Cadogan Gate, London SW1 (01-235 2282)

Industrial Tribunals for England and Wales (Central office)
93 Ebury Bridge Road, London SW1 (01-730 9161)
for local offices see the telephone directory

Joint Council for the Welfare of Immigrants (JCWI)
44 Theobald's Road, London WC1 (01-405 5527)

Law centres
there are law centres in most large towns; for a list of addresses write to the Legal Action Group – see below

Law Society
113 Chancery Lane, London WC2 (01-242 1222)

Lay Observer
Royal Courts of Justice, Strand, London WC2 (01-405 7641)

Legal Action Group (LAG)
28a Highgate Road, London NW5
initial contact should be made by letter

Magistrates' courts
see telephone directory under 'Courts'

Mail Order Traders Association of Great Britain
507 Corn Exchange Building, Fenwick Street, Liverpool
(051-236 7581)

Motor Agents' Association
201 Great Portland Street, London W1 (01-582 9122)

Motor Insurers' Bureau
Aldermary House, Queen Street, London EC4 (01-248 4477)

National Council for Civil Liberties (NCCL)
21 Tabard Street, London SE1 (01-403 3888)

National Council for One-Parent Families
255 Kentish Town Road, London NW5 (01-267 1361)

National House-Building Council
Chiltern Avenue, Amersham, Bucks (024 03 4477)

National Marriage Guidance Council
3 Gower Street, London WC1 (01-935 2838)

National Society for the Prevention of Cruelty to Children (NSPCC)
1 Riding Street, London W1 (01-580 8812)

Nationalized industries:
airlines, coal, electricity, gas, health, Post Office, railways: see the entries under each heading

Office of Fair Trading
Field House, Bream's Buildings, London EC4
initial contact should be made by letter

Ombudsman
Parliamentary Commissioner and Health Service Commissioner, Church House, Great Smith Street, London SW1 (01-212 7676)

Local Government Ombudsman:
for England:
Commissioner for Local Administration in England
21 Queen Anne's Gate, London SW1 (01-930 3333)

for Wales:
Commissioner for Local Administration in Wales
Derwen House, Court Road, Bridgend, Mid Glamorgan
(0656 61325/6)

Parliamentary Commissioner for Administration
see Ombudsman

Post Office Users' National Council
Waterloo Bridge House, Waterloo Road, London SE1 (01-928 9458)

Pregnancy Advisory Service
see under British

Press Council
81 Farringdon Street, London EC4 (01-353 1248)

Probate:
Personal Application Department
4th Floor, Adelphi Building, John Adam Street, London WC2 (01-217 5046)

Registrar General of Births, Marriages and Deaths
St Catherine's House, Aldwych, London WC2
for local offices see the telephone directory

Royal Automobile Club
89 Pall Mall, London SW1 (01-930 2345)

Royal Institution of Chartered Surveyors
12 Great George Street, London SW1 (01-222 7000)

Shelter
86 Strand, London WC2 (01-836 2051)

Trading Standards Departments
see the telephone directory under the entry for the local council

Trades Union Congress
Congress House, Great Russell Street, London WC1 (01-636 4030)

United Kingdom Immigrants' Advisory Service (UKIAS)
7th floor, Brettenham House, Savoy Street, London WC2 (01-240 5176)

Index